Marketing Research

Marketing Research

Third edition

Wong Toon Quee

MARKETING INSTITUTE OF SINGAPORE

OXFORD   AUCKLAND   BOSTON   JOHANNESBURG   MELBOURNE   NEW DELHI

Butterworth-Heinemann
Linacre House, Jordan Hill, Oxford OX2 8DP
225 Wildwood Avenue, Woburn, MA 01801-2041
A division of Reed Educational and Professional Publishing Ltd

Ⓡ A member of the Reed Elsevier plc group

First published 1999
Reprinted 1999

British Library Cataloguing in Publication Data
A catalogue record for this book is available from the British Library

ISBN 0 7506 4707 8

Composition by Genesis Typesetting, Rochester, Kent
Printed and bound in Great Britain

FOR EVERY TITLE THAT WE PUBLISH, BUTTERWORTH-HEINEMANN
WILL PAY FOR BTCV TO PLANT AND CARE FOR A TREE.

Contents

Preface _____

The approach by the book publisher, Heinemann Asia, for me to prepare a third edition of this book came much sooner than expected. In fact, it came nearly two years ago, shortly after I assumed the role of Managing Director in the Gallup-Singapore office.

This third edition, like the previous two editions, is intended for three main categories of readers. First, members of the general public who wish to acquire an overview of marketing research will find it a valuable source of reading material. It offers them an insight into the basic components of marketing research. Second, degree and diploma students in management, sales and marketing institutes can adopt it as a reading text in marketing research studies. It presents statistical procedures and techniques which students with some basic knowledge of statistics can comprehend. Third, marketing research practitioners who, at times, may wish to make references to technical aspects concerning marketing research disciplines, and will find it convenient and valuable as a desk reference book.

This new edition uses the same basic approach as its first two editions in providing a concise, easily understood coverage of marketing research activities. There have not been dramatic changes in either the material or format of the second edition, but there have been a substantial number of minor improvements. The diagrams and other learning aids in the text have been expanded and improved. More questions are included in the End-of-Chapter Revisions for readers to practise with the knowledge they have gained from each chapter.

Readers have been a continuing source of valuable comments and suggestions. I share the difficulty of most authors of giving adequate recognition to those who have contributed to this revision. In particular, I wish to convey my special thanks to Jim Clifton, President and Chief Executive Officer of the Gallup Organization, for contributing the Foreword, and Yu Yaxin, my former MBA-class student, for typing the manuscript.

I am grateful to the Literary Executor of the late Sir Ronald A Fisher, FRS, to Dr Frank Yates, FRS, and the Longman Group Ltd, London for permission to reprint Tables I, II and III from their book *Statistical Tables for Biological, Agricultural and Medical Research* (6th edition, 1974).

Wong Toon Quee

Photograph by David P.C. Tay

About the author

Wong Toon Quee received his master's degree in statistics and master's degree in mathematics from the University of Illinois, and his PhD in business administration from California Kennedy-Western University.

He is a fellow of UK Institute of Statisticians (FIS) and the President of Singapore Institute of Statistics (SIS). He was appointed Honorary Research Consultant to a number of institutions and business establishments, including the Singapore Institute of Management (SIM) and Opinion Research Consultants Pte Ltd.

He started his working career as a lecturer at the former Nanyang University. One year later, he joined the Singapore Government Service and has worked in various government ministries, departments and statutory bodies, holding key posts such as Deputy Superintendent of Census, Director of Research and Chief Executive Statistician.

He left the Singapore Government Service to join the private sector in 1975. Since then he has been working as a marketing researcher, first as Market Research Manager with Singapore Airlines, then as a director in Survey Research Singapore Pte Ltd, and later as an Assistant General Manager (Research and Information) of Singapore Press Holdings Ltd.

Currently, he is the Managing Director of The Gallup Organization (Singapore) Pte Ltd and a Senior Lecturer (Adjunct) in the Graduate School of Business, National University of Singapore. He has undertaken a wide range of research projects relating to newspaper and magazine readership, advertising and marketing, customer satisfaction, employees' attitudes and feedback, community development, public opinions and national campaigns.

He has also lectured part-time on marketing research courses offered by the University of Strathclyde, the Curtin University of Technology, the Singapore Institute of Management and the Marketing Institute of Singapore.

Foreword

When the Gallup Organization opened our Singapore office in 1996, we felt we needed to hire an expert in the field of marketing research. We wanted someone with an exceptional reputation and character who had entrepreneurial abilities, and also the best academic credentials.

We chose Dr Wong Toon Quee.

After arriving in Singapore and spending more time with Dr Wong, I was struck with a distinguishable attribute that I have rarely seen. As I moved from one speech and reception to another, many high-level executives and government leaders congratulated and gave their best wishes to our new managing director, Dr Wong. I asked everyone, 'And how do you know Dr Wong' and they would reply, 'He was a great teacher of mine'.

Through the years I have met many people around the world who felt the same way about the late Dr George Gallup. 'He was a great teacher of mine,' was a phrase echoed by many that knew him. Both Dr Gallup and Dr Wong share this common characteristic.

The core product of market research is essentially asking a question, recording the answer and teaching someone what you have learned.

Dr Wong has captured the essence of the process in this bible for market research. It is Dr Wong at his best – teaching people how to conduct near-perfect research. His revised book is extremely timely. Only through surveys of customers and employees will companies begin to see themselves move forward. This book will continue to have a profound and positive influence on world business and industry.

James K. Clifton
President and Chief Executive Officer
The Gallup Organization

1

Introduction to marketing research ____

The term 'marketing research' binds two words together: *marketing* identifies the substantive field of study, and *research* specifies the method employed to undertake the study. As the term suggests, the primary function of marketing research is to utilize research abilities/facilities for gathering facts and knowledge to support marketing decision-making. Marketing research, therefore, serves to generate essential information to help explore market opportunities and/or reduce the level of risks involved in the decision-making process. The information to be gathered in a marketing research study should be highly relevant to the specific marketing problems at hand and be able to help in identifying, analysing and solving these problems.

The marketplace of today is surrounded by a magnitude of complex marketing problems. At a time when each decision situation has its own specific requirements for information, the implications for marketing research activities have broadened. The diversity and complexity of the marketing environment underscores the importance of marketing research as a subject of study with varying applications. Some illustrative examples of marketing research studies will help demonstrate the value and versatility of marketing research, and explain why marketing research has evolved into a wide-ranging subject.

Illustrative example 1:
Concept testing

Until recently, bird's nest as a consumer product was either taken in public eating places or purchased from medical stores in its raw form for home preparation. A food and beverage manufacturer then conceived the idea of marketing bird's nest as a packaged ready-to-drink product. Before a market decision could be made, the firm wished to obtain marketing data to resolve some important issues such as:

● Would consumers accept the new product concept favorably?
● Which segments of the population would be attracted to it?
● How should the pricing be determined?

Illustrative example 2:
Advertising evaluation study

A petrol company has just completed a six-month advertising campaign for the promotion of its petrol additives. Claiming that the campaign has greatly succeeded in creating a positive impact among the motorists, the marketing manager recommended that the campaign be extended for a further period of three months to yield even better results. The management, however, asked that the marketing manager should support his claim by gathering more objective information from the market before accepting his recommendation. Essentially, the management wished to know:

- What was the level of advertising recall?
- To what extent did motorists believe the advertisement messages?
- Had the campaign been successful in attracting new users?

Illustrative example 3:
New service introduction

Growing affluence, coupled with improved standards of living and changing lifestyles, have prompted the need for automatic teller machine (ATM) services for more Singaporeans. Before introducing ATM services to its customers, the management of a regional bank chose to seek pertinent information from its customers concerning the desirability and needs for ATM services and their expectations of such service. A marketing research study was therefore commissioned to explore, among other things, the attributes and features of the intended service that would appeal to bank account holders. It also asked:

- How should its ATM services be distinct from those of its competitors?
- Where should ATM machines be strategically installed?
- Who were likely to be ATM users?

Illustrative example 4:
Advertising effectiveness study

The *Promote the Use of Mandarin* campaign, which began in Singapore in 1979, resulted in Rediffusion Services (S) Pte Ltd having to gradually reduce and finally scrap all its Chinese dialect programmes. According to traditional beliefs, Rediffusion listeners were the illiterates, the elderly Chinese who preferred dialects to Mandarin. This led the advertisers to fear a possible decline in Rediffusion listenership and, in turn, a diminishing value on their advertising. In a move to clarify the situation, Rediffusion commissioned an advertising effectiveness study to ascertain whether it still remains an effective advertising medium. The central issues addressed in this particular study include the following:

- Did the products advertised in Rediffusion register greater awareness among those who live in homes with Rediffusion sets than among those who live in homes without Rediffusion sets?
- How did *sponsored programmes* and *on spots* advertising in Rediffusion perform in terms of creating a higher product awareness?

Illustrative example 5:
Product taste test

Some years ago, a pizza eating-house contemplated establishing a foothold in Singapore in the fast-food business. Considering that pizza was relatively new to the taste of most Singaporeans, its management decided to invest in two out of the six existing flavours at the product launch. A product taste test was suggested to explore:

- Which two flavours were most palatable to the tastes of Singaporeans?
- What product modifications (e.g. toppings, sweetness level, etc.), if any, were needed?

Examples as cited above could be multiplied by thousands. They all share a common point: the pressing need for marketing research data to aid the decision-making process.

Definition of marketing research

Various institutions, organizations and individuals have defined marketing research in somewhat different ways. Appended below is a glossary of definitions which, it is hoped, would help depict the widespread usage of marketing research and offer a clearer understanding of marketing research as a subject of study.

> Marketing research is the systematic gathering, recording and analysing of all data about problems relating to the marketing of goods and services.
> (American Marketing Association)

> Marketing research is the systematic design, collection, analysis and reporting of data and findings relevant to a specific marketing situation facing the company.
> (Philip Kotler, *Principles of Marketing*)

> Marketing research is the systematic and objective search for and analysis of information relevant to the identification and solution of any problem in the field of marketing.
> (Paul E Green and Donald S Tull, *Research of Marketing Decisions*)

> Marketing research is the systematic investigation of marketing activities carried out in order to discover new information and relationships as well as to expand and verify existing knowledge. Simply put, its two major functions are to provide information for decision-making and to develop new knowledge.
> (George Kress, *Marketing Research*)

> Marketing research is the search for significant facts helpful in marketing the management of marketing activities. Marketing research is applied to every step of the marketing process.
> (Richard D. Browx and George J. Petrello: *Introduction to Business*)

Marketing research links the organization with its market environment. It involves the specification, gathering, analysing and the interpretation of information to help management understand the environment, identify problems and opportunities, and develop and evaluate courses of marketing actions.
(Thomas C Kinnear and James R Taylor, *Marketing Research: An Applied Approach*)

Four words – *systematic, objective, information and decision-making* – appear frequently in defining marketing research. Each word bears certain significance in respect of the nature and scope of marketing research and hence deserves further elaboration.

A systematic, well-organized approach is mandatory in undertaking a marketing research study. The word *systematic* suggests that:

- the research should be carefully planned and executed
- the research purpose should be clearly and concisely described
- the research design should be developed well ahead
- the data requirements should be clearly specified
- the mode of data analysis should be anticipated well in advance.

Objectivity requires an approach that is independent of the personal views of the researcher. The word *objective* implies that:

- the research should be carried out scientifically;
- the research should be carried out in an unbiased manner
- the execution of the research should not be affected by emotions.

Information brings about better knowledge and wisdom. The word *information* requires that the research information should:

- help raise the level of understanding of the marketplace and the consumers

- be pertinent to planning and control purposes
- help in the optimal allocation of marketing resources.

Finally, the word *decision-making* specifies that the research should:

- help lower the level of risk in a decision situation
- help broaden the information base for decision-making
- aid in the process of deciding on a course of action, after careful consideration of other known alternatives.

Along with these definitions come the several professional roles of a marketing researcher. He or she assumes the role of consultant as he or she specifies the various information needs. The market researcher plays the role of designer who designs survey questionnaires in their most effective formats. He or she has the role of methodologist/strategist in working out methods and strategies for collecting information – not merely data, but also information. He or she has the role of manger in planning, organizing, executing the entire research process, and undertakes the role of a quality controller who ensures the information gathered will be most accurate and reliable. The market researcher is an analyst, as he or she is expected to analyse data and turn

---

Professional Roles

- **Consultant:**
  Specify information needs.

- **Designer/Methodologist:**
  Design methods for collecting information.

- **Manager:**
  Plan, organize and control data collection process.

- **Analyst:**
  Analyse data and turn them into information.

- **Communicator:**
  Communicate findings and implications.

---

them into information, Finally, he or she must also be a communicator able to convey the research findings and implications.

Benefits of marketing research

While the principal benefit of marketing research is to reduce uncertainty or error in decision-making, the more specific benefits of marketing research include:

- helping to present a more accurate problem definition
- offering a more reliable prediction
- providing a competitive edge
- yielding a more efficient expenditure of funds
- leading to the discovery of new business opportunities
- reducing business risks
- monitoring the effectiveness of the marketing plan.

Growing importance of marketing research

Marketing research is gaining importance, a fact due mainly to the rapid changes in the business environment as witnessed since the 1960s. Some of these changes are outlined below.

1 *The shift from neighbourhood marketing to national marketing, and to global marketing.* In the past, neighbourhood residents accounted for the great majority of customers visiting a store. This proximity to the marketplace has promised the store-owner a first-hand knowledge of customers in terms of their purchasing habits, brand preferences and idiosyncrasies. The store-owner knew exactly who his customers were; how frequently they shopped; who made the purchase decisions; which brands were preferred and for what specific reasons. There was then no real need for marketing

research data. But today, marketing activities have expanded nationally and globally, and personal access to the marketplace is no longer readily available. Geographical expansion of marketing activities has brought about an extended channel of distribution which, in turn, takes the marketing manager further away from his customers. From this viewpoint, marketing research serves as an effective tool for bridging the information gap.

2 *The shift from customer need to customer choice.* Rising disposable income has led the purchasers of products and services to progressively deviate from the so-called 'need' consideration. Customers in the 1990s would seldom ponder over the basic need of owning a television set or a hi-fi radio, but rather would spend time on deciding what brand of television set or hi-fi set to purchase.

3 *The shift from price to non-price competition.* Price status as the sole determinant in product choice is being eroded, largely due to the growing affluence of consumers as well as a more complicated marketing mix. Manufacturers and service providers have come to realize the need to present and to position their products and services in the light of attributes which are non-price related. Product packaging and brand image, for example, play a significant role in influencing produce purchase.

4 *Wider acceptance of the marketing concept.* The marketing concept stipulates that customers constitute the focal point of all marketing activities. In essence, customers can dictate a product's success or failure. To be successful in the competitive marketplace, the firm must adopt a more analytical and systematic approach to the exploration of customers' needs and wants, and this can be fulfilled by the use of marketing research.

5 *Increased role of marketing research.* Until 1940, market research assumed a rather narrow scope as it was confined solely to the search for information about the consumer market. Since 1950, the scope of

marketing research has extensively widened to deal with other aspects of marketing as well, that is, *price, product, distribution* and *promotion.* The term *marketing research,* replacing the traditional term *market research,* signifies this development.

Growing Importance of Marketing Research

Neighbourhood Marketing → National/Global Marketing

Consumer Needs → Consumer Choice

Price Competition → Non-Price Competition

Wider acceptance of Marketing Concept

Higher Rate/Cost of New Product Failure

Increased Role of Marketing Research

Developing to Marketing Science

The real difference between market research and marketing research is, in fact, more than a semantic one. First, they differ in the scope of study. Traditionally speaking, market research is researching about the current and potential customers: who they are; why they buy a product or service; from where and when they buy it; what they buy and how they bought. Marketing research, in addition, deals with information relative to marketing components, namely, product, price, promotion and channel of distribution. The term 'marketing research' is therefore conceptually broader in scope and is more preferably used in modern marketing. Secondly, market research emphasizes measurements, focusing largely on quantitative dimensions. Marketing research, on the other hand, emphasizes creativity; it focuses on qualitative aspects as well. It also seeks to

1915 and earlier	**Free-For-All Stage** Scattered, unscientific surveys executed Marketing research companies did not exist
1915–1940	**Marketing Research Companies Surfaced** Surveys solely focused on consumers. Known as Market Research First book on market research published in 1921
1941–1950	**Increased Function of Market Research** Scope of studies went beyond the consumer element, and included the four marketing functions (i.e. 4Ps) Known as Marketing Research Increasingly more business organizations commissioned marketing research studies
1950–1980	**Research Methodological Advancement Stage** Improved questionnaire design Efficient and sophisticated sampling procedures Experimental research designs Scientific methodologies in data collection Qualitative research concepts and techniques
1980–	**Computer Applications and Statistical Packages** Advanced statistical analysis of research data (e.g. cluster analysis, factor analysis, multiple regression analysis) Psycho-graphic and lifestyle studies Customer satisfaction measurement models

Figure 1.1 *Historical development of marketing research*

discover unsatisfied consumer needs and wants; it tries to ferret out unsolved problems in the marketplace; and more significantly, it focuses on what could be, rather than on what is.

Over-emphasis of technological advancement in marketing research has resulted in criticism that marketing researchers in the 1990s have shown less concern over data analysis and interpretation. Some of the remarks offered by marketers about marketing researchers include:

- that marketing researchers no longer help solve problems; they apply methods. In essence, they allow methods to chase problems, rather than the other way round
- that marketing researchers are over concerned with being collectors of data; rather than being users and interpreters of data
- that marketing researchers merely dump marketers with an avalanche of data; but fail to allocate time and effort to separate the wheat from the chaff
- that consumers not only have opinions, they have passions too – an aspect which

marketing researchers sometimes neglect in the analysis and interpretation of data (e.g. the Coca-Cola fiasco)

Thus, the challenge which marketing researchers face is to return marketing research to its original role, that is, to present actionable data for marketers/management to make decisions, rather than to impress upon them with sophisticated research technologies.

Notwithstanding what has been said, marketing research should never be deemed as a substitute for management decision; rather, it should be regarded as an additional tool in making better decisions by way of providing essential information to specific marketing problems.

Main divisions of marketing research

Broadly speaking, there are five main divisions of marketing research: Market and

Main Divisions of Marketing Research

Marketing and Sales Research

Advertising Research

Product Research

Distribution Research

Price Research

Sales Research, Product Research, Price Research, Place Research and Advertising Research.

Figure 1.2 depicts the typical questions to be addressed and the research techniques which are relevant to each of these divisions. The list is by no means comprehensive and is provided for general reference only.

Users of marketing research ▬

Users of marketing research are many and varied. Key users, however, come from five broad categories:

1 *Consumer product manufacturers.* The biggest users of marketing research are the largest companies and manufacturers of fast-moving consumer products (e.g. hair shampoo, cooking oil). Generally speaking, they are physically remote from the product end-users and have a greater need to know about the market, hence their heavy reliance on marketing research.

2 *Industrial goods manufacturers.* This category of persons needs marketing research data for the following purposes: to evaluate products' performances, to suggest the machinery type to be marketed and where it should be sold. Generally speaking, industrial goods manufacturers handle only a limited range of product lines and a small number of direct clients. Additionally, the distribution channel between industrial goods manufacturers and end-users is relatively short. On this score, industrial goods manufacturers are less dependent on marketing research.

3 *Retail/wholesale intermediaries.* Agents, brokers and merchant intermediaries come under this category. They use marketing research less frequently due to their proximity to customers and their trading mentality.

4 *Media owners and business services bureaus.* Publishers of newspapers and magazines, owners of television, radio and Rediffusion stations, advertising agencies, commercial banks as well as business consultants all belong to this category. They are on a continuous search for information on consumers' profiles, attitudes and opinions, brand awareness, etc., and are heavy users of marketing research.

5 *Non-profit organizations.* Government ministries and departments, official bodies, educational institutions, charitable organizations and welfare homes come under this category.

Users of Marketing Research

Consumer Product Manufacturers

Industrial Product Manufacturers

Non–Profit Organizations

Marketing Research Users

Business Service Bureaus

Retailers and Wholesalers

Media Owners

Typical Survey Questions Addressed	Research Technique
1 Market and Sales Research This division of marketing research examines markets, that is, the characteristics of potential users of products and services. It identifies, measures and describes market segmentation, users' profiles and behaviour. Typical questions include: ● Who constitute the buyers? ● Why do some people buy and some don't? ● From which outlet(s) are the products bought? ● What are the market shares of the respective brands? ● What are the preferences of consumers?	● Market Profile Studies ● Attitude, Awareness and Usage (AAU) Studies ● Motivation Research
2 Product Research This division of marketing research deals with the evaluation of products, in particular, new products or product features, packaging, consumption pattern/rate, inventory trends and status of competing products. Typical questions include: ● Should the existing product be modified, and if so, what modifications are needed? ● What are the most favoured features of the products? ● Which package design is preferred most? ● Which brand name/logo should be used? ● What are the particular likes/dislikes about the product?	● New Product Development Research ● Product Concept Tests ● Central Location Tests ● Home Placement Tests ● Brand Image Studies
3 Price Research This division of marketing research is concerned with the price elasticity of demand for a product, and provides useful inputs to price selection. Typical questions include: ● What would be the responses to the various price levels? Are there particular prices at which large numbers of consumers would start (or cease) buying a product? ● To what extent will sales be affected by price threat from competing product(s)? What market share do my products and services start to lose? ● What pricing policy should be adopted for a new brand or service to secure maximum trial among its target group?	● Price Perception Tests ● Price Sensitivity Studies
4 Distribution (Place) Research This division of marketing research comprises channel research and location research. The former can help decide which channels to use for distribution of products and services; while the latter is concerned with decisions about warehousing, inventory and transportation. In short, it is concerned with the formation and effectiveness of distribution policy. Typical questions include: ● What channel structure should be used? ● What types of stores display the product and in what quantity? ● Where and in what volumes should the product be stocked?	● Store Audits ● Store Image/Traffic Studies ● Warehouse Withdrawal Studies
5 Promotion (Advertising) Research This division of marketing research is concerned with the persuasiveness and believability of advertising, motivation research, advertising recall, effectiveness of communications media, as well as the strengths and weaknesses of sales promotion. It also deals with the generation and evaluation of alternative advertising plans. Typical questions include: ● What advertising theme, appeal, slogan to use? ● Which is the most effective advertising mix? ● How successful are sales stimulants (e.g. discount coupons, lucky draws)? ● What product features should be emphasized?	● Readership/Audience Profile Studies ● Exposure Studies ● Advertising Recall Tests ● Communication Research ● Pre-Ad/Post-Ad Tests ● Association Tests

Figure 1.2 *Typical survey questions*

Marketing research options ▬

Marketers are constantly seeking for latest, up-to-date information on their markets at all stages of the marketing process. This ranges from market potential, brand equity, market segmentation, usage pattern, consumer profiles and attitudes. They can choose any of the three main research options to secure the valuable information needed, namely, exclusive (customized) survey, omnibus survey and syndicated studies.

Marketing Research Options

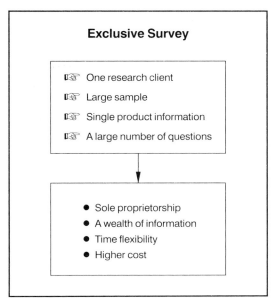

Exclusive Survey

- ☞ One research client
- ☞ Large sample
- ☞ Single product information
- ☞ A large number of questions

- ● Sole proprietorship
- ● A wealth of information
- ● Time flexibility
- ● Higher cost

without its permission. Being the sole buyer of the research, the research client can plan to include a reasonably large amount of information about the industry/product/brand to be secured from the exclusive survey.

In sum, exclusive survey is the most expensive type of research options. On the other hand, it is the most useful one since it is tailor-made and is designed to meet the exact requirements of its research client.

Exclusive (customized) survey ⎯⎯⎯

In an exclusive survey, the marketer (or research client) can engage marketing research firm to conduct a market survey in a prescribed manner. In this case, the marketer's company will bear the full cost of the survey. In return, it will specify, among other things, the survey timing, the scope and coverage of the survey in terms of the questions to be asked as well as the complexity and length of the survey questionnaire, in consultation with the marketing research firm. The marketer's company claims sole proprietorship of the survey data gathered therefrom; no other party will be allowed to release or use the survey data

Omnibus survey ⎯⎯⎯⎯⎯⎯⎯⎯⎯

An omnibus survey, as it literally means, is one whereby prior to the execution of field work, research clients are invited to 'board' the bus by adding a few questions to the common survey questionnaire. As opposed to an exclusive survey which is commissioned by one single research client, an omnibus survey takes in a number of research clients who together share the field-work costs. It is extremely cost-effective as each participating research client needs only to pay for the set of questions he requested. It constitutes a viable option for the research client who has a limited research budget and who needs only a small number of research questions, yet to be asked of a reasonably large and representative sample of respondents. Here the marketing research company sets out an omnibus time schedule and subsequently releases it to all the potential research clients. Usually, between two and six research clients would join in one omnibus survey. The marketing research company would levy the survey cost structured on a per-question basis and each research client pays only for its own set of exclusive questions. The remaining costs of field work (for example, interviewers' transport costs) are shared among the research clients participating in the same omnibus survey. As the omnibus survey involves multiclients, each research client would normally be advised to request for a small number of research questions, lest the length of survey questionnaire would become too lengthy and unmanageable.

Although there are many research clients in an omnibus survey, each research client would be provided with the research data it pays for and this would not be shared with any other research clients. Each research client will receive a report which is customized to meet its marketing needs. In other words, each research client can retain absolute confidentiality of the survey data it requested in the omnibus survey. On the part of the survey respondents, they will find themselves having to answer a large number of questions about a diverse range of topics and will possibly feel confused.

Syndicated studies

A marketing research firm sometimes conducts a large-scale syndicated study on a particular product (e.g. fast food) or service (e.g. banking) whenever it considers that the survey data gathered will be widely needed by the industry players (e.g. McDonald's, KFC, Citibank). It would, under such circumstance, undertake the survey without the prior commitment of any research client to buy the research data. The product or service to be covered in the syndicated study, the time schedule, the set of survey questions as well as the complexity and length of the survey questionnaire will fully be determined by the marketing research firm.

The marketing research firm would normally inform the potential research clients

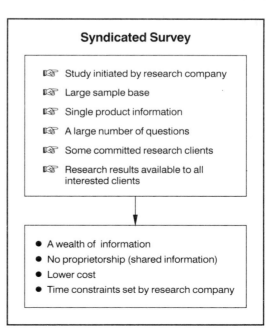

either before or after the study is undertaken. Research clients who may have a use for it are encouraged to purchase the syndicated study at a fixed cost, with an additional charge imposed if extra tabulation and/or data analysis is requested. While research clients who subscribe to the same syndicated study share the same set of information, the survey report for each research client can be customized to meet individual marketing needs.

Syndicated studies work best when it would be too expensive for a research client to absorb the full survey cost singly, as it means that a number of research clients are sharing the costs of generating the kind of original data they need.

Very often, the syndicated study is repeated over time. This periodic updating of the syndicated study provides data which become industry standards for marketers to incorporate as part of their marketing strategies database.

A list of syndicated studies conducted in 1997 in Singapore is provided in Appendix A.

Marketing research services in Singapore

Most, if not all, government ministries in Singapore have their own research and statistics departments. In the private and commercial sectors there are a number of marketing research firms offering a wide range of research services and techniques as listed below:

- personal, face-to-face interviews
- telephone interviews
- postal surveys
- central location tests
- home placement tests
- observational studies
- focus group discussions
- depth interviews.

The Marketing Institute of Singapore (MIS) undertook 'The 1996 Singapore Survey of Marketing Research Practices' to establish a profile of the marketing research activities undertaken by the companies in Singapore. The telephone interviewing method was used to reach the target sample of 156 companies in various sectors (e.g. manufacturing, publishing/broadcasting, financial services/insurance/real estate, transportation/storage, retailing/distribution, contracting, advertising, etc.) with different types of ownership (i.e. locally run, foreign-owned or joint venture). Some of the highlights of this pioneering survey are reproduced below (*MIS Marketing News*, September/October 1996).

- More than one-half of the companies surveyed allocate up to 3 per cent of the marketing budget for marketing research activities.
- About one-half of the companies based in Singapore engage in some form of marketing research.
- Manufacturers of consumer products are most active in all types of marketing research activities while, on the other hand, transportation and storage companies are the least marketing research oriented.
- Foreign-owned companies are much more likely to engage in marketing research activities than joint venture or locally owned/government-linked firms.
- Pricing studies are the most popular among companies based in Singapore, followed by studies on customer satisfaction, market potential, market share and industry/market structure and trends.
- A quarter of the respondents conduct less than three marketing research projects a year, while another quarter carry out four to six projects annually. The remaining one-half of respondents either conduct more than six projects, or carries out a variable number of projects each year.
- There exists a significant degree of formalization of marketing research in the companies surveyed, with most of them having a separate department to take charge of these activities.

● Nearly one-half of the companies surveyed indicate the use of Marketing Information System (MIS.) and databases; while 63 per cent have an access to on-line news or databases.

In-house research versus external research

Once the need for marketing research is recognized, a company next decides between undertaking its own in-house research study or employing an external research agency to perform the task. The following criteria are generally used to help make the decision:

1 *Cost.* Is it cost-effective to do it in-house? A negative answer favours the use of an external research agency.
2 *Expertise.* Is the necessary research expertise available within the company? A negative answer favours the use of an external research agency.
3 *Special equipment.* Does the research study require special research equipment (e.g. eye camera) which is not available within the company? A positive answer favours the use of an external research agency.
4 *Need for secrecy.* Is the research topic sensitive enough to raise alarm to fellow competitors when it is leaked out? A negative answer favours the use of an external research agency.
5 *Political split.* Does the study involve highly controversial issues between personalities or departments within the company? Political considerations may require the use of an outsider whose credentials are acceptable to all parties in an internal policy dispute. In this regard, a positive answer favours the use of an external research agency.
6 *Legal/promotion consideration.* Will the study results be used in litigation, legal proceedings, or as part of a promotional campaign? The credibility of the findings will generally be enhanced if the study is conducted by a respected outsider. A

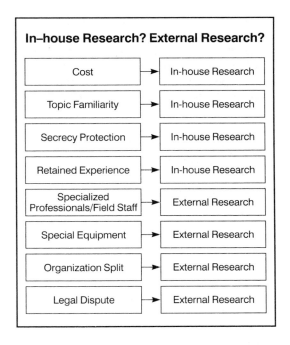

In–house Research? External Research?

Cost	→ In-house Research
Topic Familiarity	→ In-house Research
Secrecy Protection	→ In-house Research
Retained Experience	→ In-house Research
Specialized Professionals/Field Staff	→ External Research
Special Equipment	→ External Research
Organization Split	→ External Research
Legal Dispute	→ External Research

positive answer favours the use of an external research agency.
7 *Administrative consideration.* Do current workloads and time permit the execution of the research study within the company? A negative answer favours the use of an external research agency.

It is not uncommon for companies to commission marketing research studies to external firms. These companies tend to market a wide range of products/services (including new products/services) that require specialized kinds of marketing research techniques such as test marketing, consumer surveys and laboratory experiments. In sum, the use of an external research agency offers a number of advantages:

1 *Greater objectivity.* An external research agency can carry out the research study more objectively and offer independent viewpoints unaffected by controversies which may exist within the company.
2 *Availability of specialized professionals.* When it is required to adopt special qualitative research techniques (e.g. focus

group discussion) to perform the research siudy, an external agency would normally have the services of its own psychologists or behavioural scientists to handle the task. Such specialized personnel are normally not available in the user's department.

3 *Accumulated experience.* An external research agency can offer better research and analytical techniques through its varied experience accumulated over many years.

4 *Experienced field staff.* An external research agency maintains better quality field staff (e.g. interviewers) who claim long periods of relevant working experience.

In-house research study, on the other hand, is preferred for the following reasons:

1 *Cost.* In-house research studies usually cost less. External research agencies have to charge higher fees to cover their fixed costs and other operating expenses as well as to reap some profits.

2 *Subject familiarity.* In the case of an in-house research study, the marketeer is more familiar than the researcher with the background of the marketing problems facing the company, and can handle the research more realistically.

3 *Retained experience.* After the completion of each in-house research study, the experience so gained is retained within the company.

4 *Better control.* The company can exercise more contact and control while the research study is being executed.

Research brief

Prior to the commissioning of a research study, it is customary for the research client to prepare a research brief defining its research requirements and present it to the research company. The research brief specifies, among other things, the marketing problem on which the survey is expected to focus and forms the basis for briefing the

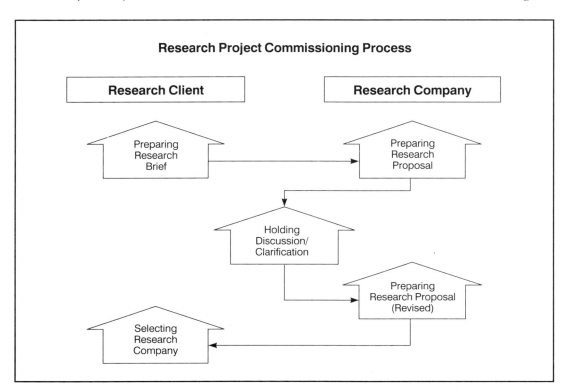

research agency. It is an extremely useful guide to the researcher. The clearer and more specific the research brief will be, the better the research agency will be able to meet the needs identified. Efforts made to prepare the research brief are fully justifiable. Some of the benefits of a research brief are described below:

1 *Data relevancy.* The research brief provides both parties – the research client and the research agency – with a clearer understanding of how the research data to be collected will help support decision-making.
2 *An overall agreement.* The research brief ensures the extent of agreement or cohesion among all parties who would be likely to benefit from the research findings.
3 *Research Programme.* The research brief helps both parties – the research client and the research agency – to plan and administer the research programme.
4 *Dispute avoidance.* The research brief can help to avoid or reduce disputes that might occur when the gaps in knowledge of the research clients are not completely 'filled' as intended.
5 *Negotiation.* The research brief can be used as the basis for negotiation with the interested research agencies.

Confusion and lack of clarity in the research brief will tend to lead to unproductive research. In preparing for the research brief, it is wise to hold discussions with the managers within the company to ensure that all parties concerned are clear of what is to be investigated, and that the eventual research program will take account of all essential information needs.

```
● Company Background
● Research Objectives
● Research Target Population
● Research Questions
● Research Data Users
● Timeline
● Budget
```

Figure 1.3 *Content outline of a research brief*

In sum, the outcome of the process should be a clear definition of the research requirements committed to paper and sanctioned by all the appropriate people/departments within the client company. Figure 1.3 presents the content outline of a research brief.

1 *Company background.* This section of a research brief describes the prevailing market situation which in turn helps the research agency to grasp a better understanding of the product/industry information. A vivid narration of the company's performance and position (e.g. market share, company's image and perception) would also be useful. In particular, any marketing problem which the company is facing with should be highlighted.
2 *Research objectives.* This section gives a clear explanation of why the research is needed. In some areas the research objectives are to assist the company to formulate marketing strategies to increase sales, to enlarge market share or, in other cases, to improve company image or to gauge the acceptance level of a new product, and so on.
3 *Research target population.* The research target population refers to the specific category of persons on and from whom the research data will be collected. In the event that the research population is targeted at the top elites, the research agency should be so informed at the outset to avoid wasting time and money collecting data from the lower- and middle-income earners. The same will hold true if the research population is directed at persons of a special gender, age, education, marital status, occupation and industry. Such specification in the research brief would also be helpful to the research agency in recommending the sample size and the sampling method.
4 *Research questions.* The research brief should provide a detailed list of questions (or topics) to be explored in the research, to help the research agency identify exactly what is required. This however does not mean writing a survey questionnaire, which is the

expertise of the research agency engaged to perform the research. The more knowledgeable is the research client about the areas of questioning, the more likely it is that the research agency will do a better job.

5 *Research data users.* In the research brief, an identification of the level of people who will ultimate study and utilize the research data would be useful. Such information provides helpful guidelines to the research agency on the types and details of the survey questions, the level of details of data analysis needed in data tabulation, as well as the type of report (i.e. technical or popular report) to be prepared.

6 *Timeline.* An indispensable section in a research brief is an indication of when the research data is required. Research data become meaningless if made available to the management only beyond the decision-making stage. The date imposition has large implications for the type of research method which can be adopted and for the factors which the research agency will need to consider in planning its research process. It is of utmost importance that the research agency would strictly adhere to the timetable specified.

7 *Budget.* Once the research brief is ready, it is almost definite that the research client would invite more than one research agencies to discuss the research undertaking. Upon distributing the research brief, the research client would ask the research companies to raise questions that they need to know to undertake a good job. The research client might in turn be informed of the possible technical problems in undertaking the research as prescribed in the research brief. The original research brief may need to be improved upon subsequent to these discussions. If so, a revised research brief will be prepared to incorporate all the changes agreed upon and resubmitted to the research companies.

The research client–research agency discussions are useful not only in producing a good final research brief, but also in facilitating the research client to assess the research agency's ability to understand the research requirements. These discussions will form the basis for subsequent working relationship between the personnel from both parties, namely the research client and the research agency.

Research proposals ▬

Upon receipt of a research brief from a research client, the research agency would proceed to write a research proposal for submission to the research client. The research proposal describes a plan for conducting a research project and acts as the first formal communication tool between the client and the research agency. It contains a record of general issues that have been agreed between the two parties (e.g. scope and objectives of the research) in order to avoid any misunderstanding or disagreement that may arise later. In reality, a research proposal should be regarded as an instrument to judge the researcher's understanding of the problem and ability to conduct the research. Very often, a research agency is selected by virtue of its research proposal. Once accepted, the research proposal becomes the basis for the contract of agreement between the research agency and the research client, and serves as a record of what was agreed on. There is not a rigid format for a research proposal as it depends on the nature of the specific research project. Figure 1.4 presents the content outline of a research proposal.

> - Introduction
> - Understanding of the Marketing Problem
> - Research Objectives
> - Research Plan
> - List of Question Items
> - Data Processing and Tabulation
> - Time Schedule
> - Survey Fee
> - Research Team

Figure 1.4 *Content outline of a research proposal*

1 *Introduction.* This section of the research proposal offers background information and introduces the general context of the research problem. Additionally, it documents the information that is needed and the specific marketing decision areas to be clarified by the research study. It explains the research in measurable terms and defines the standards of what the research should fulfil.

2 *Understanding of the marketing problem.* This section of a research proposal sets out the dimensions of the research problem and is the direct result of preliminary research work. Highlighted here are the important elements such as the history and the current marketing strategy of the prospective client company. A clear, direct description of the market problem at hand, possible reasons for the problem and decision alternatives being studied will constitute an indispensable part of this section. The research proposal is an excellent tool for the research agency to demonstrate that it has a good understanding of the problem.

3 *Research objectives.* The objectives of the research are detailed in this section of the research proposal. General statements made earlier are further expanded and relevant issues which the research aims to cover are listed. Here, specific problems confronting the management are translated into a research terminology. In the event that the research objectives are lengthy, it is advisable to break them up under distinct subheadings, e.g. demographics of the target market, purchasing behaviour, brand image, etc.

4 *Research plan.* This section of the research proposal relates the major features pertaining to the research methods proposed for the study. Justifications for the proposed methods are required. The relevant aspects to be detailed include the scope and nature of population under study, the sampling procedure, the sample size, quality control procedure and data collection technique and analysis.

5 *List of questions.* At this stage, the research agency has not yet been formally commissioned to proceed with the research project, so it would be unreasonable to expect to see a final survey questionnaire included in a research proposal. At best, there will be a suggested list of topics or questions which the research agency believes should be included in the survey questionnaire.

6 *Data processing and tabulation.* A good and comprehensive research proposal would always provide details of the work to be undertaken in data editing, coding, entry and processing in the case of a quantitative survey. For the set of statistical tabulations (which are usually included as an appendix to the survey report), the research proposal should indicate the level of cross-tabulation of data to be adopted, for example, two-way or three-way cross-tabulations, regression analysis, χ^2 tests and so on. For a qualitative survey, the research proposal should indicate how the data recorded will be expressed. For example, will the recorded tapes be transcribed, or will data analysis be done direct from the original recorded tapes?

7 *Time schedule.* A research proposal without a specification of the time schedule for each phase of the research process is never considered complete. The research client will certainly be interested in knowing when the field work is scheduled to start and end. How soon will the top-line results be made available? And by when the final report will be completed and delivered? This section provides a statement indicating the schedule of when the various research activities will be completed.

8 *Survey fee.* The research proposal must not miss mentioning the survey fee for undertaking the research as well as the benefits the client can expect to get in return. Also, the client should be told the number of copies of the report that will be made available, whether the quoted fee would include verbal presentation of the survey findings, and the cost of sample products which may be required for use during the data collection phase. It is rare for a research agency to offer open-dated

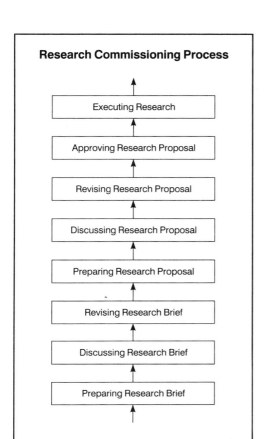

Research Commissioning Process

Executing Research

↑

Approving Research Proposal

↑

Revising Research Proposal

↑

Discussing Research Proposal

↑

Preparing Research Proposal

↑

Revising Research Brief

↑

Discussing Research Brief

↑

Preparing Research Brief

↑

cost proposals, so an indication of the validity of time period of the research cost will be included.

9 *Research team.* This section contains the list of personnel assigned to carry out the proposed study. Which research personnel will be involved in the research project is often a question that the research client asks. By presenting the curriculum vitae of its professional staff in the research proposal, the research agency is promoting its services to potential clients.

Selecting research agencies ▬

From among the research agencies which have submitted research proposals, the research client will then need to select one which can execute the study in the desired manner and at a reasonable cost. Some of the important guidelines for selection are:

1 *Research professionalism of the company.* An established research agency with a track record of numerous projects of a varied nature should be accorded high priority.

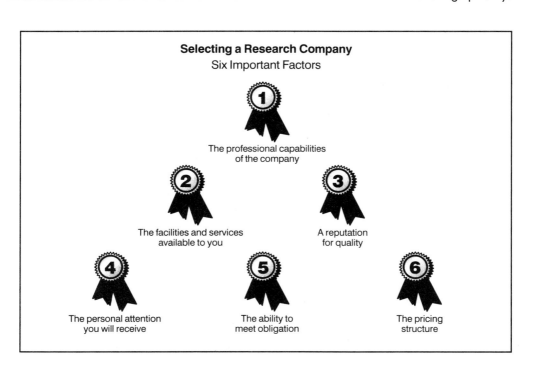

Selecting a Research Company
Six Important Factors

① The professional capabilities of the company

② The facilities and services available to you

③ A reputation for quality

④ The personal attention you will receive

⑤ The ability to meet obligation

⑥ The pricing structure

Such a research agency would normally be staffed with qualified professionals well versed with the market situations of the various products and services.

2 *Availability of research facilities.* The research agency selected possess the facilities which are fundamental for the conduct of the study. These include an updated sampling frame; experienced interviewers, coders and editors; suitably equipped chambers for special telephone interviewing; data processing equipment and software support.

3 *A reputation for quality.* The selected research agency should possess a good track record for delivering high-quality work.

4 *Personal attention expected to receive.* The selected research agency should be able to ensure a high degree of personal attention and be prompt in responding to the needs of the research client.

5 *Ability to meet deadlines.* Research data assumes near zero value if it is available only after the relevant marketing decision has been finalized. Consider only the research agencies who can submit the research findings promptly as required, after giving them time to do the job properly and thoroughly.

6 *Pricing structure.* The research client will want to pay the minimum possible costs without sacrificing data quality. Research agencies which can offer this kind of price-value combination are certainly worth considering.

Being a research client

Listed below are some courses of action which a research client should observe if he or she wishes to maximize the benefits from the research commissioned:

1 *Invite more than one research agency.* The intention here should strictly be to select the best research agency rather than to lift ideas from the many research proposals received and turn them over to the research agency which forwarded the lowest bid. To do otherwise may adversely reflect on the integrity of the research client, and at the same time lower the professional level of research agencies.

2 *Award the research early.* The earlier the research agency is informed that it has been commissioned to undertake the project, the more time it has in developing the most appropriate research programmes.

3 *Provide fullest company background.* Such information to be provided to the research agency may range from the company and product history, the nature of competition in the marketplace, to study objectives and the alternative courses of action contemplated. Remember always that even small details can sometimes help the research agency to generate valuable ideas and to propose what needs to be done.

4 *Avoid disruption.* A successful research requires the co-operation, mutual respect and confidence between the research agency and the research client. A wise and understanding research client will refrain from interfering with the operational aspects of the research once things get under way. Changes, if any, introduced by the research client at the last minute will upset the original plan and often bring more harm than good.

5 *Offer feedback on job done.* Offering compliments to the research agency on a job well done can often yield unexpected dividends for the research client in the long run. The research agency will know exactly how it has performed and may probably do an even better job the next time round. However, if the research agency has failed to execute the research study satisfactorily, the research client should make it known to the research agency as well.

6 *Regard the research agency as marketing partner.* The research agency will feel rewarded if it is regarded by the research client as an integral part of the marketing team. Such team spirit will encourage great attention and a high level of commitment from the research agency.

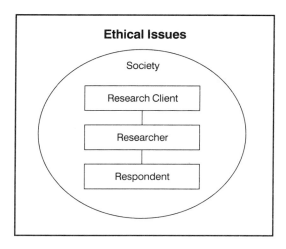

Ethical Issues

Society

Research Client

Researcher

Respondent

- confidentiality of proprietary data
- confidentiality of anonymity of client.

Additionally, the research client has the right to expect quality research from the research agency. The right includes:

- protection against unnecessary research
- protection against unqualified researcher
- protection against untruthful and/or misleading presentations of research findings.

Ethical issues

Ethics is concerned with the proper conduct of the research process in business enquiry. Ethical issues in marketing research are often discussed and brought to public's attention, as they are both necessary and desired to curb some focus of abuses.

Ethical conduct in marketing research concerns the rights and responsibilities of four parties, namely: society, the research client, the researcher and the respondent.

Societal rights

The society has the right to be informed of critical research findings. It is expected to be aware of research findings which give implications on the health and well-being of the general population. Also, the society has the right to expect objective results. In this respect, it expects the research to be unbiased and scientifically sound; and the availability of a complete reporting of the research when such a need arises.

Client's rights

The client can claim the right of confidentiality of the working relationship with the research agency. Two aspects of confidentiality are involved:

Researcher's rights

The researcher has the right to expect specific issues from both the research client, and from the respondent. From the research client, the researcher can expect him or her:

- to honestly solicit research proposals
- to have the research findings fairly and accurately dissimulated – in other words, any contingency clause attached to recommendations made by the researcher should not be deliberately omitted
- when the researcher reveals a specific analytical technique or solution strategies to the client that are competitively sensitive, he or she has the right to demand confidentiality of proprietary information.

From the respondent, the researcher can expect him or her:

- not to consciously distort or conceal data to deliberately cause confusion to the survey results
- to respect the confidentiality of the data if so requested by the organization supplying the information.

Respondent's rights

The respondent has three fundamental rights:

- the right to decide on participation
- the right to be assured of anonymity
- the right to safety in avoiding any physical or mental harm.

In other words, the respondent should be aware of the right not to participate in the research if he or she feels so, and of the opportunity to end her or his participation, if so desired. The respondent would have the guaranteed protection of anonymity, and the researcher shall hold as strictly confidential all information which tends to reveal the identity of the respondent. Finally, the respondent would be freed from stress and deception arising from her or his participation in the research study.

An abstract of Gallup's Standards and Practices in survey research is reproduced in Appendix C at the end of this chapter.

Appendix A: Syndicated studies in Singapore, 1997 ▬▬▬▬

Title of study	Sample respondents
Teens Lifestyle and Expenditure Survey	1,000 teenagers aged 12 to 19 years
Glamour Index	1,000 women aged 18 to 49 years
Sporting Life	1,000 adults aged 15 years and above
Body Power	600 mothers with children aged 0 to 3 years 11-months
Meal Cycle	1,000 adults aged 15 years and above
Interviewer's Choice	1,000 adults aged 15 years and above
Net Results	500 adults aged 15 years and above
Kids Index	600 children aged 7 to 14 years
Executive Lifestyle	500 Professionals, Managers, Executives and Business people
Consumer Electronics and Household Appliance Index	1,600 adults aged 15 years and above

Title of study	Sample respondents
Consumer Telecommunication Index	1,000 adults aged 20 years and above
Personal Computer Study	500 adults aged 15 years and above
Consumer Banking and Insurance Index	700 working adults and 300 PMEBs
Snacks Index	Six focus group discussions consisting of women, men, teenagers and children
Motoring Index	1,000 adult motorists
Residential Property Index	This index consists of a two-step survey. In the first stage, six groups of homebuyers are interviewed in a series of focus groups. The information gathered will be used to formulate the quantitative study, 300 potential homebuyers are interviewed via the telephone
Fast-Food Traffic Volume Tracking	This is an ongoing traffic monitor alone on a monthly basis at fifty fast-food outlets which are selected at random

Appendix B: Omnibus Survey Questionnaire ■■■■■■■

Introduction _____

Good morning/afternoon/evening. My name is. . . . . (**show identification card**) and I work for Frankie Research Services. This is an independent market research company in Malaysia which conducts surveys on various topics of interest. We are now conducting a survey to obtain information on personal products and services. I will be very grateful if you will help me by answering a few questions.

Contact question _____

May I know how many people aged 15 years and above are there in your household? Please tell me who they are, starting from the oldest to the youngest.

Name	Age (in years)

(*Interviewer:* Ask to speak to the selected member in the household)

A. Western fast food _____

1. Have you yourself ever visited any western fast food restaurant?
    Yes, ever visited 1
    No, never visited . . . 2 (**Go to Section B; shampoo**)

2a. Thinking about western fast food restaurants, can you name me the *first* one that comes to your mind? (*Interviewer:* **do not read out list**)
 b. Which other western fast food restaurants can you name me? Any others? (*Interviewer:* **do not read out list**)
 c. (**Show list of western fast food restaurants**). Which of the western fast food restaurants listed in this card have you ever seen or heard of? Any others?

	Q2a	Q2b	Q2c
	Top of mind	Unaided mentions	Aided mentions
A & W	1	1	1
Burger King	2	2	2
Hardees	3	3	3
Kentucky Fried Chicken	4	4	4
Long John Silver	5	5	5
McDonalds'	6	6	6
Pizza Hut	7	7	7
Shakey's	8	8	8
Wendy's	9	9	9
Other (Specify)	0	0	0
None at all	X	X	X

3. On average, about how often do you visit a western fast food restaurant?
    More than once a week 1
    Once a week 2
    About 2–3 times a month 3
    Once a month 4
    Once in every 2 to 3 months 5
    Once in every 4 to 6 months 6
    Less often 7

B. Shampoo _____

1. Do you use shampoo nowadays?
    Yes . . 1
    No . . 2 (**Go to Section C: instant coffee**)
2. Who normally buys the shampoo that you are using?
    Self 1
    Other 2

3. **(Showcard)** Here is a list of factors which people think would influence their choice for a particular brand of shampoo. As I read out each factor, please tell me how important it is in influencing your choice of a brand of shampoo. Would you say it is: Very important, Important, or Not Important at all?

	Very important	Important	Not imortant at all
Lathers easily	1	2	3
Does not cause dandruff	1	2	3
Cleans hair well	1	2	3
Has strong, lasting fragrance	1	2	3
Keeps hair in good condition	1	2	3
Has good quality	1	2	3
Is suitable for different types of hair	1	2	3
Has an attractive pack	1	2	3
Is good for regular use	1	2	3
Is not old-fashioned	1	2	3
Leaves hair feeling good	1	2	3

C. Instant coffee

1. Have you ever drunk instant coffee at home?
   Yes 1
   No .... 2 **(Go to Section D: Department store)**

2. Not counting today, thinking of the day that you last drank instant coffee, at which times of the day did you drink it?
   Before breakfast 1
   Breakfast 2
   Between breakfast and lunch 3
   Lunch 4
   Between lunch and dinner 5
   Dinner 6
   After dinner, before bed 7

3. Compared to a year ago, would you say that you are drinking More, Less or About the same amount of instant coffee nowadays?
   More 1
   About the same 2
   Less 3

D. Department store

1. When was the *last* time you visited a department store?
   A week or less ago 1
   Over 1 week to 2 weeks ago 2
   Over 2 weeks to 4 weeks ago 3
   Over 1 month to 3 months ago 4

   Over 3 months to 6 months ago* 5
   Over 6 months to 1 year ago* 6
   Over 1 year ago* 7
   *(Go to Section E: Public bus service)

2. Thinking of the last time you visited a department store, on which day of the week was it?
   Monday 1
   Tuesday 2
   Wednesday 3
   Thursday 4
   Friday 5
   Saturday 6
   Sunday 7
   Cannot remember 8

3. Again, on your last visit to a department store, at about what time of the day did you go there?
   12 noon or earlier 1
   After 12 noon–2 pm 2
   After 2 pm – 4 pm 3
   After 4 pm – 6 pm 4
   After 6 pm – 8 pm 5
   After 8 pm 6
   Cannot remember 7

4. For about how many hours did you stay in this department store on that visit?
   0.5 hour or less 1
   Over 0.5 hours – 1 hour 2
   Over 1 hour – 1.5 hours 3
   Over 1.5 hours – 2 hours 4
   Over 2 hours – 2.5 hours 5
   Over 2.5 hours – 3 hours 6
   Over 3 hours 7
   Cannot remember 8

5. If a department store runs a promotion campaign, how likely or unlikely would you make a special visit to this department store?

Very likely 1
Likely 2
Depends, not sure 3
Unlikely 4
Very unlikely 5

6. From where do you seek information *most* on department store's promotion campaign?

Newspaper 1
Television 2
Radio 3
Flyer 4
Direct mail 5
In-store posters 6
Words of mouth 7
Other (specify) 8

E. Public bus service

1. Which of the following modes of traffic transportation do you use at least 3 times a week?

Bus* 1

Mass Rapid Transportation 2
Taxi 3
Own vehicle 4
*(If not used, go to Section F: Charge/ credit card)

2. What are your reasons for taking a bus? Is it for _____ **(Read out)?**

Working 1
Studying 2
Visiting/socialising 3
Shopping 4
Other (specify) 5

3. Which of the following situations have you experienced in the past one month?

Flagged signal, but bus did not stop . 1
Pressed bell, but bus did not stop . . . 2
Rushed forward, but bus did not stop 3
Was trapped in the door of bus when boarding/alighting 4
Found bus door already open before it came into the bus bay/stop 5

Waited for 30 minutes or longer for a bus 6
Felt overcharged as demanded by bus driver 7

4. **(Show card)** Here is a list of factors that bus passnegers are usually concerned about taking a bus. How would you rate these factors in Singapore? Would you say that it is Very Good, Good, Fair, Poor or Very Poor?

	Very Good	Good	Fair	Poor	Very Poor
Punctuality	1	2	3	4	5
Stability (e.g. speed)	1	2	3	4	5
Air-conditioning	1	2	3	4	5
Cleanliness	1	2	3	4	5
Driver's mannerism	1	2	3	4	5
Waiting time	1	2	3	4	5
Frequency of bus arrival	1	2	3	4	5
Service hours	1	2	3	4	5

F. Charge/credit card

1. Do you personally own a charge/credit card?

Yes 1
No . . . . 2 **(Go to Section G: Pager)**

2. In the past *one* month, have you ever used your charge/credit card to pay for the following items?

Books 1
Clothes & accessories 2
Shoes 3
Groceries/supermarket items 4
CDs/LDs 5
Computer & peripherals 6
Sports equipment 7
Petrol 8

3. In the past *three* months, have you ever used your charge/credit card to pay for the following items?

Magazine subscription 1
Hotel accommodation 2
Household electrical appliances (e.g. hair dryer) 3
Electrical equipment 4
Furniture 5

Airline tickets 6
Restaurant meals 7
Social entertainment (pubs, bars,
KTV) 8

4. **(Show card)** I have here a list of statements about people's perception towards charge/credit cards. For each statement, please tell me whether you Strongly Agree, Agree, Neither Agree nor Disagree, Disagree or Strongly Disagree.

	Strongly Agree	Agree	Neither	Disagree	Strongly Disagree
Charge/Credit cards are a consistent way of payment	1	2	3	4	5
Charge/Credit cards are a safe way of payment . .	1	2	3	4	5
It is prestigious to own a charge/credit card	1	2	3	4	5
I prefer to own a credit card from the bank with which I have an account	1	2	3	4	5
I prefer Charge/Credit card for payment because I can keep track of my spending . .	1	2	3	4	5
I use Charge/Credit card for payment because I can make payment later	1	2	3	4	5

G. Pager

1. Do you own a pager?
Yes 1
No . . . . 2 **(Go to personal particulars section)**
2. Does you pager belong to yourself or to your company?
Yourself 1
Company 2
Other (Specify) 3

3. Do you share your pager with others for use?
Yes 1
No 2
4. Does yu pager have the following features?
Numeric paging 1
Message paging 2
Beep mail paging 3
Page talk 4
Internet E-mail alert 5
Internet paging 6
5. About how many times do you receive paging messages on an average day?
1 time or less 1
2 times 2
3 times 3
4 times 4
5 times 5
7 times or more 6

Personal particulars

1. *Record sex*
Male 1
Female 2
2. **(Show card)**
Which age group on this show card do you belong to?
Below 20 years 1
20 – 29 years 2
30 – 39 years 3
40 – 49 years 4
50 years and over 5
3. Are you **(Read out)**?
Single 1
Married 2
Divorced/separated 3
4. What is you highest educational attainment?
Primary or below 1
GCE 'O' level 2
GCE 'A' level 3
Dipoma/Polytechnic 4
Degree 5
5. Are you **(Read out)**
Working 1
A housewife 2
A student 3
A retired person 4
Unemployed 5

Administration section —————————————————————————————

Interviewer's Name: _____ Code: _____

Interview Date: _____ / _____ / _____
                  (Day)   (Month)   (Year)

Interviewing Time: From _____ to _____

Respondent's Name: _____

Respondent's Address: _____

_____

_____ (Tel. No: _____)

Best Date/Time for Making Recall (if needed): _____

THANK RESPONDENT AND TERMINATE INTERVIEW

Appendix C:
Gallup standards and policies – survey research ▬▬▬▬

Introduction

The Gallup Organization adheres to the standards set forth by the Council of American Survey Research Organizations (CASRO) as minimal requirements and is a member in good standing of this organization. In some cases, as specified, Gallup chooses to set a 'higher' standard to ensure the clearest adherence to high ethical principles.

The Gallup Organization also adheres to the Professional Code of Ethics and Practices of the American Association for Public Opinion Research (AAPOR). The following set of standards summarizes both the CASRO and AAPOR standards, but a full set of such codes are enclosed in the appendix [not included here].

This set of Standards for Survey Research sets forth the rules of ethical conduct for the Gallup Organization. Acceptance of this Code is mandatory for all CASRO members.

The Code has been organized into sections describing the responsibilities of a survey research organization to respondents, clients, and outside contractors, and in reporting study results.

1 Responsibilities to respondents

1a Confidentiality

Since individuals who are interviewed are the lifeblood of the survey research industry, it is essential that Gallup be responsible for protecting from disclosure to third parties – including clients and members of the public – the identity of individual respondents as well as respondent-identifiable information, unless the respondent expressly requests or permits such disclosure.

This principle of confidentiality is qualified by the following exceptions:

- the identity of individual respondents and respondent-identifiable information may be disclosed to the client to permit the client:(1) to validate interviews and/or (2) to determine an additional fact of analytical importance to the study. In these cases, respondents must be given a sound reason for the inquiry. In all cases, a refusal by the respondent to continue must be respected. Before disclosing respondent-identifiable information to a client for purposes of interview validation or reinquiry, Gallup must take whatever steps are needed to ensure that the client will conduct the validation or recontact in a fully professional manner. This includes the avoidance of multiple validation contacts or other conduct that would harass or could embarrass respondents. It also includes avoidance of any use of the information. (e.g., lead generation) for other than legitimate and ethical survey research purposes or to respond to customer/respondent complaints. Assurance that the client will respect such limitations and maintain respondent confidentiality should be confirmed in writing before any confidential information is disclosed.

Respondent-identifiable data may also be disclosed to clients so that they may analyse survey data in combination with other respondent-level data such as internal customer data, respondent-level data from another survey, etc. It is understood that the information will be used for model-building, internal analysis or the like, and not for individual marketing efforts. This can *only* be done with explicit respondent approval.

The identity of individual respondents and respondent-identifiable information may be disclosed to other survey research organizations whenever such organizations are conducting different phases of a multi-stage study (e.g., a trend study). Gallup should confirm in writing that respondent confidentiality will be maintained in accordance with the Code.

● In the case of research in which representatives of the client or others are present, such client representatives and others should be asked not to disclose to anyone not present the identity of individual participants or other participant-identifying information except as needed to respond, with the participant's prior specific approval, to any complaint by one or more of the participants concerning a product or service supplied by the client.

The principle of respondent confidentiality includes the following specific applications or safeguards:

● The Gallup Organization's staff or personnel should not use or discuss respondent-identifiable data or information for other than legitimate internal research purposes.
● The Gallup Organization has the responsibility for ensuring that subcontractors (interviewers, interviewing services and validation, coding and tabulation organization) and consultants are aware of and agree to maintain and respect respondent confidentiality whenever the identity of respondents or respondent-identifiable information is disclosed to such entities.
● Before permitting clients or others to have access to completed questionnaires in circumstances other than those described above, respondent names and other respondent-identifying information (e.g., telephone numbers) should be deleted.
● Invisible identifiers on mail questionnaires that connect respondent answers to particular respondents should not be used. Visible identification numbers may be used but should be accompanied by an explanation that such identifiers are for control purposes only and that respondent confidentiality will not be compromised.
● When Gallup receives from a client or other entity information that it knows or reasonably believes to be confidential, respondent-identifiable information or

lessen the importance of respondent anonymity. Consequently, if Gallup is confronted with a subpoena or other legal process requesting the disclosure of respondent-identifiable information, all reasonable steps should be taken to oppose such requests, including informing the court or other respondent anonymity and interposing all appropriate defences to the request for disclosure.

1b Privacy and the avoidance of harassment

Gallup has a responsibility to strike a proper balance between the needs for research and the privacy of individuals who become the respondents in the research. To achieve this balance:

● Respondents will be protected from unnecessary and unwanted intrusions and/or any form of personal harassment.
● The voluntary character of the interviewer-respondent contact should be stated explicitly where the respondent might have reason to believe that co-operation is not voluntary.

This principle of privacy includes the following specific applications:

● Gallup, its subcontractors and interviewers, shall make every reasonable effort to ensure that the respondent understands the purpose of the interviewer/respondent contact.
  ● The interviewer must provide prompt and honest identification of his/her research firm affiliation.
  ● Respondent questions should be answered in a forthright and non-deceptive manner.
● Deceptive practices and misrepresentation, such as using research as a guise for sales or solicitation purposes, are expressly prohibited.
● Gallup respects the right of individuals to refuse to be interviewed or to terminate an interview in progress. Techniques that infringe on these rights should not be

employed, but Gallup may make reasonable efforts to obtain an interview including: (1)explaining the purpose of the research project; (2) providing a gift or monetary incentive adequate to elicit co-operation; and (3) recontacting an individual at a different time if the individual is unwilling or unable to participate during the initial contact.

- Gallup interviewers are responsible for arranging interviewing times that are convenient for respondents.
- Lengthy interviews can be a burden. All research organizations are responsible for weighing the research need against the length of the interview, and respondents must not be enticed into an interview by a misrepresentation of the length of the interview. In general, Gallup strongly recommends telephone interviews of 15–18 minutes maximum unless appropriate incentives are provided.
- Gallup is responsible for developing techniques to minimize the discomfort or apprehension of respondents and interviewers when dealing with sensitive subject matter.
- Electronic equipment (taping, recording, photographing) and one-way viewing rooms may be used only with the full knowledge of respondents, unless such processes are for evaluation or validation purposes.

2 Responsibilities to clients _____

2a Client relationships

Relationships between the Gallup Organization and its clients for whom surveys are conducted should be of such a nature that they foster confidence and mutual respect. They must be characterized by honesty and confidentiality.

2b Specific responsibilities

The following specific approaches describe in more detail Gallup's responsibilities in this relationship:

- Gallup assists its clients in the design of effective and efficient studies. If Gallup researchers question whether a study design will provide the information necessary to serve the client's purposes, they must make such reservations known.
- Gallup must conduct the study in the manner agreed upon. However, if it becomes apparent in the course of the study that changes in the plans should be made, Gallup must make its view known promptly to the client.
- Gallup has an obligation to allow its clients to verify that work performed meets all contracted specifications and to examine all operations that are relevant to the proper execution of the project in the manner set forth. While clients are encouraged to examine questionnaires or other records to maintain open access to the research process, Gallup will continue to protect the confidentiality and privacy of survey respondents.
- When more than one client contributes to the cost of a project specifically commissioned with Gallup, each client concerned shall be informed that there are other participants (but not necessarily of their identity).
- Gallup will hold confidential all information obtained about a client's general business operations, and about matters connected with research projects conducted for a client.
- For research findings obtained by the agency that are the property of the client, Gallup may make no public release or revelation of findings without expressed, prior approval from the client.
- Gallup pledges to make every effort to meet client needs while minimizing respondent time and effort.
- In general, Gallup adheres to the basic rule of 'full disclosure' with regard to any errors or omissions. When errors or omissions are discovered, full disclosure of such errors will be made to the client in a timely manner. In addition, Gallup will make appropriate corrections.

2c Bribery and gifts to clients

Bribery in any form and in any amount is unacceptable and is a violation of Gallup's fundamental, ethical obligations. Gallup and/or its principals, officers and employees should never give gifts to clients in the form of cash. To the extent permitted by applicable laws and regulations, Gallup may provide nominal gifts to clients and may entertain clients, as long as the cost of such entertainment is modest in amount and incidental in nature.

3 Responsiblities in reporting to clients and the public

3a Accuracy of reports

When reports are being prepared for client confidential or public release purposes, it is the obligation of Gallup to ensure that the findings they release are an accurate portrayal of the survey data, and careful checks on the accuracy of all figures are mandatory.

3b Reporting survey information

Gallup's report to a client or the public should contain, or the research organization should be ready to supply to a client or the public on short notice, the following information about the survey:

- The name to the organization for which the study was conducted and the name of the organization conducting it.
- The purpose of the study, including the specific objectives.
- The dates on or between which the data collection was done.
- A definition of the universe that the survey is intended to represent and a description of the population frame(s) that was actually sampled.
- A description of the sample design, including the method of selecting sample elements, method of interview, cluster size, number of callbacks, respondent eligibility

or screening criteria, and other pertinent information.

- A description of results of sample implementation including (a) a total number of sample elements contacted, (b) the number not reached, (c) the number of refusals, (d) the number of terminations, (e) the number of non-eligibles, (f) the number of completed interviews.
- The basis for any specific 'completion rate' percentages should be fully documented and described.
- The questionnaire or exact wording of the questions used, including Interviewer directions and visual exhibits.
- A description of any weighting or estimating procedures used.
- A description of any special scoring, data adjustment or indexing procedures used.
- Estimates of the sampling error and of data should be shown when appropriate, but when shown they should include reference to other possible sources of error so that a misleading impression of accuracy or precision is not conveyed.
- Statistical tables clearly labelled and identified as to questionnaire source, including the number of raw cases forming the base for each cross-tabulation.
- Copies of interviewer instructions, validation results, code books, and other important working papers.

3c Methodological standards

The Gallup standard is based on the concept of full disclosure.

Full disclosure means Gallup explains to our clients, including the media in press releases, the quality of the results, conclusions, and inferences drawn based on the survey conducted. Full disclosure also means avoiding platitudes and general statements, to the extent possible, about the errors in surveys. It means reporting data or actualities about the quality of the data collected. This standard attempts to avoid, as much as possible, dictating how surveys must be conducted or stating benchmarks that a survey must meet in order to be defined as acceptable. The standard is (1) always fully disclose and (2) that disclosure must include statements about the following topics:

- Sample Design. This includes the time period during which the data was collected and the sampling error or some other related measure of the precision of the survey such as the margin of error – the 95 per cent confidence interval for the main item(s) of interest from the survey. Note that if an author chooses to report sampling error it must be accompanied by the statement that plus or minus sampling error gives a 675 confidence interval. Appropriate sampling weights, the inverse of the probabilities of selection, should be used in all estimation, testing and modelling done for any client.
- Non-response Error. This includes reporting the response rates, the contact rate, and the completion rate based on standard formulas. If a special study has been conducted to measure the differences between respondents and non-respondents, a brief description of the results should be included. In addition, the results of this study should be written up in detail and submitted to the *Gallup Research Journal*. In the absence of this type of study the following statement should be used in the report or press release: (a) if the data was not weighted to population (demographic) controls, 'Because respondents and non-respondents may differ in their survey characteristics, the results of this study may be biased' or (b) if weighting was used, 'The results of this study were weighted by (insert weighting variables, such as 'by age, race, ethnicity and gender') in an attempt to reduce the bias caused by non-response'. When weighting is used, the report should include weighted and unweighted results to show clients the impact of weighting.
- Coverage Error. This type of error generally occurs because of frame deficiencies. It usually appears because the frame does not cover the target population, for example, a Random Digit Dialing (RDD) survey of the US covers only households with telephones. This type of error can also appear differentially in a survey. In the above RDD example US coverage is lower among blacks, in rural areas, particularly in the south-east, and in the inner cities or urban areas. Coverage error can also occur because the frame has units in it a multiple number of times, or has out-of-scope units. For RDD surveys households with more than one residential telephone line have multiple chances to be selected, and business telephone numbers can also be selected. When these deficiencies occur, the client should be made aware, in writing, of this potential bias, through a full description of any frame deficiencies. If weighting to population (demographic) controls was used, the statement under Non-response Error should be modified to: 'The results of this study were weighted by (insert weighting variables, such as 'by age, race, ethnicity, and gender') in an attempt to reduce the biases caused by non-response and coverage error.'
- Measurement Error. This error occurs at the intersection of the questionnaire, respondent, interviewer, and mode of data collection. The impact of this type of error is very difficult to quantify without special studies, either involving reinterviews or matching to some administrative data set that is believed to contain higher quality data. In the absence of such studies, Gallup's clients must be informed of the measures taken to minimize or control measurement error. Examples of such measures include rotating response categories where appropriate for telephone surveys, interviewer training, interviewer monitoring, etc.

In summary, the Gallup standard for surveys is full disclosure of the quality of the data collected. This disclosure must be in writing and can occur as part of the body of a final report to a client, or as a technical appendix. For tracking studies, where data are regularly supplied to clients, a full disclosure report must be written and provided to the client at least annually. Because press releases usually must be fairly brief, they can refer readers to a technical document available from Gallup. However, for important or sensitive topics authors of press releases should attempt to include as much of the above full disclosure as possible. In addition, it is strongly recommended that Research Directors use a member of Galup's Methodology Department early in the design and planning of a survey to help minimize these sources of error, and to help write up the report on the quality of the survey.

Source: The Gallup Organization (1996) *The Gallup Way,* pp. 2–10.

End-of-chapter revision

Review questions
1.1 What is implied in the term *marketing research*?
1.2 What is the role of marketing research in today's marketing environment? What are the reasons for its growth in the past two decades?
1.3 Marketing research is useful in a wide variety of marketing situations. Cite three situations (real or hypothetical) to demonstrate this statement.
1.4 Give a definition of marketing research, either in your own words or quote one mentioned in the text.
1.5 Discuss the meaning and importance of each of the following words used most commonly in the definition of marketing research:
  a systematic
  b objective
  c information
  d decision-making.
1.6 What are the factors which account for the growing importance of marketing research?
1.7 Briefly explain in what ways can marketing research help managers to make:
  a pricing decisions?
  b product decisions?
  c promotional decisions?
  d distribution decisions?
1.8 There is relatively less use of marketing research by wholesalers than by retailers. What factors do you think might account for this?
1.9 Discuss the advantages and disadvantages of in-house data collection versus hiring an external research agency to collect data.

1.10 What are the major considerations involved in deciding whether to do a research project in-house, or to commission the research project to a research agency?
1.11 How should a research agency be selected?
1.12 What is a research brief?
1.13 What are the main components of a research brief? Briefly discuss each component.
1.14 Differentiate between an omnibus survey and a syndicated survey.
1.15 Differentiate between an exclusive survey and a syndicated survey.
1.16 Differentiate between an omnibus survey and an exclusive survey.
1.17 What are the advantages and disadvantages of a syndicated survey?
1.18 What are the advantages and disadvantages of an omnibus survey?
1.19 What are the advantages and disadvantages of an exclusive survey?
1.20 Identify and briefly describe the major structural components of a marketing research proposal.

True-false questions
Write True (T) or False (F) for the following:
1.21 Knowledge gained from personal experience often lacks objectivity.
1.22 Advertising agencies have very little use for marketing research.
1.23 Marketing research plays a key role in the marketing concept.
1.24 Marketing research is useful because it removes all uncertainties from a decision situation.
1.25 In-house research study is preferred over external research if the results will

be used in litigation, legal proceedings, or as part of a promotional campaign.

1.26 Marketing research is problem-oriented research whose main function is to help management make better decisions.

1.27 An exclusive survey is a viable research option for the client who has a limited research budget and who needs a few research questions.

1.28 Industrial goods manufacturers are less dependent on marketing research.

1.29 In a syndicated survey, the research client can dictate the survey timing, as well as the length of survey questionnaire.

1.30 An omnibus survey is cost-effective since a number of research clients share the field-work costs.

1.31 In-house research is preferred when the research study requires special research equipment (eg. eye camera).

1.32 In-house research is preferred from the viewpoint of cost sharing.

1.33 External research is preferred for the reason of topic familiarity.

1.34 Research brief is a document prepared by the research company.

1.35 The society has the right to be informed of critical research findings.

Multiple-choice questions

1.36 Risks arise in marketing decisions because:
a of a lack of information regarding the results
b there is more than one choice
c large amounts of money are involved
d they are often joint decisions.

1.37 Of the following, which one would have no reason to use marketing research?
a The owner of a large food chain
b The president of an alumni association
c The chief executive of a bank.
d All of the above would have reasons to use marketing research

1.38 The biggest users of marketing research are:
a manufacturers of industrial goods
b publishers and broadcasters

c manufacturers of consumer goods
d financial institutions and services.

1.39 In the marketing concept, marketing research serves the role of:
a finding out consumers' wants
b discovering the best advertising approaches for selling surplus production
c supplying data to support advertising chains
d none of the above.

1.40 Marketing research:
a emphasizes the systematic gathering and recording of data
b concerns all phases of marketing goods or services
c should be objective and accurate
d all of the above.

1.41 Marketing research involves:
a objective gathering of data
b providing information to help identify an opportunity
c providing information on which to base decisions
d all of the above.

1.42 Which of the following has not increased the importance of marketing research?
a The shift from price to non-price competition.
b Changes in consumer tastes.
c Rising corporate taxes.
d Demographic changes of the population.

1.43 From the following list, which one is not a sound reason for conducting marketing research and other surveys?
a To help clients gain a competitive edge.
b To persuade the public to buy client's product or service.
c To obtain information for executive decision making.
d To measure changes in consumer attitudes and behaviour.

1.44 From the following list, which one is a sound reason for conducting marketing research and other surveys?
a To obtain 'trade secrets' about the competition.

b To identify people's belief.

c To obtain a list of interested buyers for a research client.

d To determine the actual number of buyers of a product or service.

1.45 Which of the following results should the researcher expect from his initial project planning meetings with the research client?

a A draft questionnaire.

b Precodes for the open-ended questions.

c Pilot test results for the questionnaire.

d None of the above

1.46 The client can claim the right of expecting quality research which include:

a protection against unnecessary research

b protection against unqualified research

c protection against untruthful/misleading presentations of research findings.

d all of the above.

1.47 The survey respondent can claim:

a the right to decide on participation

b the right to be assured of anonymity.

c the right to safety in avoiding any physical or mental harm.

d all of the above.

2

Marketing research process _____

The marketing research process is a sequence of steps involved in the systematic collection and analysis of marketing data (Figure 2.1). In essence, it provides a description of how a marketing investigation is designed and implemented, which helps to guide the execution of a research study from its inception through to the final analysis and reporting of data.

The steps depicted in Figure 2.1 are sequential and interrelated. A decision made at any one step may affect the decision to be made at other subsequent steps, and any modification introduced at any one step often means that modification at other steps may be necessary.

In specific terms, the benefits of observing the marketing research process are:

● it depicts the structure on which a marketing research study can be based
● it provides a useful basis for understanding and evaluating research proposals and reports
● it helps the marketing manager to judge the extent of confidence which he can place in the research findings
● it lends support to the rationale of selecting a specific research design.

Problem definition ▰▰▰▰▰

The foremost step in the marketing research process is to define the marketing problem at hand. The adage which says, 'a problem well-defined is half solved'

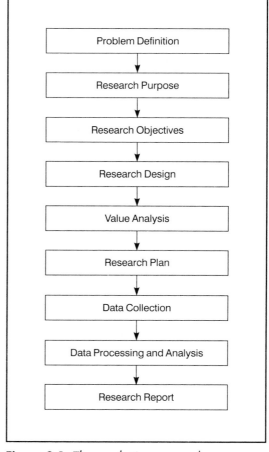

Figure 2.1 *The marketing research process*

applies well to marketing research studies, for often attention is wrongly channelled to finding solutions or evolving ideas rather than searching for the source(s) of the problem. In a situation where the research problem lacks clear definition, the task of designing a good research programme will become difficult. The prerequisite of defining the problem at hand is to identify and diagnose the problem, a process known as *situation analysis*. It is one of the most creative phases of research as it provides the key impetus in motivation and stimulation for further research.

Marketing problems exist aplenty in the marketplace and may be classified into two broad categories: difficulty-related problems and opportunity-related problems. The former concerns development surrounding the marketplace which bears negative or counter-productive consequences to the company (e.g. sales decline). The latter

category, on the contrary, originates from situations that invite benefits.

In the initial stage, a problem may only be recognized in a very general form and hence restrict the research programme from being comprehensively designed. Both the researcher and the research client (generally the marketing manager) will jointly formulate the problem into a precise and definite statement. In the process, the researcher becomes mindful of the marketing problem and the nature of decision confronting the company. At the same time, the research client is aware of what the research study can and cannot fulfil.

Hague maintained that when the research client fails to adequately define the problem either in his research brief (or verbally), it

What is the problem?	What is the cause of the problem?	What do I want to know?	What will I do with the information when I have got it?
Insufficient turnover	My sales are limited to certain industries	Market size and segments	Push into new segments
Insufficient turnover	We sell only in the South–East	Location of demand throughout the UK	Increase sales effort in other areas
Sales and profits are falling	Product is entering old age of life cycle	Future market size	Invest or sell off plant
The profit on sales ratio is falling	Our prices are too low	Price sensitivity	Adjust prices and relate them to profitability
The advertising budget is out of hand	We don't know where to get the best return	Advertising effectiveness	Modify advertisements to suit the market
Sales are falling	Our product has a quality problem	User's levels of product satisfaction	Redesign products or introduce a new range
Sales are falling	Competition has become more aggressive	Market shares and factors influencing choice of supplier	Sharpen up the marketing mix
Costs are rising	The cost of representatives has risen dramatically	Effectiveness of salesmen	Implement controls
Sales are static	We suspect we are regarded as old–fashioned	Company image	Influence by means of advertising and/or PR campaign

Figure 2.2 *Questions to ask before commissioning research – and some specimen answers.* Source: *Paul N. Hague (1987)* The Industrial Market Research Handbook. *Kogan Page.*

would be the task of the researcher to help produce the final document which leads to effective decisions. He further suggested that in order to clearly define the problem for actionable research, the researcher and the research client must jointly attempt to answer the following four questions:

1 What is the problem?
2 What is the cause of the problem?
3 What information do I require to find a solution to the problem?
4 What are the possible courses of action I could take after I am equipped with the information I want?

Some examples offered by Hague are given in Figure 2.2.

Research purpose

The purpose of research is almost always specified in the research brief provided by the research client. It would be frustrating and embarrassing for the research client and the researcher to realize that they do not fully agree on the research purpose after the research project has already commenced or been completed. Here again, if the research client is vague about his research requirements and fails to define the research purpose clearly, the researcher must seek a clarification before he proceeds with the

---

Research Purpose (Checklist of Questions)

- What decisions will be made?
- What action will be taken arising from the results of the research?
- What are the implications of this action?
- What are the alternatives available?
- What are the risks in the decision or action?
- What are the potential payoffs of the action?
- When will the decision be made?
- Are there externally enforced deadlines on the decision?

Figure 2.3 *Research purpose: checklist of questions*. Source: *Jeffrey L. Pope*, Practical Marketing Research. *Amacon, p. 48.*

---

project. In the process, the research client must supply all relevant background information to the researcher unreservedly wherever possible, and the researcher should address the research client on basic issues such as the reason(s) for wanting the research and the possible courses of action being considered by the company. (See Figure 2.3).

Research objectives

Once the research purpose is established, it will then be translated into a set of research objectives, which answer what kind of information is needed and why. Research objectives spell out the goals of the research but, unlike research purpose, they do not necessarily list out the courses of action to be considered in decision-making (e.g. the type of packaging design to be used for the new product).

When specifying research objectives, the following three fundamental areas should be covered:

- development of hypothesis
- outline of research questions
- scope (or boundary) of the research.

Though not an absolute necessity, hypothesis development helps sharpen the specific aims and the direction of a research study. As a common saying in the research circle goes: 'If you do not know what you are looking for, you won't find it.' To illustrate, if we begin with the hypothesis that sales decline is caused due to the promotional efforts introduced by competitors, then it would be absolutely necessary for the research to cover the advertising aspects. There are many ways to develop hypotheses, such as in-depth interviews, focus group discussions, experience surveys and so on.

After hypothesis development an outline of research questions will follow, which offers a clear insight into the type of information needed for the research study and serves as necessary input at questionnaire design stage. Usually, the outline of research questions will be shaped when marketing problems are translated into research problems, as exhibited in Figure 2.4.

To further enhance the precision of outlining the research questions, researchers often specify the scope or boundary of the research to include three aspects:

1 *Target segment.* This addresses the question of who constitutes the subjects of study. For example, does the study cover the entire population, or Housing and Development Board residents, or working females only?

2 *Area under study.* This concerns the areas or topics of investigation. An automobile model study, for example, may dwell on the general attitudes of motorists; or may just concentrate on motorists' attitudes towards trunk space, appearance, gas economy or styling.

3 *Accuracy level.* This concerns the desired accuracy of research results. As a general rule, the greater the risk facing the marketing decision, the higher the level of precision should be.

Marketing problems	Research problems
Develop a package for a new product	Evaluate effectiveness of new package designs
Increase market penetration through the opening of new stores	Evaluate prospective locations
Increase store traffic	Measure current image and traffic volume of the store
Increase amount of repeat purchasing behaviour	Assess current amount of repeat purchasing behaviour
Develop more equitable sales territories	Assess current and proposed territories with respect to their respective areas
Allocate advertising budget geographically	Determine current level of market penetration in the respective areas
Introduce new product	Design a test market to assess the likely acceptance of the new product
Increase in-store promotion of existing products	Evaluate the impact of present promotion scheme on sales volume
Expand current warehouse facilities	Evaluate possible warehouse locations
Adopt pricing strategy for new product	Assess the levels of potential demand associated with various price levels

Figure 2.4 *Marketing problems and research problems: examples of the relationship*

1. What specific information should the project provide?
2. If more than one type of information will be developed from the study, which is the most important?
3. What are the priorities? If none, why not?

Figure 2.5 *Research objective: checklist of questions.* Source: *Jeffery L. Pope*, Practical Marketing Research. *Amacon, p. 48.*

Research design

This step of the marketing research process involves the development of a research plan for carrying out the research study. There are alternative research designs or plans which a researcher can employ in dealing with a particular situation, the choice of which is largely dependent on the research purpose. This topic will be discussed in greater detail in Chapter 3.

Value analysis

Value analysis involves a comparison of two things: the value of research information required and the cost of acquiring such information. When the value exceeds the cost of research information, the implementation of the research is justified. When the research cost is higher than the research value, no research should be undertaken. Value analysis, also popularly known as *cost-benefit analysis*, helps determine whether the marketing research process of a proposed study should continue or halt.

Of the two components – research cost and research value – the former presents little or no difficulty in estimation. In the case of commissioned projects, the research cost would have been quoted by the research agency in its research proposal. As for an in-house research, the research cost can be computed without much difficulty

by adding up expenditures of the following items:

- Labour costs
  - Interviewing and data entry
  - Administration
  - Executive personnel
  - Quality control
- Other expenses
  - Stationery and printing
  - Travelling
  - Sampling frame
  - Computer services
  - Incentives for respondents
  - Office rentals, overheads recovery.

Computation of the value of research information is, however, not so simple and straightforward. Added to this, there is a further need to introduce subjective assumptions in the computation process. All of them will now be discussed.

At the outset, the value of research information is dependent on three major elements: the importance of the marketing information, the amount of uncertainties that surround the decision-making process and the extent of influence which the research information has on making the decision. Research information assumes a higher value when the decision on which it is based bears greater significance in terms of dollars and long-term success of the company. Secondly, when uncertainties surrounding the decision-making process are many and varied, research information would command a higher practical value. Finally, the value of research information will be increased if the research results are likely to be used to determine the ultimate marketing decision.

The reduced loss method

A crude method of computing the value of research information is the *reduced loss* method. As its name suggest, this method examines the potential loss should a wrong decision be made when no research has been undertaken. The value of research information in this case will be the difference between the expected loss incurred without research information and the expected loss incurred if research information is obtained. In mathematical terms, we have:

Value of research = Expected loss
information (without research) –
Expected loss
(with research)

The resulting value represents the potential loss which could be prevented had the research been undertaken to obtain the additional information.

Illustrative Example 1

A company is considering the launch of a new product. Based on intuition, it predicts that the probability of its new product being a failure is 35 per cent. However, if the decision to launch the new product is made after a research study has gathered the additional information, the likelihood of failure will be reduced to 30 per cent. Furthermore, it is assumed that the company would incur a loss of $400,000 if the new product should fail. The question here is: should the company commission a research study, quoted at $25,000, to gather the additional information in the decision-making process?
    We have:

Expected Loss   = $400,000 × 0.35
(without   = $140,000
research)

Expected Loss   = $400,000 × 0.30
(with research)   = $120,000

Value of research = $140,000 – $120,000
information   = $20,000

Since the value of research information ($20,000) is lower than the research cost ($25,000), the research study is not recommended.

The reduced loss method has the advantage of simplicity in application. However, it adopts a defensive approach in that it dwells on the loss aspect only and totally ignores the gain element. This explains why the reduced loss method is not frequently used. The value of research information may be insignificant when considering that it can only help to reduce the potential loss marginally, but it, at the same time, may be substantial when considering that it can help to increase the potential gains significantly. Under the reduced loss method, the research study in the above example would have been discouraged if without considering the gain aspect.

Formal analysis

A more logical computation of the value of research information is the formal or decision analysis method. This method takes into account three elements simultaneously:

1 All possible outcomes of a particular marketing action
2 The payoff associated with each possible outcome
3 The probability of each possible outcome occurring.

The application of this method can best be illustrated by an example.

Illustrative Example 2

A local manufacturer of powder detergent has just developed a new product. Its marketing manager reckons that if consumer reaction is extremely favourable (achieving more than 15 per cent of the market share), the company stands to make a profit of $300,000; if it is favourable (achieving between 5 per cent and 15 per cent of the market share), the projected profit is $100,000; but if it is unfavourable (achieving less than 5 per cent of the market share), the company will incur an average loss of $200,000. The marketing manager's best estimates of the likelihood of these occurrences are, respectively:

S_1: reaction extremely favourable;
                  probability = 0.4

S_2: reaction favourable;   probability = 0.3

S_3: reaction unfavourable;   probability = 0.3

The marketing manager's task is to decide whether or not the new product should be launched. Based on the given data, a payoff table is constructed (Figure 2.6).

For problem-solving, a common practice is to transform the payoff table into a decision tree or flow diagram (see Figure 2–7), where the problem under study is structured in the order of the alternative actions being considered, together with the possible outcomes that are associated. In Figure 2–7, the two alternative action A_1 (to launch the new product) and A_2 (not to launch the new product) are represented by two main branches, while the possible states of nature S_1, S_2 and S_3 are represented by sub-branches by a square, and the sub-branches are connected by the chance fork represented by a circle.

The decision tree is to be solved from right to left. The expected values for the respective alternatives are calculated and compared.

$$EV (A_1) = (0.4)(\$300,000) +$$
$$(0.3)(\$100,000) +$$
$$(0.3)(-\$200,000)$$
$$= \$90,000$$

		P(S)	Payoff
A_1	S_1	0.4	\$300,000
	S_2	0.3	\$100,000
	S_3	0.3	-\$200,000
A_2	S_1	0.4	\$0
	S_2	0.3	\$0
	S_3	0.3	\$0

Figure 2.7 *Decision tree*

$$EV (A_2) = (0.4)(\$0) + (0.3)(\$0) +$$
$$(0.3)(\$0)$$
$$= 0$$

Since EV (A_1) is numerically larger than EV (A_2), A_1 is the optimal alternative to be accepted; that is the decision is to launch the new product. The non-optimal alternative A_2 is rejected and is so indicated by crossing it with two short diagonal lines.

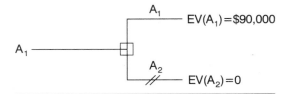

The method used in the decision-making process as described above is commonly referred to as *prior analysis*. Hitherto, the element of whether or not to conduct a research study for gathering additional information was not being considered in the calculation process.

Alternative Actions	States of nature					
	S_1: Extremely favourable		S_2: Favourable		S_3: Unfavourable	
	P(S_1)	Payoff	P(S_2)	Payoff	P(S_3)	Payoff
A_1: Launch the new product	0.4	\$300,000	0.3	\$100,000	0.3	-\$200,000
A_2: Do not launch	0.4	0	0.3	0	0.3	0

Figure 2.6 *Payoff table*

In most cases, it is reasonable to consider undertaking a research study to aid the decision-making process. Management would then make judgements about the value of the research information, and then compare it with the cost required to undertake such a research study.

Value of perfect information _____

To begin with, we assume that the research study would perfectly predict the state of nature. The decision-maker can use the additional research information to choose the best strategy (alternative) for the predicted state of nature. Had the perfect predictor indicated that S_1 (extremely favourable reaction) would occur, alternative A_1 would have been the best choice, registering an expected value of $300,000 \times 0.4 = $120,000$. Similarly, A_1 is preferred should S_2 be predicted, with an expected value of $100,000 \times 0.3 = $30,000$. Had S_3 been predicted, A_2 (with zero expected value) is preferred since the adoption of A_1 would incur loss. The expected payoff with perfect information is calculated to be $150,000 as shown in Figure 2–8.

The value of perfect information is therefore, $60,000 – being the difference between the expected payoff with perfect information ($150,000) and the expected payoff without research information ($90,000). This value is significant in that it sets the upper limit of the cost that should be spent on research, under perfect information situation. But since marketing research studies will almost never produce perfect informa-

tion, the preposterior analysis method, which is discussed next, is employed instead for estimating the value of research information.

Preposterior analysis method _____

This method is useful for estimating the value of research information under the situation of non-perfect information. The steps involved are outlined below.

Step 1

Establishing prior probabilities. Prior probabilities refer to the probabilities of the possible states of nature occurring as judged by the marketing manager. As shown in Figure 2–6, $P(S_1) = 0.4$, $P(S_2) = 0.3$ and $P(S_3) = 0.3$ are prior probabilities.

Step 2

Setting conditional probabilities. If a research study is contracted to a research agency, a wise way to classify the possible outcomes of the research would be:

- E_1: extremely favourable consumer reaction
- E_2: favourable consumer reaction
- E_3: unfavourable consumer reaction

The marketing manager next sets up the conditional probabilities matrix (see Figure 2.9) based on his assessment of the research company.

States of Nature	Probability	Maximum payoff for strategy A_1	A_2	Expected value
S_1	0.4	x $300,000		$120,000
S_2	0.3	x $100,000		$30,000
S_3	0.3	x	0	$0
			Total	$150,000

Figure 2.8 *Expected payoff with perfect information*

Research Outcomes	States of Nature S_1	S_2	S_3
E_1	0.7	0.2	0.1
E_2	0.2	0.6	0.3
E_3	0.1	0.2	0.6
	1.0	1.0	1.0

Figure 2.9 *Conditional probabilities*

The entries in Figure 2.9 are read row within column. The first column suggests that when S_1 is the true state of nature, there is a 0.7 probability that the research outcome will show E_1 (correct prediction), a 0.2 probability that it will show E_2 (incorrect prediction) and a 0.1 probability that it will show E_3 (incorrect prediction). Note that the greater the probabilities listed along the diagonal line shown in Figure 2.9, the higher confidence the marketing manager has in the research company in predicting accurate results.

Step 3

Calculating joint probabilities. The probability of each combined event between a state of nature and a research outcome is then calculated. This is known as the joint probability of the combined event. For example, the joint probability that S_1 and E_1 would simultaneously occur is $0.4 \times 0.7 = 0.28$. Other joint probabilities are similarly computed (see Figure 2.10).

The figures in the last column are known as marginal probabilities, which represent the chances of each of the research outcomes occurring. The marginal probabilities desired are:

$P(E_1) = 0.37$
$P(E_2) = 0.35$
$P(E_3) = 0.28$

Note that $P(E_1) + P(E_2) + P(E_3) = 1$, since E_1, E_2 and E_3 are mutually exclusive and exhaustive research outcomes.

Step 4

Calculating posterior probabilities. The posterior probabilities, or revised prior probabilities, refer to the probabilities that each of the states of nature occurring, under the assumption that the research outcome is E_1, or E_2 or E_3 respectively. For example, if the research outcome is E_1, the respective posterior probabilities are:

$P(S_1/E_1) = 0.28/0.37 = 0.757$
$P(S_2/E_1) = 0.06/0.37 = 0.162$
$P(S_3/E_1) = 0.03/0.37 = 0.081$

Research Outcomes	States of Nature S_1	S_2	S_3	Total
E_1	0.28	0.06	0.03	0.37
E_2	0.08	0.18	0.09	0.35
E_3	0.04	0.06	0.18	0.28
				1.00

Figure 2.10 *Joint probabilities*

Research Outcomes	States of Nature S₁	S₂	S₃
E_1	0.757	0.162	0.081
E_2	0.229	0.514	0.257
E_3	0.143	0.214	0.643

Figure 2.11 *Posterior probabilities*

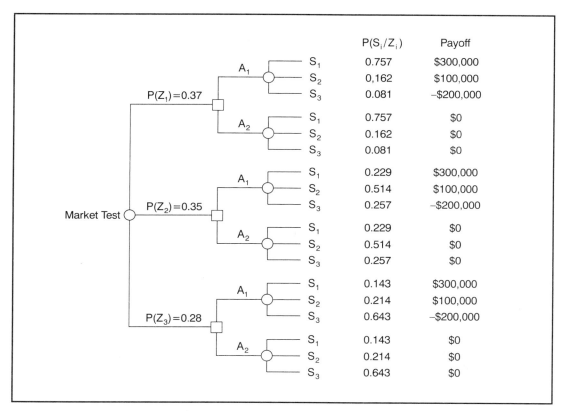

Figure 2.12 *Decision tree analysis*

The calculation of the above posterior probabilities makes use of the well-known Bayes' theorem. A full set of posterior probabilities is tabulated in Figure 2.11.

Step 5

Constructing the decision tree. All the results so far obtained can be presented in the form of a decision tree (Figure 2.12).

Step 6

Calculating expected values. This final step involves the calculation of expected values under each research outcome.

If research outcome is E_1:

$$EV(A_1) = (0.757)(\$300,000) + (0.162)(\$100,000) + (0.081)(-\$200,000)$$
$$= \$227,100$$
$$EV(A_2) = 0$$

Alternative A_1 is optimal and hence adopted.

If research outcome is E_2:

$$EV(A_1) = (0.229)(\$300,000) + (0.514)(\$100,000) + (0.257)(-\$200,000)$$
$$= \$68,700$$

$$EV(A_2) = 0$$

Alternative A_1 is optimal and hence adopted.

If research outcome is E_3:

$$EV(A_1) = (0.143)(\$300,000) + (0.214)(\$100,000) + (0.643)(-\$200,000)$$
$$= -\$64,300$$

$$EV(A_2) = 0$$

Alternative A_2 is optimal and hence adopted.

The simplified decision tree looks like this:

Finally, we arrive at the expected payoff with research information as follows:

$$EV \text{ (with research)} = (0.37)(\$227,100) + (0.35)(\$68,700) + (0.28)(\$0)$$
$$= \$108,072$$

Earlier, the expected payoff without research information (that is, prior analysis) has been calculated to be $90,000. Hence the value of research information is $108,072 − $90,000 = $18,072. In other words, no research should be undertaken when the cost of conducting it would exceed $18,072.

Research plan

A research plan is the overall framework guiding the performance of research, the processing of data, and the presentation of research findings. It is as crucial to the researcher as a blueprint is to the architect. A good research plan sets out the systematic guidelines on the approach needed to implement a research study, and steers the research towards the realization of its objectives.

The contents of a research plan will normally include the issues listed in Figure 2.13.

Data collection

Being the most active part of research activities, this phase of the marketing research process sees the research planners handing the research plan over to the field executives for actual implementation. Here, the survey methodology is put into practice and the research instruments are completed by the interviewers. Also, the supervisors will control the quality of field work. More detail of this topic can be found in Chapter 7.

Data processing and analysis

Information gathered from field research needs to be edited, tabulated and analysed before it is communicated to the research client. Depending on the complexity and quality of the collected data, the method used may range from manual processing to computer processing. Furthermore, association and relationships of variables are identified and discussed in the light of the specific marketing problem. As data are expensive to come by, they must be analysed to the fullest detail and used to the greatest advantage. Chapters 11 to 14 contain more details on this topic.

Project Title
Each research project is designated a project title for the purpose of identification.

Problem Statement
This constitutes an essential part of the research plan. It contains an outline or brief description of the general problem under consideration.

Problem Definition
This part of the research plan provides a statement on the scope of the problem, together with the goals (or objectives) of the research. Hypotheses which were earlier developed from exploratory research for further investigation are stated here.

Method and Data Sources
The types of data to be gathered are briefly identified. The methods by which the necessary information or data is gathered (for example, surveys, experiments, library search) are specified. If measurements are involved (such as consumers attitudes), the techniques adopted are explained.

Sample Design
This part specifies the universe or population under study; the sample size and the sample methodology to be employed.

Data Collection Forms
This part discusses the data collection forms needed for data gathering. Also, it specifies how these forms or instruments have been or will be validated.

Personnel Requirements
This part provides a complete list of all required personnel; and specifies exact jobs, periods of employment, and expected rates of remuneration.

Time Scheduling
This part provides the time estimates required for each research activity (e.g. draft questionnaire, interviewing etc.). The total time duration for the research study should be clearly indicated.

Tabulation Plans
This part discusses the editing of questionnaires, data entry, and the intended level of computer analysis.

Cost Estimates
An estimate of the total cost for the research study is provided here. It should among other things, include personnel costs, travel, materials, supplies, computer charges, printing and mailing costs.

Figure 2.13 *Content of a research plan*

Research report

The final phase of the marketing research process involves the preparation of a research report and its presentation to the research client. The essential factors guiding the preparation of research report are discussed in Chapter 15.

Parties involved

The marketing research process involves three parties, namely, research client, research agency and research respondent.

The research client, being the paymaster of the research, wishes to derive the maximum value for money from the research study. It is his or her desire to ensure that all the needed information is obtainable from the set of questions to be included in the questionnaire, so that the survey results will help to satisfy the management's information requirements. The researcher's main concern would be to ensure that the survey questions presented to the respondent should not be too complicated to confuse the latter, nor the questionnaire too lengthy to cause respondent's fatigue in responding to it. The questionnaire should seek to assist the interviewer to perform an efficient job with the minimum of difficulty and to be paid for it and continue in work. The respondent should not in any way be discouraged from co-operating due to any deficiency caused by the questionnaire design, in particular, he or she should not be presented with complicated or ambiguous questions in the questionnaire. Finally, the questionnaire should be designed in a way to avoid the data processor from having difficulty in coding and making unnecessary references back and forth to the questionnaire.

End-of-chapter revision

Review questions

2.1 Name and briefly describe the sequence of steps involved in the marketing research process.

2.2 What is the difference between a marketing problem and a research problem?

2.3 What characteristics should research objectives possess?

2.4 How should the research purpose be specified?

2.5 What specific research objectives need to be addressed?

2.6 What is the basic criterion for deciding whether or not to conduct a research project?

2.7 How are prior probabilities made posterior probabilities?

2.8 What is posterior analysis? What is preposterior analysis?

2.9 What is the basic nature of a payoff table?

2.10 What is meant by perfect information? How is the value of perfect information determined?

2.11 Outline the procedure necessary to determine the value of imperfect information?

2.12 What is a decision tree? How is it constructed? How is it solved?

2.13 Since there is no such thing as a perfect research study, what is the practical value of calculating the expected value of perfect information?

2.14 A marketing research analyst is assigned to recommend whether or not his firm should produce a new toy. His boss feels that a 60–40 chance exists that the toy will be successful.

Alternative actions	States of nature				
	S_1: Success			S_2: Failure	
	$P(S_1)$	Payoff		$P(S_2)$	Payoff
A_1: Produce	0.6	$150,000		0.4	–$100,000
A_2: Do not produce	0.6	0		0.4	0

Two market survey firms have submitted bids to the toy-store owner. The Aw Company is known to conduct highly accurate surveys (at rather high cost), whereas the Ben company's accuracy is somewhat lower and so is its cost. Pertinent conditional probabilities of survey results Z_i (indicating S_i) are as follows:

Firm	Conditional Probabilities	Cost
Aw Company	$P(Z_1/S_2) = P(Z_2/S_2) = 0.9$ $P(Z_1/S_2) = P(Z_2/S_1) = 0.1$	$50,000
Ben Company	$P(Z_1/S_1) = P(Z_2/S_2) = 0.7$ $P(Z_1/S_2) = P(Z_2/S_1) = 0.3$	$30,000

The marketing research analyst has the following options: conduct no survey; buy Aw's survey; buy Ben's survey.

(i) Evaluate the expected payoff of each option. Prepare appropriate decision trees.

(ii) What is the expected value of perfect information?

(iii) Would your answer to part (i) change if the prior probability assignment over S_1 and S_2 were 0.9 and 0.1 respectively? If so, how?

2.15 Who are the three parties involved in the marketing research process? Briefly describe the functions of each.

2.16 What is a turnover table and how is it read? What kinds of analysis that a turnover table can perform which other types of study cannot?

True-false questions
Write True (T) or False (F) for the following:

2.17 In prior analysis, we consider the possibility of collecting additional information before making a decision.

2.18 To achieve scientific objectivity in marketing research, the research team must not be informed of the ultimate purpose of the research.

2.19 The marketing research process comprises a series of independent steps which one can follow sequentially in designing a research study.

2.20 A research problem is essentially a translation of the decision problem into research terminology.

2.21 The fundamental difference between a marketing problem and the research problem is that the former focuses on what action needs to be taken while the latter on what information to provide and how that information can best be obtained.

2.22 The value of perfect information is calculated for the simple reason that it sets the upper limit to the value of the proposed research.

2.23 The decision tree reflects a chronological structuring of the decision problem with the most immediate decisions at the extreme left of the diagram and the most distant decisions at the extreme right.

2.24 In a decision tree, the decision forks are usually represented by circles.

2.25 A payoff table includes only two types of information: alternative courses of action and estimated probabilities with which the various outcomes will occur.

2.26 Value analysis helps decide whether or not the proposed research study should be undertaken.

Multiple-choice questions

2.27 In solving a decision tree representing a marketing decision situation, we proceed from:
 a left to right
 b right to left
 c top to bottom
 d bottom to top.

2.28 Which of the following types of analysis aid in deciding if additional information should be purchased?
 a Prior analysis.
 b Posterior analysis.
 c Preposterior analysis.
 d All of the above.

2.29 The expected value of perfect information can be important to marketing research because it tells us:
   a about how much should be spent for a given research study
   b which of two research proposals will provide the more accurate findings
   c the lower limit of expenses for any research study
   d the upper limit of expenses for any research study.

2.30 Which of the following is not a part of the marketing research process?
   a Problem definition.
   b Value analysis.
   c Preparing data collection forms.
   d They are all parts of the marketing research process.

2.31 A payoff table contains:
   a alternatives
   b states of nature
   c outcomes
   d all of the above.

2.32 The fomal analysis method takes into account:
   a all possible outcomes of a particular maketing action
   b the payoff associated with each possible outcome
   c the probability of each possible outcome occurring
   d all of the above.

3

Research design _____

Research design specifies the methods and procedures for conducting a specific research project. It is the detailed blueprint used to guide the implementation of a research study towards the realization of its objectives. A good research design serves many purposes: it forms the essential framework for research action, minimizes the danger of collecting haphazard data, ensures that the data collected meets the research objectives and more importantly, fulfils the information needs of the decision-makers.

It should be emphasized that the best research design may not be the one which offers the most accurate results. Rather, it is the one which offers the greatest value for money, or the one which can best allocate the available research funds. From this viewpoint, research design is perhaps the most difficult – but rewarding – task in a marketing research study.

Research design may be classified in a number of ways depending on the criteria considered. A research study may be quantitative or qualitative, or both in nature.

Alternatively, we call it an applied research if the research findings are expected to contribute directly to a managerial decision; or a basic research if the research findings are intended to provide answers to questions of a theoretical nature. The most common categorization of research design based upon the functional objective and research focus is presented in Figure 3.1.

These research designs are distinct but not mutually exclusive. Indeed, it has become increasingly common nowadays to engage more than one research design for a single research study. The ultimate choice will depend on the research purpose in question and to some extent, on the time and research fund available.

Exploratory research ■■■■■

Exploratory research is employed when the research purpose is to provide a greater understanding of a concept, to crystallize a marketing problem or to discover general ideas and insights relating to the subject of

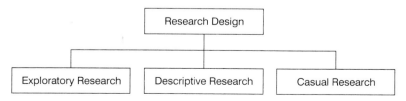

Figure 3.1 *Types of research design*

study. Situations where relatively little or absolutely nothing is known about the study subject would best lend themselves to exploratory research. Exploratory research provides background knowledge about the problem area or product field in question, and is qualitative in nature. As such, it is frequently used as the initial step in the pursuit of many research efforts. The essence of exploratory research focuses on two main ingredients, they are: listening and discovering. Exploratory research is all about observing and listening to people as they respond in a carefully-constructed environment of inquiry and gaining an understanding of their attitudes, behaviour and perception, which in turn will lead to the creation of successful strategies for marketing, communication and new product. Exploratory research often produces findings in the form of hypothesis for subsequent verification through other forms (i.e. descriptive and/or causal) of research. Another functional area of exploratory research is to break broad problem statements into smaller, more precise sub-problems.

In sum, exploratory research is favoured when the research objective is related to one or more of the following areas:

● generating new product ideas
● achieving further insight to the problem
● developing hypotheses
● enhancing researcher's familiarity with the problem area
● defining and formulating problem
● establishing priorities for further research
● defining population of interest
● Pre-testing draft questionnaire.

Exploratory research adopts an informal approach which is characterized by flexibility and versatility in use. It allows for the widest possible exploration of views, attitudes and behaviour patterns. The open-ended, flexible, interactive qualitative approach means that it is used in uncharted marketing territory in order to hypothesize about the parameters and the basic structure and dynamics of the market or the problem area. In exploratory research, structured data collection forms are seldom used. Also, controlled experiments and random sampling are not compulsory requirements. Apart from simplicity in application, exploratory research is a low-cost, minimized risk form of research which can offer a better understanding and clearer scenario of the market problem at hand.

Four key approaches in exploratory research are:

● literature search
● experience survey
● focus group discussion
● in-depth interview.

Literature search

Generally speaking, marketing research surveys are expensive undertakings. As such, they are performed only when all efforts on literature search have been exhausted. Primarily, literature search refers to a comprehensive search through secondary data sources and should include an examination of conceptual literature, trade and published statistics. Both internal and external data may be found in abundance in secondary data sources. Transport costs, sales costs, advertising and other promotional expenditures and salespersons' performances are some important internal data. External data are those extracted from outside the company and include sources from government statistical yearbooks and bulletins, journals, trade associations' reports and syndicated studies. A major benefit of literature search is that one can usually develop a better understanding of the problem area within a short period of time and at little expense.

Experience survey

Logically speaking, the first step in defining the marketing problem is for the researcher to organize informal talks with a group of resource people who can often offer a wealth of needed information. Experience survey or expert interviews, as such informal talks are normally called, focus on experts in the industry and/or persons who have experience in the field under study. The approach adopted in an experience survey should be highly unstructured to allow the respondent to offer widely divergent views. As the primary purpose here is to help formulate the problem and clarify concepts rather than to achieve conclusive evidence, experience survey does not require probability sampling techniques. Purposeful sampling is often engaged to exclude inarticulate persons or persons who exhibit little competence and/or possess limited experience in the subject of study from being interviewed. In an experience survey, researchers look for ideas, not conclusions.

Although experience survey does not qualify as being a scientifically designed research study, it contributes considerably in the discovery of ideas and underlying causes to the problem area. The term *expert* used in this context may not refer to a person who holds a high academic qualification or status. Instead, any of the following resource persons can be considered in an experience survey:

- Senior company executive – an executive in sales advertising and promotion, credit and finance, can help highlight problems concerned with his own areas of specialization.
- User/consumer – product user/consumer can offer pertinent information about product choice, usage, frequency and place of purchase. It is wise to include both contented and discontented users/ consumers in expert interviews in order to gather differing views or opinions.
- Retailer – by virtue of his proximity to the end-users, the retailer can give a good account of who his customers are, how he regards the products and what brands he pushes hard to sell; etc.
- Wholesaler – a wholesaler can offer a broader picture of what consumers are buying. Also, he can report better on

general market conditions, prices, competitive status of different brands and, perhaps, geographical or other differences among brand sales.

Focus group discussion

Focus group discussion is by far the most common method used in exploratory research. In a focus group discussion, a group of eight to ten people assemble for a free-flow conversation about the subject of interest. The conversational atmosphere permits the participants to feel relaxed and encourages them to talk spontaneously, thus helping the researcher to discover valuable insights into the problem areas which could not be obtained through other methods of data collection. Instead of attempting to obtaining measurable data about the 'who', 'what', 'when', 'how much' and 'how frequent' of consumer behaviour as in the case of other research designs, focus group discussion is primarily concerned with the 'why' aspect of consumer behaviour. It is particularly used to get below the sometimes superficial and rational responses and, in turn, to explore and establish the underlying feelings, ideas, beliefs and motivations of consumers. A fuller discussion of focus group discussion method can be found in Chapter 5.

In-depth interview

In-depth interviewing is a special form of focus group discussion in which one, and only one, participant takes part in the discussion session with the interviewer (or moderator). The same relatively free-ranging, qualitative interviewing technique is used as in a focus group discussion. In-depth interviewing is preferred over focus group discussion when the topic involves intimate subject matter (e.g., contraception) or very personal views (e.g., attitudes towards management; political opinions); or when the subject matter is potentially embarrassing (e.g., sanitary towel protection). Situations when there are difficulties in assembling the desired participants (e.g., travelling business people) at specified time and place will call for in-depth interviewing method. A fuller description of in-depth interviewing can be found in Chapter 5.

Descriptive research ▬▬▬▬▬

Descriptive research, as the name implies, aims at describing the characteristics of the population under study. Many marketing research studies are primarily concerned with providing up-to-date and detailed information on total market size and brand share, customers' profiles, preferences and buying habits. For such studies, descriptive research suits best as it provides reliable estimates of the relevant environmental variables. As a general rule, studies which involve one or more of the following research objectives will require descriptive research:

● To establish potential market size and brand share of a product.
● To describe the characteristics of the various population groups (e.g. users and non-users).
● To explore product purchase patterns.
● To determine the degree of association between marketing variables (e.g. price and sales).
● To predict future sales level.

As opposed to exploratory research, descriptive research is primarily concerned with the gathering of numeric, measurable data. This is the type of research when one is most likely to see quoted by product manufacturers and service providers regarding the number and incidence of consumers who use a certain brand of shampoo, or who have acted in a certain way (e.g., used almost everyday).

Descriptive research is recommended when the research purpose is centred on providing accurate, statistically reliable data – how much, how many, how often, what

brand and when bought? Generally speaking, descriptive research is the method of choice when the following situations arise:

● gauging the overall market size
● estimating the market share of a particular brand
● testing the level of customer acceptance of a new product
● tracking the performance of a particular brand
● evaluating the effectiveness of an advertising/promotion campaign
● changing product ingredients/formulae, tag prices, flavours or packaging design.

Data collection techniques adopted for descriptive research include personal interviews, mail surveys and telephone interviews. A fuller description of each of these data collection methods can be found in Chapter 5.

From an operational viewpoint, descriptive research is particularly different from descriptive research. First, descriptive research requires a reasonably large number of respondents (i.e., sample size) to supply the needed information. Secondly, the selected sample of respondents must be representative of the 'parent' population intended for the research study. Thirdly, a standard questionnaire is adopted for all sample respondents throughout the entire data collection process.

In sum, descriptive research necessitates formal, structured interviews – a feature which distinguishes it from exploratory research in character and purpose. Strict sampling procedures are essential to mini-

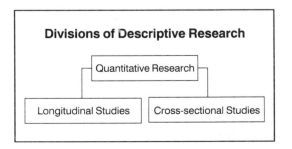

mize systematic errors on the one hand, and to maximize data reliability on the other. The sample should normally be reasonably large and be representative of the population under study in all possible aspects (e.g. age, sex, education, etc.).

A comparison of the distinct features of exploratory research and descriptive research is shown in Figure 3.2.

Longitudinal studies

Trend data that relates what and how market changes occur over time can offer a better appreciation of the marketing problem at hand. Research studies which are designed for providing repeated measurements of an event over a period of time are known as longitudinal or time series studies. There are two ways in which longitudinal studies are carried out: the independent sample method and the consumer panel method.

Independent sample method

This method is characterized by a sample of respondents independently selected for

each round of the survey. For an illustration of this method, we turn to the following example.

Illustrative example 1

A market research study on dish-washing liquid was conducted at two points in time, T_1 and T_2, six months apart. Each time, a random sample of 1,000 households was independently chosen for interview and the results in terms of *brand used most often* in households for the two surveys are tabulated on page 000:

Brand used most often

	At T_1	At T_2
Brand A	250 (25%)	300 (30%)
Brand B	350 (35%)	330 (33%)
Brand C	200 (20%)	180 (18%)
Brand D	100 (10%)	90 (9%)
Others	100 (10%)	100 (10%)
	1000 (100%)	1000 (100%)

Exploratory Research	Descriptive Research
It is used to "get below" the sometimes superficial and rational responses.	It is used to provide accurate statistical information on consumers and consumerism.
It is concerned with the "why" aspects or consumer behaviour, that is, it deals with the understanding and not the measuring of data.	It is concerned with statistical indicators on "how many", "how often", "what" or "when" of consumer behaviour.
It does not require a large sample of respondents.	It necessitates a reasonably large sample of respondents.
The sample of respondents does not need to be representative of its "parent" population under study.	The sample of respondents must be representative of its "parent" population under study.
There is no need for a standard questionnaire for the purpose of data collection.	There should be a standard questionnaire for the purpose of data collection.
The data collection methods are: • Literature search • Experience survey • Focus group discussion • In–depth interview	The data collection methods are: • Personal interview • Mail survey • Telephone interview
In Exploratory Research, the respondent rules.	**In Descriptive Research, the questionnaire is king.**

Figure 3.2 *Comparison of exploratory research and descriptive research*

Between the time period T_1 and T_2, Brand A has shown an improvement on market share from 25 per cent to 30 per cent, while that of major competing brands B, C and D have dipped. Meanwhile, the market share of 'other brands' remains unchanged. Thus it would appear that Brand A secured a higher market share at the expense of its major competitors, as observed from the independent sample method.

Consumer panel method

The consumer panel method gets a panel (e.g. persons, stores, dealers or households) committed to agreeing to supply information on two or more occasions over a period of time. To encourage participation, monetary incentives and/or gifts are normally offered to panel members.

Coming back to the previous example, let us now assume that a panel of 1,000 households were interviewed both at T_1 and T_2 and that the survey results in terms of *brand used most often* in households at T_1 and T_2 were in a matrix form (Figure 3.3).

This matrix is commonly known as a turnover table. The turnover table offers a wide scope of data analysis reflecting the loss aspect and the gain aspect as well as the loyalty of each brand.

The loss aspect

Brand A lost	15 households to Brand B
	5 households to Brand C
	5 households to Brand D
Brand B lost	15 households to Brand C
	15 households to Brand D
	10 households to 'Others'
Brand C lost	5 households to Brand D
	45 households to 'Others'
Brand D lost	10 households to Brand C
	25 households to 'Others'
'Others' lost	75 households to Brand A
	5 households to Brand B

The gain aspect

Brand A gained	75 households from 'Others'
Brand B gained	15 households from Brand A
	5 households from 'Others'
Brand C gained	5 households from Brand A
	15 households from Brand B
	10 households from Brand D
Brand D gained	5 households from Brand A
	15 households from Brand B
	5 households from Brand C
'Others' gained	10 households from Brand B
	45 households from Brand C
	25 households from Brand D

Brand used most often (at T_1)	Brand used most often (at T_2)					
	A	B	C	D	Others	Total
A	225	15	5	5	0	250
B	0	310	15	15	10	350
C	0	0	150	5	45	200
D	0	0	10	65	25	100
Others	75	5	0	0	20	100
	300	330	180	90	100	1,000

Figure 3.3 *Turnover table*

It now becomes clear that Brand A has gained its market share from 'Others', and lost some of its customers to its major competitors, namely Brands B, C and D. These observations invalidated the earlier conclusion reached by using the independent sample method.

Brand loyalty

Turnover tables offer yet another benefit; namely an understanding of brand loyalty (defined as the percentage of households using the same brand of product both at T_1 and T_2).

	Loyalty level
Brand A	225/250 = 90%
Brand B	310/350 = 89%
Brand C	150/200 = 75%
Brand D	65/100 = 65%
Others	20/100 = 20%

Brand A enjoys the highest level of brand loyalty (90 per cent) while 'Others' the lowest (20 per cent).

The consumer panel method offers the following advantages over the independent sample method:

- It suggests a relationship between variables for further examination.
- It offers a larger pool of data to be gathered, since panel members are more willing to co-operate.
- It brings a higher level of statistical precision.

On the other hand, the consumer panel method suffers from the following limitations:

- Difficulties in recruiting panel members.
- Difficulties in retaining panel members (e.g. deaths).
- Attitudes of panel members can be consciously created rather than unconsciously changed. Being conscious that their responses can cast influences on the decision-makers, panel members might respond differently from their usual behaviour.
- Panel membership may not be representative of the intended population. Those who agreed to be panel members may in many ways be different from those who declined to participate, or who dropped out subsequently.

Cross-sectional studies

While longitudinal studies provide measurements of an event at successive points of time, cross-sectional studies on the other hand, describe an event at one particular point of time only. Cross-sectional studies are useful in facilitating comparisons between different population subgroups and will usually require a much larger sample so that the data pertaining to population subgroups can be meaningfully analysed. While a turnover table constitutes a key ingredient in longitudinal studies, cross-tabulation of data plays a crucial role in cross-sectional studies. As evidenced from Figure 3.4, data descriptions become more revealing when the data on car ownership is cross-tabulated by ethnic group and by house type.

In summary, descriptive research studies are scientifically designed studies conducted in a formal, structured manner in order to yield an accurate description of the characteristics of whatever universe it purports to describe. In such studies, issues that relate to questionnaire design, sample representation, response rate, field administration and control, etc. may become extremely complex. Cost also presents an important limiting factor in adopting a descriptive research design. The leading argument against the use of descriptive research studies is that they can at best yield measurable data only, but fail to address the *why* aspect of a certain behaviour.

	All households	Ethnic group			House Type		
		Chinese	Malay	Indian/others	HDB flats (1–3 rooms)	HDB flats (4&5 rooms)	Landed Properties
Own cars	33%	37%	15%	29%	12%	35%	88%
Do not own cars	67%	63%	85%	71%	88%	65%	12%
	100%	100%	100%	100%	100%	100%	100%

Figure 3.4 *Incidence of car ownership in Singapore, 1991*

Causal research

Longitudianal studies and cross-sectional studies are instrumental in marketing research as they suggest the relationship, if any, between marketing variables. Both, however, fail to conclusively establish a direct cause-and-effect relationship between marketing variables. The survey results may show that car ownership and household income have both risen over time, yet one cannot say with certainty that car ownership increase is a direct result of the rise in household income. A lower road tax, better road facilities and other factors could have resulted in the increased car ownership.

Two (marketing) variables or factors are said to have a cause-and-effect relationship when, and only when, a change in one variable will lead to a corresponding change in the other variable, independent of the environmental conditions. The primary goal of causal research is to explore and establish a cause-and-effect relationship, if any, between variables. This can be achieved through experimentation, involving manipulation of one or more variables by the experimenter so that the effect(s) on other variable(s) can be measured. The underlying principle here is, 'When a single independent variable is manipulated while all other variables are controlled over a period of time, any observed change in the dependent variable will be attributable entirely to the independent variable'.

Causal research designs involve laboratory and/or field experiments. The fundamental difference between a laboratory experiment and a field experiment lies in the environment under which the experiment is executed. In a laboratory experiment, the researcher creates a situation which simulates, as much as possible, the real conditions and he or she controls some variables while manipulating the others. Thus laboratory experiments are characterized by a relatively high degree of artificiality. A field experiment, on the other hand, refers to a real-life situation in which one or more independent variables are manipulated under as carefully controlled conditions as the situation will permit. Unlike a laboratory experiment, it depicts a high degree of realism.

Compared with field experiments, laboratory experiments usually require considerably less resources and time and, more importantly, industry competitors are less likely to be aware of such experiments taking place. On the other hand, a field experiment enjoys the realism of the situation, and benefits from the generalities of the results. The strengths and weaknesses of laboratory and field experiments are summarized in Figure 3.5.

Terms and notations

Prior to a discussion of the various experimental research designs, it is necessary to

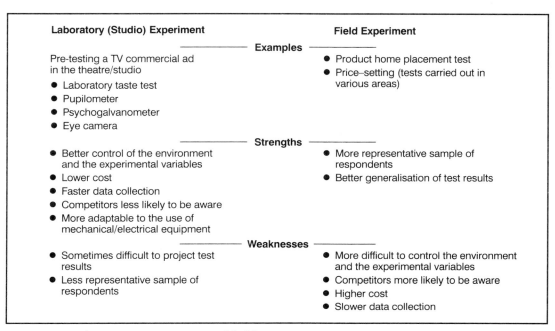

Figure 3.5 *Laboratory experiment and field experiment*

review some common terms and notations used in the literature of experimental research design.

- *Experimental treatment*. This refers to the manipulation of an independent variable whose effects on the dependent variables are to be measured. Some examples of experimental treatments are: pricing strategy, advertising/promotion campaign etc. Experimental treatment is denoted by the letter X.
- *Experimental group*. This refers to the group of respondents or test units who are exposed to the experimental treatment. The experimental group may be newspaper readers, radio listeners, television viewers or customers. Experimental group is denoted by the letter E.
- *Control group*. This refers to the group of respondents or test units who are not exposed to the experimental treatment. Control group is denoted by the letter C.
- *Measurement*. This refers to the numerical values observed for the dependent variable (e.g. sales volume) in the experimentation.

Measurements made before and after the experimental treatment are termed before-measurements and after-measurements respectively.

Types of experimental research design

The major types of experimental research designs are listed in Figure 3.6

In the discussion that follows, the symbol 0_i will be used to indicate the observed values of measurement. A horizontal arrangement of 0's and X's running from left to right signifies the movement of time. Thus the following symbolic arrangement:

$$0_1 \qquad X \qquad 0_2$$

means that 0_1 is the observed measurement of the dependent variable before experimental treatment X is introduced (thus called before-measurement), whereas 0_2 is the observed measurement of the dependent

---

One-group experimental designs
- After-only design
- Static-group comparison design
- Before-after design

Two-group experimental designs
- After-only with control group design
- Before-after with control group design
- Solomon four-group six-study design

Statistical experimental designs
- Completely randomised design
- Randomised complete block design
- Latin square design
- Factorial design

Figure 3.6 *Main types of experimental research design*

variable after the experimental treatment X is introduced (thus called after-measurement). We are now ready for the discussion on the various experimental designs.

One-group experimental designs _____

After-only design

This is the simplest and most dubious of all experimental designs. In this design, no attempt is made to adjust for the influence of other variables. The symbolic arrangement of an after-only design is:

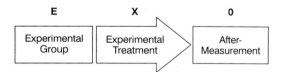

Here, the experimental group is exposed to an experimental treatment (X), after which a measurement (0) on the dependent variable is made. This design is sometimes called *one-shot case study* design because throughout the entire experimentation, only one measurement is observed.

Illustrative example 2

The Singapore National Productivity Month Campaign has been launched annually since 1980 to help promote the productivity concept at work. In 1982, a Knowledge, Attitude and Practice (KAP) survey on productivity was conducted to measure the level of understanding the productivity concept among Singapore workers.

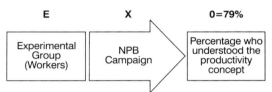

Thus, two years after the campaign was first launched, 79 per cent of Singapore workers were reported to have understood the productivity concept. But since before-measurement was not available, the extent which the campaign has contributed to raising the level of understanding the productivity concept could not be determined. The after-only design thus fails to establish the validity of hypothesized causal relationships between the campaign and the level of understanding the productivity concept. Strictly speaking, the after-only design is not regarded as an experimental design as the researcher lacks a basis to compare what had happened in the presence of the experimental treatment with what had happened in the absence of the experimental treatment. Despite this, after-only design is useful in suggesting hypothesis (rather than in testing the validity of these hypothesis) and is more appropriate for qualitative research.

Static-group comparison design

Also known as ex-post-facto experimental design, the static-group comparison design is an extension of the after-only design. Like after-only design, this design involves only one group (E) of respondents, which is later categorized into two subgroups for which measurements are made. In the event that experimental treatment is a printed advertisement, the two subgroups to be categorized might be:

Group A: those who remembered having seen the printed advertisement

Group B: those who did not remember having seen the printed advertisement.

The symbolic arrangement of static-group comparison design is:

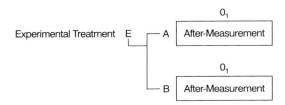

The effect of the experimental treatment is:

$$d = O_2 - O_1$$

Illustrative example 3

After a three-month period of an advertising campaign in a local newspaper, the manufacturer of SOOTHE shampoo commissioned a research study to evaluate its advertisement effectiveness. A sample of 300 housewives were interviewed on the following two questions:

Q1: Have you purchased this brand (SHOWCARD) of shampoo in the past three months?

Q2: Can you tell me whether you remember seeing this advertisement (SHOW AD) in the newspapers?

The respondents were categorized into two groups, A and B, based on their responses to Q2:

A: Those who said they remembered seeing the newspaper advertisement (assuming 100 housewives said so)

B: Those who said they did not remember seeing the newspaper advertisement (assuming the remaining 200 housewives said so).

The incidence of SOOTHE shampoo purchase for each group is tabulated and shown below.

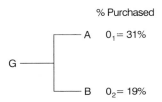

Thirty-one per cent of those who remembered seeing the newspaper advertisement had purchased the shampoo, while only 19 per cent of those who did not remember seeing the printed advertisement purchased it. Thus, the newspaper advertisement has increased the incidence of purchase by $d = O_2 - O_1 = 12$ per cent.

The static-group comparison design is often used in situations when it is too late to secure a before-measurement of a variable and is regarded as a remedial design. This design is often criticized for its lack of assurance that the two subgroups of respondents are statistically identical on all the variables under study. For example, it may be argued that those who purchased the shampoo are more likely to recall seeing the newspaper advertisement than those who did not purchase the shampoo.

Before-after design

This design involves a before-measurement and an after-measurement on the experimental group. The symbolic arrangement of before-after design is:

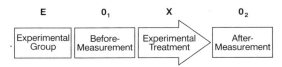

The effect of the experimental treatment is expressed by:

$$d = O_2 - O_1$$

Illustrative example 4

A National Road Safety Campaign was launched. Quarterly statistics on road accidents occurred before and after the campaign were compiled below:

	No. of road accidents
Before-measurement campaign	$O_1 = 2,148$
After-measurement campaign	$O_2 = 1,992$

$$d = 1,992 - 2,148 = -156$$

Numerically speaking, there was a reduction of 156 road accidents over a three-month period after the launch of the National Road Safety Campaign.

Simple in application as it is, the before-after design cannot claim to be one of the better experimental designs. The control elements of a true experiment fails to exist because not all variables that might affect the dependent variable are identified and considered. In the above example, extraneous factors such as improved weather conditions and fatal road mishaps etc. which occurred during the campaign period could have helped prevent or minimize road accidents. More conclusive and perhaps more complex experimental designs are needed to establish the causal relationship. Before we proceed further to discuss these better-controlled experimental designs, we pause here to review the major types of extraneous variables that may exist in an experiment.

Extraneous variable

This refers to any factor which does not constitute a part of the experimental treatment but none the less accounts for the effects on the dependent variable. Weather changes and competitors' reactions are examples of extraneous variables. Experi-

mental designs which will alienate or eliminate the effects caused by extraneous variables can definitely strengthen the decision to accept or reject a hypothetical statement.

Researchers have to live with the unfortunate fact that extraneous variables do exist in almost all experiments which in turn disturb data validity. Experimental data can be impaired by extraneous variables in two aspects, namely external validity and internal validity. The former has to do with the interpretation of the cause and effect relationship in the experiment and occurs when the group of test units does not truly represent the population which it purports to describe, and/or when the various selected groups involved in the experimentation do not match each other in terms of the key characteristics under study. It is, strictly speaking, a sampling problem.

Internal validity of data, on the other hand, refers to the question of whether the experimental treatment was the sole contributor to the observed changes in the dependent variable or, alternatively, to the correctness of the apparent relationship between the experimental treatment (or independent variable) and the dependent variable. Campbell and Stanley have identified some variables influencing internal validity of data. (See Figure 3.7.)

- History
- Maturation
- Mortality
- Instrumentation
- Testing effect
- Regression
- Selection

Figure 3.7 *Extraneous variables affecting internal validity of data. Source: D. T. Campbell and J. C. Stanley (1963) Experimental and Quasi-Experimental Designs for Research on Teaching. In* Handbook of Research on Teaching *(N. L. Gage, ed.) pp. 171–246, Rand McNally.*

● *History.* History refers to external events which occurred during the experimentation beyond the control of the experimenter and can produce effects on the dependent variable. A typical example is when competitors deliberately alter their marketing strategies to cause confusion/changes to the market situation during a test-marketing period. Note that the term 'history' is not used in the usual sense as it does not mean past events that occurred before the experiment.

In the National Road Safety Campaign example cited earlier, new speed regulation, improved weather conditions are history factors that may explain partly or fully the observed decline in the number of road accidents. History can be better controlled for laboratory experiments than field experiments, although room temperature, lighting conditions and the like could still affect the results in the former. The longer the duration of an experiment, the more likely it will be for history to compound the experiment.

● *Maturation.* Maturation refers to the biological and physical changes in the test units throughout an experiment. Test units become older, tired and get bored – all these are signs of maturation. Experimentations which last for a considerably long period of time are prone to maturation effect.

● *Mortality.* Mortality refers to loss of test units. During the experiment, test units may choose to quit due to boredom, illness, deaths and so on. As a result, the test units at the beginning stage of the experiment may be markedly different from those at the end of the experiment.

● *Instrumentation.* Instrumentation, or instrument effect, refers to the changes in the measuring instruments (e.g. observers or scores) over time. Variability among observers usually exists. Even for the same observer, his standard of measurement may differ from one stage to the next. As the experiment progresses, the observer may improve on his recording ability or usage of the recording devices. Finally, the differing personalities among observers can also cause the test units to react in different manners.

● *Testing effect.* Testing effect is concerned with the possible effects caused by the learning process of the test units. When the test units know their behaviour is being observed, or had become more familiar with the testing procedures, they tend to change their usual behaviour and this will affect the measurements. For example, students who sit for an IQ test a second time will usually do better than when they took it the first time. In a product taste test, if the cake mix earlier tested tastes too spicy, the next cake mix will tend to taste plain even though it too may be spicy.

● *Regression.* Generally speaking, people with extreme characteristics tend to move towards a more average position over time or within a group. A poorly performing salesperson may improve his or her skill as he or she deals more frequently with clients; while a star athlete may decline in prowess after some time. This phenomenon, known as regression, suggests that when a disproportionate number of test units hold extreme views, it is likely that the regression will induce a shift in the opposite direction towards the norm. Regression may be viewed as a special form of maturation, where the change in the test units is the result of their becoming more normal.

● *Selection.* Selection effect is a sample bias resulting in improper choice of test units for the various treatments. Whenever the test units are allowed to select their groups, self-selection bias is created. Random assignment of test units to various groups can help minimize the selection effect.

Two-group experimental designs

All one-group experimental designs described earlier are appropriate when extraneous variables causing changes in the dependent variable do not exist. The respondents for the experiments are not selected from a common pool of subjects nor are they randomly assigned to one group or another. On this note, they are not considered true experimental designs.

Two-group experimental designs are used principally to take into account the effect of extraneous variables on the experimental treatment. An assumption made here is that all the test units are randomly assigned to the treatment groups. We shall now discuss the following kinds of two-group experimental designs:

- after-only with control group design
- before-after with control group design
- Solomon four-group six-study design.

After-only with control group design

The symbolic arrangement of after-only with control group design is:

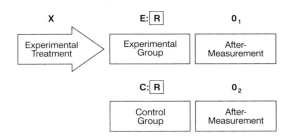

The effect of the experiment is: $d = O_1 - O_2$.

The notation $\boxed{R}$ signifies the randomization of assigning the subjects.

This design resembles the after-only design, except that it involves an additional group of subjects called the control group, denoted by C, who are not exposed to the experiment. The experimental group E and the control group C are supposedly matched samples.

Illustrative example 5

In July 1983, Rediffusion Singapore commissioned a research study to demonstrate the strength of Rediffusion as a medium of advertising. Two groups, E and C, of Chinese people aged 15 years and above were selected to match each other in terms of age, sex, dwelling type and household income as closely as possible.

- E = 404 Chinese living in homes with a Rediffusion set
- C = 413 Chinese living in homes without a Rediffusion set.

Products already advertised in Rediffusion for a period of more than three months at the time of the survey were examined in the light of having their levels of awareness measured. The results showed that, for some advertised products, their levels of awareness were substantially higher among those living in homes with a Rediffusion set than among those who lived in homes without a Rediffusion set.

Brand	Experimental Treatment	Groups	After–Measurement	
Cherina	X	E	$O_1 = 90\%$	d=3%
		C	$O_2 = 87\%$	
Bubbles	X	E	$O_1 = 48\%$	d=14%
		C	$O_2 = 34\%$	
Menard	X	E	$O_1 = 97\%$	d=4%
		C	$O_2 = 93\%$	
Yamano	X	E	$O_1 = 70\%$	d=37%
		C	$O_2 = 33\%$	

Since a before-measurement is absent in this design, the degree of change in the dependent variable cannot be traced in either group. Only the change which is relative to the control group is measured instead. Additionally, without a measure of change in the control group, there is no sign showing that extraneous factors are not present, or the magnitude of change to be accounted for by the control group.

Before-after with control group design

With this design, the experimental group and the control group both receive two sets of measurement, one before and the other after the experimental treatment. The symbolic arrangement of before-after control group design is:

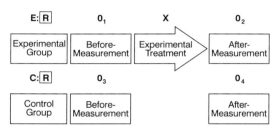

The effect of the experimental treatment is:

$$d = d_1 - d_2$$

where $d_1 = 0_2 - 0_1$ represents the combined effect caused by the experimental treatment and the extraneous variables, and $d_2 = 0_4 - 0_3$ represents the effect caused by the extraneous variables.

The premise of before-after control group design assumes that all extraneous variables operate equally on the experimental group as well as the control group.

Solomon four-group six-study design

This design is a combination of the two designs just discussed and provides a means for controlling the interactive testing effect as well as the effects of other extraneous factors. This particular design involves four groups and six studies, hence its name. The symbolic arrangement of this design is shown below.

This design provides the means to calculate the effects of the following factors which are responsible for changes in the dependent variables:

● effects of experimental treatment
● effects of extraneous variables

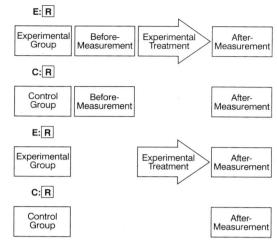

● effects of the pre-measurement
● any compounding of the effects of the before-measurement and the effects of the experimental variable.

The Solomon four-group six-study design is not commonly used in marketing research studies because it is highly expensive to conduct. On the other hand, it does allow control of mortality and interaction error which the before-after control design does not. Nevertheless, these errors are generally small or unlikely for most experiments.

Statistical experimental designs

All the experimental designs discussed so far are collectively referred to as quasi-experimental designs, whereby the researcher has control over data collection procedures (i.e. the *when* and *to whom* of measurements) but does not have complete control over the scheduling of the treatment (i.e. the *when* and *to whom* of exposure) as well as the ability to randomize test units' exposure to treatment.

We shall now turn to the discussion of statistical experimental designs which are extensions of the experimental designs earlier described. In a statistical experimental design, experimental treatments are randomly assigned to randomly selected test units. By means of a statistical procedure called the *analysis of variance*, the results of the experiment would be analysed to determine whether one experimental treatment significantly influences another experimental treatment, or whether the observed association could have been due to chance or some other factors.

Four statistical experimental designs are now discussed:

Completely randomized design

Randomized complete block design

Latin square design

} Only one (independent) experimental factor is studied

Factorial design

} Two or more (independent) experimental factors are simultaneously studied

Completely randomized design _____

This is the simplest and least costly of all statistical experimental designs, the objective of which is to investigate the impact of a single independent variable. Here, experimental treatments are randomly assigned to test units and in so doing, the researcher attempts to control all extraneous variables while manipulating the treatment variable, since these extraneous factors will not affect one group in any different way. The number of test units receiving one experimental treatment need not be equal to that of the test units undergoing different experimental treatments.

Consider the case of k experimental treatments on n test units. Experimental treatment i $(1 \leq i \leq k)$ is randomly assigned to n_i test units so that $kn_i = n$. The results obtained from a completely randomized design may be summarized as shown below:

Experimental treatment	No of test units	Measurements/ observations on treatment	Treatment total	Treatment mean
1	n_2	$x_{11}, x_{12}, \ldots x_{1n1}$	$T_{1+} = \Sigma X_{1i}$	x_{1+}
2	n_3	$x_{21}, x_{22}, \ldots x_{2n2}$	$T_{2+} = \Sigma X_{2i}$	x_{2+}
3	n_1	$x_{31}, x_{32}, \ldots x_{3n3}$	$T_{3+} = \Sigma X_{3i}$	x_{3+}
.	.	....	....	....
.	.	....	....	....
.k	n_k	$x_{k1}, x_{k2}, \ldots x_{knk}$	$T_{k+} = X_{ki}$	x_{k+}

The null hypothesis H_0 that there is no significant difference between experimental treatments can be tested by the analysis of variance method with one-way classification.

_____

Illustrative example 6

A supermarket chain has decided to introduce a new toilet soap but has yet to set its unit price. Four price levels – $1.80, $1.90, $2.00 and $2.10 – are considered and randomly assigned to twenty-two selected retail stores for one-calendar week. Weekly sales at these retail stores were recorded as follows:

Unit price	No. of stores	Sales in each retail store	Total sales	Average sales
$1.80	4	98, 73, 68, 85	324	81
$1.90	6	67, 83, 80, 76, 75, 69	450	75
$2.00	5	72, 69, 82, 65, 72	360	72
$2.10	7	81, 59, 61, 76, 63, 63, 66	469	67
	22			

Note that the completely randomized design is appropriate when we have essentially similar test units and homogenous treatment groups; or equivalently, no single group will differ vastly from another in terms of any important extraneous variables. Unfortunately in real-life situations, these hypothesized situations will almost not exist. In the above example, store size may influence sales performance and distort the results of the experiment. When it is obvious that one or more extraneous variables do exist which exert great influence over the test units, alternative designs as described below are used instead.

Randomized complete block design ____

This design makes it possible to control a single extraneous variable that might otherwise compound the experimental results. The test units are stratified in terms of an extraneous variable (e.g. store size) into blocks before being randomly assigned to the experimental or control groups. Each block has the same number of test units, and each experimental treatment appears only once in every block.

Take k experimental treatments for our illustration. The n test units are stratified to form b blocks comprising k units each (n = k × b). The experimental treatments are then randomly assigned to the test units within each block. Note that each experimental treatment is replicated b times. The data collected from a randomized complete block design may be summarized as follows:

Experimental treatment	No of test units	Observed measurements in block no. 1 2 3 . . .j . . . b	Treatment total	Treatment mean
1	n_1	$X_{11} X_{12} X_{13} \dots X_{1j} \dots X_{1b}$	T_{1+}	X_{1+}
2	n_2	$X_{21} X_{22} X_{23} \dots X_{2j} \dots X_{2b}$	T_{2+}	X_{2+}
i	n_i	$X_{i1} X_{i2} X_{i3} \dots X_i \dots X_{ib}$	T_{i+}	X_{i+}
k	n_k	$X_{k1} X_{k2} X_{k3} \dots X_{kj} \dots X_{kb}$	T_{k+}	X_{k+}
Block total		$T_{+1} T_{+2} T_{+3} \dots T_{+j} \dots T_{+b}$	T_{++} Grand total	
Block mean		$X_{+1} X_{+2} X_{+3} \dots X_{+j} \dots X_{+b}$	X_{++} Grand mean	

The null hypothesis H_0 stating that there is no significant difference between experimental treatments and between blocks can be tested employing the analysis of variance method; this time under a two-way classification.

With small samples, randomized block design is superior to completely randomized design in much the same way as stratified random sampling is to simple random sampling. In a randomized block design, the researcher can consider only one blocking factor (e.g. size of store) at a time. Although he can define the blocking factor in the form of a combination of one or more variables (e.g. location and size of store), yet only the effect of the combined blocking factor can be measured, as it is not possible to isolate the effect caused by each variable in the blocking factor. The Latin square design described below provides a partial solution.

Latin square design

The Latin square design may be viewed as an improvement of the randomized complete block design in that it allows the researcher to control or block out the effects of two or more extraneous variables that are likely to compound the results of an experiment. To apply the Latin square design, the following four requirements must all be fulfilled.

1 The number of categories of both control variables must be equal, yielding n × n square matrices.
2 The number of experimental groups must be equal to the number of categories of the control variables.
3 Each experimental group must appear in every row.
4 Each experimental group must appear in every column.

Procedurally, the experimental treatments are randomly assigned to the square matrices, under the requirements specified in (3) and (4) above. Assume that we have four experimental treatments A, B, C, D and sixteen test units. The two control variables are Q_1 and Q_2, each being classified into four categories. The arrangement of experimental treatments will constitute a 4×4 Latin square design as shown below:

$Q_2 Q_1$	1	2	3	4
1	A	D	C	B
2	B	A	D	C
3	C	B	A	D
4	D	C	B	A

Here, the effects of extraneous variables (e.g. store size and store location) on the dependent variable (e.g. sales) are both controlled. Two kinds of interactions that might occur but however are not considered in this design are: (a) interactions between these two extraneous variables; and (b) interactions between extraneous variables and the treatment levels. Despite these potential weaknesses, the principal strength of the Latin square design makes it a very popular experimental design used in marketing research studies.

In general, the analysis of variance table of a $k \times k$ Latin square design takes the following form:

Analysis of variance table of a k x k Latin square

Source of variation	Sum of squares	Degrees of freedom	Mean square	F ratio
Between treatments	SS_t	$k-1$	$MS_t = SS_t/k-1$	MS_t/MS_E
Between rows	SS_R	$k-1$	$MS_R = SS_R/k-1$	MS_R/MS_E
Between columns	SS_C	$k-1$	$MS_C = SS_C/k-1$	MS_C/MS_E
Residual	SS_E	$(k-1)(k-2)$	$MS_E = SS_E/(k-1)(k-2)$	
Total	SS_T	k_2-1		

Null hypothesis H_0:

- There is no difference between treatments.
- There is no difference between rows.
- There is no difference between columns.

The data collected from a Latin square design allows for the computation of treatment totals T_A, T_B, T_C and T_D in addition to the row totals and column totals.

Total sum of squares, denoted by SS_T, is:

$$SS_T = \sum_i^k \sum_j^k (X_{ij} - \bar{X}_{++})^2 = \sum_i^k \sum_j^k X_{ij}^2 - \frac{(T_{++})^2}{k^2}$$

The total sum of squares can be broken up into four parts: Sum of squares between treatments, sum of squares between rows, sum of squares between columns, and residual sum of squares. These can be computed as follows:

Treatment sum of squares:

$$SS_t = k \sum_t^k (\bar{X}_t - \bar{X}_{++})^2$$

$$= \sum_t^k \frac{T_t^2}{k} - \frac{(T_{++})^2}{k^2}$$

Row sum of squares:

$$SS_R = k \sum_i^k (\bar{X}_{i+} - \bar{X}_{++})^2$$

$$= \sum_i^k \frac{T_{i+}^2}{k} - \frac{(T_{++})^2}{k^2}$$

Column sum of squares:

$$SS_R = k \sum_i^k (\bar{X}_{+i} - \bar{X}_{++})^2$$

$$= \sum_i^k \frac{T_{+i}^2}{k} - \frac{(T_{++})^2}{k^2}$$

Residual sum of squares:

$$SS_E = \sum_i^k \sum_j^k (\bar{X}_{ij} - \bar{X}_t - \bar{X}_{i+} - \bar{X}_{+j} + 2\bar{X}_{++})^2$$

$$= SS_T - SS_t - SS_R - SS_C$$

In the above expression, the subscript t denotes treatments A, B, C and D: $\bar{X}_t$ represents the treatment means $\bar{X}_A$, $\bar{X}_B$, $\bar{X}_C$ and $\bar{X}_D$; and T_t represents the treatment totals T_A, T_B, T_C and T_D.

Factorial design

All the preceding experimental designs have allowed us to measure the effects of only one single independent (experimental) variable. Very often, it is required to investigate the simultaneous effects of two or more independent variables (e.g. price changes and promotion), each of which at two or more treatment levels. Factorial designs are intended for these situations and have significant value in marketing experiments where there is likely to be at least some interaction between the treatment variables.

Let us consider two independent factors – factor A (pricing level) and factor B (media type) each of which has two levels:

Factor A	Factor B
a_1: high-price policy	b_1: print advertisement
a_2: low-price policy	b_2: broadcast advertisement

This constitutes the simplest case known as a 2^2-factorial experiment. All levels of factor A are combined with the different levels of factor B to yield four district combinations: a_1b_1, a_1b_2, a_2b_1, a_2b_2. The factorial design specifies that at least one observation must be made for each possible combination.

	Factor B	
Factor A	b_1: print advertisement	b_2: broadcast advertisement
a_1: high-price policy	a_1b_1	a_1b_2
a_2: low-price policy	a_2b_1	a_2b_2

Analysis of the results of a factorial experiment provides two types of measurements: (a) interactive effects, resulting from two variables interacting to produce an effect that is greater than the simple sum of their individual effects; and (b) main effects, that is, the effects of each independent variable individually. In the above example, there are four sets of interactive effects as expressed below:

- Simple effect of Factor A at $b_1 = a_2b_1 - a_1b_1$
- Simple effect of Factor A at $b_2 = a_2b_2 - a_1b_2$
- Simple effect of Factor B at $a_1 = a_1b_2 - a_1b_1$
- Simple effect of Factor B at $a_2 = a_2b_2 - a_2b_1$

The main effect of each factor is calculated by computing the average of the simple effect of that factor. Thus:

Main effect of factor A

$$= 1/2\,[(a_2b_1 - a_1b_1) + (a_2b_2 - a_1b_2)]$$

Main effect of factor B

$$= 1/2\,[(a_1b_2 - a_1b_1) + (a_2b_2 - a_2b_1)]$$

Two principal strengths of factorial design are evident. First, it requires a smaller number of test units for estimating the simple and main effects of independent factors. A 2^2-factorial experiment, say, requires only four test units rather than eight test units as they are in a single-factor experimental design. Two test units would be needed to determine the simple effect of Factor A while Factor B is kept constant at b_1 level, and another two units to determine the simple effect of Factor A at b_2 level. The same number of test units would be required to determine the simple effects of Factor B, at a_1 level and a_2 level respectively. Secondly, this design can estimate the interaction between independent factors which a single-factor experiment fails to. In practice, the treatment combinations of a factorial experiment may be replicated over test units either by the use of a completely randomized design, or a randomized block design, or a Latin square design. Let us consider the 2_2-factorial experiment with the four treatment combinations: a_1b_1, a_1b_2, a_2b_1 and a_2b_2, each of which being replicated n times. The completely randomized design is used and no restriction is imposed on the randomization process except that each treatment combination has n replications. The analysis of data is then described on page 70.

The total sum of squares, denoted by SS_T, has $(4n - 1)$ degrees of freedom and can be partitioned into two components:

Source of Variation	Sum of squares	Degrees of freedom	Mean square	F Ratio
Between Treatment Combinations	$SS_t = \dfrac{T_{11}^2 + T_{12}^2 + T_{21}^2 + T_{22}^2}{n} - \dfrac{T_{++}^2}{4n}$	3	$MS_t = SS_t / 3$	
Main Effect A	$SS_A = \dfrac{T_{1+}^2 + T_{2+}^2}{2n} - \dfrac{T_{++}^2}{4n}$	1	$MS_A = SS_A$	MS_A / MS_E
Main Effect B	$SS_B = \dfrac{T_{+1}^2 + T_{+2}^2}{2n} - \dfrac{T_{++}^2}{4n}$	1	$MS_B = SS_B$	MS_B / MS_E
Interaction AB	$SS_I = SS_t - SS_A - SS_B$	1	$MS_I = SS_I$	MS_I / MS_E
Within Treatment Combinations	$SS_E = SS_T - SS_t$	4n - 4	$MS_E = SS_E /(4n-4)$	
Total	SS_T	4n -1		

Figure 3.8 *Analysis of variance table (A 2_2 factorial with n replications)*

- the between treatment combination sum of squares, denoted by SS_t with 3 degrees of freedom
- the within treatment combination sum of squares, denoted by SS_E, with $(4n - 4)$ degrees of freedom.

Thus $SS_T = SS_t + SS_E$ are to be computed in the same way as in the one-way classification analysis of variance. Next, the component SS_t can be further partitioned into three parts, each with one degree of freedom:

- the main effect A sum of squares, denoted by SS_A
- the main effect B sum of squares, denoted by SS_B
- the interaction AB sum of squares, denoted by SS_I

Thus $SS_t = SS_A + SS_B + SS_I$.

If we denote T_{11}, T_{12}, T_{21}, T_{22} to represent the totals of the n observations on a_1b_1, a_1b_2, a_2b_1, a_2b_2 respectively; T_{1+}, T_{2+}, T_{+1} and T_{+2} to represent the totals of the 2n observations involving a_1, a_2, b_1 and b_2 respectively; and

finally T_{++} to represent the grand total of all 4n observations, we can arrange these into a 2×2 table:

a_1	T_{11}	T_{12}	T_{1+}
b_2	T_{21}	T_{22}	T_{2+}
	T_{+1}	T_{+2}	T_{++}

We are now able to express the main effect and interaction sum of squares in the form of the formulae below:

$$SS_A = T_{21+}/2n + T_{22+}/2n - T_{2++}/4n$$

$$SS_B = T_{2+1}/2n + T_{2+2}/2n - T_{2++}/4n$$

$$SS_I = SS_T - SS_A - SS_B$$

These sums of squares can be summarized into the analysis of variance table in Figure 3.8.

The significance of main effect A, main effect B and interaction AB can be tested at a predetermined level by the respective F-ratios.

End-of-chapter revision

Review questions

3.1 What is research design? What is its role in marketing research?

3.2 What are the different types of research design? What is the basic purpose of each?

3.3 What are the steps involved in the research design process?

3.4 In what situations may it be likely that exploratory research is sufficient, and that the researcher need not proceed with a large-scale project?

3.5 What are the basic uses of exploratory research? Name and discuss three approaches used in exploratory research.

3.6 What are the key characteristics of exploratory research?

3.7 What is experience survey? How can it be useful as a form of exploratory research?

3.8 What is descriptive research?

3.9 How does the descriptive research design differ from exploratory research design?

3.10 Differentiate between cross-sectional and longitudinal research designs.

3.11 What advantages does the longitudinal research design offer relative to the cross-sectional research design?

3.12 What is meant by a consumer panel?

3.13 What are the reasons that a consumer panel may not be representative of the population from which it is drawn?

3.14 What are the main problems associated with the use of consumer panels for the collection of marketing research data?

3.15 Explain clearly what experimentation involves.

3.16 What is the difference between a laboratory experiment and a field experiment?

3.17 What are the strengths and weaknesses of field experiments?

3.18 What are the strengths and weaknesses of laboratory experiments?

3.19 Describe the following experimental designs using the appropriate symbols:
- After-only without control group design
- Before-after without control group design
- Before-after with control group design
- After-only with control group design
- Static-group comparison design
- Solomon four-group six-study design

3.20 Under what circumstances is an after-only without control group design appropriate?

3.21 Describe and give an example of each of the following:
- Maturation
- History
- Instrumentation
- Selection
- Mortality

3.22 How do statistical designs differ from basic designs?

3.23 Describe and discuss the important characteristics of each of the following:
- Randomized block design
- Latin square design
- Factorial design

3.24 Under what circumstances might one wish to use:
- The completely randomized design?
- The randomized block design?
- The Latin square design?

3.25 What is a 4 × 4 Latin square design? What is a 2 × 2 × 3 factorial design?

3.26 What are the strengths and weaknesses of a:
- Latin square design?
- Factorial design?

3.27 Assume a particular research problem, for example, finding the type of persons who buy *Her World* magazine at news-stands. Can you suggest a research plan to obtain this information?

3.28 Describe and contrast, using examples, qualitative research and experimental design research.

True-false questions

Write True (T) or False (F) for the following:

3.29 Logitudinal studies are those which are designed for providing repeated measurements of an event over a period of time.

3.30 The consumer panel method is characterized by a sample of respondents being independently selected for each round of the survey.

3.31 Causal research adopts an informal approach which is characterized by flexibility and versatility in use.

3.32 Exploratory research allows for the widest posible exploration of views, attitudes and behaviour patterns.

3.33 In exploratory research, structured data collection forms are seldomly used.

3.34 The approach adopted in an experience survey should be highly unstructured to allow the respondent to offer widely divergent views.

3.35 Experience survey requires probability sampling techniques.

3.36 Causal research aims at describing the characteristics of the target population.

3.37 Descriptive research is recommended when the research purpose is centred at providing accurate, statistically reliable data.

3.38 Exploratory research necessitates a reasonably large sample of respondents.

3.39 The randomized block experiment can reduce the effects of one or more extraneous variables that are related to the independent variable.

3.40 Qualitative research is often used to clarify concepts and to establish priorities for further research.

3.41 Subjects in the control group are exposed to the experimental variable.

3.42 A probability sample is imperative in qualitative research.

3.43 Panel members are generally willing to fill out questionnaires and grant interviews that are longer and more demanding than members of the general public would find acceptable.

3.44 The most important advantage of the panel design is analytical.

3.45 Experimentation is a popular technique in qualitative research.

3.46 A research study which is aimed at making predictions is a causal research study.

3.47 A descriptive study demonstrates direct cause-and-effect relationships.

3.48 A qualitative study is used to measure brand's share of a market.

3.49 The testing effect refers to the influence of a measurement on the values obtained in subsequent measurements.

3.50 The laboratory experiment is likely to allow subjects to function in a natural setting, such as their homes or supermarkets.

3.51 In the static-group comparison design, individuals are not randomly assigned to experimental and control groups.

3.52 The Latin square design makes it possible for the researcher to control the effects of two extraneous variables.

3.53 The main purpose of a qualitative study is to draw conclusions upon representative evidence.

Multiple-choice questions

3.54 The experimental method is superior to other research methods because:
a it can establish a cause-and effect relationship
b it can establish a direct relationship
c it has minimum error
d it is very cheap to set up and administer.

3.55 Consumer panels are used in marketing research because:
a they constitute an unbiased sample
b the set-up and maintenance costs are low
c they have many applications in cross-sectional research
d they are effective in generating data measuring change over time.

3.56 In a field experiment a change in a competitor's price is likely to be:
a an independent variable
b an extraneous variable
c a dependent variable
d none of the above.

3.57 The effects of two interacting independent variables can best be measured using:
a the static-group comparison design
b the randomized block design
c the Latin square design
d the factorial design.

3.58 To become familiar with the problem situation and identify important variables, we may wish to conduct:
a a predictive study
b a causal study
c a qualitative study
d a descriptive study.

3.59 An area of concern when using consumer panels is:
a possible lack of representation on the part of panel members
b the inability to perform field experiments
c the inability to gather market-share information
d low rate of response.

3.60 During an experiment, subjects or test units may change in some way that influence the results. This is referred to as:
a history
b mortality
c maturation
d testing effect.

3.61 Randomization is the:
a random assignment of subjects to groups in an experiment
b random decision as to whether a given variable will be included in the experiment
c unethical practice of falsifying experimental data by using random numbers instead of actually collecting real data
d random method of deciding whether or not to tell subjects which group they are in.

3.62 Which one of the following experimental designs would be best if we wish to control the effects of just one extraneous variable?
a Latin square.
b Randomized complete block.
c Factorial.
d Completely randomized.

3.63 Which one of the following experimental designs would be best if we wish to examine interaction between different levels of two or more independent variables?
a Latin square.
b Randomized complete block.
c Factorial.
d Completely randomized.

3.64 The experience survey is a procedure most appropriate for:
a qualitative research
b descriptive research
c causal research
d all of the above.

3.65 The panel in a longitudinal study has:
a a fixed sample of members
b periodic additions to replace dropouts
c members that are measured repeatedly
d all of the above are true.

3.66 Exploratory research is adopted when the research purpose is:
 a to provide a greater understanding of a concept
 b to crystallize a marketing problem
 c to discover general ideas and insights relating to the subject of study
 d all of the above.

3.67 Descriptive research is favoured when the research purpose is:
 a generating new product ideas
 b developing hypothesis
 c defining and formulating problems
 d none of the above.

3.68 The effects of two interacting independent variables can best be measured using:
 a the static-group comparison design
 b the randomized block design
 c the Latin square design
 d the factorial design.

3.69 To become familiar with the problem situation and identify important variables, we may wish to conduct:
 a a predictive study
 b a causal study
 c a qualitative study
 d a descriptive study.

3.70 An area of concern when using consumer panels is:
 a possible lack of representation on the part of panel members
 b the inability to perform field experiments
 c the inability to gather market-share information
 d low rate of response.

3.71 During an experiment, subjects or test units may change in some way that influence the results. This is referred to as:
 a history
 b mortality
 c maturation
 d testing effect.

3.72 Randomisation is the:
 a random assignment of subjects to groups in an experiment
 b random decision as to whether a given variable will be included in the experiment
 c unethical practice of falsifying experimental data by using random numbers instead of actually collecting real data
 d random method of deciding whether or not to tell subjects which group they are in.

3.73 Which one of the following experimental designs would be best if we wish to control the effects of just one extraneous variable?
 a Latin square
 b Randomised complete block
 c Factorial
 d Completely randomised

3.74 Which one of the following experimental designs would be best if we wish to examine interaction between different levels of two or more independent variables?
 a Latin square
 b Randomised complete block
 c Factorial
 d Completely randomised

3.75 The experience survey is a procedure most appropriate for:
 a qualitative research
 b descriptive research
 c causal research
 d All of the above.

3.76 The panel in a longitudinal study has:
 a a fixed sample of members
 b periodic additions to replace dropouts
 c members that are measured repeatedly
 d All of the above are true

3.77 A large-scale study was undertaken to gauge how students currently rate the prestige of various secondary schools; which of the following type or research is it?
 a Exploratory research.
 b Longitudinal research.
 c Cross-sectional research.
 d Causal research.

3.78 In-depth interviewing is preferred over focus group discussion when the topic of study involves:
 a intimate subject matters (eg. contraception)
 b highly personal views (e.g. attitudes toward management or government)
 c embarrassing question items (e.g. sanitary towel protection)
 d all of the above.

3.79 The independent sample method offers advantages over the consumer panel method because:
 a it suggests a relatioinship between variables under investigation
 b it offers a larger pool of data to be gathered
 c it does not need to retain the respondents for subsequent interviews
 d it brings a higher level of statistical precision.

4

Basics of sampling ─────────────────

The concept and application of sampling are commonplace in our daily life. We take the first sip from a cup of coffee cautiously to gauge how hot (or cold) it is. Shoppers sample a small piece of biscuit to know what it tastes like before making a purchase. The doctor takes a sample of blood to examine the patient's physical condition. Quality control inspectors test the life span of light bulbs. Examples of sampling practices can run into an endless list. We are, indeed, samplers ourselves.

Sample originates from the word 'example'. Ideally, the sample should be a good example of the defined universe (or population) so that the values of the population (e.g. age, income, percentage of smokers, etc.) may be estimated from the corresponding sample data.

Since sampling plays a vital role in marketing research, a basic understanding of its function and principal methods is of particular use to both marketing managers and researchers. In this chapter, we will confine the discussion to the fundamental aspects of sampling, and leave the readers to refer to the appropriate textbooks for a more intensive study of this subject.

General principles of sampling ■

Statistical theory on sampling methods is based upon the following basic principles:

1 *The principle of statistical regularity.* It states that if a reasonably large sample is selected at random from a population, this sample will generally possess characteristics which closely resemble those of that population.
2 *The principle of inertia of large numbers.* It states that larger aggregates of individual elements generally exhibit a higher degree of stability in measurements, with abnormalities of elements in one direction (e.g. exceptionally large values) more likely to be balanced by abnormalities of elements in the opposite direction (e.g. exceptionally small values).
3 *The principle of normal frequency.* It states that if natural phenomenon (e.g. weights, heights, etc.) are plotted in terms of frequencies of occurrences, a symmetrical *bell-shaped* curve, or the *normal curve*, will generally be exhibited.

Benefits of sampling ■■■■■

Compared to a complete enumeration of the population units (i.e. a census), sampling has a number of advantages:

1 *Cost.* First and foremost, sampling is much less expensive. The cost of interviewing a fraction of the population will certainly be lower than that of interviewing the entire population. Sampling will also mean a lower data processing cost, since only a smaller number of data collection forms will be handled.

2 *Speed.* Much shorter time is needed to interview a sample than the entire population. Furthermore, tabulation and analysis of sample results can be performed earlier and faster.

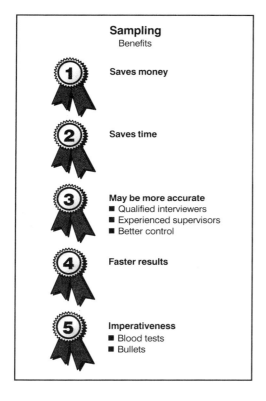

3 *Accuracy.* Since sample interviewing will require a much smaller group of interviewers, only the more skilled and qualified interviewers will be recruited to undertake the interviewing work. This will help increase the accuracy of results.
4 *Destructive nature of elements.* Sampling presents the only feasible alternative if the research study entails destructive elements (e.g. blood, electric bulbs, bullets etc.). If each element is to be tested, there would be no element left after the testing.

Limitations of sampling

Sampling is not without shortcomings, some of which are listed below:

1 It demands a more rigid control in undertaking the sample operations.
2 The study of minority subgroups is often suspect, due to the small number of sample elements belonging to the subgroups.
3 When the sample data is subjected to the weighting procedure, accuracy level is affected. Moreover, data processing and tabulation become extremely cumbersome.
4 Sample results are, at best, approximations.

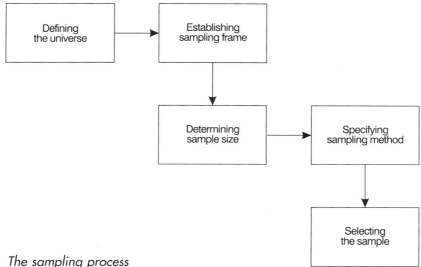

Figure 4.1 *The sampling process*

The sampling process ▬▬▬

The sampling process is described in Figure 4.1.

Defining the universe _____

A basic consideration in the sampling process concerns the identification of the target population or universe. The question of 'Who do we want to study?' must first be established. The universe (or population) of a research study, in sampling terminology, refers to the totality of elements about which measurements are to be made. This phrase outlines the extent or scope of subjects (e.g. persons, users, households, newspaper subscribers, etc.) to be studied and about whom sample results will be inferred. A well-defined universe specifies the following:

1 What constitute the units of analysis (e.g. HDB homes)?
2 What are the sampling units (e.g. HDB homes occupied in the past six months)?
3 What is the specific designation of which units are to be covered (e.g. HDB in town area)?
4 What is the time boundary, that is, what time period does the data refer to (e.g. 1 January 1997)?

Establishing sampling frame _____

A sampling frame is a list of all elements in the population from which the sample may be drawn and hence serves, in a sense, as the boundaries that circumscribe the population. Telephone directories, electoral registers and club membership lists are examples of sampling frames commonly used in marketing research studies. Without a sampling frame, researchers will find it difficult to assure that the sample elements are chosen with equal probabilities. When the sampling frame available for use does not fully represent the intended population, the observed difference between them (known as the frame error) can adversely affect the degree of reliability of sample results. Such discrepancy constitutes the first potential source of error associated with sampling.

Determining sample size _____

The determination of sample size follows after the sampling frame has been established. The required sample size would normally depend on the desired level of data precision, the degree and nature of the analysis, the extent of homogeneity of population elements, the amount of research funds provided, as well as the length of time allowed for the study.

Specifying sampling method _____

This step specifies the method under which the sample elements are to be selected (e.g. probability sampling or non-probability sampling).

Selecting the sample _____

This step illustrates the operational procedures of selecting the sample.

Sampling error and non-sampling error ▬▬▬

The use of good sampling methods produces accurate results. Unfortunately, no sample is totally error-free since it would not likely be an exact replica of the population from which it is drawn. Sampling error, known as the difference between the sample value and its corresponding population value, will always exist.

Apart from sampling error, any sample survey is subjected to non-sampling error as well. [*Note*: A census is free from sampling error and so is subjected to non-sampling error only.] As the sample size increases, sampling error gets smaller while non-sampling error becomes larger. Interestingly though, the total error (sum of sampling error and non-sampling error) of a sample survey may be smaller than the single non-sampling error of a census (see Figure 4.2).

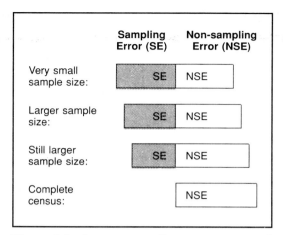

Figure 4.2 *Components of error in a research study*

The US Bureau of Census uses the sample to check the accuracy of the census data and in the event that the sample shows a possible source of error, the census may need to be re-done. The nature of non-sampling error will be discussed in further detail in Chapter 7.

Probability sampling

Sampling methods used in marketing research are basically of two types: probability sampling method and non-probability sampling method. Either sampling method can be justified provided one is sure about the likely risks. We begin with the discussion of probability sampling method.

Probability samples are based on chance selection procedures. In probability sampling, every element in the population has a known non-zero probability of being selected, and the selection of probability samples will always observe certain mathematical or mechanical decision rules which are not subjected to the discretion of the researchers.

Probability samples are designed to be *measurable*, that is, statistical inferences to the population values can be logically made based on measures of variability (e.g. standard errors) derived from the sample data. Until 1950, probability sampling as a sampling procedure was little known in field studies. Modern advancements in sampling theory, coupled with the improved techniques employed in field work, have greatly enhanced the practical value of probability sampling. Today, the probability sampling method is widely used in marketing research.

Probability sampling includes the following:

1 Simple random sampling.
2 Stratified sampling.
3 Cluster sampling.
4 Systematic sampling.

Simple random sampling

The simplest of all probability sampling methods is simple random sampling. In this method, usually called for brevity the method of random sampling, each possible sample will have an equal probability of being chosen, and each element in the population will have an equal chance of being included in the sample. As the name suggests, simple random sampling is operationally convenient and simple in theory.

Simple random sampling is the purest form of sampling and does not require any prior knowledge or assumptions about the population profile. (*Caution*: The term *random sampling* should not be taken to mean haphazard sampling; instead it should be regarded as a sampling procedure with strict adherence to a scientific plan.) Simple random sampling is most appropriate when the universe under study is reasonably small and/or the population elements are either pre-listed or readily identifiable.

Illustrative example 1

To select a simple random sample of two typists from a pool of six typists represented by the letters A, B, C, D, E and F.

Method 1
- *Step 1*. Take six identical marbles, each to represent a particular typist in the given universe.
- *Step 2*. Mark each marble with a serial number from 1 to 6 (i.e. 1 to represent typist A, 2 to represent typist B, etc.) and mix the marbles thoroughly in a drum.
- *Step 3*. Select two marbles from the drum at random, one at a time without replacement.

Assume that marbles 1 and 5 are chosen consecutively. The selected sample, denoted by S, will comprise typist A and typist E. Note that the probability of selecting S = [A,E] is:

$$P(S) = P \text{ (1st draw is marble 1 while 2nd draw is marble 5)} + P \text{ (1st draw is marble 5 while 2nd draw is marble 1)}$$
$$= (1/6 \times 1/5) + (1/6 \times 1/5)$$
$$= 1/15$$

Method 2
- *Step 1*. List out all the possible samples comprising two typists. There are $_6C_2 = 15$ different samples as exhibited below:

List of samples		Sample elements
S_1	=	[A,B]
S_2	=	[A,C]
S_3	=	[A,D]
S_4	=	[A,E]
S_5	=	[A,F]
S_6	=	[B,C]
S_7	=	[B,D]
S_8	=	[B,E]
S_9	=	[B,F]
S_{10}	=	[C,D]
S_{11}	=	[C,E]
S_{12}	=	[C,F]
S_{13}	=	[D,E]
S_{14}	=	[D,F]
S_{15}	=	[E,F]

- *Step 2*. Take 15 identical marbles, each to represent one of the above samples.
- *Step 3*. Mark each marble with a serial number from 1 to 15 (e.g. 1 to represent S_1, 2 to represent S_2, etc.) and subsequently mix them thoroughly in a drum.
- *Step 4*. Select one marble at random from the drum. Assume that the marble 10 is chosen, the selected sample S comprises typist C and typist D.

The probability of selecting S = [C,D] (in fact, any one of the random sample above) is 1/15.

For a large population size, both methods of selection as described above become tedious. A population comprising 400 elements, for example, will generate a total of 79,800 different samples of size n = 2, which would be administratively cumbersome to execute if the two methods previously described are used. Random number tables offer a partial solution to this situation.

Random number tables

Random number tables contain numerous columns and rows of single-digit numbers without any regular or systematic pattern. Any number, or sequence of any two or more numbers in a random number table, can occur as frequently in a random manner. The primary benefit of random number is to dismiss the inaccuracies or bias of a sample which is selected via personal judgement.

The numbers in a random number table are mechanically or mathematically generated and may be read in any way: horizontally, vertically, diagonally, forward, backward and so on. The number 1 will be

---

1. **Assign a unique number to each population element. It is common practice to start with serial number 1, or 01, or 001, etc upwards depending on the number of digits involved.**

2. **Choose a random starting position.**

3. **Select serial numbers systematically across rows or down columns.**

4. **Discard numbers which are not assigned to any population element.**

5. **Ignore numbers which have already been selected.**

6. **Repeat the selection process until the required number of sample elements is selected.**

Figure 4.3 *Procedures for using random number tables*

represented by 01 if two-digit serial numbers are involved; by 001 if three-digit serial numbers are involved and so on.

The procedures involved in using random number tables are outlined in Figure 4.3.

Illustrative example 2

To select a simple random sample of 10 members of PR Recreational Club which has 100 members, using the random number table method.

We begin by assigning each club member a two-digit serial number from 00 to 99 as shown below:

00(C)	20(M)	40(C)	60(I)	80(M)
01(C)	21(I)	41(I)	61(M)	81(C)
02(I)	22(C)	42(I)	62(M)	82(C)
03(C)	23(I)	43(C)	63(C)	83(M)
04(C)	24(C)	44(M)	64(C)	84(I)
05(C)	25(M)	45(C)	65(I)	85(C)
06(M)	26(C)	46(I)	66(M)	86(C)
07(M)	27(M)	47(M)	67(C)	87(M)
08(C)	28(I)	48(C)	68(M)	88(I)
09(C)	29(C)	49(C)	69(C)	89(C)
10(M)	30(C)	50(C)	70(C)	90(I)
11(C)	31(C)	51(M)	71(C)	91(C)
12(I)	32(C)	52(I)	72(M)	92(M)
13(M)	33(M)	53(M)	73(C)	93(C)
14(C)	34(C)	54(C)	74(I)	94(C)
15(M)	35(M)	55(C)	75(C)	95(I)
16(C)	36(C)	56(M)	76(C)	96(C)
17(I)	37(C)	57(C)	77(M)	97(C)
18(I)	38(I)	58(M)	78(M)	98(M)
19(M)	39(I)	59(M)	79(C)	99(C)

where C indicates Chinese = 50 (50%)
M indicates Malays = 30 (30%)
I indicates Indians = 20 (20%)

$$\overline{}$$
100 (100%)

Adopting the random number table provided in Appendix C at the end of this chapter, randomly choose two columns, say 41 and 42, and work downwards, say, from Row 12.

	Column No.	
	41	42
Row 12	2	4
	8	8
	8	8 (note: already
	2	3 selected)
	8	4
	8	3
	4	4
	9	9
	0	8
	5	5
	1	0

The selected sample would be:

$$S = (24, 88, 23, 84, 83, 44, 99, 08, 55, 10)$$

There are a number of disadvantages in the adoption of random number tables. First, the task of serializing all the population elements can quickly become boring. Secondly, the rate of rejecting invalid numbers will be high in some cases. A population which contains, say 1,036 elements, will usually be assigned serial numbers from 0001 to 1036, hence all selected four-digit numbers greater than 1036 will be rejected, resulting in a wastage rate of nearly 90 per cent. To avoid such wastage, marketing researchers sometimes resort to computers to generate the number of pseudo-random numbers desired within the limits specified. In practice, there is no perceptible difference between pseudo-random numbers and random numbers.

Stratified sampling

In stratified sampling, the population is divided into subgroups or strata, each to be as homogeneous as possible in terms of some desired characteristics (e.g. age, income). Within each stratum, a sample of elements is selected. These samples are then aggregated to constitute a stratified random sample. A stratified sample is a restricted random sample from the viewpoint that its sample elements are drawn from each stratum rather than from the entire population. While the probability of selecting any element within a stratum is equal and known, that of selecting any item in the population is unequal but known. Stratified sampling works best when the population under study is heterogeneous in nature.

In brief, stratified sampling involves the following steps:

1 Subdivide the population under study into homogeneous, mutually exclusive subgroups or strata based on certain criteria (e.g. age, income).
2 Select a sample of elements from each stratum.
3 Combine all sample elements so selected to form a stratified random sample.

The selection of sample elements from each stratum may be carried out using either proportionate allocation or disproportionate allocation. With proportionate sampling, the number of sample elements to be selected from each stratum is in direct proportion to the stratum size. This ensures that each stratum is proportionally represented in the ultimate stratified sample – a crucial consideration for eliminating any possible difference that may exist between strata. In the case of disproportionate sampling, the number of sample elements selected from each stratum is not proportionate to its stratum size but varies with the extent of variation within each stratum. In other words, if a stratum exhibits greater variation, a larger number of sample elements will be selected, and vice versa. The primary purpose of disproportionate sampling arises from the desire to over-sample some specific subgroups as well as to reduce variance within each subgroup. Very often, researchers may want to oversample a certain subgroup whose sample elements would not otherwise be sufficiently large for any meaningful analysis of data.

Illustrative example 3

To select a proportionate stratified sample of 100 members from PR Recreational Club mentioned in the previous example.

1 Subdivide the club members into three homogeneous subgroups or strata by ethnic origin: Chinese, Malays and Indians.

Chinese members					Malay members			Indian members	
00	22	40	64	82	06	35	66	02	42
01	24	43	67	85	07	44	68	12	46
03	26	45	69	86	10	47	72	17	52
04	29	48	70	89	13	51	77	18	60
05	30	49	71	91	15	53	78	21	65
08	31	50	73	93	19	56	80	23	74
09	32	54	75	94	20	58	83	28	84
11	34	55	76	96	25	59	87	38	88
14	36	57	79	97	27	61	92	39	90
16	37	63	81	99	33	62	98	41	95

2 Calculate the overall sampling fraction, f, as follows:

$$f = n/N = 10/100 = 1/10$$

where n = sample size
N = population size

Determine the number of sample elements (n_1) to be selected from the Chinese stratum. In this example, n_1 = 50 × f = 5. We then assume that a simple random sample comprising of members 03, 24, 57, 69, 97 are selected from the Chinese stratum. Next, determine the number of sample elements (n_2) to be selected from the Malay stratum. In this example, n_2 = 30 × f = 3. We then assume that members 06, 51, 98 are selected from the Malay stratum. Similarly, determine the number of sample elements (n_3) to be selected from Indian stratum. In this example, n_3 = 20 × f = 2. We then assume that members 41, 74 are selected from the Indian stratum.

3 The ultimate stratified sample is

S = (03, 24, 57, 69, 97, 06, 51, 98, 41, 74).

If we pause a while and compare the *ethnicity* distribution of the simple random sample and the stratified sample of the population under study (see below), we will discover that the simple random sample has under-represented the Chinese and over-represented the Indians. The stratified sample, on the other hand, exhibits a perfect match with the population in this respect. This feature will always (or almost always) be true in proportionate stratified sampling in respect of the specified criteria adopted.

	Simple random sample	Stratified random sample	Population under study
Chinese	40%	50%	50%
Malays	30%	30%	30%
Indians	30%	20%	20%

Stratified sampling has some inherent limitations. The basic requirement for stratified sampling is the availability of the needed information (such as ethnicity in the above example) about the population under study. When the needed information is not available, the adoption of stratified sampling would necessitate the collection of such basic data which means longer time in the research process. Data tabulation becomes difficult when a large number of strata are involved. On the positive side, a stratified sample will normally yield more precise survey results. Another advantage of stratified sampling is that information pertaining to the subgroups can be more meaningfully analysed.

Cluster sampling

Cluster sampling bears a unique characteristic which distinguishes it from all other types of probability sampling methods, and that is: the sample elements are selected in groups or clusters, instead of one element at a time. The primary reason for cluster sampling is economy, while the characteristic of a probability sample is retained. The procedures involved in selecting a cluster sample are outlined below:

1 Subdivide the population under study into a number of mutually exclusive and collectively comprehensive clusters, or subgroups.
2 Select a simple random sample of clusters.

Illustrative example 4

Referring to the same example of PR Recreation Club members:

1 Subdivide the club members into 10 (heterogeneous) clusters, each cluster containing 10 members.

Cluster no.	Chinese	Malays	Indians
1	00, 22, 40, 64, 82	06, 35, 66	02, 42
2	01, 24, 4, 67, 85	07, 44, 68	12, 46
3	03, 26, 45, 69, 86	10, 47, 72	17, 52
4	04, 29, 48, 70, 89	13, 51, 77	18, 60
5	05, 30, 49, 71, 91	15, 53, 78	21, 65
6	08, 31, 50, 73, 93	19, 56, 80	23, 74
7	09, 32, 54, 75, 94	20, 58, 83	28, 84
8	11, 34, 55, 76, 96	25, 59, 87	38, 88
9	14, 36, 57, 79, 97	27, 61, 92	39, 90
10	16, 37, 63, 81, 99	23, 62, 98	41, 95

<table>
<tr><th>Stratified sampling</th><th>Cluster sampling</th></tr>
<tr><td>
1. The population under study is sub-divided into a few strata, each containing a large number of elements.

2. Within each stratum, the elements are homogeneous. Between strata, there is a high degree of heterogeneity.

3. A sample element is selected each time.
</td><td>
1. The population under study is sub-divided into a large number of clusters, each containing a few elements.

2. Within each cluster, the elements are heterogeneous. Between clusters, there is a high degree of homogeneity.

3. A cluster is selected each time.
</td></tr>
</table>

Figure 4.4 *Stratified sampling versus cluster sampling*

2 Proceed to choose one of the 10 clusters. Assume that cluster 8 is selected, then all its elements (i.e. Club Members 11, 34, 55, 76, 96, 25, 59, 87, 38, 88) are selected.

Where the entire set of elements in the selected cluster is considered in the ultimate sample (as in the above example), we have a one-stage cluster sample. On the other hand, if the elements in a selected cluster are subject to further sampling, we have a multistage cluster sample.

The essence of cluster sampling is that each cluster must be as heterogeneous as the population on the variables of interest. It can be seen that the requirement of forming the clusters is exactly opposite to that of forming strata. Contrasting features between stratified sampling and cluster sampling are summarized in Figure 4.4.

Compared with simple random sampling, cluster sampling is more prone to sampling error, since neighbouring elements within a cluster are likely to possess somewhat similar characteristics. This phenomenon is commonly referred to as *cluster effects*. On the other hand, economy and feasibility favour the adoption of cluster sampling.

Systematic sampling

Systematic sampling resembles simple random sampling with one exception. Unlike simple random sampling where a random number is drawn each time to select a sample element, systematic sampling needs only to pick one random number throughout the process. Once the first sample element is selected, subsequent sample elements are selected systematically one at a time after a fixed interval; hence its name systematic sampling. This fixed sampling interval, I, is determined by the following formula:

$$I = N/n$$

where N = population size; and
       n = sample size

The reciprocal of I is called the sample fraction:

$$f = 1/I = n/N$$

A step-by-step account of systematic sampling procedures is outlined in Figure 4.5.

1. Decide on the desired sample size;
2. Calculate the fixed sampling interval I;
3. Select a random start number r(0<r<I); and
4. Select the r-th element from the population list. Subsequently, proceed to select other elements at every I-interval until the population list is exhausted.

Figure 4.5 *Procedures of systematic sampling*

Systematic sampling offers a number of advantages:

1 *Speed.* Since only one random number is required in the entire selection process, a systematic sample can be chosen much more speedily than a simple random sample.
2 *Administrative convenience.* Simple random sampling necessitates the sampler to refer to the population list (or sampling frame) forward and backward each time when a random number is selected. In systematic sampling, the sample elements are selected orderly in one fixed direction.
3 *Sampling frame.* Systematic sampling is the only probability method for which the availability of a comprehensive sampling frame may not be required. For example, if a particular block of public housing units is selected, the interviewer selects at random the first housing unit for interview, and thereafter proceeds to interview all other housing units located at a fixed interval. In this case, there is no real need to possess a list of all the housing units to facilitate selection.

Systematic sampling suffers from two major drawbacks, both of which are related to the inherent nature of the population list, or sampling frame:

1 *Monotonic data.* If the elements in the sampling frame appear in some uni-directional order of their values, a smaller (larger) random start number would result in a lower (higher) value for the population estimate when these elements are arranged in ascending (or descending) order of their values.
2 *Periodicity.* When the elements in the population display a certain cyclical pattern, there will be bias in the systematic sample. For example, if the cinema operator wishes to estimate annual cinema attendances based on a sample of, say fifty-two days, with each sample day selected from a calendar week. In the event that the first day selected is a Saturday, all other Saturdays of the year will systematically be included. This would lead to a higher estimation of attendances since Saturday is usually the most popular day for cinema-going.

Non-probability sampling ▬▬

In non-probability sampling, the selection of sample elements depends, in some part, on the personal judgement of the researcher or field interviewer. Also, the probability of any particular element being selected is unknown. No statistical techniques are appropriate to calculate the magnitude of sampling error, so that the level of accuracy of sample estimates cannot be determined. Any attempt to project data beyond the sample itself is statistically inappropriate. These shortcomings, however, should not be over-emphasized so as to totally deny the values of non-probability sampling. There are many occasions when non-probability samples are best suited for a researcher's purpose. If carefully selected, non-probability samples can yield data no less accurate than probability samples.

Non-probability sampling is a cheaper form of sampling method. It does not typically identify particular units to the interviewer. Instead, the interviewer is given a set of general guidelines only, and the selection of specific units is entirely left to his or her own discretion. Some special marketing studies rely heavily on the non-probability sampling method. Examples are shopping centre interviews, depth interviews, focus group discussions, product taste tests and so on.

The main types of non-probability sampling methods are:

● convenience sampling
● judgemental sampling
● quota sampling.

Convenience sampling ―――――

Convenience sampling, as it name implies, is one where convenience is the key criterion considered in the selection of sample elements. It involves selecting people who are most conveniently available to the interviewers. In convenience sampling, hardly any attempt is made to come up with a representative sample, as there is no defined population for which statistical inferences can be made.

Convenience sampling is commonly used in exploratory research to generate hypotheses, to test pilot questionnaires, and so on. Intercepting shoppers and recruiting passers-by to participate in a product taste test are common practices used for convenience sampling so that a larger number of interviews can be completed quickly and economically. As remarked earlier, the nature of convenience sampling does not allow the computation of sampling error, nor a conclusive statement to accompany the sample results.

Judgemental sampling

With judgemental sampling, the interviewer exercises his or her own judgement, and perhaps experience, to select sample elements with the intent that the sample so selected would be a good representation of the population under study. A frequent area of its application is test marketing, when test markets are purposely selected because they are viewed as closely matching with the demographic as well as socio-economic profiles of the entire market. Judgemental sampling is also frequently used to select stores for the purpose of trying out a new display. So long as the basis of judgement made is sound and valid, a judgemental sample is an improvement over a convenience sample.

Quota sampling

Quota sampling is the most sophisticated among all non-probability sampling methods. Here the researcher exercises rigid control over the selection of sample elements on the basis of one or more known parameters (called control characteristics) of the population. This sampling procedure demands that the number of sample elements possessing a certain control characteristic (e.g. female) in the sample will be in the same proportion as the number of elements possessing that same control characteristic in the population. In this manner, the sample derived will be a close replica of the population of interest, at least from the viewpoint of the control characteristics. The procedures involved in quota sampling can be best illustrated by the following example.

Illustrative example 5

To select a quota sample comprising 2,000 persons in Singapore with due regard to the three control characteristics: sex, age and race.

Case I: Independent control characteristics
In this case, the three control characteristics are considered independently of one another. The distribution pattern of the general population in Singapore in terms of each control characteristic is examined (see table below), in order to calculate the desired number of sample elements possessing the specified control characteristics.

	Population distribution	Sample elements
Sex		
Male	51%	2000 × 51% = 1020
Female	49%	2000 × 49% = 980
Age		
15–19 years	13%	2000 × 13% = 260
20–39 years	53%	2000 × 53% = 1060
40 years and over	34%	2000 × 34% = 680
Race		
Chinese	77%	2000 × 77% = 1540
Malay	15%	2000 × 15% = 300
Indian	6%	2000 × 6% = 120
Others	2%	2000 × 2% = 40

Case II: Interlocking control characteristics
Here the cross-tabulation of data on the general population in Singapore by sex, age and race (see Table 4.1) is examined. (*Note:*

Table 4.1

| | (Percentage) | | | | | | | |
| | Chinese | | Malay | | Indian | | Others | |
	Male	Female	Male	Female	Male	Female	Male	Female
15–19 years	4.7	4.4	1.1	1.1	0.4	0.4	0.1	0.1
20–39	21.2	20.2	4.3	3.9	1.8	1.6	0.5	0.5
40 years and over	12.6	13.9	2.1	2.0	1.5	0.8	0.5	0.4

In the table above, each figure is expressed as a percentage of total population.)

By multiplying these percentages in the above table with the sample size (i.e. 2,000), we obtain the number of sample elements required in each of the corresponding cells (see Table 4.2). Thus for a quota sample of size n = 2,000, the sample should include, for example, 94 persons who are Chinese, male and aged 15–19 years.

It is common practice to validate the quota sample after it has been selected. This might be performed by comparing the distribution of the achieved quota sample with that of the total population in respect of some *non-control* characteristics (e.g. marital status, education, income, etc.). If the two sets of distribution compare reasonably well in terms of non-control characteristics, the selected sample would more likely be a good sample.

The major benefits derived from quota sampling are:

1 It dismisses the need for call-backs when the selected person is not available for interview during the interviewer's visit.
2 It allows the interviewers greater flexibility and freedom to recruit respondents.
3 The quota sample would always, or almost always, be a good representation of the population, from the viewpoint of the control characteristics.
4 It is cheaper to execute.
5 It does not require a comprehensive sampling frame.

On the other hand, the disadvantages of quota sampling are:

1 It is prone to interviewers' bias as interviewers may avoid interviewing some categories of persons, or choose to interview nearby respondents.

Table 4.2

| | (Number) | | | | | | | |
| | Chinese | | Malay | | Indian | | Others | |
	Male	Female	Male	Female	Male	Female	Male	Female
15–19 years	94	88	22	22	8	8	2	2
20–39 years	424	404	86	78	36	32	10	10
40 years and over	252	278	42	40	30	16	10	8

Quota sampling

👍 Advantages	👎 Disadvantages
■ No call-backs	■ Interviewer's bias
■ Greater flexibility	■ Not-at-home
■ Representativeness by control characteristics	■ Recruitment difficulty (end of fieldwork)
■ Cheap	■ Outdated control data
■ Sampling frame (not required)	■ Sampling error cannot be measured

2 The *not-at-homes* may be left out and hence will likely be under-represented.
3 Quota requirements become increasingly difficult to accomplish towards the tail-end of the interviewing period. Interviewers may have to spend much time trying to scout for respondents who fit the quota requirements.
4 Available data relating to the control characteristics may be outdated.
5 Sampling error cannot be computed.

Determination of sampling size

It becomes obvious that the smaller the sample size, the lower will be the probability of detecting a real relationship between variables because random chance variation in a small sample masks the effect. Big samples, however, mean high cost. The determination of sample size constitutes an important consideration in the sampling process. First, it is necessary to decide on the precision required to estimate the characteristics concerned. The second decision relates to the probability or assurance (i.e. the confidence level) that the sample will actually fall within the required range (measured as the sampling error) from the true population value.

Essentially, the concept of confidence interval may be used to determine the sample size required in estimating the population value with a specified degree of precision and a predetermined level of

confidence. Suppose that we wish to estimate the mean of a population and e is the permissible error. We want to be 95 per cent confident that our estimate will not differ from the population mean by more than e. This means:

$$z \times \sqrt{\frac{\sigma^2}{n}} \leq e$$

where z = 1.96 at 95 per cent confidence level.

Solving for n, we then have:

$$n = 3.84\sigma^2/e^2$$

where the population variance σ^2, which is usually unknown, can be estimated from previous studies or from other similar populations.

In the case of population proportion, the precision e is given by the formula:

$$e = z \times \sqrt{\frac{p(1-p)}{n}}$$

where z represents confidence level, p represents sample proportion and n represents sample size.

Solving for n, we have:

$$n = \frac{z^2 \times p(1-p)}{e^2}$$

It now becomes obvious that sample size is dependent on three factors: the confidence level, the sample proportion and the permissible precision of the sample results. Although the values for z and e can be pre-assigned, the value of p is unknown. The latter may be estimated from past studies or pilot surveys. Nevertheless, the largest value for n will occur when p = 0.5.

$$n \ (max) = \frac{z^2 \times 0.5 \times (1-0.5)}{e^2}$$

Illustrative example 6

A random sample survey has been planned to determine the proportion of households which consumed a specific brand of health food drink during a particular week. The client who commissioned the research wanted a 95 per cent level of confidence that the sampling error of the derived proportion is kept within 2 per cent. How many households should be selected for interview?

The given data are:

$z = 1.96$
$e = 2$ per cent

If it were estimated that about 70 per cent of households consumed the specified brand of health food drink, this value can be substituted for p, and the sample size required would be:

$$n = \frac{z^2 \times p \times (1 - p)}{e^2}$$

$$= 2{,}017 \text{ households}$$

Appendix A: Random sample selection of 1,200 households in Singapore

- Step 1: Divide Singapore into 2,750 Reticulated Units (RUs) where (a) each RU is featured by one housing type (e.g. HDB, etc.) and (b) each RU comprises about 300 housing units.
- Step 2: Arrange and stratify the 2,750 RUs according to housing type:
  - HDB (1–3 rooms)   1485
  - HDB (4.5 rooms)   715
  - Landed property/private apartment   399
  - Attap/zinc-roofed   69
  - Other types   82
  - Total   2750
- Step 3: Select a random sample of 48 RUs. This sample is formed by combining the sub samples of RUs selected from within each stratum.
- Step 4: Prepare a comprehensive listing of all housing units located in the 48 RUs selected. (*Note*: An expected number of 14,400 housing units will be included in this list.)

- Step 5: Choose a systematic sample of 1,200 housing units.(*Note*: Sampling interval $k = N/n = 14,400/1,200 = 12$. Choose a random start number, say 3, and select housing units accordingly. For example, in the following list, an arrow sign ➡ indicates that the housing unit is selected.)

RU No: 0125

Electoral Division: Clementi

Postal address	House type
02-209 Blk 324 Clementi Ave 5 (0512)	HDB 3-room
02-211 Blk 324 Clementi Ave 5 (0512)	HDB 3-room
➡ 02-213 Blk 324 Clementi Ave 5 (0512)	HDB 3-room
02-215 Blk 324 Clementi Ave 5 (0512)	HDB 3-room
02-219 Blk 324 Clementi Ave 5 (0512)	HDB 3-room
02-221 Blk 324 Clementi Ave 5 (0512)	HDB 3-room
02-223 Blk 324 Clementi Ave 5 (0512)	HDB 3-room
02-225 Blk 324 Clementi Ave 5 (0512)	HDB 3-room
02-227 Blk 324 Clementi Ave 5 (0512)	HDB 3-room
02-229 Blk 324 Clementi Ave 5 (0512)	HDB 3-room
02-231 Blk 324 Clementi Ave 5 (0512)	HDB 3-room
03-209 Blk 324 Clementi Ave 5 (0512)	HDB 3-room
03-211 Blk 324 Clementi Ave 5 (0512)	HDB 3-room
03-213 Blk 324 Clementi Ave 5 (0512)	HDB 3-room
➡ 03-215 Blk 324 Clementi Ave 5 (0512)	HDB 3-room
03-217 Blk 324 Clementi Ave 5 (0512)	HDB 3-room

Appendix B: Random sample selection of 1,200 adults in Singapore

- Steps 1–5: Select 1,200 housing units as described in Appendix A.
- Step 6: Visit all these 1,200 housing units and list out all adults (aged 15 years and above) living in each of these selected housing units. (*Note*: An expected number of 3,600 adult persons will be listed.)
- Step 7: Choose a systematic sample of 1,200 adults.
  (Note: Sampling interval I = 3,600/1,200 = 3. Thus choose a random start number, say 2, and select adult members accordingly. For example, in the above list, adult members indicated by an arrow sign ➡ are selected.)

01	S/N	Name	Sex	Age
	01	Chow San Wah	M	50
➡	02	Yeo Eng Leong	M	56
	03	Chow Fong Ye	F	21
	04	Chow Ju Chuan	M	20
➡	05	Chow Ju Huat	M	16

02	S/N	Name	Sex	Age
	01	Yip Swee Cheng	M	34
	02	Ang Ee Ngor	F	32

03	S/N	Name	Sex	Age
➡	01	Teo Tai Keow	M	74
	02	Lim Chin Nea	F	64
	03	Teo Teck Meng	M	44
➡	04	Teo Teck Wah	M	34

04	S/N	Name	Sex	Age
	01	Madam Goh	F	79
	02	Yeo Eng Leong	M	56
➡	03	Yeo Poh Leong	M	55
	04	Mrs Yeo Eng Leong	F	53
	05	Mrs Yeo Poh Leong	F	52
➡	06	Yeo Li Chin	F	48
	07	Yeo Teck Watt	M	24
	08	Yeo Ah Lan	F	23

Appendix C: Random number table

Row		Column Nos.			
	1-10	11-20	21-30	31-40	41-50
1	55 74 30 77 40	68 34 30 13 70	44 22 78 84 26	04 33 46 09 52	68 07 97 06 57
2	59 29 97 68 60	74 57 25 65 76	71 91 38 67 54	13 58 18 24 76	15 54 55 95 52
3	48 55 90 65 72	27 42 37 86 53	96 57 69 36 10	96 46 92 42 45	97 60 49 04 91
4	66 37 32 20 30	00 39 68 29 61	77 84 57 03 29	10 45 65 04 26	11 04 96 67 24
5	68 49 69 10 82	29 94 98 94 24	53 75 91 93 30	34 25 20 57 27	40 48 73 51 92
6	40 33 20 38 26	70 29 17 12 13	13 89 51 03 74	17 76 37 13 04	07 74 21 19 30
7	96 83 50 87 75	56 62 18 37 35	97 12 25 93 47	70 33 24 03 54	97 77 46 44 80
8	88 42 95 45 72	99 49 57 22 77	16 64 36 16 00	04 43 18 66 79	94 77 24 21 90
9	33 27 14 34 09	16 08 15 04 72	45 59 34 68 49	12 72 07 34 45	99 27 72 95 14
10	50 27 89 87 19	31 16 93 32 43	20 15 37 00 49	52 85 66 60 44	38 68 88 11 80
11	36 96 47 36 61	03 47 43 73 86	46 98 63 71 62	33 26 16 80 45	60 11 14 10 95
12	42 81 14 57 20	97 74 24 67 62	42 53 32 37 32	27 07 36 07 51	24 51 79 89 73
13	56 50 26 71 07	16 76 62 27 66	32 90 79 78 53	13 55 38 58 59	88 97 54 14 10
14	96 96 68 27 31	12 56 85 99 26	05 03 72 93 15	57 12 10 14 21	88 26 49 81 76
15	38 54 82 46 22	55 59 56 35 64	31 62 43 09 90	06 18 44 32 53	23 83 01 30 30
16	49 54 43 54 82	16 22 77 94 39	17 37 93 23 78	87 35 20 96 43	84 26 34 91 64
17	57 24 55 06 88	84 42 17 53 31	77 04 74 47 67	21 76 33 50 25	83 92 12 06 76
18	16 95 55 67 19	63 01 63 78 59	98 10 50 71 75	12 86 73 58 07	44 39 52 38 79
19	78 64 56 07 82	33 21 12 34 29	52 42 07 44 38	15 51 00 13 42	99 66 02 79 54
20	09 47 27 96 54	57 60 86 32 44	49 17 46 09 62	90 52 84 77 27	08 02 73 43 28
21	44 17 16 58 09	18 18 07 92 46	79 83 86 19 62	06 76 50 03 10	55 23 64 05 05
22	84 16 07 44 99	26 62 38 97 75	83 11 46 32 24	20 14 85 88 45	10 93 72 88 71
23	82 97 77 77 81	23 42 40 64 74	07 45 32 14 08	32 98 94 07 72	93 85 79 10 75
24	50 92 26 11 97	52 36 28 19 95	00 56 76 31 38	80 22 02 53 53	86 60 42 04 53
25	83 39 50 08 30	37 85 94 35 12	42 34 97 96 88	54 42 06 87 98	35 85 29 48 39
26	83 62 64 11 12	16 90 82 66 59	67 19 00 71 74	60 47 21 29 68	02 02 37 03 31
27	06 09 19 74 66	11 27 94 75 06	02 94 37 34 02	76 70 90 30 86	38 45 94 30 38
28	33 32 51 26 38	25 24 10 16 20	79 78 45 04 91	16 92 53 56 16	02 75 50 95 98
29	42 38 97 01 50	38 23 16 86 38	87 57 66 81 41	40 01 74 91 62	48 51 84 08 32
30	96 44 33 49 13	31 96 25 91 47	34 86 82 53 91	00 52 43 48 85	27 55 26 89 62
31	64 05 71 95 86	66 67 40 67 14	11 05 65 09 68	76 83 20 37 90	57 16 00 11 66
32	75 73 88 05 90	14 90 84 45 11	52 27 41 14 86	22 98 12 22 08	07 52 74 95 80
33	33 96 02 75 19	68 05 51 18 00	07 60 52 93 55	59 33 82 43 90	49 37 38 44 59
34	97 51 40 14 02	20 46 78 73 90	04 02 33 31 08	39 54 16 49 36	47 95 93 13 30
35	15 06 15 93 20	64 19 58 97 79	01 90 10 75 06	40 78 78 89 62	02 67 74 17 33
36	22 35 85 15 13	05 26 93 70 60	92 03 51 59 77	59 56 78 06 83	52 91 05 70 74
37	09 98 42 99 64	07 97 10 88 23	61 71 62 99 15	06 51 29 16 93	58 05 77 09 51
38	54 87 66 47 54	68 71 86 85 85	73 32 08 11 12	44 95 92 63 16	29 56 24 29 48
39	58 37 78 80 70	26 99 61 65 53	42 10 50 67 42	32 17 55 85 74	94 44 67 16 94
40	87 59 36 22 41	14 65 52 68 75	26 78 63 06 55	13 08 27 01 50	15 29 39 39 43
41	71 41 61 60 72	17 53 77 58 71	12 41 94 96 26	44 95 27 36 99	02 96 74 30 83
42	23 52 23 33 12	90 26 59 21 19	96 93 02 18 39	07 02 18 36 07	25 99 32 70 23
43	31 04 49 69 96	41 23 52 55 99	10 47 48 45 88	13 41 43 89 20	97 17 14 49 17
44	31 99 73 68 68	60 20 50 81 69	35 81 33 03 76	24 30 12 48 60	18 99 10 72 34
45	94 58 28 41 36	91 25 38 05 90	45 37 59 03 09	90 35 57 29 12	82 62 54 65 60
46	98 80 33 00 91	34 50 57 74 37	09 77 93 19 82	74 94 80 04 04	45 07 31 66 49
47	73 81 53 94 79	85 22 04 39 43	33 62 46 86 28	08 31 54 46 31	25 99 32 70 23
48	73 83 97 22 21	09 79 13 77 48	05 03 27 24 83	72 89 44 05 60	35 80 39 94 88
49	22 95 75 42 49	88 75 80 18 14	39 32 82 22 49	02 48 07 70 37	16 04 61 87 87
50	39 00 03 06 90	90 96 23 70 00	55 85 78 38 36	94 37 30 69 32	90 89 00 76 33

End-of-chapter revision

Review questions

4.1 What is a census? What is meant by sampling?

4.2 Sampling methods are often used in marketing research to gather data. What are the reasons for using sampling techniques instead of taking a census?

4.3 What are the steps in the sampling process?

4.4 What is a probability sample? Describe the difference between a probability sample and a non-probability sample.

4.5 What are the major factors to consider when choosing between a probability sample and a non-probability sample?

4.6 Why is probability sampling considered superior to non-probability sampling in marketing research?

4.7 What is meant by a sampling frame?

4.8 What are the necessary parts of the definition of a population?

4.9 What are the distinguishing features of a simple random sample?

4.10 How should a simple random sample be selected? Briefly describe the procedure.

4.11 What is the formula for the standard error of the proportion of a simple random sample?

4.12 What are the specifications that must be made in order to determine the sample size required to estimate the population proportion using a simple random sample?

4.13 What is stratified sampling? What are the objectives of stratified sampling? How is a stratified sample selected? How will you stratify a population in a market research study pertaining to demand of cellular phones in Singapore?

4.14 What is a proportionate stratified sample? Describe the procedure for selecting a proportionate stratified sample.

4.15 What is a disproportionate stratified sample? Describe the procedure for selecting a disproportionate stratified sample.

4.16 Under what circumstances might a researcher wish to use a proportionate sample or a disproportionate sample? Illustrate each case by using your own hypothetical data.

4.17 What is cluster sampling? What are the benefits of cluster sampling? Comment on the similarities and differences between cluster sampling and stratified sampling.

4.18 What is the nature of error generated by a non-probability sampling procedure?

4.19 Since non-probability samples do not yield a measure of sampling error, why are these procedures so often used in practice?

4.20 What is a purposive sample and under what circumstances might a researcher wish to employ this approach? Provide an example of such a circumstance.

4.21 What is a convenience sample? In what situations should such a sampling method be used?

4.22 What is a judgemental sample? Cite some situations in which this sort of sampling technique might be used.

4.23 What is a systematic sample? How are the random start number and sampling interval determined with a systematic sample?

4.24 What is periodicity in respect of systematic sampling? How is it caused and corrected?

4.25 Describe the procedures for selecting a quota sample. Why is a quota sample a non-probability sample?

4.26 What are the potential weaknesses of quota sampling?

4.27 A quota sample controlled by sex and age of respondents is planned for a campus survey. How can this non-probability sample be validated in terms of its representativeness?

4.28 A researcher wishes to use systematic sampling to interview shoppers leaving a bookstore. How would you advise the researcher to proceed?

4.29 Discuss and contrast telephone directory and non-telephone directory sampling methods.

True-false questions
Write True (T) or False (F) for the following:

4.30 A sample is a portion or subset of a larger group or universe.

4.31 A good sample is a miniature version of the population.

4.32 When drawing a simple random sample from an infinite population, it is assumed that every item has an equal chance of being selected for every draw.

4.33 It is not necessary to know the total number of items in a population to select a simple random sample from that population.

4.34 In systematic sampling, the probability of selecting any item in the population is equal and known.

4.35 With proportionate allocation, the sampling fraction for each stratum differs from the overall sampling fraction.

4.36 To achieve random sampling from clusters, each cluster must contain the same number of sampling units.

4.37 Sampling error occurs because the researcher has taken a sample instead of a complete census of the population.

4.38 Sampling error would still be present even if we took a complete census of the population.

4.39 A census typically has a smaller total error than a sample.

4.40 Members of a convenience sample are selected primarily because they are readily available.

4.41 Members of a purposive sample are generally highly representative of the population.

4.42 A sampling frame is a list of elements from which the sample will be drawn.

4.43 With quota sampling, many not-at-homes are left out and hence will be underrepresented in the achieved sample.

4.44 Random digit dialling (RDD) allows the researcher to select persons who have changed their addresses.

4.45 The maximum sampling error occurs when the survey result is $p = 0.25$.

Multiple-choice questions

4.46 For a defined population, any statistic is:
a subject to sample error
b biased
c a constant
d relationship.

4.47 Sampling error is present in the results of a typical marketing research survey because:
a a question may be ambiguous
b only a small part of all persons is interviewed
c some respondents move to new addresses
d all of the above.

4.48 One of the following is not an advantage of probability samples compared with non-probability samples:
a They are less expensive to develop and administer.
b They produce unbiased estimates of parameters.
c Sampling size can be determined to meet information needs.
d Sampling error can be measured.

4.49 With stratified random sampling, the probability of selecting any item from the population is:
a equal but unknown
b equal and known
c unequal but known
d unequal and unknown.

4.50 Stratified random sampling is more efficient than simple random sampling because:
a it minimizes intra-stratum variance
b it minimizes inter-strata variance
c it maximizes intra-stratum variance
d it maximizes inter-strata variance.

4.51 Of the following, which one is not a probability sample?
a Quota sample.
b Systematic sample.
c Cluster sample.
d Stratified sample.

4.52 The difference between the sample result and the results of a census using identical procedures is referred to as:
a sampling error
b non-response error
c sampling frame error
d non-sampling error.

4.53 Which one of the following is a probability sample?
a Quota sample.
b Cluster sample.
c Convenience sample.
d Judgemental sample.

4.54 If the research question is to determine the level of interest in buying retirement housing in Singapore, which of the following sample respondents matches the target population?
a The Chief Executive Officers (CEOs).
b The X-generation (20–29 years old).
c The 50+ years old.
d The car owners.

4.55 If the research question is to determine the future trends in business investments in China, which of the following sample respondents matches the target population?
a The Chief Executive Officers (CEOs).
b The X-generation (20–29 years old).
c The 50+ years old.
d The car owners.

4.56 Which of the following is a 'limitation' of proper sampling?
a Shorter timelines for a study.
b Increased accuracy of results.
c Rigid control standards are required.
d Lower cost.

4.57 Which of the following is a 'benefit' of proper sampling?
a Results are approximations.
b Subgroups are sometimes too small for data analysis.
c Questionnaires are streamlined as a result.
d None of the above.

4.58 The population is divided into definite segments, and a random sample is obtained from each segment. This sampling method is known as:
a systematic sampling
b convenience sampling
c stratified sampling
d quota sampling.

4.59 Every twentieth shopper leaving a local shopping mall was stopped for an interview until 500 mall shoppers had participated in the study. This sampling method is known as:
a systematic sampling
b convenience sampling
c cluster sampling
d simple random sampling.

4.60 Everyone in the defined population has an equal chance of being selected for the study. This sampling method is known as:

a judgemental sampling
b quota sampling
c convenience sampling
d simple random sampling.

4.61 Each mobile phone user is asked to help recruit other mobile phone users to be interviewed for the study. This sampling method is known as:

a quota sampling
b convenience sampling
c snowball sampling
d stratified sampling.

4.62 Friends, relatives and family members who fit the selection qualifications are recruited to participate in questionnaire pre-test. This sampling method is known as:

a simple random sampling
b cluster sampling
c stratified sampling
d convenience sampling.

4.63 Duplication of sampling units in the sampling frame results in:

a refusal errors
b response errors
c coverage errors
d all of the above.

5

Data collection methods _____

This chapter reviews the various methods employed in marketing research for the gathering of data through direct questioning of respondents, observing subjects' behaviour and conducting experiments. Potential advantages and disadvantages associated with the application of each method will also be discussed.

Marketing data may be classified into two basic types: primary data and secondary data. Primary (or original) data refer to those which are collected to meet the specific research needs at hand. Secondary data, on the other hand, refer to existing information which has previously been collected and reported by some individual or organization, and which are other than the research problem at hand. Thus, the principal distinction between primary data and secondary data lies in the original purpose of data collection and is in no way related to the relative importance of the information.

Secondary data can be obtained rapidly and inexpensively. Sometimes, the researcher may find his or her data requirements totally met from available secondary data; in which case there is no need to generate primary data. The golden rule is to exhaust all possible means to explore secondary data before deciding to mount on a comprehensive plan for primary data collection. As such, we begin with a discussion on secondary data.

Secondary data ▬▬▬

The importance of secondary data should not be underestimated. The existence of secondary data can, in many instances, dismiss the need for potentially expensive and time-consuming field work. Secondary data exists aplenty from internal and external data sources as presented in Figure 5.1.

Appendix A at the end of this chapter presents a summary of secondary data sources in Singapore. Apart from time-saving and cost economics, secondary data is less subject to intentional bias. Also as certain types of information may be impractical or virtually impossible to gather through primary data approach, secondary

---

Internal data sources

- Sales records (invoices, inventory records)
- Cost information (budget, production cost)
- Marketing activity (advertising, promotion)
- Distributors' reports
- Consumers' reports

External data sources

- Government agencies' reports
- Trade associations' reports
- Books, periodicals and newspapers
- Companies' annual reports
- Syndicated research reports/information
- Academic studies and dissertation abstracts

Figure 5.1 *Sources of secondary data*

data sources are the only alternative. Typical examples are: internal and external trade statistics, tourist arrival statistics and census information. But secondary data suffers from pitfalls as detailed below:

1 *Obsolescence.* Secondary data quickly becomes outdated in an ever-changing environment. The rapid changes of consumers' attitudes, values and demographic factors can quickly make secondary data obsolete or reduce the desired reliability.
2 *Unmatched classification.* Very often, secondary data was earlier collected without due consideration of the researchers' present specific needs. The value of secondary data is grossly diminished if the data grouping or classification fails to meet the researchers' specific requirements. Age of the population in secondary data source, for example, may be expressed in five-year age groups (0–4 years, 5–9 years, 10–14 years, and so on) whereas the researchers may be specifically interested in consumers aged between 12 and 17 years. Similarly, geographical boundaries (e.g. blocks, counties) tabulated in census reports may not match with researchers' requirements.

Figure 5.2 shows the advantages and disadvantages of using secondary data.

Secondary data should be appraised before use. Users of secondary data should at least raise the following questions when assessing data reliability and suitability:

- WHO collected the data?
- WHY were the data collected?
- HOW were the data collected?
- WHAT types of data were presented?
- WHEN were the data collected?
- ARE the data consistent with those obtained from other sources?

Primary data

In many cases, marketing research is concerned with obtaining information on new products or services, or evaluating some proposed marketing strategies. As a result, the required information is often not available from secondary data sources. So, while secondary data may occasionally prove sufficient for marketing problems, more often than not primary data are further needed. The nature and type of primary data required would depend largely on the research objectives and vary from one project to another. Such data can be classified into the following basic kinds:

1 *Attitudinal data.* Attitudinal data reflects the respondent's feelings and convictions towards a product or service. Marketers generally look upon consumers' attitudes as a fore-runner of consumers' behaviour, and tend to interpret a favourable attitude towards a product to mean possible intent to purchase or use it. This hypothetical relationship between attitudes and actual behaviour highlights the importance of attitudinal data in identifying market segments, developing product positioning strategies, evaluating advertising effectiveness and so on.
2 *Awareness data.* Data on consumers' awareness (or knowledge) of some phenomenon under study can generate a great amount of interest among marketers. Understanding the consumers' level of awareness of an advertisement, a promotion slogan, or a particular brand can help marketers map out their

---

Advantages

- Faster
- Cheaper
- Inaccessible information
- Less bias

Disadvantages

- Out-dated
- Differences in classification or measurement
- Lack of accuracy

Figure 5.2 *Secondary data: advantages and disadvantages*

marketing strategies more realistically and effectively.

3 *Purchase intention data.* In the study of psychology, a person's intention reflects his anticipated or planned behaviour. Purchase intention, in particular, is of paramount importance to marketers for estimating the potential market size. A word of caution is needed though: Purchase intention does not always mean purchase action. A respondent who had earlier given a *definitely/probably would buy* response might not buy whereas the respondent who said *definitely/probably would not buy* might turn up to be a buyer of a new product or service.

4 *Motivational data.* Motivational data helps explore the underlying reasons as to why consumers behave in the way they do. In addition, they offer explanations to consumers' rejection or acceptance of a particular product.

5 *Behavioural data.* Many scientists examine past behaviour with the intention of predicting future behaviour. Marketers are no exception. They are keen to gather information concerning the past behaviour of consumers (e.g. how much were consumed, who made the purchase decision, where was the product last purchased from, etc.) in order to plan their marketing strategy. Questions which are designed to gather behavioural data usually begin with *what, how much, when* and *who.*

6. *Classification data.* Responses gathered from the main questions in the survey questionnaire are normally analysed together with the basic data (e.g. sex, age, race, education) pertaining to the respondent. These basic data are called classification data as they are not directly related to the subject under study. Classification data broadens the base for data analysis, and is particularly useful for market segmentation studies.

Figure 5.3 provides a list of typical questions which are addressed for gathering the various kinds of primary data.

Methods of data collection ■■■

The basic methods employed in the collection of marketing data can be grouped into three broad categories (see overleaf).

Attitudinal data	'Do you agree or disagree that smoking should be forbidden in public places?' 'Can you please tell me whether you consider it right or wrong to look at pornographic magazines?'
Awareness data	'What brand of petrol can you name that has petrol additives in it?' '(SHOWCARD) Which one of the following themes is used by Singapore Airlines?'
Purchase intention data	'If you were to see this product available in the market, how likely do you think you would be buying it?'
Motivtional data	'I have here a list of main reasons why people say they work hard. Can you please show me from this showcard, which reasons you have in mind when you work hard at your job?'
Behavioural data	'Which brand do you usually purchase?' 'Where did you last purchase your shampoo?' When was the last time you or someone in your family purchased fruit juice?'
Classification data	'Can you show me, in this showcard, which household income group you belong to?' Please tell me in this showcard, which age group you belong to?'

Figure 5.3 *Typical questions addressed in primary data collection*

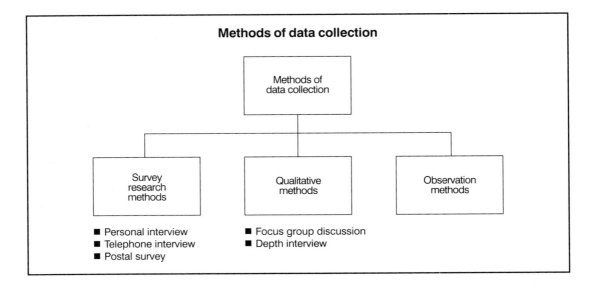

No single data collection method is always superior to any other methods, nor does one method preclude the other. In fact, multi-mode interviewing is becoming increasingly common nowadays. Payne had described a product home use test to include (a) personal placement of products, self-administered questionnaires and returned envelopes; (b) postal returns of questionnaires; and (c) telephone follow-up interviews. (see Stanley L. Payne [1964] Combination Survey Method. *Journal of Marketing Research*, **1**, May, 61–2.). Which data collection method to use will depend on a host of factors, such as time and budget available, topics to be covered and the required precision of survey results. With the introduction of technological innovations to provide new forms of data collection method, the traditional methods of personal, telephone interviews and postal questionnaires may be becoming less distinctive in the future. The mixed-mode approach of asking respondents to tune-in to a cable television channel in which the interviewer can be seen is a typical example of such development. The telephone, in this case, takes on some of the dimensions of a personal interview.

Survey research method

The survey research method refers to a systematic gathering of primary data through the use of structured questionnaires and communication with a reasonably large number and a highly representative sample of respondents. Three types of survey research method may be identified: personal interviewing, telephone interviewing and postal survey.

Personal interview

A personal interview involves face-to-face communication between two persons – an interviewer and a respondent – during which the interviewer initiates the gathering of primary data from the respondent. It is a purposeful and directed conversation, whose purpose is to gather information by means of administering the same set of questions in a consistent way to all selected respondents. These respondents presumably are representative of the population of interest, or target population. Personal interviewing works best when the survey questionnaire is too long to conduct over the telephone or when there is a need to show survey material (e.g. advertising copy) to the respondent. In a personal interview, the initial concern should be to ensure the full co-operation of the respondent in providing the needed information. Next, the interviewer focuses his or her attention on the interviewing process and data collection instrument. He or she has to ask the survey questions in the proper sequence, use the exact wording as phrased in the questionnaire and record the responses given by the respondent to the best of his or her belief and knowledge.

The full session, or part thereof, of the interviewing session may be tape-recorded but prior consent from the respondent must be obtained. Personal interviews may be held at the respondent's home or place of work, on pavements, in public places (e.g. shopping centres, departmental stores) or at street junctions.

The personal interviewing method has several advantages and disadvantages over the other methods of data collection.

Advantages	
Flexibility	Response rate
Exhibit	Sequence bias
Observation	Rapport
Quantity of data	Clarity
	Respondent identification

Disadvantages	
Higher cost	Interviewer cheating
Longer time	Time dimension
Interviewer bias	Field control
Anonymity	

1 *Flexibility.* A distinct feature of personal interviewing is the physical presence of an interviewer during the data collection process. This direct interaction between interviewer and respondent allows the former to perform functions which other data collection methods cannot do; for example, distributing sample products to the respondent in a product taste test, requesting the respondent to view a television commercial or print ad, etc.

2 *Exhibits.* A related advantage concerns the display of visual exhibits (e.g. new product sample, sketches of proposed advertising, etc.) to the respondent. From the viewpoint of controlling the order of presentation, and of the time duration of exposure of these exhibits, personal interviewing method is the most appropriate and effective.

3 *Observation.* Observation is a bonus to personal interviewing. Information on sex, race, house type, etc. of the respondent can be observed and recorded without the need to ask such questions. Moreover, The behavioural aspects and facial expression of the respondent can also be observed and recorded.

4 *Quantity of data.* Personal interviewing is less restricted by the length of the survey questionnaire than any other data collection method and thus permits a much wider range of questions to be investigated. A respondent may be reluctant to spend, say half an hour, responding to a telephone interview, or filling out a self-administered questionnaire, but would be quite prepared to oblige the interviewer in a personal interview.

5 *Pantry checks.* Where a check in the pantry is dictated by the research client to confirm home availability of the claimed

product, personal interviewing method is the only choice.

6 *Response rate.* The physical presence of an interviewer helps maintain respondent's interest in the survey which in turn helps secure a higher response rate. In a personal interview, the respondent is generally not required to do any writing or reading, except to talk. People normally enjoy sharing views with pleasant and friendly interviewers.

7 *Sequence bias.* With personal interviewing, the sequence in which the survey questions are asked is fully administered by the interviewer. The respondent cannot answer the questions in any other order that he or she wishes.

8 *Establishing rapport.* A rapport developed between the interviewer and the respondent helps dispel the natural suspicion that surrounds the interviewer.

9 *Clarity.* With personal interviewing, there is less likelihood of misunderstanding/misinterpreting the survey questions.

10 *Identifying respondents.* Personal interviewing offers the opportunity for the interviewer to identify the respondents in cases of follow-up contacts.

Against the above-mentioned advantages, personal interviewing encounters a number of disadvantages as discussed below:

1 *High cost.* The principal disadvantage of personal interview relates to cost, primarily due to interviewing and travelling. Under cost-per-interview consideration, personal interview is highest among all survey methods, more so for a geographically-dispersed sample.

2 *Longer time.* A personal interview demands much longer time to accomplish, particularly when the selected respondent resides in distant, isolated areas (e.g. offshore islands, rural areas etc.).

3 *Interviewer bias.* The presence of an interviewer may create interviewer (or interviewer-respondent) bias. By a mere change of his or her tone, an offer of undesired prompts, or a show of facial expressions, the interviewer can untruthfully influence the respondent's answers. Also, interviewers may differ in the way they listen to the respondent and record the responses.

4 *Anonymity.* Personal interviewing deprives the element of anonymity – at least psychological anonymity – from the respondent. As such, it may deter respondents from admitting socially undesirable behaviour and views, or offering truthful answers on sensitive and embarrassing questions.

5 *Interviewer cheating.* A personal interviewer will usually conduct field interviews alone unaccompanied by his or her superior or anyone. Short of direct supervision, an insincere interviewer is prone to cheating in questionnaire completion.

6 *Time dimension.* Personal interviewing suffers from time and situational dimensions. Early morning interview is not recommended, while late evening interviews can arouse respondents' objections. Respondents loathe being interrupted at meal times by interviewers, and daytime interviewing with working respondents will meet with low success rate.

7 *Field control.* Personal interviewing can hardly claim to have strict field control. Supervisors have great difficulties in locating their interviewers at work, let alone witness the interview sessions. The interviewer might complete the questionnaires without contacting the intended respondent, or by making guesses concerning some parts of the questionnaire. Moreover, the interviewer may accept 'Don't Know' or 'No Opinion' answers too readily or ignore probing instructions for detailed responses.

Telephone interview

Telephone interviewing involves administering questionnaires by the interviewer over the phone. The increased popularity of telephone interviewing as a research tool has been frequently documented and there are many varied reasons behind this growing popularity. A higher incidence of telephone ownership and the escalation of field operation costs have provided the impetus for the use of telephone interviewing method. The invention of advanced telephoning techniques (e.g. random digit dialling) has further enhanced its popularity. The CATI (Computer-Assisted Telephone Interviewing) system introduced in the 1970s was described in the *Market Research Society Newsletter* as the 'acronym of the year'. [*Note*: Essentially, the CATI system operates by showing the questionnaire on a visual display unit from which the questions are read by the telephone interviewer. Answers given by the respondent are keyed directly into the computer, and subsequently the next question will appear on the screen. Since the computer can handle the skip and filtered instructions, only the appropriate or relevant question is displayed on the screen, and the possibility for interviewer error is much reduced. Data processing is virtually instant with the CATI system.]

Telephone interviewing lacks the face-to-face interaction of personal interview, and therein lies both its strengths and weaknesses. We shall first begin by enumerating the advantages and disadvantages derived from the application of telephone interview.

Advantages	Disadvantages
Faster results	No exhibits
Lower cost	Longer time
Wide geographical coverage	Data limitation
Imperativeness or irresistibility	
Access to hard-to-reach people	
Early/late interviews	
Privacy	
Coincidental data	
Better control	

1 *Faster results.* Speed is perhaps the greatest advantage of telephone interviewing. Telephone contact and recall can be established almost instantly. Travel time between consecutive interviews is not needed; also eliminated is the time spent on waiting for the intended respondent or for the return of mailed questionnaires (postal surveys). When research data is urgently required for decision-making, telephone interviewing emerges as the natural choice.

2 *Lower cost.* As the cost of personal interviews escalates, telephone interviews become relatively inexpensive. Cost of economies are realized because travel time and cost are eliminated. Telephone recalls can be made at minimum cost. Overall cost per telephone interview is relatively low. In a study which compared the cost differential of personal interview with telephone interview, the results showed that the latter was 40 per cent lower (Robert M. Groves and Robert L. Kahn [1979] *Surveys by Telephone, A National Comparison with Personal Interviews.* Academic Press).

3 *Geographical coverage.* All intended respondents that have telephones at home can be reached regardless of where they are located. Geographical dispersion of respondents is no longer a factor of concern in the choice of sampling methods. This means that the researcher is not confined to a few sampling methods (e.g. area sampling, cluster sampling) to gain administrative convenience.

4 *Imperativeness or irresistibility.* People will answer the telephone call under normal circumstances when they would not open the door to an interviewer, let alone invite him or her inside the house for an interview. In short, telephone calls command definite attention.

5 *Access to hard-to-reach people.* People who reside in isolated or rural locations are difficult to reach in a personal interviewing situation. Also, personal interviewers may be denied entry into high class condominiums guarded by security officers. The effect of urbanization on non-response

rates has been documented in several studies using the personal interviewing method. Telephone interviewing technique can uplift these barriers.

6 *Early/late interviews.* Few people would want to be approached by strangers (including personal interviewers) after they have put on their nightwear and/or have settled themselves in front of a television set. Thus, telephone interviewers are more acceptable than personal interviewers for early and late hours.

7 *Privacy.* Privacy in terms of interview content can be secured with telephone interviews, for at least the interviewer's side of the conversation will not be heard by any family member other than the respondent himself or herself. Embarrassing or sensitive questions may be answered more willingly in a telephone interview than in a personal interview.

8 *Coincidental data.* Telephone interviewing is most suitable for securing coincidental data. The question, such as 'Can you tell me whether you are now watching the Prime Minister's address to Parliament on TV?' is a typical example. Telephone interview technique can provide immediate feedback on a recent advertising campaign, and quick estimates on the ownership of household durables. Other data collection methods to address such issues could encounter memory loss and/or create extraneous factors (e.g. competitors' promotions) which may invalidate the survey results.

9 *Better control.* Many research firms provide special chambers exclusively for conducting telephone interviews. With all interviews conducted in a centralized location, the supervisors could closely monitor/witness the interviewing process to ensure that the prescribed set of interviewing procedures are being followed.

The main disadvantages of telephone interviewing are:

1 *No exhibits.* The principal disadvantage of telephone interviewing lies in its inability to present visual aids, showcards, test packages, test ads, sample products, etc., to the respondents. For some research studies such as product taste test and advertising copy test, the telephone interviewing method is instantly ruled out for this reason. Also, attitudinal questions which involve presenting rating scales to the respondents should not rely on telephone interviewing.

2 *Length of interview.* Telephone interviewing suffers greater restriction on the length of interview than other methods of data collection. A telephone interview has to be kept brief and short (preferably not more than 10 minutes) as few people can tolerate a lengthy and laborious telephone interview, who may merely hang up the telephone before the interview ends, especially when the survey topic does not appear interesting to them.

3 *Data limitation.* Confronted by time constraint, a telephone interview questionnaire will need to be short and can only secure a limited amount of data. Hence, the depth of information sought may have to be sacrificed.

4 *Others.* Inability to conduct pantry check, shortage of highly-qualified telephone interviewers are some other disadvantages.

Telephone directory sampling

A common and natural tool used for telephone interviews is telephone directory sampling. This approach takes the form of selecting telephone numbers from telephone directories under the systematic sampling procedures described earlier. The telephone directory, which used to be a complete source of information about all telephones in an area, is far less reliable today. In the event that telephone directory sampling is used, further disadvantages of telephone interviewing will emerge:

1 *Incomplete universe.* Not every household has a telephone – a common criticism cited whenever telephone directory sampling is used. Only persons living in homes/offices equipped with telephones can then be selected in the sample. This brings about a

serious limitation as the characteristics of telephone households and non-telephone households may differ significantly. Empirical data has shown that low-income households are likely to be under-represented if telephone directory sampling is adopted. Non-owners of telephones tend to be less affluent, and this phenomenon is likely to produce bias in the survey results. In Singapore today, this limitation is less significant as the majority (about 95 per cent) of homes have telephones.

2 *Unlisted subscribers.* In the old days, popular personalities (e.g. movie stars, politicians, etc.) chose to have their names omitted from the phone directories to avoid unnecessary calls. An increasing number of telephone subscribers now join in this practice. In Singapore, it was reported that 14 per cent of telephone numbers were unlisted in 1990. They kept the telephone numbers out of the telephone directory for a combination of reasons. Some simply wanted privacy while others cited bad experiences with nuisance calls that made them apply for unlisted telephone numbers. In the USA the corresponding figure was 28 per cent. Empirical results gathered from various studies showed that unlisted households tend to have younger heads and more household members in the 18–34 age group. A survey on telephone subscribers conducted in 1988 in Singapore by Quah Siam Tee concluded that relatively more Chinese and Indians but fewer Malays were among the unlisted subscribers. The unlisted subscribers were also better educated; had more administrators, managers and executives; but included fewer sales and services workers. The popularity of paging services can also cause the unlisted numbers to surge upwards at an even faster rate. Consequently, one takes quite a gamble in using a telephone directory sample in this day and age.

3 *Multiple listings.* This occurs when a person has more than one telephone number listed in the telephone directory. Statistically speaking, the multiple listing of telephone numbers lends him/her a higher chance of being selected.

4 *Telephone directory obsolescence.* Phone directories are usually updated annually. After publication, they become outdated with the passage of time arising from the exclusion of new subscribers on the one hand, and the failure to delete lapsed subscribers on the other. Also, for administrative reasons, publishers cease to incorporate new subscribers in the phone directory a few months before printing. A survey conducted in the USA revealed that 15 per cent of listings were outdated on the very day of release of the phone directory!

Notwithstanding the above-mentioned shortcomings, past studies have shown that samples originated from phone directory sampling produce virtually the same results as including unlisted telephone numbers. For many types of studies, telephone directory sampling is quite adequate and its lower cost makes it attractive.

Random digit dialling (non-directory sampling)

Notwithstanding aforesaid, it is always theoretically sound to adopt a sampling technique which includes households with unlisted numbers. To overcome the problem of unlisted numbers in the telephone directory, a special technique known as random digit dialling (RDD) or non-directory sampling was introduced in the early 1960s. Essentially, RDD involves generating telephone numbers (either by a random or systematic process) so that any working telephone number, listed or unlisted, will have an equal chance of being selected. The obvious disadvantage of the random digit dialling method is that it may generate a large number of random numbers which do not correspond to any working telephone number. While the research results from random digit dialling may correspond to those obtained by telephone directory sampling, random digit dialling does come closest to being a probability sample. As a matter of fact, it is the only telephone sampling method that permits the researcher to reach virtually all households with a telephone. Hence it is the surest way to achieve a sample that is as closely representative as possible of its parent population under study.

In short, the use of a random-digit-dialling method offers other important advantages:

- The sample is highly representative.
- Unlisted telephone numbers have the same probability of inclusion in the sample as listed numbers. This is particularly important in reaching both high income and minority cohorts.
- Respondents are geographically dispersed, rather than clustered.
- Households with multiple phone listings have the same probability of being included in the sample as households with a single phone listing.

Some procedural modifications to random digit dialling have been introduced to reduce the occurrence of non-working (non-assigned) telephones. 'Add-one' sampling is a method of telephone sampling that incorporates some of the characteristics of random digit sampling on the one hand, while avoids some of the shortcomings of that technique on the other hand. 'Add-one' sampling involves adding 1 to the numbers selected from the phone directories. For example, the number 987–6265 becomes 987–6266 and 653–1219 becomes 653–1220 under the add-one sampling technique. From the practical point of view, add-one sampling is more efficient than random digit dialling. It however suffers from problem of a different kind: Any number (listed or unlisted) which precedes a non-listed number will not be selected. But this is a relatively less serious problem, and add-one sampling generally produces a high contact rate as well as claims some of the advantages of randomness while still remaining cost-efficient.

Postal survey

Unlike personal or telephone interviewing, a postal (or mail) survey does not involve verbal conversation between interviewer and respondent. Here the respondent is required to complete a postal questionnaire and to return it either by post, or by leaving it at a designated location for collection. It should be noted that a postal survey does not necessarily need to use the facilities of a post office. Thus the postal survey would include questionnaires that are placed in house magazines, newspapers or other publications, or that are placed on a hotel's reception counter. Perhaps a better descriptive term for postal survey is *self-administered* survey since it necessitates the individual to administer the survey form himself without the help of the interviewer. Robert Ferber once said: 'The postal questionnaire has been the subject of extensive controversy over the past two decades. Some have hailed it as the ultimate data collection technique while others have condemned it as an instrument of the devil.' Whatever it may be, postal or self-administered questionnaires rely largely on the efficiency of the written word rather than an interviewer. This presents several advantages and disadvantages of a postal survey.

Advantages	Disadvantages
Wider geographical coverage	Absence of mailing list
Data collection methods	Unidentifiable respondents
Thoughtful answers	Questionnaire exposure
Sensitive questions	Data limitation
No interviewer bias	No interviewer assistance
Lower cost	Assumed literacy
Control	Low response rate
Anonymity	Shorter answers
Easy reach	Longer time
Clarity	

1 *Wide geographical coverage.* Postal surveys can reach people almost simultaneously and at relatively lower cost. Wide geographical spread of sample

elements poses no disadvantage to postal survey, and there is no need for researchers to limit to area sampling or cluster sampling. Respondents in remote, outlying areas can be contacted as easily as those in metropolitan locations.

2 *Thoughtful answers.* A postal respondent can choose to complete the questionnaire at his or her own time. He or she can ponder over the questions attentively for more thoughtful answers. Besides, the respondent can, if he or she wishes, check relevant documents (e.g. warranty cards, receipts, etc.) or seek help from others at his leisure, with regard to answers or responses about which they are uncertain of.

3 *Sensitive questions.* Postal surveys have a clear edge over personal and telephone interviews when dealing with sensitive questions. The physical appearance (or the voice of a telephone interviewer) can inhibit the respondent from offering truthful answers to sensitive questions. Furthermore, the anonymity of postal surveys can encourage respondents to freely divulge private or socially undesirable information (see example below).

Illustrative example 1

In 1973, a study of Boston residents was undertaken using three different approaches: Personal interviews, telephone interviews and postal survey. In terms of the neutral and non-sensitive questions asked, the data obtained via all three methods matched very well. However, when it comes to the sensitive questions (e.g. on legal abortion), the results differed considerably between the three methods.

	Percentage favouring legal abortion
Postal survey	89
Personal interview	70
Telephone interview	62

---

4 *No interviewer bias.* It is generally believed that interviewers who hold a definite opinion on a certain issue tend to bias the responses given in favour of his or her own opinion (known as interviewer bias). Postal survey is free from any interviewer-respondent interaction and can avoid such interviewer bias. In a conversational situation with a personal interviewer, few respondents would want to appear ignorant, poor or boastful and hence may be tempted to give untruthful, socially desirable responses.

5 *Lower cost.* Economy appeals most for postal surveys and constitutes a major reason for the extensive use of postal survey method for social research. The cost of a postal survey includes the mailing piece, postage, self-addressed envelope and perhaps cash incentives; but all these combined are usually far lower than the cost incurred for personal or telephone interviews.

6 *Control.* Most of the control problems in collecting marketing research data originate from the employment of field staff. Such problems do not exist in a postal inquiry as its only control involves the outgoing and incoming of questionnaires – a relatively simple and easy exercise. Indeed, procedures for postal surveys are often deemed simple enough that individuals and organizations conduct their own postal survey rather than relying upon survey research organizations.

7 *Anonymity.* It guarantees anonymity of the informant.

8 *Easy reach.* It provides easy reach to residents in security-tight condominiums and avoids the intrusion of interviewers at inconvenient hours.

9 *Clarity.* Postal questionnaires are typically highly structured, clear-cut and easily understood by the respondents.

The disadvantages of a postal survey are:

1 *Absence of mailing list.* The prerequisite of a postal survey is the availability of a

comprehensive mailing list of potential respondents. It is almost impossible to undertake a postal survey without a proper mailing list. Sometimes, such a mailing list may not be available.

2 *Unidentifiable respondents.* A postal survey does not guarantee that the returned questionnaire is completed by the intended respondent himself. The wife may have filled in the questionnaire which is addressed to her husband, or a secretary on behalf of his or her employer. In short, a researcher is not assured that the intended subject will actually fill out the questionnaire himself/herself.

3 *Questionnaire exposure.* Often, the respondent is tempted to browse through the whole questionnaire before he begins to complete it. This is absolutely undesirable as answers given to the latter questions in a questionnaire can be influenced after the respondent has glanced through the questions which appear in the earlier part of the questionnaire. Having been exposed to the whole set of questions, the respondent is apt to react to a filter (or skip) question in a way that he or she can be conveniently spared from having to respond to follow-up questions. In a smoking habit survey, for example, a smoker may falsely declare himself or herself as a non-smoker to avoid having to respond to a full set of questions on smoking behaviour and habits which appear in the latter part of the questionnaire.

4 *Data limitation.* Few respondents are willing to spend much time and effort on an unreasonably long questionnaire. As a general rule, postal questionnaires should not exceed six to eight pages of A4 size, and this limits the amount of data to be sought. The length of the questionnaire poses a restricting factor with postal survey.

5 *No interviewer assistance.* In a postal survey situation, no interviewer is nearby to provide explanations and clarifications when needed by the respondents. Under this circumstance, the researcher will have to be extra careful to ensure that the survey questions are clearly worded and properly structured.

6 *Assumed literacy.* Postal survey method presumes that the respondent will be sufficiently literate to self-administer the questionnaire without any assistance. This assumption cannot be universally valid.

7 *Response rate.* Non-response is the most critical problem with postal survey. Low response rate, more than any other issue, has given postal surveys a poor image among social researchers. The lack of motivation and persuasion from the interviewer, coupled with the reluctance of the respondent to complete and return the questionnaire, can cause a lower level of response. Given that the questionnaire is returned, the incidence of item non-response – which occurs when the respondents leave some parts of the questionnaire unfilled – may be high, especially for sensitive or personal questions. A poorly designed postal questionnaire may at best be returned by 15 per cent of intended subjects. A noted authority on postal survey once said: 'No mail survey can be considered reliable unless it has a minimum of 50 per cent response, or unless it demonstrates with some form of verification that the non-respondents are similar to the respondents.' (Paul L. Erdos [1970] *Professional Mail Surveys.* McGraw-Hill, p. 144.) In short, the few who do respond to a postal survey might be atypical.

8 *Shorter answers.* The answers offered in the postal questionnaire are likely to be short and brief, or even incomplete. To a large extent, information obtained from a postal survey has to be accepted at its face value.

9 *Longer time.* Odd as it may seem to be, a postal inquiry may take a longer time to execute. This happens because after the questionnaires are mailed out, the researcher can virtually do nothing but wait for the return of completed

Comparative assessment of survey research methods			
Advantages	Personal interview	Telephone interview	Postal survey
Administration consideration			
■ Cost	High	Intermediate	Low
■ Speed	Fair	Fast	Intermediate
■ Supervision over interviewer	Bad	Good	Poor
■ Control over targeted time	Intermediate	Good	Poor
Sampling consideration			
■ Geographical dispersion	Poor	Good	Good
■ Control over respondent's identity	Good	Intermediate	Poor
■ Response rate	Good	Intermediate	Poor
■ Call-backs	Intermediate	Good	Poor
■ Access to hard-to-reach people	Poor	Good	Intermediate
■ Item non-response	Low	Low	High
Data consideration			
■ Quantity of data	Good	Fair	Intermediate
■ Full classification data	Good	Fair	Intermediate
■ Complete information	Good	Fair	Poor
Interview consideration			
■ Interview bias	Poor	Intermediate	Good
■ Interviewer cheating	Poor	Intermediate	Good
■ Control over speed of interview	Good	Intermediate	Poor
■ Length of interview	Good	Intermediate	Fair
■ All-item response	Good	Intermediate	Poor
■ Thoughtful answers	Poor	Intermediate	Good

Figure 5.4 *Comparative assessment of survey research methods*

questionnaires. Few people respond to a postal survey instantly, and most would oblige only after repeated reminders.

10 *Others.* These include inability to probe into extensive answers and uncertainty over whether or not the respondents will constitute a representative sample.

A comparative assessment of the three types of survey research methods is presented in Figure 5.4.

Quantitative versus qualitative research

Basically, research can be classified into two very distinct types: quantitative research

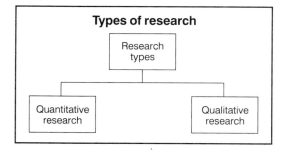

and qualitative research. Sometimes, research clients are confused and put off by the apparent diversity, scope and complexity of research techniques. A discussion on each of these two types of research is therefore warranted.

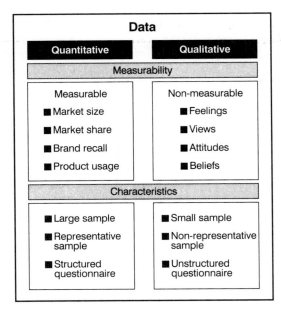

Data	
Quantitative	**Qualitative**
Measurability	
Measurable ■ Market size ■ Market share ■ Brand recall ■ Product usage	Non-measurable ■ Feelings ■ Views ■ Attitudes ■ Beliefs
Characteristics	
■ Large sample ■ Representative sample ■ Structured questionnaire	■ Small sample ■ Non-representative sample ■ Unstructured questionnaire

Quantitative research

Quantitative research is used when the primary research objective is to wanting to derive numeric or quantifiable data which is statistically accurate and reliable. Examples include: market size estimation, brand share analysis, percentages of people who smoke, level of consumer acceptance of new products, profiles of product users/now-users, and so on. Quantitative research is recommended when there exists a need for accurate numeric data: how much, how many, how often, what type/brand?

The techniques of data collection most commonly used in quantitative research

---

Quantitative research

Features:

■ Numerical data

■ Large sample

■ Representative sample

■ Structured questionnaire

■ Data collection methods:
  I personal interviews;
  I telephone interviews; and
  I postal surveys.

---

include personal interview, telephone interview and postal survey which have been detailed earlier.

Qualitative research

Briefly put, qualitative research is a form of exploratory research involving small samples of respondents and non-structured data collection procedures. In qualitative research, respondents provide diagnostic information regarding their thoughts, views and feelings that are not easily projected to the whole population.

Qualitative research provides an excellent tool for gathering data which is rich in insight, understanding and depth of information. This form of data collection necessitates a small number of interviews – often less than thirty. Although its database may be too small to justify valid statistical statements, the information generated by qualitative research is not of lesser importance or value than quantitative research. They are a different form of data used to accomplish quite different objectives. For this reason, qualitative research may turn out to be very useful in giving clues to the thinking of the population under study.

Qualitative research was first popularized in the 1950s during an immense interest in something labeled 'motivation research'. When first introduced shortly after the Second World War as a method of data collection, qualitative methods came under attack by the conservative researchers who condemned it as unscientific and untrustworthy. The major criticism is that such new methods collect information from only a very small sample of people and then attempt to generalize it to the entire population. In addition, some of the conclusions derived from qualitative research have gained increasing recognition and wide acceptance by marketers with the passage of time. It has proven to be a useful tool to explore more than the functional benefits of products, and has introduced a variety of new techniques to the field of marketing research that permit in-depth gathering of information. Today, qualitative methods emerged as one of the data collection techniques most widely used in marketing research, particularly in the areas of generating new product ideas, in developing hypothesis, in discovering new uses for existing products, and in advertising copy research studies.

We shall now discuss three main types of qualitative research. They are: focus group discussion, individual depth interviews and projective techniques.

Focus group discussion

Features

- 6–12 participants
- Comfortable setting
- Views, frustrations, attitudes, etc.
- DEPTH but not BREADTH of information
- Unstructured questionnaire
- One-way mirror

Focus group discussion

Focus group discussion, as its name implies, refers to the assembly of a carefully selected group of people to talk freely on certain subjects of interest. It is an informal session of listening to people (e.g. customers or prospects) on their views, feelings, frustrations, attitudes and is concerned more with the depth rather than the breadth of information.

Within the one to two hours of deliberation, a focus group discussion can yield unexpected dividends. It helps generate new or different ways of looking at an old (existing) subject, and gains insights into relationships and contingencies of consumer attitudes and behaviour. Product faults or virtues that seem unimportant to respondents in a postal survey or telephone study may be unfolded, and human buying motivations that may not have been realized may be discovered. It is not absolutely necessary to prepare a formal questionnaire for such a free-ranging discussion.

The interviewer (or the moderator) of a focus group does not need a standard questionnaire to include a specific set of questions that must be answered by all respondents (or participants). Instead he or she is guided by a discussion guide, and he or she is free to create questions and probe those responses that appear relevant.

Apart from the benefit of probing and achieving beneath superficial answers, focus group discussion offers some strong reasons for its use in marketing research:

1 *Group stimulation.* The foremost benefit of focus group discussion is the element of stimulation among participants. The stimulation and spontaneity of the group environment can motivate a high number of creative responses. Here, the group members stimulate, encourage and spark ideas off each other. A casual remark by one participant can trigger off a stream of opinions and feelings from other participants. The feeling of security with a group also helps encourage the shy participants to speak up.

2 *Hypothesis generation.* Focus group discussion churns out new, fresh thinking and is a superb mechanism for developing hypotheses. Hypotheses generated from a group discussion may subsequently be tested in follow-up quantitative studies.

3 *Idea generation.* A focus group can be a sort of 'think-tank'. A constant flow of new ideas may be generated by listening to a group of persons talking about new, alternative uses of existing products and/or services. Advertising agencies frequently depend on focus group discussions to obtain input for the creation of new advertising ideas. This synergistic effect of the group setting may result in the production of data or ideas that might not have been uncovered in individual interviews.

4 *Speed.* Another distinct benefit of focus group discussion is speed. Focus groups derive data from a group of people much more quickly than would be the case if each individual were interviewed separately. The whole process of a focus group discussion, from organizing it to submitting final report, may take only two or three weeks. This enables the management to initiate remedial marketing actions, if any, almost immediately.

5 *Cost.* Focus group discussion is a relatively inexpensive form of research, considering the richness of information output.

6 *Client rapport.* The client can observe the discussion session either in an adjacent room equipped with a one-way mirror (or a closed circuit television), or personally participate (without revealing his or her identity to the group) in it. This allows the client to secure a high degree of rapport with the participants.

7 *Flexibility.* Focus group discussion offers maximum flexibility in speech. Both the moderator and the participants are not restricted by any structured questionnaire; nor are they under pressure to give spontaneous answers. The discussion is free-flowing and unhampered, so long as the moderator keeps it focused on the subject of interest.

8 *Questionnaire structure.* Focus group discussion is a good prelude to questionnaire construction for large-scale quantitative research. The manner in which the participants talk about something – in their exact words – can provide useful guides for phrasing the survey questions and at the same time suggest the range of answers for a closed-end question.

9 *Research report.* Research report prepared for a quantitative study, is often flooded with numerical data and percentages, much to the annoyance of administrators who read them. A focus group discussion report, on the other hand, contains minimum numerical data and percentages, and incorporates verbatim quotes from the participants which make it look very real and alive. This is not always the case with more sophisticated survey research that employs complex statistical analysis.

It might now appear that focus group discussions have much to offer (and they

```
┌─────────────────────────────────────────┐
│         Focus group discussion          │
│               Moderator                 │
│  ┌──────────────────┐ ┌──────────────┐  │
│  │    Advantages    │ │ Disadvantages│  │
│  ├──────────────────┤ ├──────────────┤  │
│  │ ■ Group stimulation│ │ ■ Non-measurable│ │
│  │                  │ │   data       │  │
│  │ ■ Generating     │ │ ■ Assembly of│  │
│  │   hypothesis     │ │   participants│ │
│  │ ■ Generating ideas│ │ ■ The "Loud-Mouth"│ │
│  │ ■ Speed          │ │              │  │
│  │ ■ Cost           │ │              │  │
│  │ ■ Rapport        │ │              │  │
│  │ ■ Report         │ │              │  │
│  └──────────────────┘ └──────────────┘  │
└─────────────────────────────────────────┘
```

do!), but some problems with focus group discussions also exist, as listed below:

1 *Unquantifiable data.* Focus group discussion produces information of a qualitative nature, usually inappropriate for statistical analysis. Marketing research projects which aim for quantitative data (e.g. market size, market share, brand awareness and the like) would instantly rule out the use of this approach. The small number of participants in the focus group and the convenience nature of focus group recruiting practices significantly limit generalization to a larger population.

2 *Assembly of participants.* The participants in a focus group discussion are required to assemble in a specific location at a time agreed upon. Organizing such an assembly can present some difficulties, particularly if the participants are senior executives.

3 *Loud-mouth effect.* Quite frequently, a focus group session is dominated by one or a few participants. These so-called *loud-mouth* participants deprive their fellow participants of a chance to talk and worse still, may influence their opinions and views. An experienced moderator should tactfully rectify the situation. Another related problem is that a very dominant or opinionated participant may cause bias to the results obtained in a focus group, as

the more-reserved participants may be hesitant to express their views.

4 *Free responses.* The open-ended nature of responses obtained in focus groups often makes summarization and interpretation of results difficult.

5 *Moderator's bias.* The moderator may bias results by knowingly or not knowingly providing clues about what types of responses and answers are desirable.

6 *Capping participants.* Sometimes participants try to cap each other and they may do this to the extent of offering over-exaggerating responses, or worse still, lying.

Keeping participants informed. Participants should be informed in advance of the informal nature of the focus group discussion in order to put their minds at ease. This will ensure that they will be more relaxed and not be left in a state of anxiety. It is psychologically comforting for the participant to feel that his or her fellow participants will also be similar to himself or herself. The recruiter may briefly mention the discussion topic when he or she recruits the participant but he should always remind the latter that no homework or preparation of any kind is expected from him or her. The recruiter should also assure the participant that no selling of any product/service will be involved during the focus group discussion, as people may shy away from places where they are pressurized to buy products or services.

Participant's recruitment. A properly organized and effective focus group discussion will always impose some basic requirements on the selection of participants. At the outset, it is undesirable to recruit a participant who knows any other person in the same focus group; and unless specifications call for it, no two participants in the group should be related (e.g. mother and daughter, husband and wife, etc.) to one another. A person who has attended a focus group discussion in the past twelve months should not be considered, even if earlier group discussions he or she attended involved a completely different topic. It is

---

Focus group discussion

About participants

- Unknown to one another
- Unrelated to one another (e.g. mother-daughter, husband-wife)
- Non-professional
- Same background
- Contrasting behaviour

---

wise to form an appropriate mix of participants who posses similar socio-economic characteristics on the one hand, and display contrasting behaviour on the other. Similarity in socio-economic status reduces communication gap and psychological barriers between the participants so that they can feel free to make their points without inhibition; while contrasting behaviour (product users and non-users) will promise an interesting and fruitful debate.

A screener questionnaire is sometimes prepared to specify the criteria used in recruiting participants (e.g., must be male, shampoo users, teenagers, etc.). Generally speaking, the stricter the criteria specified, the more difficult it will be to organize a focus group. None the less, the overriding factor in formulating the criteria requirements is the research objectives, and not recruiting difficulty.

other events may result in recruits having to pull out at short notice. A common practice is to remind the participants on the very day of the focus group discussion. There is no *correct size* for a focus group, the number of participants required may vary depending on the type of participants needed, the discussion topic as well as the moderator's preference. A focus group is typically composed of seven to ten people, but the actual size can range from as few as four (e.g., senior management participants) to as many as twelve (e.g., student participants). The size is conditioned by two factors. First, it must be small enough to develop empathy, and for each participant to have opportunity to share insights. Secondly, it must be large enough to explore diversity of perceptions and to stimulate interaction and generate ideas. When the group size becomes too large, there is a tendency for the group participants to fragment into subgroups. They start to whisper to the participants seated next to them once they fail to talk openly as there is just not a sufficient pause in the group discussion. In short, the size (number of participants) in a focus group can vary depending on the discussion topic, the preference of the moderator, the availability of participants, and the survey objective.

The discussion venue, usually a conference room or a hotel, should be easily accessible to the participants and is conducive to creating a relaxed and informal atmosphere throughout the discussion.

Preparatory work

Before the discussion session begins, the organizer should arrange the seating of participants in some form of a circle and ensure that participants are all seated at about the same head-level. Participants who sit out of line tend to participate inactively, or slow down the discussion. Set up the cassette tape-recorder and microphones in full view and always check that there are sufficient number of tapes for use. It is a good idea to over-recruit, lest illness, accidents or some

The moderator

The moderator plays a critical role in promoting the desired interaction among the participants. He or she should preferably be a trained social scientist with an open mind and can be either from the research company, or an outside research expert who can readily make people feel relaxed and anxious to talk. A moderator who speaks in a monotone and is lifeless in body language does little to motivate the participants to offer their responses.

Among others, the tasks of a moderator include the following:

- On arrival of the participants, he or she should *introduce* them to one another and appear warm and friendly. He or she can create an informal and relaxed atmosphere by keeping the introduction to a first name basis.
- He or she should *explain to the participants that he or she is not seeking correct or incorrect answers* and urge them not to hesitate to disagree with what other participants might say. He or she should also request them to talk one at a time.
- He or she should always present himself or herself as someone who wishes to learn from the discussion, and *refrain from giving others the impression that he or she is an expert on the discussion topic,* lest he or she might intimidate the participants.
- He or she should attempt to *tone down the few participants who dominate the discussion.* He or she can do so by *encouraging other participants to speak up* whenever they have differing experiences, or if they see things differently. At the close of the session, he or she may ask each participant to summarize what the group has resolved. This helps encourage the shy participants to express their viewpoints.
- He or she should *curtail discussion when it digresses from the subject,* and lead it back tactfully. When a topic is no longer generating fresh ideas, the moderator should quickly switch to another topic of discussion.
- He or she should *always assume the role of a willing/patient listener.* Under no circumstances should the moderator show disinterest or argue with the participants, even when he or she disagrees strongly with their views. The moderator must be sensitive to participants' feelings and comments.
- Before concluding the discussion, he or she must *thank the participants for their valuable comments and time.*

Discussion guide

A discussion guide is a document prepared by the moderator before conducting the discussion session. It is by no means a structured questionnaire with carefully crafted questions. Rather, it is an agenda for a focus group discussion, often in a outline form. It enumerates the research objectives and ensures that the major areas are not omitted or inadequately covered during the group discussion. The discussion guide should be in considerable detail to contain a comprehensive list of relevant topics, yet flexible enough to be adjusted as the discussion progresses. A discussion guide should be developed jointly by the research client and the researcher (moderator) so that both parties feel contented and comfortable with it. An example of a discussion guide is given in Appendix B at the end of this chapter.

Individual depth interview

Depth interview is a special form of focus group discussion which involves only one participant at a time. It is an unstructured personal interview utilizing extensive probing technique, to get the respondent to talk freely and to express his or her beliefs and feelings at great length. Its name suggests a pattern of questioning which encourages the respondent to go deeper and deeper into his or her thoughts in order to discover the real motives and explanations for his or her behaviour. Depth interview is often used in motivational research to descend beneath the superficial answers provided by respondents.

Depth interview

- A special form of focus group discussion
- Privacy of conversation
- Acute personal differences
- Unstructured-questionnarie (Discussion guide)

This method is most appropriate for exploring political, sensitive and personal issues (e.g. pre-marital sex) where privacy is essential. Also, it is instrumental in exploring subjects in which personal differences are so acute that the interaction in a focus group discussion situation may prove to be more destructive than useful.

The advantage of individual depth interview lies in its ability to discover greater depth of insight and to associate the response directly with the respondent. Unlike focus group discussion, the one-to-one dialogue session may facilitate a respondent's revelation of attitudes or motives which might not be forthcoming in a group setting.

Like focus group discussion, individual depth interview requires a well-trained and highly qualified moderator. Ideally, the moderator should possess reasonably good knowledge of psychology, be imaginative as well as alert in probing the leads offered by the respondents. By the large, individual depth interview shares most of the merits and demerits of focus group discussion.

Projective technique

A common tool used in qualitative research method is the projective technique which was originated by clinical psychologists. It is an indirect interviewing method in which the respondent is presented with an ambiguous or unstructured object, activity or person, and is asked to project beliefs and feelings on to a third party, or into a task situation. It involves the setting up of a situation for the respondent to express his or her own point of view, or to interpret/complete an ambiguous stimulus presented to him or her. Photographs, drawings, print advertisements and storyboards are typical examples of visual stimuli. The respondent draws on his or her own attitudes, opinions and motivations and project these on to some other persons or objects. The underlying assumption behind projective technique lies in Oscar Wilde's phrase: 'A man is least himself when he talks in his own person; when he is given a mask he will tell the truth.' With direct questions, the respondents might be embarrassed to express their true feelings through answers that reflect unfavourably on their image. But if they are presented with unstructured, ambiguous stimuli, they can be encouraged to describe a situation in their own words with minimum prompting by the interviewer. Psychological skills are needed, however, to interpret the responses given. Projective techniques were popularized in the 1950s amidst a wave of motivation research. We shall now discuss the most common projective techniques.

Free word association

Free word association is among the oldest forms of projective techniques. A list of words or phrases, carefully selected to reveal attitudes or feelings towards the subject of research, is read out one at a time to the respondent who is asked to respond with the first word or phrase that emerges from his or her mind. The interviewer records each response before reading the next word. If a response follows the stimulus word by more than two or three seconds, it is rejected as it is not regarded as true reaction. With free word association, the respondent's subconscious thoughts are revealed since the conscious mind would not have enough time to think up something else. Free word association is frequently used in testing potential brand names, advertising themes, promotion slogans, etc. It can also be used to pretest words or concepts to be included in questionnaires; to enable the researcher in determining the extent to which the meaning of a word is understood in the context of a survey. The list of words presented should contain a mixture of test words and neutral words so as to bypass mental defences. For example, if a researcher is interested in people's beliefs about home economists, the stimulus words might be:

Stimulus word	Response
Bread	_____
Home economist	_____
Season	_____
Advertisement	_____
Flower	_____
Book	_____
Kitchen	_____
Cake mix	_____
Honesty	_____

Word association

- Read out a list of words/phrases
- For each word read, respondent to respond instantly with a word/phrase

An example

Stimulus word	Responses
Flower ◄──────►	Smell
Flower ◄──────►	Beauty
Flower ◄──────►	Funeral
Flower ◄──────►	Valentine

In free word association, both verbal and non-verbal responses (e.g. hesitation) are recorded. Interpreting its test results may be difficult, and researchers generally make use of these methods:

- compiling the frequency of each word given as a response
- analysing the amount of lapsed time
- counting the number of respondents who fail to give a response after a specified period of time.

The frequency of a word given as a response reflects a basic attitude towards the test word presented. Such information enables the researcher to check the reactions towards the brand name (existing or intended) against those of the competitors;

or to assess the implications of essential words in an advertising copy, theme or slogan. Alternatively, response may be grouped according to favourable-unfavourable; pleasant-unpleasant; masculine-feminine classifications. The time between reading the test word and receiving a response is recorded by the use of a stopwatch or by the interviewer counting seconds. A *hesitation* is defined when a respondent takes longer than the specified time (usually three seconds) to respond.

While single word association yields top-of-the-mind response, successive word association – double/triple – is used to gather additional information. The latter technique analyses responses in the same way as single word association, that is, by way of tabulation and timing of responses.

Sentence completion

An extension of the free word association test is the sentence completion technique. Here, the respondent is presented with a sentence (or sentences) expressing incomplete ideas (or stimuli) and is asked to complete each sentence with whatever thoughts that come first to his or her mind. Answers given to sentence completion questions tend to be more extensive than those given in word association. On the other hand, the intent of sentence completion is more apparent to the respondents.

Care must be exercised to ensure that sentences are phrased in the most simple and unambiguous form to facilitate rapid completion. The researcher should attempt

---

Sentence completion

- Read out an incomplete sentence
- Respondent to complete the sentence

Examples

A married woman who never cooks …

People who drive convertibles …

Teenagers who smoke …

to vary the nature of the ideas presented without allowing the respondent to be aware of any research intent and thus causing bias in the response. The mode of analysing sentence completion results follows that of free word association.

Cartoon technique

With the cartoon technique, the respondent is shown a cartoon similar to a comic strip with a *balloon* indicating a speech. Usually, two people appear in conversation with balloons above their heads. The speech of one is shown in a balloon, and the other balloon is left blank for the respondent to fill in with words or sentences. The cartoon characters are generally drawn to appear neutral (e.g. no facial expressions such as a smile or a frown). A common practice is to use stick figures.

From next month, petrol price will be increased by ten cents per litre.

Cartoon technique

■ Present a cartoon drawing

■ Show individuals with conversational balloons. One balloon is blank

■ Respondent fills words in the blank balloon

Observation method

Instead of asking customers on how much time they spend on shopping, a supermarket manager might prefer to observe and record the time interval between a shopper's entry into and departure from the store.

Observation is an alternative to direct questioning. Under this approach, trained observers/interviewers are assigned, or mechanical devices installed at strategic locations (e.g. supermarkets, road junctions) to observe and record people's behaviour, action or events at the time of their occurrences. The unobtrusive or non-reactive nature of the observation method often produces data without the knowledge of the subjects. Alfred Politz studied advertising exposure to posters on the outside of buses by installing movie cameras which film people looking towards the buses as the vehicles travelled along their routes (Alfred Politz [1959] *A Study of Outside Transit Poster Exposure*, National Association of Transportation Advertising, Inc.).

Advantages of the observation method

Observation is favoured for specific marketing research studies as the only possible method of gathering data. A study aiming at investigating how infants select their favourite toys would invariably use this method.

Observation method provides objectivity in reporting events as it avoids interviewer-interviewee bias. There is no need to seek the co-operation of the respondent and many of the problems related to field work (e.g. refusals, not-at-homes, untruthful responses and the like) would readily disappear.

Observation produces greater accuracy of data than direct questioning. Imagine a group of students is asked whether they would cheat in an examination when no invigilator is around. Certainly observational devices (e.g. hidden cameras) can do a better job here.

Disadvantages of the observation method

Observation fails to record an important aspect of consumer action: the *why* aspect of human behaviour. Setting up observation at the exit of a supermarket can at best reveal what have been purchased by the consumer, but it does not explain why these items were purchased. In other words, observation method can only yield information that is primarily descriptive in nature, but fails to provide explanation of observed behaviour. The researcher has to infer or draw own conclusions to determine motivation that may underlie the behaviour observed. Observation method also suffers from venue restriction, as it is not possible to observe subjects' activities, behaviour in their homes objectively. The subject, once aware of being observed, might behave differently.

The observer may have to spend a considerable amount of time waiting for the anticipated events to occur. The inability to achieve a representative sample of subjects observed and the inability of observers to record all details are the other disadvantages. Last but not least, observation method becomes useless if the interviewer (observer) allows personal bias or lack of objectivity to influence them.

Recording observation

Under the observation method of data collection, there may simply be too much for the observer to record in details. Variation in recording contents may arise from differing abilities of the observers. Selltiz, Wrightsman and Cook ([1979] *Research Methods in Social Relations*. 3rd edn, Holt, Rinehart and Winston, pp. 271–3) noted that a detailed description of a behaviour incident may involve the following factors:

- the participants (who they are; how are they related; and how many)
- the setting (location)
- the purpose (why these participants have been brought together)

- the social behaviour (what occurs in terms of stimulus; objectives of behaviour; form of activity of the behaviour)
- the frequency and duration of the behaviour and situation (when; for how long; and recurrence).

Delens defines observation techniques as 'those whereby the investigator is placed in a position from which he can observed and note the actions and behaviour of respondents'. This definition has three implications:

- The activity and behaviour of the respondent should be observable.
- The observer should note the observations either simultaneously with the action or immediately after.
- The respondent (or the person under observation) should not be aware of him or her being so observed.

Open or disguised observation

Open (or visible) observation takes place when the presence of the observer, or the observation instrument, is known to the subject. It has the potential bias as the subjects may behave differently once they take note of such presence. In some studies, therefore, observers disguised themselves as shoppers; or hidden mechanical devices (e.g. hidden cameras) are being used. With hidden observation method, respondent error is minimized, but it also raises an ethical issue concerning the privacy of the person being so observed.

Human or mechanical observation

With human observers, the problems associated with inaccuracies and inabilities will always exist. Furthermore, human observers can be expensive to employ. Instead, mechanical observation using various devices described below is preferred.

The audimeter

Introduced by A C Nielson Company, the audimeter is connected to the television set and records when the television set is on, or off, and the channel which is tuned to. The major weakness of this equipment is that while it can continuously monitor and record when the set is on, it does not indicate whether anyone is actually watching the programme. Thus, a diary panel using the survey method is additionally employed to supplement the observed data.

The people meter

This is an improved audimeter with a remote-control handset about the size of a hand calculator which contains numbered buttons to identify viewing by family members/guests. Each family member is pre-assigned a number. When a person starts to watch television, he/she presses his/her number, and when that person stops watching, he/she presses that number again. In this manner, information on audience size as well as audience profiles can be analysed.

The pupilometer

The pupilometer observes and records changes in the diameter of the subject's pupils as he or she is presented with an ad, a package design or a product design. Subjects are instructed to look at a screen on which an ad or other stimulus is projected. A progressive change in the size of pupils is presumed to reflect the varying of interest in the observed object, if brightness and distance of observation remain unchanged.

The eye camera

This records the gaze movements of the subject's eyes while he or she is looking at a stimulus (e.g. print advertisement, package). This instrument registers the amount of time spent in looking at the stimulus, and indicates which part of the stimulus is looked at first, etc.

The psychogalvanometer

This records emotional responses to various stimuli by measuring changes in one's galvanic skin response (GSR), or the rate of his or her perspiration. The instrument is attached to the subject's palm when measurements are made. Excitement towards the stimulus speeds up the perspiration rate of the body which in turn increases the electrical resistance of the subject.

Critical evoked potential (CEP)

This is a specific brain wave showing the extent to which a person reacts to a stimulus. It is used primarily to test responses to television programming content as well as commercials. The brain patterns can be identified by attaching small electroids to the subject's head and then identifying the amount of right and left brain activity occurring while the subject views an advertisement.

Normal or controlled environment

It would be ideal to observe activities in a real (i.e. not contrived or artificially created) environment. But this means much time would be spent in waiting for the subject (e.g. shopper) to appear. Thus it is often necessary to observe an activity in an artificially created situation in order to permit more efficient and effective observation to take place. For example, a diner complaining about a bad meal or service given by the waitress may actually be the researcher him or herself who attempts to record the waitress' reactions.

Appendix A: Statistical sources in Singapore ▬▬▬▬▬

Publication	Frequency	Source
General		
Yearbook of Statistics	Annually	Department of Statistics
Singapore Statistical Charts	Annually	Department of Statistics
Singapore Facts and Pictures	Annually	Ministry of Information and the Arts
Singapore in Brief	Annually	Department of Statistics
Singapore Key Indicators	Monthly	Department of Statistics
Monthly Digest of Statistics	Monthly	Department of Statistics
Population and vital statistics		
Report on the Census of Population	Decennially	Department of Statistics
Report on the Registration of Births and Deaths	Annually	Registrar-General of Births and Deaths
Statistics on Marriages and Divorces	Annually	Department of Statistics
Population Report	Annually	Ministry of Health
Singapore Demographic Bulletin	Monthly	National Registration Office
Labour		
Singapore Yearbook of Labour Statistics	Annually	Ministry of Manpower
Report on the Labour Force Survey	Annually	Ministry of Manpower
Report on Wages in Singapore	Annually	Ministry of Manpower
Manufacturing		
Report on the Census of Industrial Production	Annually	Economic Development Board
Index of Industrial Production, Singapore	Annually	Economic Development Board
Report on the Survey of Business Expectations of Industrial Establishments	Quarterly	Economic Development Board
Transport and communications		
Road Traffic Accidents Statistical Report, Singapore	Annually	Traffic Police Department
Telecoms Statistical Yearbook	Annually	Singapore Telecommunication Pte Ltd
Singapore Shipping and Cargo Statistics	Monthly	Port of Singapore Authority
Air Transport Statistics	Monthly	Civil Aviation Authority of Singapore

Publication	Frequency	Source
Construction, building and housing		
Construction Manpower Update	Annually	Construction Industry Development Board
Yearbook of Construction and Real Estate Statistics	Annually	Ministry of National Development
Report on the Occupancy of Private Residential Properties, Offices and Shopping Space	Half-yearly	Ministry of National Development
Construction and Real Estate Statistics	Quarterly	Ministry of National Development
Real Estate Statistics Quarterly	Quarterly	Urban Redevelopment Authority
PWD Cost Information Quarterly	Quarterly	Public Works Department
Monthly Bulletin of Construction Statistics	Monthly	Urban Redevelopment Authority
Consumer expenditure and prices		
Report on the Household Expenditure Survey	Quin-quennially	Department of Statistics
Consumer Price Index	Monthly	Department of Statistics
External trade		
Singapore Trade Statistics – Imports and Exports	Monthly	Singapore Trade Development Board
Singapore External Trade	Monthly	Singapore Trade Development Board
Finance		
Monthly Statistical Bulletin	Monthly	Monetary Authority of Singapore
Economics		
Singapore Input-Output Tables	Quin-quennially	Department of Statistics
Economic Survey of Singapore	Annually / Quarterly	Ministry of Trade and Industry
Commerce and services		
Report on the Survey of Wholesale Trade, Retail Trade, Restaurants and Hotels	Annually	Department of Statistics
Report on the Survey of Services	Annually	Department of Statistics
Survey on Business Expectations of the Commerce and Service Sectors, Singapore	Quarterly	Department of Statistics
Education		
Education Statistics Digest	Annually	Ministry of Education
Key Statistics on Vocational Training	Annually	Vocational and Industrial Training Board
Tourism		
Singapore Annual Report	Annually	Singapore Tourism Board
Survey on Overseas Visitors to Singapore	Annually	Singapore Tourism Board
Singapore Monthly Report on Tourism Statistics	Monthly	Singapore Tourism Board

Appendix B: Discussion guide (shampoo advertisement study) ■■■■■■■

Introduction

1 Welcome and thank respondents for coming.
2 Introduce respondents to each other and try to create a friendly and relaxed atmosphere.
3 Explain the nature of the company and research purpose/method:
   a Market research: Interested in people's thoughts and impressions; carry out studies to help manufacturers.
   b Different approaches: door-to-door interviewing; group discussions – purpose is to provide environment for exchange of views.
   c Feel free to express personal opinion. No right or wrong answers.

General

1 Let us start by talking about television viewing. Do you watch television at home?
   (*PROBE BRIEFLY: Types of programmes Viewing hours*)
2 Do you enjoy watching TV commercials appearing in between the shows?

Reactions to advertisements

1 Right, why don't you try to imagine yourself as being at home now and you are watching your favourite television programme. As usual, there is the commercial break and this is what comes on the air . . .
   (*Show 3 commercials and note spontaneous reactions.*)
2 I would like to know what thoughts went through your minds as you were watching these advertisements.
   (*PROBE: Any particular likes/dislikes?*)
3 Can you remember what was advertised?
   (*PROBE: brand; shampoo/conditioner?*)

4 Would you like to describe to me what was shown/said in the advertisement? Let's look at each of the advertisements again one at a time.
   (*Show ads and for each ad, ask questions that follow*)
   What do you think this ad is trying to tell you about the product?
   (*PROBE: Are there any special features of the product?*
   Any differences/similarities to other products?
   Anything you particularly like/ dislike?)
5 Thinking about the advertisement, are there any advantages/disadvantages of using (*Mention brand*)
6 Is there anything that people may not understand?
   (*PROBE: What is it that they may not understand?*
   In what way?)
7 What other impressions do you have of the product? How would you, in your own words, describe the product now?
   (*PROBE: Good quality?*
   Effective?
   Expensive?
   Suitable for particular hair type?)
8 Who do you think would be attracted to using this product after looking at the advertisement?
   (*PROBE: Type of person?*
   Young vs old?
   Working vs non-working?
   Sophisticated vs conservative?)
9 For those who don't use this brand (*State whichever applicable*), does the advertisement interest you in trying the products?
   (*PROBE: Reasons for interest/lack of interest*)
10 How do those of you who are currently using this brand feel about the product after seeing this advertisement?
   PROBE: Assured?
   Proud/pleased?
   Any negative comments?)

Hair care and shampoo usage

11 Having discussed at length about shampoo advertising, I wonder what your views are towards hair care?
(PROBE: *How do you take care of your hair?*
What products do you use?)

12 Would you like to describe in detail what you do when you wash your hair?
(PROBE: *Number of times hair is washed*
Frequency
Visits to the salons
Massage
Conditioner
Tonic
Hot/cold water)

13 What is your idea of an ideal shampoo? What do you expect from it?
(PROBE: *Cleans hair*
Makes hair shiny
Softness
Manageability
Nourish/condition?)

14 To what extent are you satisfied with the shampoo that you are currently using?
(PROBE: *Advantages/disadvantages?*
Likes/dislikes?
Price – expensive/reasonable?
Suits particular hair types?)

Brand image

15 Let's try to name some of the various brands of shampoo which you are currently using.
(PROBE: *What others have you tried before?*
Any others that you have seen/ heard of?)

16 I have with me some of these brands that you have named.
(DISPLAY: *Countess, Kao, Sunsilk, Clairol (Herbal Essence), Wella and Revlon-Flex*)
NOTE ANY SPONTANEOUS REACTIONS
What are your impressions/thoughts and feelings about these products here? Are they similar/different?

(PROBE: *Wide range*
Price differentiation
Suitable for different hair types
Country of origin)

17 Which of these products would you like to talk about first?
(COVER: *Countess, Sunsilk, Kao in depth*)

ASK THE FOLLOWING QUESTIONS FOR EACH BRAND

18 Can you tell me your thoughts and feelings abut this/these product(s)?
(PROBE: *Likes/dislikes*
Brand trial
Interest in trying? Why/why not?)

19 What do you think are the advantages of using this range of product(s)? Are there any benefits?
(COVER: *Ingredients used?*
Useful/advantages?
Do they appeal?
Fragrance?)

20 Is this product similar or different from other products on the market?
(PROBE: *Similar to which brand?*
In what ways similar/different?)

21 What about the pack design?
(PROBE: *Attractive?*
Good quality?
Classy?
Any negative comments?)

22 How much does this product cost? How much are you prepared to pay?
(PROBE: *Reasonable?*
Expensive/cheap?)

23 Who do you think would find this particular product appealing?
(PROBE: *Those with problem hair/what problems?*
Younger vs older women
Single girls vs families)

24 To those of you who have never tried this, I would like to know why this is so?
(PROBE: *Attracted but loyal to current brand*
Confused/unsure about suitability

*Unimpressed by fragrance/
pack/advertisement
Never seen/heard
Not interested?)*

25 Would you be interested in trying now?
(*PROBE: Why/why not?*)

26 What about those of you who have tried
this brand before? Why have you
stopped using this brand?
(*PROBE: In what way is your current
brand different from this brand?
Any change in the condition of
hair as a result of the switch?*)

27 Have you ever considered changing from
your current brand?

(*PROBE: Why/why not?
If yes, do you ever consider
buying this brand again?
Why/why not?*)

Conclusion

28 Do you have any other comments to
make before we close the discussion?
Anything else to say about hair
care/these products/the advertisements?

THANK PARTICIPANTS AND CLOSE
DISCUSSION

End-of-chapter revision

Review Questions

5.1 What are secondary data? What is the role of secondary data in the research process?

5.2 Differentiate between internal and external secondary data.

5.3 Name and briefly discuss the shortcomings of secondary data.

5.4 What are some of the advantages of secondary data relative to primary data for a market research study?

5.5 What features should the researcher look for in evaluating secondary data?

5.6 Define each of the following:
a Personal interview
b Postal survey
c Telephone interview

5.7 What are the strengths and weaknesses of personal interview as a method of data collection?

5.8 Identify the social and technological changes that suggest a continuing increase in the use of telephone interviewing in marketing research.

5.9 List out and explain some of the probable differences between respondents with listed telephone numbers and respondents with unlisted telephone numbers.

5.10 What are the two types of unlisted telephone numbers?

5.11 What is random digit dialling? Outline the steps in random-digit dialling.,

5.12 What is add-one dialling? What advantages does the add-one approach have over random-digit dialling?

5.13 What does CATI mean in respect of telephone interviewing? What are its advantages?

5.14 Name and discuss the main advantages and disadvantages of postal surveys.

5.15 What is meant by a–g and which interview method(s) deal with it most effectively?
a Complexity of the questionnaire.
b Required amount of data.
c Time requirements.
d Level of response.
e Sample control.
f Accuracy.
g Cost.

5.16 Describe the degree and nature of the effect of a–h on the response rate of postal surveys:
a respondents' interest in topic
b physical aspects of the questionnaire
c questionnaire length
d anonymity/confidentiality
e return deadline
f advanced notification
g monetary incentives
h follow-up reminders.

5.17 What is a focus group discussion? What uses in marketing research can it serve?

5.18 Discuss the key issues involved in carrying out a focus group discussion.

5.19 What are the major limitations of focus group discussion?

5.20 List out some of the desirable characteristics for focus group moderators. What are the tasks that the moderator need to perform to ensure a fruitful focus group discussion?

5.21 Why must attention be paid to the composition of focus groups? What factors should be considered when determining the composition of a particular group?

5.22 What is the purpose of a focus group discussion guide? How does such a guide differ from a survey questionnaire? And what are the reasons for this difference?

5.23 How does the depth interview method differ from the focus group method?

5.24 What is meant by observation method and why is it sometimes considered a desirable alternative to direct questioning?

5.25 Identify and discuss the advantages and disadvantages of observation method.

5.26 What are some of the commonly used mechanical and/or electronic observational devices? What advantages and disadvantages do they have compared to human observation?

5.27 Distinguish between open and disguised observation; between direct and indirect observation.

5.28 Under what situations would you recommend that a depth interviewing method be adopted rather than focus group discussion?

5.29 Describe and illustrate the major types of projective interviewing technique?

5.30 When choosing between personal, telephone interviews and postal survey, what are the factors to be considered?

5.31 What is projective technique? Which are the main types of projective technique?

5.32 Develop a projective technique to determine students' attitudes towards littering.

5.33 Describe and give examples of each of the following types of projective techniques:
a Word association.
b Sentence association.
c Cartoon completion.

5.34 Describe the information provided by the psychogalvanometer. Of what value is it to marketing researchers?

5.35 What principle underlies the use of an eye camera?

5.36 Describe the information provided by the pupilometer. Of what value is it to marketing researchers?

True-false questions

Write True (T) or False (F) for the following:

5.37 The respondent is a person who conducts an interview as a part of the survey.

5.38 A survey interview is a purposeful conversation in which the interviewer asks a set of prepared questions and the respondent answers them.

5.39 Surveys done by personal interviewing are usually more expensive.

5.40 Telephone interviews have advantages over postal surveys in terms of the ability to use visual aids.

5.41 The reasons why telephone interviewing is being used are its cost efficiency and speed of data collection.

5.42 If a respondent must consult records for needed information, the postal survey method is superior to telephone interviewing.

5.43 Compared to primary data, secondary data usually takes less time and money to collect.

5.44 Random-digit dialling is used only when a telephone directory is not available for the locality being surveyed.

5.45 Focus group discussion is useful in exploratory research situations where statistical extrapolation to the larger population is not necessary.

5.46 It is usually a good idea to have friends participate in the same focus group.

5.47 In disguised observation, persons being observed are unaware that they are being observed.

5.48 Add-one sampling allows the interviewer to reach persons who have changed addresses.

5.49 Postal surveys generally cost less than telephone surveys

5.50 Call-backs are usually easiest with face-to-face interviews.

5.51 Data quality is usually best when collecting data through telephone interviews.

5.52 Respondents tend to give more thoughtful answers in postal surveys.

5.53 Generally, it is never sure who completed the postal survey questionnaires.

5.54 Face-to-face interviews are generally much more costly than telephone and postal surveys.

5.55 Response rates for postal surveys are generally higher than those of face-to-face and telephone interviews.

5.56 Interviewing bias and cheating are usually greatest for face-to-face interviews.

5.57 Hard-to-reach people are equally difficult to locate for telephone, postal and face-to-face interviews.

5.58 It is usually quite easy to supervise face-to-face interviewers.

5.59 Quantitative research is generally exploratory in nature. It describes, rather than presents numeric outcomes of interest to managers.

5.60 Qualitative research is generally descriptive in nature, and outcomes of interest are presented to managers in tabular, graphic and statistical formats.

Multiple-choice questions

5.61 The observation method is appropriate to gather:
a opinions
b attitudes
c preferences
d facts.

5.62 Attractive appearance of a questionnaire is essential when data collection is done through:
a personal interview
b self-administered postal questionnaire
c telephone interview
d focus group discussion.

5.63 Compared to primary data, secondary data is:
a gathered more quickly and inexpensively
b more relevant to the problem at hand
c more up-to-data
d none of the above.

5.64 Random-digit dialling:

a allows the interviewer to reach persons who have moved to new addresses
b involves the use of the phone book
c is especially useful when the survey involves product purchase intention
d allows the interviewer to reach unlisted persons in the phone book.

5.65 Compared to random digit dialling, add-one dialling has the advantage of:
a being able to contact individuals owning more than one telephone
b reducing the number of not-at-homes
c obtaining a greater proportion of working numbers
d minimizing the number of persons who do not co-operate.

5.66 A strength of the depth interview is:
a ease in data tabulation
b ability to provide insights into motivation
c economy in terms of time
d need for a skilled interviewer.

5.67 A researcher wishes to estimate the number of readers of *The Straits Times* who have read or seen the Dragonfly Cream advertisement which appeared in a particular day. He or she should preferably use:
a postal survey
b personal interview
c observation method
d telephone interview.

5.68 Which of the following is an advantage of telephone interviewing method?
a It costs less and can be completed quickly.
b It is easy to supervise.
c Wide scatter of respondents is no obstacle.
d All of the above are advantages.

5.69 Which of the following survey methods are used in qualitative research?
a Postal survey, using both closed-ended and open-ended questions

b Telephone survey, using both closed-ended and open-ended questions

c Face-to-face interview, using both closed-ended and open-ended questions

d None of the above.

5.70 Which of the following survey methods are used in qualitative research?

a Face-to-face interview, using both closed-ended and open-ended questions

b Focus groups, using open-ended questions

c Depth interviews, using open-ended questions

d b and c above.

5.71 Pilot interviews is a brief pre-study to examine:

a the time needed to conduct an interview

b the non-response rate

c the logical sequence of questions

d all of the above.

6

Designing data collection forms _____

A data collection instrument is a document used for the gathering and recording of data in a research study. It constitutes a central component of marketing research studies, whatever the method of data collection is adopted. In particular, when the data collection instrument is administered by survey research methods – personal interview, telephone interview or postal survey – we call it a *questionnaire*. Survey guides, tally sheets, observational forms, etc., constitute other data collection instruments.

Since questionnaire is the main data collection instrument in marketing research, we will devote this chapter to the issues involved in questionnaire construction, together with the activities that go with it. A brief discussion on the development of data collection forms for observation is provided towards the end of this chapter.

Questionnaire ▬▬▬▬▬

The questionnaire is a document on which the interviewer records the answers given by the respondents. A questionnaire may be defined as a formalized schedule or form which contains an assembly of carefully formulated questions for information-gathering. *Webster's New Collegiate Dictionary* defines it as 'a set of questions for obtaining statistically useful or personal information for individuals'. An effective questionnaire is much more than what is implied in the above definition, for it necessitates thoughtful design not only to suit the research aims but also to elicit cooperation from the respondent. A major concern in questionnaire design is measurement error. If poorly designed, a questionnaire can hamper response rates, create bias and invite misleading responses. The questionnaire is probably the most crucial single element in the entire marketing research process.

A distinguishing feature of a well-designed questionnaire is its ability to convey the proper message clearly. Questionnaire design is more an art than a science. There is no standard set of principles or guidelines to guarantee an effective and efficient questionnaire. Most textbooks will readily advise on the dos and don'ts in questionnaire design, but to acquire the necessary skills for it will need experience and practice. A wise approach is to draft the questionnaire personally, then test it on a small sample of respondents, examine its flaws or weaknesses, revise it again and again if necessary.

If the questionnaire is to achieve the desired purposes, two basic criteria are to be met – relevance and accuracy. (Donald P. Warwick and Charles A. Linger [1975] *The Sample Survey: Theory and Practice*. McGraw-Hill, p. 127). A questionnaire is said to be relevant if no redundant information is collected, and if all the needed information is obtained. Accuracy of questionnaire means that the information gathered therefrom is reliable and valid. These two criteria are often referred to as the goals of questionnaire design.

The designing work on a questionnaire becomes somewhat complicated as there are five distinct parties involved, particularly so when the needs and wants of each party are not necessarily the same, but often conflict. These five parties are: the research client, the researcher, the interviewer, the respondent and the data processor.

The research client, being the paymaster of the research, wishes to derive the maximum value for money from the research study. It is his desire to ensure that all the needed information are obtainable from the set of questions to be included in the questionnaire, so that the survey results will help to satisfy the management's needs of information. The researcher's main concern would be to ensure that the survey questions presented should not be too complicated thus confusing the respondent, nor the questionnaire be too lengthy thus causing respondent's fatigue in responding to it. The questionnaire should seek to assist the interviewer to perform an efficient job with the minimum of difficulty. The respondent should not in any way be discouraged to co-operate due to any deficiency caused by the questionnaire design, in particular, he should not be presented with complicated

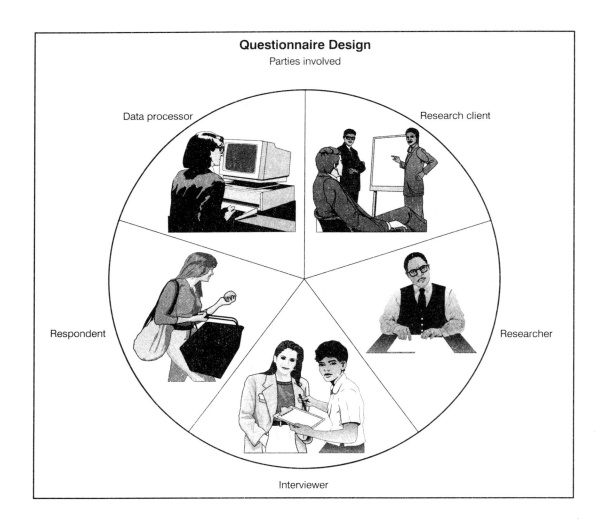

Questionnaire Design
Parties involved

Data processor

Research client

Respondent

Researcher

Interviewer

or ambiguous questions in the questionnaire. Finally, the questionnaire should be designed in a way to help the data processor without having difficulty in coding and unnecessary references back and forth of the questionnaire.

Categorization of questionnaire

The general form of questionnaire may be categorized in two ways: the degree of structure and the degree of disguise. First, structure refers to the amount of freedom the interviewer has in executing the questionnaire to meet the unique situation posed by each interview. In a structured questionnaire, all questions are prearranged in some specified order; furthermore, the range of possible responses for each question is provided. Using this approach, a standardized set of questions is administered for each and every respondent. An unstructured questionnaire, on the other hand, contains mostly (if not all) open-ended questions. This offers the respondent great latitude in answering as well as affording the interviewer the opportunity to probe in great length into the underlying aspects of the answers given. Most questionnaires used in marketing research studies combine structured and unstructured questions.

Whether or not a questionnaire is disguised or undisguised will be determined by how likely the respondent is aware of the nature and purpose of the survey. An undisguised questionnaire reveals the research purpose clearly either in an introductory statement or from the questions asked. A disguised questionnaire is one which the research purpose is obscured to the respondent.

A cross-classification of the two criteria mentioned above yields four general categories of questionnaires as presented in Figure 6.1.

Procedures for designing questionnaires

The procedures for the design of a questionnaire is illustrated in Figure 6.2.

Information needs

The first step in questionnaire design is to determine the specific information needed to achieve the research objectives. Here the researcher must critically review the research purpose and ensure that essential questions are included. Once the interviews begin, or the questionnaires are mailed out, it will be too late to take in any additional question. The researcher must also decide on the level of data analysis planned for the research study. For instance, would it require only simple cross-tabulation of data, or would advanced statistical procedure such as regression analysis, Chi-squared test or analysis of variance be applied? Unless the information needs are examined, the researcher would fail to gather data in the form suitable for the desired analytical technique.

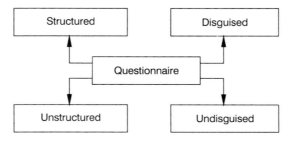

Categories	Features/Characteristics
Structured–Undisguised	A standard set of questions for each respondent
	The most commonly used questionnaire in research
	Exact question wording reduces the possibility of misunderstanding
	Most effective when range of possible responses is limited
	Simple to administer, code, tabulate and analyse
	Less opportunity for probing is provided
	Inappropriate for personal and motivational questions
Structured–Disguised	A standard set of questions for each respondent
	The least often used questionnaire in marketing research
	Easy to administer, code, tabulate and analyse
	Eliminates respondent's bias
Unstructured–Undisguised	Free from the restrictions imposed by a standard formal set of questions
	Most appropriate for in-depth interviews and focus group discussions
	Interviewer is given only general instructions on the types of information required
	Deeper and more accurate responses can be obtained, especially for sensitive and complex issues
	Difficult to code, tabulate and analyse
	Higher cost per completed interview
	Not frequently used
Unstructured–Disguised	Free from the restrictions imposed by a standard formal set of questions
	Most appropriate for in–depth interviews and focus group discussions
	Most often used in motivational research to explore the 'whys' of an individual's behaviour
	Difficult to code, tabulate and analyse

Figure 6.1 *Categorization of questionnaire*

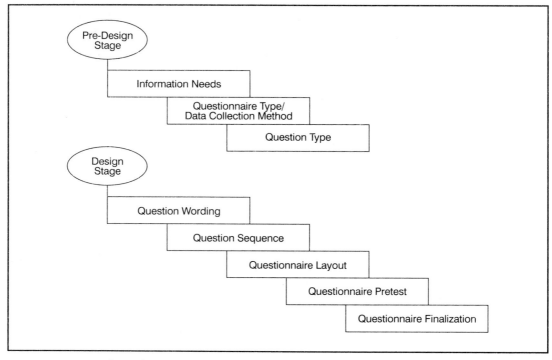

Figure 6.2 *Procedures for designing questionnaires: procedural steps*

Questionnaire type/data collection method

Once the information needs are established, the researcher next decides whether a structured or unstructured, a disguised or undisguised questionnaire, is most appropriate. This is much dependent on whether a personal interview, telephone interview or postal survey method is used. Such a decision will hinge on three key factors, namely, type of information sought, nature of intended respondents, and research fund and time available.

Question type

All questions in a questionnaire may be categorized into one of three basic types – open-ended questions, close-ended (or checklist) questions and scaling questions – dependent on the amount of freedom given to respondents in offering responses. The type of questions for use will be determined by the form of responses sought, the nature of the respondents and their ability to answer the questions.

Main types of Questions

Open–Ended Questions
- Basic open–ended questions
- Probing questions
- Clarifying questions

Closed–Ended Questions
- Dichotomous questions
- Multiple–choice questions

Scaling Questions
- Behavioural/Attitudinal questions
- Buying–intent questions
- Agree/Disagree questions
- Preference questions
- Ranking questions
- Semantic differential questions
- Constant–sum questions

Open-ended questions

An open-ended question is one which allows the respondent to answer it freely in his or her own words, and to express any ideas generated from the question itself. The respondent is given free latitude to offer responses that seem appropriate in the light of the questions posed, uninhibited or constrained in any way. Open-ended questions are appropriate when the pattern of responses is least known to the researcher, or when no fixed pattern of information, attitude or opinion is anticipated. Responses to open-ended questions are usually recorded verbatim without summarizing or omission. Sufficient space for writing should be provided in the questionnaire for a complete and accurate record of the responses presented. Open-ended questions are further subdivided into three categories: basic open-ended questions, probing questions and clarifying questions.

Basic open-ended questions

Basic open-ended questions are used when the respondent's opinions or views are sought at some length. They enable the researcher to detect trends and attitudes which normally would not come to light. These questions often begin with words such as What, Why, How, etc. For example: What do you particularly like about Wella shampoo? Why did you say you would not buy it when it is available in the market?

Probing questions

At times, researchers may not be satisfied to obtain only the first answer given to an open-ended question. Probing questions are used as a standard technique to follow up a basic open-ended question. They are intended to urge a fuller and more complete response than was given earlier. Many ideas which the respondents thinks of, even though he or she does not pour them all out instantly, may then be obtained through a probing question. For example: What do you particularly like about Wella shampoo? PROBE: What else?

Effective probing requires high-level interviewing skills. While it is essential for the interviewer to continue probing until he is satisfied that the respondent truly has nothing more to offer, the interviewer should refrain from putting words into the respondent's mouth. It is essential that the probing question should not influence the respondent's replies any more than the original open-ended question did. Typical probing questions are: What else? Anything else? Are there any others? Probing should only be exercised when specific instructions to do so are printed in the questionnaire. [*Note*: Instructions for the interviewer, including probing instructions, are usually printed in capital letters.]

Clarifying questions

A clarifying question, as its name suggests, seeks to clarify or obtain a clearer explanation from the respondent, when the responses given are considered to be vague or too general. For example: In what way would you say it is too oily? What exactly do you mean by saying that this brand name is difficult to remember?

Advantages of open-ended questions

- It does not restrict the respondent's response, the widest scope of response can thus be attained.
- It is appropriate where the range of possible responses is broad, or when a fairly comprehensive set of possible responses cannot be predetermined.
- It is less subject to interviewer bias.
- Its responses are recorded verbatim, thus making it possible to insert relevant *direct quotes* to bring realism and life to the written report.

Disadvantages of open-ended questions

- The interviewer may not record the responses at verbatim, but instead give a summary of them. The recorded information thus combines the respondent's ideas with the interviewer's ideas, and in so doing the essential richness of the respondent's real ideas will be lost.
- Since the responses offered by respondents differ, it is difficult to categorize and summarize the responses given. An editor is required to scan a sample of responses in order to classify them into a given scheme; later all the responses are coded according to the classification scheme.
- The respondent cannot be bothered telling the interviewer all his or her ideas. He or she gives out just one or some of his or her ideas and thinks that is enough. Also, the interviewer is in a hurry to end the interview and does not push the respondent to go on giving ideas. Under these circumstances, the percentage of respondents offering any particular idea on an issue (e.g., reasons for quitting smoking; likes about a particular brand of hair shampoo) is far smaller than the percentage who actually believe that idea or view. The open response questioning system is therefore not suitable for quantitative research.
- In the event that open-ended questions are used too often, the respondent may become frustrated and annoyed, and eventually decide to terminate the interview, or ignore the postal questionnaire.
- An open-ended question is inappropriate for self-administered questionnaire since people tend to write more briefly than they speak. Also, there is a possibility of the respondent's illegible handwriting.

Closed-ended questions

A closed-ended or checklist question, as its name suggests, is one where a predetermined list of alternate responses is presented to the respondent for checking the appropriate one(s). This list of alternate responses is sometimes printed on a showcard for respondent's to view or is read out to the respondent as part of the question.

How satisfied or dissatisfied are you with the overall services provided by the MRT in Singapore? Would you say that you are . . . (READ OUT)?

Very satisfied 1
Satisfied 2
Neither satisfied nor dissatisfied . . . 3
Dissatisfied 4
Very dissatisfied 5

A code or number is attached alongside each alternate response in the questionnaire and all that the interviewer (or the respondent in the case of a self-administered questionnaire) needs to do is to circle the code which corresponds to the response given.

Checklist questions are appropriate when the range of alternate responses is limited, or when the majority of responses can be foreseen. A checklist question falls into one of two categories: dichotomous question and multiple-choice question.

Dichotomous questions

A dichotomous question, the simplest of all types of questions, contains two (usually opposing) alternatives in the predetermined list of responses. Typical examples are *yes-no, true-false, agree-disagree, like-dislike, fair-unfair* and so on. This type of question is favoured for its simplicity in administration. A third (neutral) category of response designated as *no opinion, don't know, neither, both*, etc., may be added to the checklist of responses. Some researchers, however, are reluctant to provide this neutral category as they fear the respondent may choose to remain non-committal to the question asked.

Without neutral response:

Do you have a bank account?
Yes 1
No 2

With neutral response:

Is it likely that your household will purchase a personal computer in the next six months?
Yes 1
No 2
Not sure 3

A major pitfall of dichotomous question is that very often they fail to fulfil marketing data requirements. Furthermore, limiting the respondent to polarized responses only can give rise to measurement errors.

Multiple-choice questions

As opposed to dichotomous question, a multiple-choice question offers more than two responses (not counting the neutral response) in the predetermined list of alternate responses. There are two categories of multiple-choice questions: *single-coded question* and *multi-coded question*. In a single-coded question, the respondent is permitted to check one and only one response. A multi-coded question, on the contrary, allows the respondent to select as many responses that are applicable.

Single-coded question:

Can you please tell me how much an average, your household spend on water, electricity and gas in a month?
Would you say it is . . . .
(READ OUT)?
Less than $50 1
Between $50 and $99 2
Between $100 and $149 3
Between $150 and $199 4
$200 or more 5

[*Note*: In a single-coded question, the responses provided in the checklist must be both mutually exclusive and collectively comprehensive.]

Multi-coded question:

Which brand, or brands, of plaster listed in this card does your household have?
(SHOW CARD)
Elastoplast 1
Handyplast 2
Currad 3
Band-Aid 4
Johnsonplast 5
B B Band 6
Others (Specify _____) . 7

It is common practice to include an *Others* category in the checklist to cater for responses which do not fall into any of the categories listed earlier.

Advantages of closed-ended questions

Closed-ended questions overcome many of the disadvantages associated with open-ended questions. Specifically, the main advantages of a closed-ended question are:

- It necessitates all respondents to reply in a uniform manner and in standard wording. Its standard set of alternative responses allows comparability of responses, which facilitates coding, tabulating and interpreting the data.
- It is easier to administer to the extent that a less skilled interviewer may be engaged.
- The checklist of responses helps reduce difficulty in memory-recall that respondents might encounter in responding to open-ended questions.
- It is most suited for self-administered questionnaire.

- It requires shorter interviewing time
- It is faster for data tabulation.

Disadvantages of closed-ended questions

- It is time-consuming to prepare the checklist of responses. Exploratory studies are often carried out as an initial step to provide the required inputs.
- A long checklist of responses can cause confusion to the respondent.
- The checklist of responses may not be comprehensive.
- The respondent cannot freely express himself, and often detailed information is missed.
- The order in which the alternate responses appear in the checklist can create what is called the position bias. Past studies have shown that responses which appear at the top or bottom of the checklist are more likely to be mentioned. This order (or position) bias can be overcome by rotating the order of responses in the checklist for different sets of questionnaires.

Scaling questions

In recent years, the academic world has spent considerable amount of time reviewing questions where opinions, attitudes and other subjective evidences can be fruitfully compiled. These are special types of closed-ended questions and in view of their inherent features, deserve some mention.

Behavioural/attitudinal questions

Such questions aim to measure the degree of feelings, interests, convictions and intentions. The respondent is presented with a scale from one end of a spectrum to the other to indicate his response. Population subgroups who are favourably inclined towards a product, service or issue can hence be identified.

Buying-intent questions

Such questions come closest to evaluating the sales potential. Here, the respondent is presumed to have already possessed sufficient knowledge (e.g. price, size, colour etc.) of the product in order to form an intelligent opinion about buying interest.

Which one of the statements in the showcard best describes how interested you would be in buying this product?

(SHOWCARD)

I definitely would buy 1
I probably would buy 2
I might or might not buy 3
I probably would not buy 4
I definitely would not buy 5

Agree/disagree questions

This category of questions seeks to measure the relative weight of attitudinal response. The respondent is asked of the extent he agrees or disagrees with a particular statement which is read out to him or her.

I have here a list of statements regarding quality control circles (QCC). When I read out each statement, can you please tell me whether you agree or disagree with it? PROBE: Strongly/Somewhat

(READ OUT STATEMENT ONE BY ONE)

QCC is a waste of time.
Strongly agree 1
Somewhat agree 2
Neither agree nor disagree 3
Somewhat disagree 4
Strongly disagree 5

QCC can help boost teamwork.
Strongly agree 1
Somewhat agree 2
Neither agree nor disagree 3
Somewhat disagree 4
Strongly disagree 5

When analysing such data, one must realize that disagreement with a negative statement does not necessarily mean agreement with its opposite (i.e. positive) statement, and vice versa.

Preference questions

These questions are used to establish direct comparison between products or services. Here, the respondent is asked to indicate his preference for products or services based on his or her own impressions of them.

Would you please tell me which brand of petrol you prefer in terms of . . . (READ OUT THE ATTRIBUTES IN SHOWCARD ONE BY ONE)?

	BP	Caltex	Esso	Mobil	Shell
a. most miles per litre	☐	☐	☐	☐	☐
b. best engine power	☐	☐	☐	☐	☐
c. best engine protection	☐	☐	☐	☐	☐
d. keeping engines cleanest	☐	☐	☐	☐	☐
e. reducing air pollution best	☐	☐	☐	☐	☐

Preference question has an obvious weakness: it fails to indicate the intensity of preference. When Brand A is preferred over Brand B, for example, it may be that Brand A is wonderful and Brand B horrible; or that Brand A is just the lesser of two evils; or that both brands are good with Brand A being relatively better.

Ranking questions

A preference question is suitable when the study involves only a pair of products/services. When a study involves more than two products/services, ranking questions should be used instead.

Here is a stack of five cards. Each has the name of a major oil company printed on it. Can you please arrange these cards in the order of concern expressed by the oil companies with regard to encouraging motorists to save energy. Place the card in the 1st position (i.e. on top) if it concerns most, and the card in the 5th position (i.e. at the bottom) if it concerns least, etc. RESHUFFLE THE STACK OF CARDS THOROUGHLY BEFORE PASSING IT TO THE RESPONDENT.

ALLOW TIME FOR THE RESPONDENT TO THINK OR TO CHANGE HIS OR HER MIND. CIRCLE THE APPROPRIATE CODES ONLY AFTER FINAL RANKING IS REACHED.

	Most	2nd Most	3rd Most	4th Most	Least
BP	1	2	3	4	5
Esso	1	2	3	4	5
Shell	1	2	3	4	5
Caltex	1	2	3	4	5
Mobil	1	2	3	4	5

Ranking questions share the same pitfall as preference questions in that they fail to indicate the interval measurement between ranked subjects. Furthermore, the task of ranking can quickly become tedious and less accurate if it involves a large number of products/services.

Semantic-differential questions.

A semantic-differential question is one of the most common scaling techniques used in marketing research studies to determine the direction as well as the intensity of the respondent's attitude towards the subject under study. An area of particular use is to establish the *image profiles* of a product, a brand, an advertisement or a company. The respondent is required to evaluate the subject under study by means of ratings offered on a set of monopolar and/or bipolar adjectives.

Examples of monopolar adjectives	*Examples of bipolar adjectives*
High class – Ordinary	High Class – Low class
Sweet – Not sweet	Sweet – Bitter

Please insert a cross 'X' in the appropriate space provided above the broken lines which best describes your opinion of The First National Bank.

Friendly	__:__:__:__:__:__	Unfriendly
Old-fashioned	__:__:__:__:__:__	Modern
Reliable	__:__:__:__:__:__	Unreliable
Secure	__:__:__:__:__:__	Insecure

Profile analysis is often performed for semantic differential questions. Essentially, it involves computing the mean (or median) value assigned to each adjective pair for an object by a specified group of respondents. This profile can then be compared with the profile of another object, or another group.

Constant-sum questions

Constant-sum questions are popularly used in marketing research for its simplicity. The respondent is given a number of points – typically 10 to 100 – to be distributed over the set of alternate responses to reflect the relative magnitude regarding some attitudinal characteristics.

Can you please assign a total number of 100 points across the five oil companies to reflect your relative like/dislike for them?

BP	. . . .	S_1
Caltex	. . . .	S_2
Esso	. . . .	S_3
Mobil	. . . .	S_4
Shell	. . . .	S_5
Total	. . . .	100

Question wording

Wording questions is not as simple a task as it might seem to be. All survey questions must mean the same to both the respondent and the researcher, a task which is by no means easy to accomplish. Alex Gallup, Co-Chairman of The Gallup Organization, has become concerned that the survey research industry may be straying from its fundmentals, specifically the most basic component of survey research: good survey questions. Alex says:

'If you look at the whole discipline, probably the most dramatic area of improvement would be that sampling is more sophisticated than ever before. And certainly computers have helped our industry with the ability to conduct sophisticated analytical procedures. But if there is an area that's been almost ignored by the whole survey research industry, it's question wording.'

Alex Gallup emphasizes the basic concept of the clear expression of meaning when he says:

'A lot of people are far more worried about whether the question is grammatical than they are about whether it communicates. It should be conversational, you love to use language that will be understood by the lowest common denominator. It's not going to hurt a well-educated person to hear a question that is phrased for the least educated person.'

As a medium of communication, words have a variety of meanings as defined in the dictionaries and by different persons as well. Research questions, therefore, must be clearly worded so that they convey the same meaning to the respondent as they do to the researcher; otherwise, research findings would not be homogeneous and relevant. Different words can generate different results. A study was undertaken covering three matched samples of respondents. Each respondent was asked one of the following three questions:

1 Do you think anything *should* be done to make it easier for people to pay consultation or hospital bills?
(82 per cent replied 'Yes')
2 Do you think anything *could* be done to make it easier for people to pay consultation or hospital bills?
(77 per cent replied 'Yes')
3 Do you think anything *might* be done to make it easier for people to pay consultation or hospital bills?
(63 per cent replied 'Yes')

(*Source*: Green, Paul E. and Tull, Donald S. (1988) *Research for Marketing Decisions.* 5th edn, Prentice Hall, New Jersey.)

The above three questions are identical except for one single word – *should, could* and *might*. The results to these questions, at the extreme, are 19 percentage points apart. This finding illustrates the importance of question wording in obtaining information from the respondent. Many experts in survey research generally believe that improving the wording of questions can contribute far more to accuracy than can improvement in sampling.

Use short, simple questions

Survey questions should be short, simple and readily understandable to the respondent. Jargon and technical words should be avoided at all times. Instead of asking 'What is your economic status?', its equivalent 'Are you working, unemployed or retired now?' is preferred.

Likewise, such terms as *martial status, occupation*, etc. should be avoided. As a general rule, survey question must communicate effectively with even the least-educated respondent.

Avoid vague words

To assume that respondents will always understand the question asked of them is a common and serious error. Questions with vague words can invite vague (if not misleading) responses. The question 'Did you go to the cinema frequently?' is vague because the word *frequently* does not specify a fixed or standard time reference. One respondent would regard a *once a week* visit as frequent while another respondent would not. So long as respondents are allowed to exercise their own interpretation of the word *frequently,* confusion and uncertainty in the research results would invariably occur.

Avoid leading questions

A leading question is one which is framed in a manner that invites some expected responses. A leading or loaded question is a major source of bias in question wording, and should not be used in the interview. It does not elicit information, instead it is inclined to suggest to the respondent what the researcher thinks he or she should answer and usually he or she will answer accordingly.

Don't you agree that the Save Energy Campaign is a success?

Yes 1
No 2

The above question induces the respondent to give a *Yes, I do* answer, and is therefore a leading question. A better question would be: 'Do you agree or disagree that the Save Energy Campaign is a success?'

Avoid estimation.

Questions which demand the respondent to compute estimates should be avoided.

How much do you spend on car petrol in a year?

(RECORD IN $)

Yearly expenditure: $ _____

Under normal circumstances, the respondent (i.e. motorist) confronted with such a question would first start thinking of his expenditure on petrol per month and then multiply it by twelve to arrive at the annual estimates of expenditure on petrol. In the process of multiplying, the respondent may inadvertently commit an error without the knowledge of the interviewer. In this instance, it is advisable to ask and record the monthly expenditure, and leave it to the office staff to convert it to annual expenditure.

Avoid double-barrelled questions

A double-barrelled question is one which combines two or more distinct questions into one single question.

How do you like hot and crispy pizza?

Like it very much 1
Like it somewhat 2
Don't like it at all 3

The above question is double-barrelled because a respondent who likes hot pizza may loathe crispy pizza and vice versa. In this case he or she would be confused and undecided as to which answer he or she should offer. A double-barrelled question should rightfully be split into separate questions.

Any attempt to use double-barrelled questions to save cost and time will always turn out to be false economy.

Avoid presumptuous questions

A presumptuous question is one which makes assumptions on the respondent.

How many cigarettes do you smoke a day?

(*RECORD NUMBER OF CIGARETTES*)

No. of Cigarettes:_____

The above question is a framed one because it assumes that the respondent is currently a smoker. A lapsed smoker should not be asked to answer this question lest he or she might be caused to give an answer which relates to habits during his or her smoking days. Presumptuous questions can be avoided by asking a *filter question* preceding it (see example below).

Do you smoke nowadays?

Yes 1
No . . . . 2 (GO TO Q5)
IF YES

How many cigarettes do you smoke a day?

(*RECORD NUMBER OF CIGARETTES*)

No. of Cigarettes:_____

Use split-ballot technique

This technique is used whenever it is required to analyse the results of two different words used in two separate questionnaires. Each questionnaire is tested on half the respondents.

Many experiments and studies were carried out to illustrate the effects caused by question wording. Some of these studies are reproduced below.

1 *Presenting only one alternative.* Two questions, A and B, each comprising one alternative only, were presented to two independent groups of respondents:

A: Do you think the United States should allow public speeches against democracy?
B: Do you think the United States should forbid public speeches against democracy?

These two questions are identical except for one opposing word. The results obtained were remarkably different as shown below:

Question A
Should allow 21%
Should not allow 62%
No opinion 17%

Question B
Should not forbid 39%
Should forbid 46%
No opinion 15%

(*Source*: Donald Rugg [1941] Experiments in Wording Questions: 11. *Public Opinion Quarterly*, **5**, March, pp. 91–2.)

Perhaps a neutrally-phrased question in the form of 'Do you think the United States should allow or forbid public speeches against democracy?' would be preferred.

2 *Presenting more than one alternative – token vs. substantive.* Consider the question: 'Are you in favour of giving special priority to buses in the rush hour?' This question was reworded in two different ways as follows:

With token alternative: 'Are you in favour of giving special priority to buses in the rush hour OR not?'

or

with substantive alternative: 'Are you in favour of giving special priority to buses in the rush hour OR should cars have just as much priority as buses?'

Somewhat differing results were obtained from this experiment:

	Token alternative (% said Yes)	Substantive alternative (% said Yes)
All respondents	69	55
Males	74	66
Females	65	49
Car owners	66	54
Non-car owners	73	55

(*Source*: Graham Kalton [1977] Martin Collins and Lindsay Brook Methodological Working Paper No. 7. November.)

3 *Inclusion of* neutral response *category.* The following two differently worded questions were presented to two matched samples of respondents:

A (without neutral response alternative): 'Do you think that giving buses priority at traffic signals would increase OR decrease traffic?'

B (with neutral response alternative): 'Do you think that giving buses priority at traffic signals would increase OR decrease, OR would it make no difference to traffic congestion?'

Somewhat differing results were obtained and tabulated as follows:

Response	Without neutral	With neutral
All respondents who said would increase OR decrease traffic	53%	37%
Respondents who said would increase traffic	33%	25%
Respondents who said would decrease traffic	20%	12%
Respondents who gave neutral answer	29%	47%
Respondents who were unable to answer	18%	16%

(*Source*: Graham Kalton [1977] Martin Collins and Lindsay Brook Methodological Working Paper No. 7. November.)

4 *Inclusion of no opinion option.* The following two differently worded questions were presented to two matched samples of respondents:

A (without *no opinion* option):'Do you think special bus lanes are a good thing OR a bad thing?'

B (with *no opinion* option):'Do you have an opinion as to whether special bus lanes are a good thing OR a bad thing?'

Again, somewhat differing results of the above experiment were:

	Without 'no opinion' option (% said Yes)	With 'no opinion' option (% said Yes)
All Respondents	85	74
Males	88	81
Females	82	67

(*Source*: Graham Kalton (1977) Martin Collins and Lindsay Brook Methodological Working Paper No. 7. November.)

Questions sequence

Ensuring that the survey questions are properly worded is but one step towards producing a sound questionnaire. Of equal importance is the decision on the sequence of questions. Such a decision specifies the order of questions within each section of the questionnaire as well as the order of sections. Sequence of questions can influence the respondent's answers and is a frequent source of error in survey undertaking. Some general principles to be observed in the sequencing of questions are provided.

The earlier questions should be less complex, less sensitive, easy to answer and unbiased towards the answers that follow. A few openers for a *Yes-No* answer can help in injecting the respondent's confidence that it is within his capacity to participate in the study. Such opening questions may not be related to the subject of study, but are usually good starters. A smooth start helps set the tone for the remaining part of the interview, establishing a rapport effect that gains trust and enhances willingness to participate fully in the interviewing process.

Question Sequence
Things to Remember

- Begin with simple/easy question
- Smooth/logical transition of topics
- Place general question first
- Place sensitive/embarrasing question last

Ask general questions first. General (broad) questions should always precede the specific (narrow) ones. Known as the *funnel approach*, this principle stipulates that question sequencing should begin with broad questions and progressively limit its scope to narrow questions. It minimizes the likelihood of answering a general question which is biased towards the answer he or she gave earlier to a specific question.

Illustrative example 1

A: 'What improvements to your car would you like to have?'
B: 'How many miles per litre does your car get?'

If Question B precedes Question A, *economy* would be mentioned more frequently in Question A than it would be when the order of the two questions were reversed.

The transition from one topic to another should be smooth and logical. Questions covering one common topic (e.g. buying habits) should be grouped together.

Shifting unnecessarily among topics (e.g. brand preference, perception) may disrupt the thinking process, reduce rapport and cause confusion to the respondents.

Sensitive or embarrassing questions should be placed last. Only after good interviewer-interviewee rapport has been established would the respondent be less apt to object to such questions. In the event that the respondent refused to co-operate at this stage of the interview, the researcher is at least satisfied that most of the essential issues have been addressed.

As a general rule, classification questions (e.g. those on age, sex, education, income and marital status) should be left to the end of the interview. An exception to this rule is when quota sampling is used. Here, classification data is asked first in order to check the eligibility of respondents. When classification data is sought, the interviewer should explain its purpose because respondents may wonder why it is necessary to provide their personal particulars to the interviewer. The interviewer should assure the respondents that the information will be treated with utmost confidentiality. To avoid irritating the respondent, classification questions which are not absolutely essential should be avoided at all costs.

Randomized response technique

Sensitive and embarrassing questions such as 'Have you ever been involved in premarital sex?' or 'Do you smoke marijuana nowadays?' can rarely elicit frank replies from the respondent.

A special interviewing device has been developed to handle such questions. Called the randomized response technique, it essentially involves presenting the respondent with two questions, one being the sensitive question under study and the other an innocuous or non-sensitive question. The respondent answers only one of the two questions, to be determined by the outcome of the flipping of a coin, or based on whether his or her identity card number is odd or even, or in some other random manner with a *Yes* or *No* response. The respondent does not tell the interviewer which question he or she answered. As the interviewer does not know which of the two questions is being answered by the respondent, under this circumstance the respondent is more willing to put forward a truthful answer.

Illustrative example 2:

Marijuana tracking study

In a national study to estimate the extent of marijuana smokers, a random sample of 1,000 respondents were interviewed. Each respondent was presented with a showcard containing the two questions:

A: 'Is the last digit of your birth certificate a six?'

B: 'Do you smoke marijuana nowadays?'

The respondent was asked to flip a coin: If the outcome was a head, he or she answered Question A; and if it was a tail; he or she answered Question B. The respondent should not inform the interviewer which question he was to answer.

Seventy-five respondents gave *Yes* answers while the remaining 925 gave *No* answers. To arrive at the incidence of marijuana smokers, we proceed with the following calculations:

	All respondents	Answered Question A	Answered Question B
Sample size	1,000	X_1	X_2
Yes answers	75	Y_1	Y_2

If the coin is unbiased:

$$X_1 = 1,000 \times P \text{ (Head)} = 500$$
$$X_2 = 1,000 \times P \text{ (Tail)} = 500$$

Furthermore

$$Y_1 = 500 \times P \text{ (last digit of birth certificate is a 6)}$$
$$= 500 \times 1/10$$
$$= 50$$

Therefore $Y_2 = 75 - Y_1 = 25$.

Thus out of an estimated number of $X_2 = 500$ respondents who answered Question B (i.e. sensitive question), twenty-five offered *Yes* replies. The incidence of marijuana smokers is therefore $25/500 = 5$ per cent.

Questionnaire layout

The physical layout of a questionnaire is important for a number of reasons:

● To promote fluent presentation of questions to the respondent (in personal and telephone interview) or smooth completion of questionnaire by the respondent (in postal survey).

- To facilitate full and accurate recording of responses.
- To make the interview more interesting and stimulating.
- To facilitate speedy tabulation of data.

Some measures which can help achieve the above objectives are:

1 *Provide sufficient space.* Space is one criterion of good layout, it is unwise to design a *crammed* questionnaire which is difficult for the interviewer/mail respondent to identify the instructions, and which in turn lead to errors in questioning and recording. Sometimes, a researcher designs a crammed questionnaire because he or she fears that the large number of pages may prevent the respondent from wanting to participate in the study. Obsessive saving of space in questionnaire layout can create adverse effects and should be discouraged.

2 *Use prominent print for instructions.* A questionnaire usually contains survey questions (and their corresponding checklists of responses) and instructions to the interviewers/postal respondents. There must be a clear distinction between survey question and instruction. A sensible rule is to print instructions in bold and capital letters.

3 *Do not split the same question over two pages.* All parts of a question should preferably appear on the same page. To do otherwise would present difficulty in

questionnaire completion and in turn give rise to errors. Likewise, each section of a questionnaire should start on a new page.

4 *Use filtered questions.* Filtered questions are meant to be asked of a specific group of respondents only. The filtered instruction '*Go to QX,*' is shown on the right-hand side of the response:

```
8 a. Have you ever seen
      this slogan before?
   Yes. . . . . . . . . . . . . . . 1
   No. . . . . . . . . . . . . . . 2 GO TO Q9
   IF YES
   b. Where did you see the
      advertisement with this
      slogan?
      (SHOW CARD)
   From newspaper . . . . 1
   From television . . . . . 2
   From poster . . . . . . . 3
   From others (specify) . 4
9 ASK ALL
   Does your household own a car?
   Yes . . . . . . . . . . . . . . 1
   No . . . . . . . . . . . . . . 2
```

Thus Question 8b is conditional upon the response to its preceding question (i.e. Question 8a). *Skipping* questions may also depend on the type of respondents being interviewed, and on whether a certain question or section of questions is relevant to certain types of respondents:

```
ASK THOSE WHO ARE WORKING

Can you please tell me for whom do
you work? Are you working in
(READ OUT)
A government ministry/dept . . . . . . 1
A statutory board . . . . . . . . . . . . 2
A public limited company . . . . . . . 3
A private limited company . . . . . . . 4
Others (specify) . . . . . . . . . . . . . 5
```

Questionnaire Layout

Guidelines

- Provide sufficient space
- Be consistent in positioning questions
- Use prominent print for instructions
- Do not split one question over two pages
- Use filtered questions

5 *Insert running prompt when necessary.* Sometimes respondents need to be directed to answer in a certain way. Otherwise, if they were asked the question: 'About how often do you use hair tonic?' some respondents would give the specific day of the week ('almost every Saturday'), others would say 'not very often' etc. To standardize the answers given, it will be appropriate to have a forced-choice question, followed by running prompts. However, the predetermined checklist of responses should not be used as prompts unless the instruction *READ OUT* is clearly indicated:

About how often do you use hair tonic?
Do you normally use it . . . (READ OUT)

Three times or more a week 1
Twice a week 2
Once a week 3
Once every two weeks 4
Once every three weeks 5
Once a month 6
Less often 7
Never 8

Another way of dealing with forced-choice question is to prepare a prompt card containing the checklist of responses, to be read out or shown to the respondent to elicit the appropriate answer(s).

6 *Single-coded question.*

What would you say about the colour of the shampoo? Would you say the colour is . . . (READ OUT)

Very bright 1
Somewhat bright 2
Somewhat dull 3
Very dull 4

---

7 *Multi-coded question.*

Which things do you sometimes use when you set your hair at home?
(SHOW CARD)

Setting lotion 1
Ordinary rollers/curlers 2
Heated rollers 3
Hand-held hair dryer 4
Portable hair dryer 5
Curling tongs 6
Others (specify) 7

---

8 *Use broken lines for a battery question.* When a question embraces a long battery of attitudinal or behavioural statements/items, the interviewer may inadvertently record the response against the wrong item. This risk can be reduced if broken lines are provided separating the long battery into groups with three of four statements/items in each groups:

I have in this card a list of statements about frozen food. When I read out each statement, can you please indicate whether you agree of disagree with it.

	Agree	Disagree	No opinion
Frozen food saves time	1	2	3
Frozen food can be just as nutritious as fresh food	1	2	3
Frozen food is cheaper	1	2	3
I buy frozen food to use keep for emergency use	1	2	3
Frozen food should not be kept in a freezer for more than two weeks	1	2	3
I am worried that the frozen food I buy may not be fresh	1	2	3

- -

I buy frozen food only when fresh food is not available	1	2	3
Frozen food contains a lot of preservatives and other chemicals	1	2	3
Most of my friends buy frozen food nowadays	1	2	3

For a precoded question, it should be made explicitly clear to both interviewer and respondent whether one answer or more than one answer is acceptable. Instructions such as *PLEASE TICK ONLY ONE ANSWER* or *PLEASE TICK ALL ANSWERS THAT APPLY* should be highlighted in bold typeface in the questionnaire:

Which of these credit or charge cards do you have now?

(PLEASE TICK ALL ANSWERS THAT APPLY)

Visa 1
Diners 2
Master Charge 3
American Express 4
Others (Specify _____) 5

Which one of the following credit or charge cards do you use most often nowadays?

(PLEASE TICK ONLY ONE ANSWER)

Visa 1
Diners 2
Master Charge 3
American Express 4
Others (Specify_____) 5

In the case of verbatim responses, a generous amount of writing space should be provided. It is rather frustrating for interviewers to have too little space to record answers. For self-administered

questionnaires a customary practice is to print the instruction *PLEASE RECORD ANSWERS FULLY BELOW*.

What do you particularly like about POSB?
    (PLEASE RECORD ANSWERS FULLY BELOW).

Finally, the layout and printing of a questionnaire should be such that editing and coding of data can proceed smoothly. Code numbers should stand out clearly for the convenience of key-punch operators. Bad questionnaire layout slows down data entry, which is an expensive undertaking. A common convention is to position the codes under a separate column from which the data is to be punched:

Now thinking of the T-shirt you last bought, what type of shop did you buy if from?
(SHOW CARD)

Roadside stall 1
General clothing store 2
Departmental store 3
Sports shop 4
Chinese emporium 5
Others (Specify _____) 6

9 *Self-administered questionnaires.* These are administered by the respondent without the assistance of an interviewer. A postal questionnaire is a typical example of a self-administered questionnaire. The layout requirements for self-administered questionnaire parallel those for interviewer-administered forms, but greater

attention is needed to make the self-administered questionnaire and its accompanying document look more attractive and straightforward.

The layout and physical appearance of a self-administered questionnaire are of crucial importance and can affect the level and accuracy of response. An attractive questionnaire helps encourage a response considerably. Some characteristics of a self-administered questionnaire are listed below.

- The paper should be of good quality and pleasant-looking. A postal questionnaire with good appearance gives the impression that the researcher cares about standards.
- The postal questionnaire should be printed, not cyclostyled.
- The size of the postal questionnaire should not appear unusually big to cause inconvenience in handling. A six-page postal questionnaire of $8\frac{1}{2} \times 11$ inches is normally considered the upper limit in length.
- Each question should be numbered, making it easier for editing, coding and tabulating responses.
- It is helpful to use the arrow sign to direct respondents to proceed to the next question.
- The covering letter should be brief but include the essential points: sponsor of the research, subject of the research and what the respondents are required to do.
- The questionnaire may contain coloured pages to distinguish general instruction page from question page(s).

- In the event that a postal questionnaire runs into several pages, it is advisable to present it in a booklet form rather than many sheets of paper clipped or stapled together. A booklet is easier to handle and does not tear easily.
- It is usual to provide boxes for respondents to record their answers by placing a tick rather than following the interviewer's convention of circling codes. Some respondents do not understand what code numbers are meant for: placing ticks in boxes in probably less confusing and is a familiar process:

Which of these publications do you read regularly?

(PLEASE TICK BOXES THAT APPLY)

Time Magazine . . . .☐
Newsweek . . . .☐
Readers' Digest . . . .☐
Asia Magazine . . . .☐
Far Eastern Economic Review . . . . . .☐
Asian Wall Street Journal . . . .☐
Others (Specify _____)☐

It is helpful to include some notes at the end of the mail questionnaire – a request to respondents to recheck their responses, an invitation to comment on the subject of study, a message of thanks and a plea for a prompt return of the completed questionnaire.

Respondents may be put off from completing the mail questionnaire if he or she discovers that the questions run up to number 72. Psychologically, he or she reckons that there are too many questions and time-consuming to fill in the questionnaire. An advisable thing to do would be to number questions within unitary portions of the questionnaire, returning to 1 for the first question of each unitary portion. This will avoid using high numbers in a long questionnaire.

Self-Administered Questionnaire
Guidelines

- Paper be good quality
- Typeset (not cyclostyled)
- Size not unduly large
- Introduction should be brief
- Coloured pages for distinction
- Provide "Ticking off" boxes
- Number questions within sections

Questionnaire pretest

Hardly would a questionnaire be ready for fieldwork without a pretest. A questionnaire pretest is a virtual necessity. During the pretest, a questionnaire may be found lengthy, its words vague, ambiguous or incomplete. This process is exceedingly useful and leads to rephrasing of biased questions. The question sequence or the style of composition may need to be altered as well. Making a mistake with say twenty or so respondents in a questionnaire pretest can avoid the potential disaster of administering an invalid questionnaire to a much larger sample of respondents.

A further pretest is often recommended should the previous pretest suggest that the test questionnaire needs to undergo extensive changes. The number of pretests needed will depend on the accuracy required in the results, and the time, cost as well as other resources available.

The first pretest is best conducted using the personal interviewing technique, even if the study is to be administered by a different method of data collection. Here, only the best interviewers are assigned to pretest work because they can detect areas of confusion as well as probe into the nature of such confusion.

Where the survey is to be executed by telephone interviewing or mail survey, the pretest questionnaire should further be tested using the intended method of data collection. This move seeks to explore whether the intended data collection method is suitable, and to uncover any weakness that may exist. A questionnaire pretest does not require a reasonably large sample – about tenty interviews are considered adequate. Also, a representative sample is not absolutely necessary, but it is advisable to have a sample which includes the various population subgroups under study, though their correct proportions are not required.

The benefits of questionnaire pretest are summarized below:

- To uncover biased or ambiguous questions.
- To assess the logical sequence of questions.
- To assess the efficiency of questionnaire layout.
- To modify interviewers' manual of instructions.
- To review the suitability of the intended data collection method.
- To assess response rate.
- To estimate the duration needed for questionnaire completion.
- To review data collection method.
- To devise a classification scheme for open-ended responses.

Questionnaire finalization

The pretest provides the researcher with the final opportunity to introduce changes and revisions in the questionnaire before administering it in the field for survey research. Usually a questionnaire goes through several pretests. The exact number of pretests required will depend on the researcher's and client's judgement. After both parties agree that the desired information is being collected in an unbiased manner, and that no obvious flaws in design and wording are detected, the questionnaire is finalized and ready for use.

The introduction section ▬▬

This beginning section of a questionnaire is intended for the interviewer to introduce him or herself by name to the potential respondent, as well as to acquaint the latter with the research company that is undertaking the research study. Very often, the broad objective of the research is stated in this introduction section. It is also a tool for the interviewer to establish rapport with the respondent, and to elicit the latter's cooperation and assistance in responding to the survey.

Survey Questionnaire

Main Sections

- The Introduction
- The Body
- The Classification Section
- The Administration Section

Illustrative example 3

Good morning/afternoon/evening. My name is . . . . (SHOW I.C.) from WTQ Research Pte Ltd. This is a market research company which conducts surveys of all kinds in Singapore. Today, we are talking to people about The New Paper. The research purpose is to know who read The New Paper and how they read it. I will be grateful if you will help by answering some questions.

The body section ▬▬▬▬

It is in this section that most, if not all, of the information needed to meet the research objectives is included in the form of survey questions. This is likely to be the longest section of the questionnaire.

Question Wording

Guidelines

- Use short, simple questions
- Avoid vague words
- Avoid leading questions
- Avoid estimation
- Avoid double–barrelled questions
- Avoid presumptuous questions

Filter Question

An Example

Q1. Do you smoke nowadays?
　　　　Yes . . . . . 1 (Smokers)
If no,　　No. 2

Q2. Have you ever smoked before?
　　　　Yes . . . . . 1 (Lapsed smokers)
　　　　No. . . . . . 2 (Non-smokers)

Ask if smokers
Q3. On an average day, how many cigarettes do you smoke nowadays?
Q4. How long ago did you start smoking?

Ask if lapsed smokers
Q5. How long ago did you stop smoking?
Q6. What are your reason(s) for stopping smoking?

Ask if non–smokers
Q7. If your friend happens to smoke in a smoking-free area, would you ask him/her to stop smoking?

Illustrative example 4:

Instant coffee market study

1 Did you drink Instant Coffee in past week?

　　Yes 1
　　No 2

ASK IF DRINKERS

2 Which one of the following brands of Instant Coffee do you consume MOST OFTEN nowadays?

　　Nescafe 1
　　Maxwell House 2
　　Indocafe 3
　　Boncafe 4
　　Blueorient 5
　　Etc.

3 Do you drink Instant Coffee during breakfast?

　　Yes 1
　　No 2

4 From which type of shop do you usually buy Instant Coffee for home consumption?

　　Provision shop 1
　　Supermarket 2
　　Others 3

5 When was the last time you bought Instant Coffee for home consumption?

　　A week or less ago 1
　　8 days – 4 weeks ago 2
　　1–3 months ago 3
　　Longer ago 4
　　Don't know/Can't remember　5

ASK IF NON-DRINKERS

6 a. Have you ever drunk Instant Coffee regularly before?

　　Yes 1
　　No 2

IF YES (i.e. Lapsed Drinkers)

b What are the reasons for not drinking Instant Coffee nowadays? (PROBE: Any other reasons?) _____

IF NO (i.e. Never Drinkers)

c What are the reasons for never drinking Instant Coffee? (PROBE: Any other reasons?) _____

ASK ALL

7 Do you agree or disagree that 'Instant Coffee is nutritious'?

    Agree. 1
    Disagree 2

8 Do you agree or disagree that 'Instant Coffee is thirst-quenching'?

    Agree. 1
    Disagree 2

9 Do you agree or disagree that Instant Coffee is quick to serve'?

    Agree. 1
    Disagree 2

The classification section ▬▬

This section includes questions on the demographic, economic and social characteristics of the respondent.

Illustrative example 5

RECORD SEX   Male 1
                 Female 2

RECORD RACE   Chinese 1
                 Malay 2
                 Indians 3
                 Others 4

(SHOWCARD 23)

Please show me on this card which age group you fall in?

    Below 20 years 1
    20 to 29 years 2

30 to 39 years 3
40 to 49 years 4
50 years and over 5

The administration section ▬▬

This section is intended to record information needed to exercise the control of the collection of data and to manage the interviewer. It contains the name of the interviewer and the time and date the interviews were conducted. It also contains the name, address and telephone number of the respondent to facilitate subsequent recall by the field supervisor.

Illustrative example 6

Interviewer's Name   : . . . .
Interviewer Date   : . . . .
Interviewer Time   : . . . .
                     (Started) (Ended)
Respondent's Name   : . . . .
Respondent's Address : . . . .
Respondent's Tel. No. : . . . .

A questionable questionnaire _____

Suppose a beer manufacturer prepared the following survey questionnaire for use to interview beer-drinkers. What do you think of this questionnaire?

Have you ever got drunk?

This is a personal question. A questionnaire should never begin with such a question as it would cause refusal, non-response.

What is your annual income to the nearest dollar?

People don't necessarily know their income to the nearest dollar, nor do they want to reveal their income to the detail requested.

Are you a heavy or a light beer-drinker?

How do you define heavy versus light beer-drinkers? It is risky to leave the definition to the respondent.

How much beer did you drink in March last year?

Can the respondent recall how much beer he or she drank then?

How many beer advertisements did you see on television in the month of March last year?

Again, can the respondent remember this?

Do you think it's right to buy a foreign beer brand and put our own people out of employment?

This is a loaded question, forcing a 'NO' answer.

Question Wording
Some common errors

Double–barrelled question
Wrongly combine two or more questions into one single question.

Examples
Q. Do you think Coke has the right level of *carbonation* and *sweetness*?
Q. Do you think menthol candy is *good* and *necessary* for your throat?

The technique of designing a good questionnaire is more an art than a science. It requires constant practices and observation before such an art is developed. The following is a set of useful guidelines to observe for becoming a good designer of a questionnaire:

- Draft the questionnaire YOURSELF.
- Apply the draft questionnaire to YOURSELF.
- Apply the draft questionnaire to OTHERS.
- Enjoy discovering flaws/mistakes in questionnaires.
- Amend the questionnaire YOURSELF.
- Remember flaws/mistakes made in questionnaire.
- Enjoy studying other people's questionnaires.
- Criticize other people's questionnaires.

Semantic confusion

The misunderstanding of questions by respondents often can be humorous. Consider the following cases of misunderstandings:

1 During advertising research for a disinfectant, the copy showed a housewife referring to the product as a 'bathroom sanitizer'. The housewife said: 'Yes, I'm certainly for that. I think we do need sanity in the bathroom.'
2 In a consumer survey for a new detergent, the question concerned locations of use of detergents within the home. A specific reference was to 'germ-ridden areas'. 'I want a germ-ridden kitchen,' one woman said to the interviewer. 'What do you mean by that?' dutifully probed the interviewer. 'Well, I want to be ridden of all my germs.'
3 An insecticide marketer wished to learn the meaning attached to the term 'residual insecticide'. They found out that the term not only meant what they always thought it meant but also meant:

'has no residual'
'for insects that reside'
'more powerful'
'powdered form'

Research can be fun. (*Source*: Lee Adler [1966] Confessions of an Interview Reader. *Journal of Marketing Research*, May, 1194–5.)

Observational forms

Data collection forms for use in observational research studies are generally much easier to design than questionnaires. Since observation eliminates the process of questioning and answering, the design problems associated with the control of non-sampling errors in direct questioning will not exist.

In an exploratory study situation, observers are required to record a variety of the subject's behaviour that seems significant. In this case, observational forms will be quite simple to design and may contain relatively few structured questions and instructions. In situations other than exploratory research, the researcher may be interested in specific behaviour and so the observer will be expected to monitor explicitly those specific events. This will call for numerous structured questions and instructions in the data collection forms. An observational form which follows closely the *structured* questionnaire format will permit quantitative analysis of data. If such a form is used, the observer must be clearly instructed on the types of observations that need to be recorded, and the actual manner in which these observations are to be measured. If the observational form follows closely the design of an unstructured questionnaire, data analysis will only be interpretative and qualitative in nature.

An observed event can be recorded in a multitude of ways. When watching a customer makes a talcum powder purchase, for example, an observer might record any one of the following:

Checklist for Observational Forms

Who is to be observed?
(e.g. purchasers, shoppers, onlookers, couples, children, etc)
What is to be observed and recorded?
(e.g. brand purchased, size, brand considered but rejected, etc)
When is observation made?
(e.g. days of week, hours, time of purchase, etc)
Where is observation made?
(e.g. kind of store, location, etc)

Figure 6.3 *Checklist for observational forms*

- The person purchased one tin of talcum powder.
- The young lady purchased one tin of talcum powder.
- The young lady purchased one tin of Amami talcum powder.
- The young lady purchased one tin of blue Amami talcum powder.
- After consulting with her shopping companion, the young lady purchased a tin of blue Amami talcum powder.
- Some other ways.

Variations to the above can be endless, such as recording the type and name of product, the type and location of the store where behaviour was observed, etc. It is obvious, therefore, that the researcher must determine in advance what aspects of the observed behaviour are relevant for recording purposes. A suggested checklist is provided in Figure 6.3.

Review questions

6.1 What is a questionnaire?

6.2 Name and describe an orderly series of steps in developing a questionnaire.

6.3 What are the preliminary decisions that must be made before a questionnaire can be developed?

6.4 What is meant by the degree of structure of a questionnaire? What are the advantages and disadvantages of a structured questionnaire?

6.5 What is meant by the degree of disguise of a questionnaire? What are the advantages and disadvantages of a disguised questionnaire?

6.6 Describe each of the following:
a Structured-undisguised questionnaire.
b Unstructured-undisguised questionnaire.
c Unstructured-disguised questionnaire.
d Structured-disguised questionnaire. Under what circumstances might it be most desirable to use each?

6.7 How does the method of administering a questionnaire affect the content of the questions? And the type of questions to be employed?

6.8 What is an open-ended question? What are its advantages and disadvantages?

6.9 What is a closed-ended question? What are the advantages and disadvantages associated with it?

6.10 What is a dichotomous question? What are its advantages and disadvantages?

6.11 Distinguish between single-choice question and multiple-choice question. Illustrate each with an example.

6.12 What is meant by position bias with respect to closed-ended questions?

6.13 Under what conditions would dichotomous questions be inappropriate?

6.14 What are the general issues involved in the phrasing of a question? What is a double-barrelled question?

6.15 Give three examples to illustrate each of the following:
a Presumptness question.
b Double-barrelled question.

6.16 What are the major sections of a survey questionnaire?

6.17 What are the things that should be avoided in questionnaire design? Give an example each to illustrate.

6.18 Develop an appropriate introduction for a questionnaire dealing with commuter's attitudes toward MRT service.

6.19 Develop four double-barrelled questions and corrected versions of each.

6.20 What is a leading question? Give two examples to demonstrate when such a question may occur.

6.21 What is a *branching* instruction? A *skip* instruction?

6.22 In what way can one secure *embarrassing* information from respondents? What is randomized response technique?

6.23 In a survey of 600 students, each was given a card with the following two questions, and asked to flip a coin:
'If heads, answer Question A: Have you ever cheated in an examination?'
'If tails, answer Question B: Have you visited a library in the last month?'

The results of the study were: 225 answered *yes* and 375 answered *no*. In a recently completed survey with a comparable sample of students, 55 per cent indicated that they had visited a library within a month. Using the randomized response approach, and the above information, what percentage of students just surveyed have ever cheated in an examination?

6.24 What is meant by split ballot method? Why is it employed?

6.25 One general rule for sequencing questions in a questionnaire is to proceed from the general to the specific. What rationale is there for this rule?

6.26 What is the proper sequence when asking for classification information?

6.27 Provide an example of each of the following:
   a A survey question which is ambiguous.
   b A survey question which may be beyond the ability of a typical respondent to answer.
   c A survey question which may unduly require the respondent to provide estimations.

6.28 What information is usually collected in the Administration Section of a questionnaire?

6.29 What strategies should be followed in selecting questions to place:
   a at the beginning of the questionnaire?
   b in later stage of the questionnaire?
   c at the end of the questionnaire?

6.30 Evaluate the following section of a questionnaire. The questions were presented orally.
   a 'Is there enough space in your study room?'
   b 'What improvements would you like to introduce in your study room?'

6.31 What is questionnaire pretesting? Why is it important?

6.32 Who should administer the questionnaire in a pretest?

6.33 Design a short questionnaire on the topic of employee attitudes towards the management ability of senior staff in your company. Include questions dealing with open-ended responses, single-choice responses and multiple-choice responses. Design a complete (but short) questionnaire to measure commuter satisfaction with the MRT.

6.34 Design a short questionnaire to include, among others, the following topics of information on credit cards:
   a Number of credit cards owned;
   b Advertising recall of brands (i.e. AMEX, Visa, Diner, Charge Card);
   c Card usage;
   d Attitudes toward the major credit cards: status prestige, receptability and credit limit allowed.

True-false questions

Write True (T) or False (F) for the following:

6.35 A badly designed questionnaire constitutes one of the major sources of errors in marketing research studies.

6.36 The method of data collection must be determined before a questionnaire can be written.

6.37 A well-organized questionnaire will lead the respondent from general questions to specific questions.

6.38 An unstructured questionnaire is typical of a market study gathering quantitative information.

6.39 Classification data should be recorded before any effort is made to gather a respondent's attitudes.

6.40 Pretesting is unnecessary with highly structured questionnaires to be sent/returned by mail.

6.41 The degree of disguise of a questionnaire refers to whether the respondent is likely to be aware of the purpose of the study.

6.42 The structured questionnaire is especially useful in conducting exploratory research.

6.43 Open-ended questions offer respondent the freedom to answer in his or her own words.

6.44 Multiple-choice questions minimize the effects of respondent articulateness.

6.45 Multiple-choice questions are relatively inexpensive to develop.

6.46 Open-ended questions tend to minimize interviewer bias.

6.47 Data generated by a semantic differential scale is often assumed to be interval in nature.

6.48 Open-ended questions are used as a follow-up to an important question to obtain the reasons for the answers given.

6.49 Less-skilled interviewers are needed to conduct surveys with open-ended questions.

6.50 Open-ended questions are best suited for focus group discussions.

6.51 Survyes are often shorter in duration when many open-ended questions are asked.

6.52 A limited number of response choices are available for a closed-ended question.

6.53 The respondent cannot freely express himself or herself when answering a closed-ended question.

6.54 Closed-ended questions often begin with the words 'how','what' or 'why' and allow for free expression of ideas from the respondent.

6.55 Closed-ended questions are most appropriate for self-administered (e.g. postal) questionnaires.

Multiple-choice questions

6.56 The document used in conducting a survey of respondents is called a . . . ?
a survey
b interview
c questionnaire
d all of the above.

6.57 The demographics of survey respondents will be recorded in the . . . . of the questionnaire.
a Introduction.
b Body.

c Classification section.
d Administration section.

6.58 Highly-structured questions:
a are easier to tabulate
b are useful in measuring attitudes
c are used to stimulate respondent interest
d cannot be used as cheater question.

6.59 Regardless of the data collection method to be used, most survey questionnaires are pretested using:
a personal interview
b telephone interview
c group discussion
d postal survey.

6.60 The question form that is most subject to interviewer bias is the:
a dichotomous question
b free response question
c constant-sum question
d preference question.

6.61 A questionnaire is said to be undisguised if:
a it contains questions that are formal and standardized
b respondents are aware of the purpose of the research study
c respondents are unaware of the purpose of the research study
d it contains questions that are vague.

6.62 The questionnaire form that is most frequently used in marketing research is:
a structured undisguised
b structured-disguised
c unstructured-undisguised
d unstructured-disguised.

6.63 Closed-ended questions are difficult to formulate and arrange, but:
a are able to collect more extensive information than open-ended questions
b are more effective than other question types when used in exploratory research studies
c allow the researcher to disguise the intent of the questionnaire
d make it easier to analyse the results of the survey

6.64 What is wrong with this question:
'What is your age?'

    10–20 years   1
    20–30 years   2
    35–50 years   3
    Over 50 years 4.

a The categories are not of equal intervals.

b The categories are not exhaustive.

c The categories are not mutually exclusive.

d Both b and c above.

6.65 Multiple-choice questions:

a require longer coding time

b do not permit respondents to elaborate their true position

c both a and b above

d None of the above.

6.66 Which of the following is not an advantage of open-ended question?

a They elicit a wide range of responses.

b They minimize the respondent's frustration.

c They provide a 'feel' of the respondent's views.

d All of the above are advantages

7

Fielding data collection forms _____

We now come to the most vulnerable phase of the research process: the fielding of data collection forms. A marketing research project is no better than the data collected in the field. All efforts made through the use of an excellently conceived questionnaire may go to waste if the field operations are not performed correctly. The right question becomes an incorrect one when it is improperly administered at the field-work stage.

Planning of field work must be organized early in order to minimize the problems that may be encountered at the data-gathering stage. The kind of planning work needed will vary, depending on the type of data collection method.

Planning field operations ▬▬▬

The basic issues which are relevant to the planning of field operations comprise the following:

- scheduling activities
- preparing budgets
- recruiting interviewers
- conducting basic training and project briefing.

Time scheduling _____

Scheduling for field operations must take into account two key aspects: List of research activities involved and approx-

imate time needed to perform each activity. A specimen of time scheduling for a typical personal interview study is exhibited in Figure 7.1.

A bar chart approach in presenting the time schedule was developed by Henry L. Gantt (see Figure 7.2). The Gantt chart shows a more realistic time span (21 weeks instead of 32 weeks) taking into account the overlapping of research activities.

Another planning tool known as the Network Analysis or Programme Evaluation Review Technique (PERT) is also frequently used. (See Figure 7.3.) The researcher traces each possible path of research activity through the network, and calculates the total time required by each. The path which records the greatest total time is called the critical path along which a delay in the completion of any activity will cause a corresponding delay in the completion of the project.

Preparing budgets _____

Budget preparation involves the assignment of cost to each research activity. It is usually prepared simultaneously with time scheduling, for a change in one will result in a corresponding change in the other. In a personal interviewing situation, the main expenditure items include office wages and salaries, survey materials and supplies, supervisory and interviewing costs as well as costs for the reproduction of questionnaires and other administrative forms.

Activities	Time Needed
A. Formulate survey objectives	1 week
B. Formulate survey methodology and design	1 week
C. Recruit and train interviewers	3 weeks
D. Draft pilot questionnaire	2 weeks
E. Pretest questionnaire	2 weeks
F. Finalise questionnaire	3 weeks
G. Compile sampling frame	7 weeks
H. Select the sample	2 weeks
I. Collect the data	5 weeks
J. Transfer data to diskettes/tapes	2 weeks
K. Process the data	3 weeks
L. Prepare the report	1 week
	Total 32 weeks

Figure 7.1 *List of research activities (a personal interview study)*

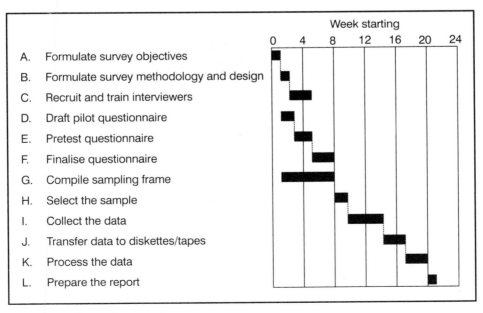

Figure 7.2 *Gantt chart of research activities*

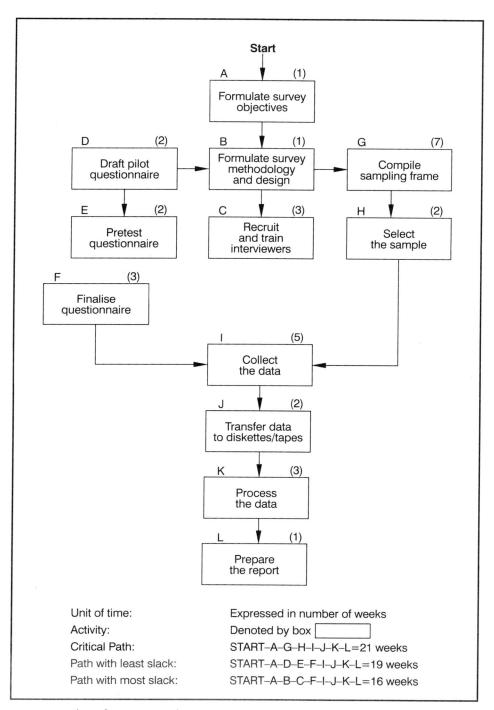

Figure 7.3 *PERT chart for a research project*

Interviewer recruitment _____

Field interviewing is an art – only persons with the right calibre are considered for employment to perform the task. Adequate effort must be made in the selection of field staff responsible for data collection. Generally speaking, persons who possess the required aptitude will find interviewing work a satisfying and enjoyable activity. On the contrary, a person who lacks the required temperament is not suited for the job and field interviewing can thus turn out to be a cause of much anxiety. The duties of an interviewer include searching for obscure addresses, securing co-operation from respondents and administering questionnaires. The work of an interviewer is very different from that of a person who works in the office. In most instances, interviewers perform their tasks without direct supervision.

Role of the interviewer

The primary role of an interviewer is to gather data. Such information upon which major marketing decisions may hinge, is only as good as the field interviewer who gathers the information. Hence the conscientiousness and skill of the interviewer in conducting interviews in a correct and precise manner, and in recording the answers correctly are of critical importance. The value of the information obtained depends on his or her skill, good sense and accuracy. To do a worthwhile job, the interviewer must be well informed about the survey and its objectives. With random sampling, each interviewer is given a list of selected persons/households to execute field work. In the case of quota sampling, however, interviewers are not given such a list and therefore their foremost task would be to search for respondents within the limit of quota controls as predetermined by the researcher.

The interviewer must establish good relations with the respondent, avoid arousing unnecessary prejudice, confusion or resentment, and always respect the confidence on which the respondent has given information. The interviewer should make the respondent aware that all information collected will be treated as strictly confidential, and that data will never be linked to individual names.

In the course of performing his or her duties, the interviewer must motivate the respondent to supply comprehensive and accurate answers. Normally he or she begins the interview by assuring the respondent that all information given will be treated with strict confidence and that the data pertaining to any respondent would not be divulged without the respondent's prior consent. The interviewer should never reveal or give hints to the respondent who the survey client is. (*Note*: The identity of the survey client may appear obvious from the questions asked, but it could well be that the survey client is a competitor.) The interviewer must be totally familiar with the questionnaire and be skilful in handling all the survey materials (e.g. showcard.) He or she should be able to *talk* to the respondent and not merely read the survey questions; in this manner, the interviewer makes the interviewing situation more alive and interesting. He or she should always be ready to display interest in the answers given by the respondent and to sustain the respondent's enthusiasm throughout the interview. In addition, the interviewer should plan his or her work schedule systematically and efficiently, and observe the survey control procedure honestly.

Qualities of field interviewers

It is imperative to employ interviewers who meet certain job requirements. A good interviewer is one who can communicate effectively with the respondent from various backgrounds. The following qualities are expected of an interviewer:

1 *Appearing confidence.* The respondent's immediate reaction to the request for an interview is likely to be a mixture of curiosity and suspicion. Thus the first

> ### Interviewers
> #### Qualities
> - Being confident
> - Appearing relaxed
> - Being neutral
> - Conscientious regard for detail
> - Absolute honesty and integrity
> - Work under difficult conditions
> - Abide by instructions
> - Write legibly
> - Pleasant appearance and manner

impression made by the interviewer is of utmost importance. A confident interviewer can help in winning the trust and co-operation of the respondent. He or she must be confident in what he or she is doing and always ensure that people will talk to him or her.

2 *Being relaxed.* The relaxed appearance of the interviewer is a sure sign of confidence and will help to put the respondent at ease. This should not however be overacted, as a sense of seriousness in interviewing is still a necessity. Generally speaking, if the interviewer looks relaxed and confident and is a pleasant person to meet, the respondent will act more happily than if the interviewer looks tense and nervous.

3 *Being neutral.* The interviewer must remain completely neutral. He or she should put personal feelings aside and obtain information as others see it. The interviewer should avoid deliberate changes in his or her tone or facial expressions which would influence the respondent's answers.

4 *Possessing a conscientious regard for details.* The interviewer should be on surveillance at all times and be able to *read* the respondent so as to react according to interviewing situations. His or her ability to observe if the respondent is aggressive, timid, doubtful or showing off will be an added asset.

5 *Absolute honesty and integrity.* Because the scope of field work is often spread geographically and supervision of the interviewer is difficult, the interviewer may be tempted to cheat by submitting completed questionnaires based on interviews which were never conducted. Interviewers who are so discovered should have their services terminated immediately.

6 *Being prepared to work under difficult conditions* Most field work requires a great deal of travel, walking, night work, unpleasant remarks from the respondent and visits to notorious neighbourhoods. These difficult conditions can put off a number of interviewers.

7 *Being able to abide by instructions* Instructions and information schedules pertaining to field work are often extensive. Thus ability to follow instructions and to pay attention to details are necessary. The interviewer should always remember to ask questions using the exact words printed on the questionnaire and in the exact sequence.

8 *Being able to write legibly.* Legibility is essential in questionnaire completion. The bad handwriting of an interviewer can present difficulty to the office staff in deciphering the entries made, and in turn, cause a delay in data processing work.

9 *Showing a pleasant appearance and pleasing personality.* These qualities can help in handling aggressive or difficult respondents.

10 *Holding an enthusiastic and positive attitude.* Attitudes are contagious. If the interviewer appears enthusiastic and adopes a positive approach in his or her work, the respondent will be more willingly to co-operate.

In sum, the recruitment of interviewers is by no means an easy task considering the difficulty in assessing the suitability of a candidate. Some people possess the required qualities of an interviewer, while some interviewers are better suited for specific surveys. In a study undertaken in 1951 of the relation between interviewer

Interviewer Recruitment
An Advertisement

Singapore Press Holdings
requires

PART–TIME INTERVIEWERS

to conduct house–to–house interviews

Requirements:
- Above 18 years of age
- Completed GCE 'O' level
- Able to speak English, Mandarin and Chinese dialects

Interested applicants are invited to come personally for an interview TODAY and TOMORROW between 9.30am and 12 noon, or between 2pm and 4pm at:

Marketing Services & Research Department
Singapore Press Holdings Ltd
82 Genting Lane
Level 6, News Centre
Singapore 349567

*SBS bus number 8, 61, 66, 151, 154
(alight in front of Mcpherson POSB) or
SBS bus number 40, 62, 64, 100, 135, 154, 155
(alight at Aljunied junction off Kallang Way)*

characteristics and performance, Sheatsley discovered that women were better interviewers than men; that married men were superior to single women; that college majors in psychology or sociology scored best.

Interviewer training

Interviewers differ in interviewing qualities. Upon recruitment, they must receive training to fully understand the project and data requirements before they proceed to do field work. Training is as important as recruitment. The depth and detail of the training materials will vary with the survey project. An untrained interviewer is more likely to misrecord responses, fail to probe for adequate answer and would be easily satisfied with a *don't know* response.

There are two main forms of interviewer training: basic training and project briefing. Basic training is designed to prepare the interviewer for general interviewing techniques such as how to elicit a response, when to exercise probing techniques and how to avoid interviewer's bias. Project briefing, on the other hand, deals with more specific topics such as method of selecting respondents and the manner to complete the questionnaire used for a particular survey, to ensure that the data is collected in a uniform manner from all respondents.

Basic training usually takes the form of classroom lectures, visual displays, demonstration and open discussions. Interviewers may be briefed on the structure of the research company, the nature of marketing research and the broad aspects of interviewing. During the sessions, the following specific points are to be emphasized:

- importance of interviewers in marketing research studies
- methods of introducing oneself to the respondents, and of establishing a good rapport with them
- tact in dealing with possible refusals, and ways to accept refusals graciously
- sampling procedures available
- desirability to follow instructions.

Demonstration or mock interviews constitute a principal part of basic training as they offer the interviewers a clear and vivid idea of what field work entails. Research companies usually stipulate that an interviewer conducts some mock interviews to familiarize himself or herself with the questionnaire and to build up his or her confidence before commencing field work. Instruction manuals on interviewing are also printed for further references whenever necessary. (See Appendix A at the end of this chapter.)

While basic training helps familiarize the interviewer on the general aspects of interviewing, project briefing is concerned with specific issues pertaining to a particular survey. Though basic training may be optional to the more experienced interviewers, project briefing is absolutely compulsory to all interviewers employed for the

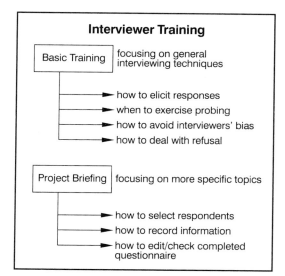

Interviewer Training

| Basic Training | focusing on general interviewing techniques |

→ how to elicit responses
→ when to exercise probing
→ how to avoid interviewers' bias
→ how to deal with refusal

| Project Briefing | focusing on more specific topics |

→ how to select respondents
→ how to record information
→ how to edit/check completed questionnaire

the researcher who is in charge of the particular survey takes over the task. Dummy interviews are commonly practised, with the researcher playing the role of a respondent, responding initially to a single interviewer on a small part of the questionnaire, while the other interviewers observe and record the response given. A post-mortem follows once the interviewer has finished his or her round. This process is repeated for other interviewers on other parts of the questionnaire. The project briefing session should create an informal and relaxed atmosphere lest the trainees would be too mindful of making mistakes.

Themes of interviewers

Gallup has identified, in its *Interviewer Ttraining Manual*, nine themes (talents) that contribute to the success of a telephone interviewer:

Work orientation – You view your work as a natural expression of yourself. Your work is more than 'just a job'. You are attracted to opportunities where you can be personally productive. You have belief in what you do . . . 'MISSION'.

Teamwork – Every person is a 'partner' on your team. You work well with managers and co-workers to complete a job. You are the ultimate team player and form good relationships with others.

Audience – You have a natural affinity toward market research, and a real attraction to the specialty of phone work and collecting people's opinions.

Pride – You are positive, quality-conscious and productive. You know that what you do makes a difference' You like to be recognized for a job well done.

Discipline – You 'plan your work and work your plan'. You stay in focus to complete a task and achieve big things.

Third ear – You have the ability to recognize your respondents' individuality over the phone and tailor your presentation

particular survey. The topics covered in project briefing include:

- survey objectives
- method of data collection adopted
- coverage of respondents
- sample design and methodology, procedural aspects
- administration of questionnaires.

The session leaders of project briefing should normally possess more advanced skills and knowledge on marketing research than the instructors of basic training. Ideally

Interviewer Manuals

- What is the survey about?
- When will the survey start/end?

About the respondents:

- How many?
- Where and how to select?
- What to do with not-at-homes?

- How to introduce oneself and initiate the interview?
- How each question should be asked?
- Methods of probing, encouraging responses and aiding memory.
- How to edit questionnaires?
- What to do with completed questionnaires?
- When/how will interviewer be paid?
- Basis on which work quality will be appraised?

accordingly. You can empathize with respondents to get the best data possible, but also know how to keep a swift pace.

Command – You can 'take charge'. You can turn refusals around by conveying the purpose of the survey and its importance. You are not afraid to call a stranger on the phone and keep them focused throughout the interview.

Woo – You like to **W**in **O**thers **O**ver! People who might not otherwise respond will talk to you because you are so convincing and positive on the phone. You have low refusal rates because people like you!

Ethics – You are honest! You collect 100 per cent accurate data and expect others to do so as well. You produce high quality work consistently!

The interview

The interviewer is responsible for collecting data from the respondent in the most accurate and efficient manner using proper interviewing techniques. This section breaks down the survey and describes the characteristics and appropriate techniques of each component.

Introduction

The introduction is always provided in the survey questionnaire and is the first words the interviewer reads to the respondents. Here the interviewer has the opportunity to sell him or herself to the intended respondent in a friendly and professional manner.

> Good morning/Afternoon/Evening, I am
> _____ (NAME OF INTERVIEWER)
> working for The Gallup Organization(s)
> Pte Ltd. We are conducting a survey to
> listen to people's opinions about MRT
> services in Singapore. The interview will
> take between five and ten minutes. All
> information provided by you will be kept
> strictly confident. I would be grateful if you
> could help us in this survey by answering
> some questions.

At this point, the interviewer will usually show his or her identification card to support this statement.

Doorstep introduction should be brief. At the doorstep, the interviewer should not attempt to ask for gaining permission for interview, but instead to indicate the course of action he or she has wished for. Thus, instead of asking the respondent: 'May I come in to interview you?' to which the respondent could easily give a 'No' reply, the interviewer should simply say: 'I would like to come in and talk with you about this'. Other examples of questions for the interviewer to avoid using are:

- 'Are you busy now?'

  (Expected answer: 'Yes, I am.')

- 'Could I take this interview now?'

  (Expected answer: 'No, not now.')

Likewise, questions which invite negative reactions are liable to lead the respondent into refusing to be interviewed. Sometimes the respondent will not have the time for an interview when the interviewer contacts him or her. It may not be advisable for the interviewer to press on for an interview at a time which may be inconvenient for the respondent; instead to make an appointment to call back at a more suitable time when the respondent can give unhurried and undivided attention. Once the appointment has been made, the interviewer must ensure that he or she will keep it.

Reading verbatim

Each question in the survey questionnaire must be read verbatim (i.e. word for word) at all times. The interviewer should not add to, delete from, or paraphrase any question. (*Exception*: Information in parenthesis and in bold prints refers to instruction/guide to the interviewer and is not to be read aloud.)

How satisfied or dissatisfied are you personally with the overall level of MRT services?

Are you . . . . . (READ OUT)?

Very satisfied	1
Somewhat satisfied	2
Somewhat dissatisfied	3
very dissatisfied	4

Never explain a question. If a respondent does not understand, patiently reread it. If the respondent still does not understand, enter this as a 'don't know' response and continue with the next survey question.

Also, never interpret any terms. If the respondent asks for a definition, simply reply that there is none provided in the survey questionnaire. Encourage the respondent to answer the question according to his or her own interpretation.

For an open-ended question, recording an answer verbatim can be difficult if it is lengthy. It is therefore a good idea to let the respondent know you are recording the answer word for word so they slow down. You may not paraphrase, summarize, correct grammar, or in any other way alter the response. It is utterly important that on an open-ended question the answer is in the respondent's own words.

Can you please tell me why you said that you were not satisfied with the MRT services?

_____
_____
_____
_____

Probing

An important aspect of the interviewer's work is getting the respondent to answer the question which was asked. Answers which are incomplete, irrelevant or vague must be probed further for clarity to be of use. The quality of the interview depends a great deal on the interviewer's ability to use probing techniques successfully.

The interviewer should at all times watch that he or she repeats the respondent's own words in any probe that he or she makes – if he or she paraphrases the respondent, he or she will probably be prompting.

Good probes

For CLOSED-ENDED questions:

- 'If you had to make a choice, what would it be?'
- 'If you had to choose between the two, which would you say?'
- 'Which would be closer to the way you feel?'
- 'For the sake of the survey, what would you say?'

For OPEN-ENDED questions:

- 'Why do you feel that way?'
- 'Could you be more specific about what you've just said?'
- 'From anything you've read, seen or heard, what would you say?'
- 'What comes to your mind when you said so?'
- 'There is no right or wrong answer to this question. It is just your opinion that we want to know.'

Avoiding prompting

The interviewer should never attempt to suggest a particular answer to the respondent, or to suggest how the respondent might feel about a subject.

Arranging/organizing the interview

At times, the respondent will not have the time to be interviewed when the interviewer first contacts him or her. If this situation occurs, the interviewer should never attempt to persuade the respondent to be interviewed but instead to make an appointment to come back at a more suitable time when the respondent can give his or her unhurried and undivided attention to the interviewer. Once an appointment has been made the interviewer must ensure that he or she will keep it without fail. Do not accept a refusal too easily. The respondent will almost certain ask if it is all right not to respond to the interview. The most common reason given for refusing interview is lack of time. Some respondents plead ignorance about the survey subject under study, while others claim that they are non-typical and hence ineligible for interview. Elderly people may insist that at their advanced age, their opinions and views are not worth having. Yet others complained that they've been seasonal respondents having participated in too many surveys already. The important task for the interviewer is to find out the reason for refusal, and in doing so, he or she will have a starting point for persuading a person to change their mind about responding to the interview.

Rotating the scale

This is a technique in which the interviewer is required to rotate the order of the list each time the question is asked, to ensure that the respondent does not favour items toward the beginning or end of the list.

What is your most favourite flavour of ice-cream.

Is it . . . . (READ OUT AND ROTATE)?

Chocolate	1
Mint	2
Strawberry	3
Vanilla	4
(Don't know)	5
(Refused)	6

If the interviewer were on his or her fourth interview for the day, he or she would start on 'Vanilla' (code 4) and finish with 'Strawberry' (code 3).

Demographics

Demographics is the last set of questions asked (except perhaps for quota interviews), in body part section of the survey. They are designed to classify the respondent by gender, age, race, education, marital status or income bracket. Here, it is crucial that the interviewer reassure the respondent that this information is all confidential and in no way associated with him or her as an individual. The main purpose is to make sure that a wide range of respondents are covered in the survey.

The interview is almost finished and I really appreciate your opinions and the time you've given me. I just have a few questions on personal data left to classify your answers.

Which of the following age group do you belong to? Is it . . . . . (READ OUT)?

10 years and below	1
Over 20 years–30 years	2
Over 30 years–40 years	3
Over 40 years–50 years	4
Over 50 years	5

Concluding the interview

Before leaving, always remember to thank the respondent. The success of an interview is dependent on the respondent's goodwill and the interviewer should make a point of saying so to the respondent. It is always wise to let the respondent feel that the interview has really been worth his or her time, and that talking with him or her has been an enjoyable experience. The aim is to leave every respondent feeling willing to co-operate in survey undertaking again.

Field work problems ▬▬▬

Two major problems are commonly encountered by researchers in marketing research studies involving field interviewing. Very often, they are also regarded as interviewer-related problems and respondent-related problems. (See Figure 7.4.)

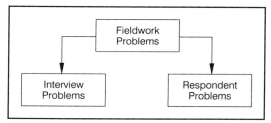

Figure 7.4 *The nature of field-work problems*

Interviewer problems ▬▬▬▬▬

As mentioned earlier, competent interviewers and extensive training can help reduce field work problems and raise the level of data reliability. It is almost impossible to avoid interviewer problems completely. Some inherent problems which deserve special mention are:

- errors in asking questions
- errors in recording responses
- cheating by interviewers
- interviewers' variability
- errors in respondent selection

When the interviewer forces a gesture or a facial expression to encourage (or discourage) a particular response, he or she has in fact created errors in the interviewing process. Errors may also occur due to the interviewer's failure to present the survey questions in the manner as worded or sequenced in the questionnaire, and his or her inability to record the exact responses supplied.

Open-ended questions and attitudinal questions, in particular, require much time

in attending to the responses given and are more prone to recording errors. This problem may be overcome by tape-recording the entire interview.

Interviewer cheating is an interviewer problem and, strictly speaking, is not an interviewer error. The interviewer fills in answers in the questionnaire without contacting the respondent as he should do. In personal interviewing where an interviewer works in some distant parts of the country and cannot be easily supervised, the temptation to cheat is even greater. The following are cases of interviewer cheating:

- The entire questionnaire is filled up fictitiously without an interview.
- Only some parts of the questionnaire are completed through an interview.
- The interviewer, for convenience's sake, deliberately chooses to interview an unselected person. In a survey on chief executives, for example, the interviewer resorts to interviewing their secretaries when the former are not available for interview.

The most effective way to curb interviewer cheating is to implement the *spot check* system for the purpose of verifying a claimed interview. Spot checks may be carried out by field supervisors through personal interview or telephone call made to the respondent. Prior warning to the interviewer that spot checks will be made is itself effective in deterring him or her from making any attempt to cheat.

No two interviewers can be alike in all aspects. They may differ in their ways of handling an interviewing situation and of interacting with the respondent. The nature of such differences together with anything that goes with it, is known as interviewer variability. The problem associated with interviewer variability lies in the difficulty of predicting its pattern or direction, as well as in measuring its magnitude. A study designed to demonstrate interviewer variability was carried out by the Social and Community Planning Research (SCPR) in North Yorkshire. This study involved a

Table 7.1

| | Prefer A | | Prefer B | | | | |
	Strongly %	Not strongly %	Strongly %	Not strongly %	Don't know %	Prefer A at all %	Prefer either strongly %
	(1)	(2)	(3)	(4)	(5)	(6)	(7)
Interviewer #							
19	86	10	0	3	0	96	86
1	60	17	3	20	0	77	63
14	60	27	6	6	0	87	66
10	57	30	3	9	0	87	60
17	54	35	4	4	0	89	58
4	53	25	8	8	6	78	61
16	48	28	8	12	4	76	56
12	47	27	3	17	7	74	50
2	46	34	0	14	6	80	46
15	45	26	3	23	3	71	48
11	43	30	4	20	2	73	47
5	41	34	9	12	3	75	50
18	39	41	15	5	0	80	54
6	33	40	5	18	5	73	38
9	30	57	3	7	3	87	33
3	26	52	7	10	5	78	33
8	26	42	0	26	3	68	26
7	25	50	4	21	0	75	29
13	4	74	0	22	0	78	4
Average	43	36	4	14	2	79	47
Mean deviation	13	11	3	6	2	6	13

Source: Adapted from Interviewer Variability: The New Yorkshire Experiment. Methodological Working Papers (No. 13) by Martin Collins.

group of twenty interviewers, each issued with forty addresses of respondents; each selected from one of forty designated sampling points in order to ensure an even distribution of workload among the interviewers.

The test question of relevance presented to the respondents was:

On the whole, which of the following two options would you prefer to happen?

And, do you feel strongly or not strongly about this?'

Option A: Protect historic buildings.
Option B: Provide modern facilities.

The answers offered by the respondents in respect of each interviewer are tabulated in Table 7.1.

The findings exhibited wide variations amongst interviewers. In terms of *strong preference* response (Column 7) for example, the range varied from 86 per cent reported by interviewer #19 to only 4 per cent reported by interviewer #13. Also, in the case of interviewer #19, almost all prefer Option A (96 per cent) while the corresponding level was only 68 per cent under interviewer #8. These findings suggest the presence of interviewer variability.

Respondent problems

Respondent problems, unlike interviewer problems, are error-related. They can be broadly classified into two categories: response error and non-response error.

Response error

Response error originates from inaccurate information supplied by the respondent and comprises semantic error and false reporting error.

Semantic error refers to misinterpretation of questions on the part of the respondent. It occurs when the respondent who misunderstands the question unconsciously and provides a wrong answer. Inadequate wording of question is the main cause of semantic error; for this reason, survey questions must be worded so that the respondent can fully understand what is being asked and share the researcher's meaning of the term used. Very often, semantic error occurs without the knowledge of both the interviewer and the respondent. Such error can be reduced by organizing extensive training programmes, conducting questionnaire pretests etc. to ensure a clear understanding of the survey questions. Some respondents are *yea sayers* who tend to accept all statements they are asked about. Others tend to disagree with all questions. Both are referred to as acquiescences.

False reporting, on the other hand, is an intentional act by the respondent to forward incorrect or false responses. Such error occurs when the respondent fully understands the question and knows the answer but chooses to give incorrect information. This happens most frequently in the case of relatively sensitive and/or personal topics. In some cases, a respondent distorts his or her responses to make his or her self-image more acceptable to others. Generally speaking, false reporting error presents a less serious problem than semantic error. It is believed that once the respondent accepts an interview or agrees to fill in a self-administered questionnaire, he or she is unlikely to falsify responses without good reasons.

Non-response error

Commercial marketing research studies are sometimes perceived as invasion of privacy and thus encounter a high level of non-response. It is almost impossible to achieve a 100 per cent response rate regardless of what data collection technique is used.

Non-response error occurs when the group of respondents differs from that of non-respondents with respect to the characteristics under study. In a personal interview situation, for instance, the not-at-homes are likely to differ in a number of ways from persons or families who are usually available for at home interview. Researchers very often fail to gauge the magnitude of non-response error, as the essential data pertaining to the non-respondents are absent. Apart from not-at-homes, other major components of non-response are refusals, unsuitables, etc.

Not-at-homes refers to selected respondents who are not present at the time of interviewer's visit. In Singapore, not-at-homes are on the increase, especially for daytime visits by the interviewer due to the high employment rate. Apart from the working population, the not-at-homes are likely to be the better educated, the young ones and the urban residents. Married

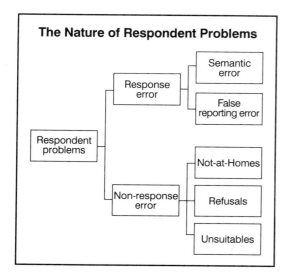

Figure 7.5 *The nature of respondent problems*

couples without children are less likely to be at home than those who have children.

Since revisit to the respondent helps considerably in reducing non-response, major research companies in Singapore stipulate a minimum of three visits (initial one plus two revisits). Understandably, this additional measure incurs extra cost and prolongs the survey field work.

In a situation where the intended respondent is contacted but refused to respond, we refer to it as a refusal. Refusals not only increase data-collection costs but also bias the survey results, because those who refuse to respond may differ from the respondents along the criterion variables being measured. Refusal errors plague all three survey research methods – especially postal survey.

The main reasons given for refusals include:

- No free/spare time to respond.
- Not interested in the survey topic.
- Fear of house-breaking.
- Fear of being identified.
- Wish to avoid obscene telephone calls.
- Wish to avoid abuse by salesperson.

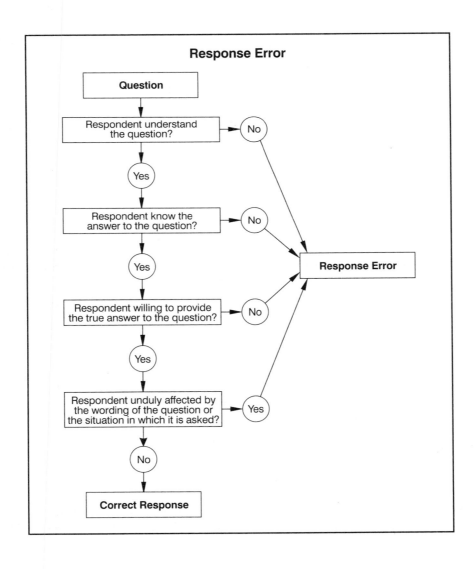

Finally, unsuitables refer to intended respondents who are ill, deaf or have suffered recent death in their families, thus rendering a non-interviewing situation. There is little that the interviewer can do about unsuitables which can cause respondent error.

Methods of determining response rate ▄▄▄▄▄▄

The term *response rate* is generally accepted to mean the percentage of respondents interviewed, and constitutes the single most important factor for measuring the reliability of survey results. Ironically, researchers themselves have yet to agree on the formula for the calculation of response rate. A study has brought their diverging practices to light.

The primary objective to the study was to explore the formulae adopted by research companies in calculating response rate. A field-work summary sheet (see below) of a hypothetical telephone survey was presented to selected research companies to indicate what they would consider is the response rate of the particular survey.

Out of the forty research companies that responded to the study, twenty-nine different formulae were discovered to have been used to calculate response rate!

The three most frequently used formulae were:

1 One which defines response as any contact made. The response rate is:

$$r = \frac{\text{Items } [(d) + (e) + (f) + (g) + (h) + (i)]}{\text{Item } (a)}$$

$$= 48 \text{ per cent}$$

2 One which considers response as a contact with the appropriate individual. The response rate is:

$$r = \frac{\text{Items } [(d) + (f) + (g) + (h) + (i)]}{\text{Item } (a)}$$

$$= 44 \text{ per cent}$$

3 One which defines response as a completed interview. In this case, the response rate is:

$$r = \frac{\text{Item } (i)}{\text{Item } (a)}$$

$$= 12 \text{ per cent}$$

Another study which compared the nature of non-response in a telephone interview study and a personal interview study provided the following results:

	Telephone interview (%)	Personal interview (%)
Completed interviews	55.9	74.3
Partial interviews	3.4	–
Respondent refusal	7.5	10.9
Refusal by other member of the household	4.3	1.9
Non-interview for other reasons (deaf, etc.)	8.0	9.6
No answer or not at home	20.7	3.3
Total	99.8	100.0

Source: Robert M. Groves and Robert L Kahn (1979) *Survey by Telephone.* Academic Press, pp. 66–7.

**Field-work summary sheet
(telephone survey)**

		No. of cases
a	Total number dialled	4,178
b	Disconnected, non-working number	426
c	No answer, busy, not at home	1,757
d	Interviewer reject (e.g. language barrier, deaf)	187
e	Household refusal	153
f	Respondent refusal	711
g	Ineligible respondent	366
h	Termination by respondent	74
i	Completed interview	504

Non-sampling error

All error, apart from sampling error, that arise from a research study are collectively called non-sampling error. Interviewer problems and respondent problems consititute a part of the overall non-sampling error in survey work. Unlike sampling error, the magnitude of non-sampling error is usually non-measurable.

Coverage error stems largely from the inadequacy (e.g. ommission, duplication, or ineligibility) of the sampling frame used. The adoption of telephone directories for the selection of respondent is a typical example of coverage error.

The sources of questionnaire error include: poor design; excessively long questionnaire; inadequate interviewer instructions; or wrong measurement/attitudinal scales used.

Data processing error may be caused by: error in editing data; error in coding; error in computer data entry and error in tabulation.

Finally, analysis (reporting) error refers to the inappropriate statistical methods used in the interpretations of data.

Methods to increase response rate

To achieve a 100 per cent response rate for a research study has always been the researcher's dream, though this is a remote

possibility. Nevertheless, researchers strive to increase response rate for obvious reasons. First, a higher response rate diminishes the impact of non-response bias. Secondly, a high response means a larger achieved sample, which in turn provides a higher degree of data reliability. In the case of personal/telephone interviewing, the key to increasing response rate often hinges on the interviewer's ability to communicate successfully with potential respondents.

Some of the more useful tips for achieving high response rate are offered below:

- Send an advanced notification letter.
- Send personalized cover letter.
- Assure respondent of anonymity and confidentiality of data.
- Offer tokens and/or monetary incentives.
- Make recalls/revisits.
- Keep questionnaire short.
- Issue identification/authorization card to interviewer (in case of personal interviewing).
- Provide training on proper telephone etiquette (in case of telephone interviewing).
- Promise to provide summary of survey results to the respondent.

The most effective method for increasing response rate is perhaps that of making revisits. Most research companies insist on a minimum of three visits made to the respondents at different times of the day and on different days of the week, before allowing the interviewer to treat it as a non-response. On the other hand, most of the efforts made in increasing the response rate of mail surveys centre on the motivational aspect. These include:

- An advance communication with the respondent (telephone call, postcard, letter, etc.).
- A cover letter to accompany the questionnaire.
- Inclusion of a stamped, self-addressed envelope for returning the completed questionnaire.

Components of Non-Sampling Error

Non-Sampling Error

Non-Observational | Observational

Non-Observational:
- Interviewer error
- Respondent error
- Coverage error

Observational:
- Questionnaire error
- Data processing error
- Analysis (Reporting) error

- Send personalized letter.
- Send reminder letter.
- Offer monetary incentives.
- Promise to provide survey results to respondents. (S. S. Robin [1965] A Procedure for Securing Returns to Mail Questionnaire. *Sociology and Social Research*, **50**, October, 24–35.)

The effect of making successive recalls is evident from the field work summary of a Newspaper Readership Survey which is reproduced in Table 7.2. (*Note*: The figures shown are cumulative percentages.) It is readily noted that *four calls* present the most cost-effective option. In personal or telephone interviews, the interviewer should note the day and hour when unfruitful attempts were made. With personal interviews, the neighbours may be approached to suggest an appropriate time to call again.

The recall method helps improve data reliability. As the following study shows, median income of respondents tended to be higher among those who were interviewed after repeated visits. Had the interviewing efforts been terminated after the first call, the median income of the population under study would have been grossly underestimated.

Median Income Variation of Respondents

No. of calls at which interviewed	No. of achieved interviews	Median income ($)
1st call	427	4,188
2nd call	391	5,880
3rd call	232	6,010
4th call	123	6,200
5th call	77	6,010
6th and subsequent calls	59	7,443
All interviews	1,309	5,598

Source: J. B. Lansing and J. N. Morgan (1971) *Economic Survey Methods*. The University of Michigan Press, p 161.

None the less, the above observation should not be used to generalize that high non-response rate means high non-response error and vice versa. It is true only when the respondents and the non-respondents differ substantially on the variables of interest.

Given a fixed budget, an advisable thing to do would be to plan for a smaller sample imposing on three or more recalls, rather than to begin with a large sample but no follow-up calls are intended at all. This is

Table 7.2

(As percentage of final sample)

	Total		Men		Women	
	No.	%	No.	%	No.	%
1 call	1,326	40	390	27	936	50
2 calls	2,520	76	1,018	70	1,503	80
3 calls	3,075	93	1,316	91	1,759	94
4 calls	3,220	97	1,398	97	1,822	97
5 calls	3,284	99	1,431	99	1,853	99
6 calls	3,307	100	1,442	100	1,865	100
7 calls	3,315	100	1,445	100	1,870	100
8 calls	3,316	100	1,446	100	1,870	100

because in the event that non-respondents differ significantly from the respondents, substitution of additional respondents will merely increase the size of the final sample, but in no way help reduce the non-response error.

The weighting method

Non-response, as mentioned earlier, may lead to an underrepresentation of certain segments of the intended population on the one hand, and an over-representation of certain segments of the population on the other. To rectify this unbalanced situation, researchers will normally introduce, at the data processing stage, a technique whereby the under-represented segments are appropriately adjusted upwards, and the over-represented segments are appropriately adjusted downwards. Called the weighting method, this technique aims to assign appropriate representation to various segments of the population when the data is being tabulated. An example displaying the use of the weighting method is given below.

Illustrative example 4

A random survey with an initial sample of 1,000 adults (consisting of 501 males and 499 females) was conducted to establish the incidence of reading a particular magazine. A total of 850 adults responded, of whom 153 read the magazine. The results of the survey were tabulated by sex of respondents as show below:

	No. achieved sample	No. read magazine	Incidence of reading (%)
Male	370	33	8.9
Female	480	120	25.0
	850	153	

Without weighting, the incidence of reading the magazine is 153/850, that is 18.0 per cent.

If we pause here and compare the distribution of the achieved sample and the intended sample in terms of sex, we will notice that the former is far from being a representative sample, as female adults were over-represented and male adults under-represented.

	Achieved sample	Intended sample
Male	370 (43.5%)	501 (50.1%)
Female	480 (56.5%)	499 (49.9%)
Total	850 (100%)	1,000 (100%)

Under the weighting method, the incidence of magazine reading is calculated to be:

$$8.9\% \times 50.1\%) + (49.9\% \times 25.0\%) = 16.9\%$$

Quality control

Interviewers are not infallible; no one can expect their work to be absolutely error-free at all times. There is absolute necessity to implement devices to ensure the quality of field work to be at the highest possible standard. One way is to impose quality control on the work of the interviewer. The primary objectives of quality control are:

- To confirm that a claimed interview has actually been honestly made.
- To monitor the response rate achieved by each interviewer.
- To ensure interviews are conducted in the manner required.

Due to cost constraints, field check can only be done on sample basis. Most research companies stipulate that at least 15 per cent of all claimed interviews should be subjected to field checks.

Other useful devices to exercise quality control on the work of the interviewer include:

1 *Field-witnessing.* This means supervisor's presence at the interviewing situation. Only with field witnessing can the supervisor be satisfied that his interviewer carries out the field work in the manner as specified. Field-witnessing is most essential at the initial stage of field work as common interviewing errors can be spotted early for rectification.

2 *Personal recall.* Quality controllers, supervisors or senior interviewers check on the claimed interview by making revisits to the respondent (or household).

3 *Postal check.* Postcards are sent to the respondent claimed to have been interviewed. Postal check is less costly but may suffer from low response rate. It is also argued this measure produces limited result as the respondent tends to ignore postcards sent to them.

4 *Telephone checks.* Telephone check has the advantages of being inexpensive and speedy in obtaining the required information. The feasibility of telephone check will, however, depend on the availability of telephone number in the questionnaire as provided by the respondent.

5 *Scrutiny of questionnaire.* This method offers a very good opportunity for the supervisor to uncover the errors in the questionnaire made by the interviewer. If it is discovered that a particular interviewer has been recording an excessive number of *don't know* replies, or a much higher item non-response, the supervisor immediately call for a performance review of that interviewer.

Appendix A: Instruction manual for interviewers

1. The role of the interviewer

1.1 Remember always you (the interviewer) play a very important and crucial role in a survey. Incorrect and biased interviews conducted by you will wipe off all efforts made during the planning stage.

1.2 Establish good relations with respondents, avoid arousing prejudice, confusion or resentment.

2. Before approaching the respondent

2.1 Read and understand all instructions/guidelines carefully.

2.2 Carry out a few *dummy* interviews before you conduct an actual interview.

2.3 Always check that you bring along all the materials – authorization card, questionnaire, show cards and so on.

2.4 Always wear appropriate clothing. Aim for simplicity and comfort – a simple suit or dress is best.

2.5 Avoid anything that appears like a salesperson. It is unwise to carry a basket or a briefcase.

3. Upon meeting the respondent

3.1 Your first contact with a respondent is of vital importance. Briefly introduce yourself and the company you work for. Show your authorization card at this juncture to support your identity.

3.2 Approach the respondent in a confident and positive manner. The positive attitude on the part of the interview is promptly transmitted to the respondent and helps achieve a satisfactory completion of the interview. The hesitant or nervous interviewer will always end up with more refusals than the confident one.

3.3 After introducing yourself, immediately proceed to ask the first question. A pause at this juncture would only invite refusal.

3.4 Introduction at doorsteps should be brief. Since this is not a very convenient place to carry on a conversation, always ask if you may enter the house for a short while for the interview.

3.5 Remember always that questions which permit negative responses can lead the respondents into refusing to be interviewed. For example, instead of asking 'May I interview you?' to which a respondent could easily say 'No', you should say, 'I would like you to assist us in this survey by answering a few questions'. Other examples of questions to avoid are : 'Are you busy now?' (A 'Yes, I am ' answer is expected), 'Could I take this interview now?' (A 'No, not now' answer is expected). Questions which permit negative responses can lead the respondent into refusing to be interviewed.

3.6 Tell the respondent approximately how long the interview will take and ensure him or her that the information provided by him or her will be kept strictly confidential.

4. Conducting the interview

4.1 At all times of the interview, make the respondent feel that his or her contributions are valuable.

4.2 Speak slowly but clearly. Adjust the pace of the interview to suit your respondent.

4.3 Do not skip any questions in the questionnaire. Follow the question sequence without fail.

4.4 Ask the question exactly as they appear on the questionnaire, without attempting to add or omit any word or phrase. Remember that a change in the wording of questions may introduce bias. If your respondent has not fully understood a survey question, simply repeat the question slowly and clearly. Never try to explain the question or suggest answer(s) to him or her.

4.5 Ask the questions in the order as they appear in the questionnaire.

4.6 Remember always that for questions concerning opinions/attitudes, there are no *right* or *wrong* answers. Do not therefore show, by expression or tone, your approval, disapproval or surprise at a respondent's answer.

4.7 Record the responses legibly.

4.8 Contact your supervisor or office by telephone if you have any queries or clarifications to make.

4.9 Do not pause unnecessarily between questions.

4.10 Concentrate on the survey topics and do not allow the respondent to stray. Be tactful to lead the respondent back to the questionnaire and do not engage in extraneous conversation.

4.11 Do not reveal the questionnaire to the respondent. Always choose to sit facing opposite the respondent – but near to him or her – with the questionnaire slightly tilted.

4.12 Always interview a respondent alone. The presence of other people may influence the respondent's answers. The interviewer should explain to the other members that it is the respondent's view, and his only, which is required.

4.13 When it is required to present respondents with show cards, always allow the respondents sufficient time to view the show card/exhibit in full. Only read out the show card contents if the respondent is illiterate, blind or without his or her glasses on.

4.14 If the *selected* respondent is out, or if the respondent does not have the time to be interviewed on your first contact, make an appointment to call back at a more suitable time.

4.15 When fixing an appointment, start off by suggesting times which suit your field work/schedule, otherwise you may find yourself having to turn down a succession of times, thus giving the respondent the impression that you are not very interested.

4.16 Keep your appointment with the respondent without fail. However, treat respondents who break their appointment with as much patience as you can.

5. Concluding the interview

5.1 Before leaving, check to ensure that you have asked all the questions and recorded all the answers.

5.2 Never leave any questionnaire or other survey materials behind with the respondent.

5.3 Ensure that all questionnaires are signed and dated.

5.4 Before leaving, do not forget to thank the respondent for his or her co-operation and assistance. Let the respondent feel that the interview has really been worthwhile, and that you have enjoyed talking to him or her. Leave with the feeling that he or she would like to be interviewed again.

6. After the interview

6.1 Return all the completed questionnaires to your supervisor or office according to the scheduled arrangements.

6.2 Return all documents pertaining to the survey to your supervisor or office at the end of the survey.

End-of-chapter revision

Review questions

7.1 What are the four important issues in the planning of field operations?

7.2 For what purposes is Gantt chart used?

7.3 How might a critical path network be a practical aid in controlling research? State its benefits.

7.4 What are the characteristics of a good interviewer? In what ways can training improve the performance of an interviewer?

7.5 In what ways can the interviewer contribute to minimizing measurement error?

7.6 What guidelines should be given to interviewers regarding the asking of questions?

7.7 What are the problems peculiar to the use of personal interview in field operations?

7.8 List and discuss the tasks involved in data collection using field interviewers.

7.9 What basic types of interviewer behaviour can lead to response bias?

7.10 Which is the purpose of field control?

7.11 What are the main sources of error in field operations?

7.12 What is a non-sampling error? What are the properties of such an error?

7.13 Define and give an example of each type of non-sampling errors discussed in the text.

7.14 What is non-response error?

7.15 What are the basic types of non-response errors? Are they equally serious for personal interview, telephone or mail studies? Explain your answer.

7.16 Evaluate the use of the telephone interview in field operations.

7.17 Is the biasing effect of an interviewer more serious in a personal or a telephone interview? What steps can be taken to minimize this biasing effect in these two types of interviews?

7.18 Why do most researchers who adopt the personal or telephone interview method insist on having 10 per cent to 15 per cent of completed interviews validated?

7.19 What are the advantages of the telephone advanced notification approach over the conventional postal survey?

7.20 What can be done to reduce non-response rates for postal surveys?

7.21 What is meant by item non-response? What alternatives would you suggest to treat item non-response?

7.22 What can be done to reduce the incidence of non-response errors associated with postal surveys?

True-false questions

Write True (T) or False (F) for the following:

7.23 The Programme Evaluation Review Technique (PERT) is often used to trace the nature of non-response error.

7.24 Errors in data collection can be remedied by applying advanced statistical techniques in tabulation and analysis.

7.25 The interviewer should not reveal or give hints to the respondent on who the survey client is.

7.26 Response errors can be eliminated if we take a complete census of the population.

7.27 Because of the generally low refusal rate, the personal interview tends to have less non-response error than other survey approaches.

7.28 Unsuitables refer to selected respondents who are not present at the time of the interviewer's visit.

7.29 Response bias is a major problem in most observational studies.

7.30 Semantic error arises from the misinterpretation of questions by the respondent.

7.31 A 'not-at-home' respondent is one who has changed address and cannot be contacted by the interviewer.

7.32 Response rate is the percentage of qualified respondents who declined to respond.

7.33 The crucial component of the interview for capturing the respondent's interest is the introductory statement by the interviewer.

7.34 In the case of telephone interviewing, respondents have time to observe the interviewer and to listen to the introductory statement.

7.35 Non-response error is more serious when the respondent group vastly differs from the non-respondent group with respect to the variables under study.

Multiple-choice questions

7.36 Which one of the following is not a reporting error?
   a A respondent gives an incorrect answer.
   b A respondent does not wish to answer truthfully, and makes up an answer instead.
   c A respondent cannot remember, so he or she makes a guess.
   d A respondent does not know the answer and says no.

7.37 Of the following types of errors, which one can be reduced by increasing the sample size?
   a Non-sampling error.
   b Sampling error.
   c Response bias.
   d None of the above.

7.38 Non-response error in survey research is present:
   a when a respondent doesn't know the answer, but makes up a response that he or she thinks will please the interviewer
   b only when small sample sizes are

employed
   c when those who respond are different from those who don't
   d none of the above.

7.39 Non-response error can occur:
   a when some persons refuse to take part in a personal or telephone interview
   b as a result of some mail questionnaire recipients misplacing their questionnaires
   c when a person is not at home when called during a telephone survey
   d all of the above.

7.40 Which of the following survey technique tends to have the least difficulty with response error?
   a Personal interview.
   b Telephone interview.
   c Postal questionnaire.
   d None of the above.

7.41 Which of the following survey technique tends to have the greatest difficulty with non-response error?
   a Personal interview.
   b Telephone interview.
   c Postal questionnaire.
   d None of the above.

7.42 The response rate to a mail questionnaire can be increased by:
   a making the questionnaire as brief as possible
   b using a stamped, self-addressed return envelope
   c including a cover letter
   d all of the above.

7.43 The desired qualities of an interviewer include:
   a being confident
   b being neutral
   c being able to write legibly
   d all of the above.

7.44 A good interviewer is one who:
   a uses unbiased questioning techniques
   b uses correct question order
   c establishes rapport with the respondents
   d all of the above.

8

Attitude measurement ─────────────

In the middle and late 1950s, there emerged as Joyce put it, a 'wholesale introduction' of behavioural research techniques (Timothy Joyce [1963] The Role of the Expert in Market Research. Market Research Society, Summer School, July). The mushrooming of these techniques had much improved the measurement of the consumer's behaviour and attitudes. Furthermore, development in this direction has expanded the theory and practice of marketing research which in turn enriched the planning aspects of marketing strategy.

An understanding of consumers' attitudes in reality often lead to explain the *why* aspect of consumers' past, present and future behaviour. Such understanding can, however, be achieved through some complicated means, which necessitate a more subtle approach than direct questioning. It is so primarily important because attitude variables (e.g. belief, preference, motivation and intention) are conceptual ideas which are not only hard to explore, but also difficult to record the responses accurately and comprehensively.

Attitudes are multidimensional, for there is always more than one aspect that make up one's attitudes. The researcher should examine all relevant aspects if he or she wishes to evaluate consumers' attitudes towards a product, brand or service. This chapter is primarily concerned with an introduction and application of research techniques that are most commonly employed in measuring attitudes.

Types of numbers ▬▬▬▬

The term *scaling* is often used in the process of measuring attitudes, where numbers are assigned to describe or represent objects, persons, households or events according to a fixed set of rules. Numbers may be numeric or simply symbolic; alternatively they can be classified under one of the following four types (see page 183); each possesses some inherent properties which govern the type of mathematical operations that can be performed.

Nominal numbers ───────────

Nominal numbers are categorical data which have no numerical value. Hence, they are the most primitive and least sophisticated among all types of numbers. Mathematically they are weak in that no arithmetical operations (i.e. addition, subtraction, multiplication and division) can be applied to them. The primary functions of nominal numbers are: (a) identification of objects or events; and (b) classification of objects or events.

─────────────────

Illustrative example 1:
Identification of objects/events

Birth Certificate Number:	6721859/B
Football Jersey Number:	12
Bank Account Number:	6682954/E

─────────────────

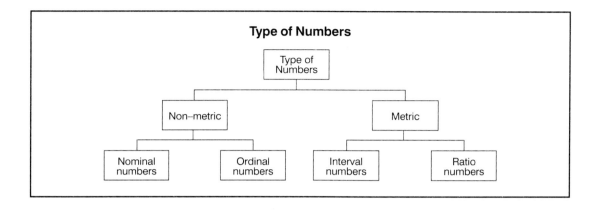

An identification number bears no significance other than for identification purpose. In the above example, jersey numbers merely serve to identify the players or their positions in the field but do not imply a superior characteristic in terms of their skills, speed etc. A football player wearing jersey number '12' for example, is not necessarily superior to his team-mates who are assigned lower jersey numbers. These numbers are arbitrary and have no inherent value.

Illustrative example 2:

Classification of objects/events

	Codes
Chinese	1
Malay	2
Indian	3
Others	4

In the above example, respondents are categorized into various ethnic groups by virtue of classification numbers, often referred to as *codes*. Code assignment is arbitrary, that is, the number 1 could be assigned to the Chinese category or any other category. Nothing can be said that the ethnic group represented by the number 1 is anything more, or less than other ethnic groups represented by numbers 2, 3, etc. Once a particular code has been assigned to,

say, Chinese respondents, the same code cannot be subsequently assigned to non-Chinese respondents. Nominal numbers permit only the most primitive mathematical operations, such as a simple count of the number of elements that fall into each category and their respective percentages, as well as an indication of the modal category. The scope of analysis for nominal numbers is thus very limited.

Ordinal numbers

Ordinal (or ranking) numbers indicate position or order of objects under investigation according to some specific characteristics. These numbers describe whether or not an object has *more, the same* or *less* of a specific characteristic than some other objects.

Illustrative example 3:

Scoreboard of a 400 m race

Tom	1
Henry	2
Victor	3

The scoreboard indicates the positions of the three runners at the finishing point. Tom, at first position, ran faster than Henry at second position who, in turn, was a faster runner than Victor who was third.

A rating scale using ordinal numbers provides more information than one using nominal numbers. Statistical techniques related to positional measures (e.g. median, quartile and mode) are now permissible. Ordinal numbers are therefore a high-level number type than nominal numbers. Marketing research studies, particularly those concerned with consumers' preferences, rely much on ordinal numbers.

Ordinal numbers, however, do not provide measurement on the distance between the two ordered objects. For this reason, the interval (or distance) between objects in unknown. The earlier example reveals nothing about the distances between the three runners at the finishing point, and leaves one to wonder whether the race was a close or lop-sided one. The numerical difference between any two ordinal numbers bears no meaning at all. Calculation of arithmetic mean is hence prohibited for ordinal numbers.

Interval numbers

Interval (or cardinal) numbers not only arrange objects in a specified order, but also measure the distance between them. Hence interval numbers are superior to ordinal numbers in the quality of information for which they can provide. Statistical measures (e.g. arithmetic mean, standard deviation, correlation coefficient and test of significance) are performable with interval numbers. The thermometer is a typical example of objects which use interval numbers. In thermometer reading, one can assert that 50°F is warmer than 40°F; that the difference (or distance) between 80°F and 60°F is the same as the difference between 50°F and 30°F, or betweeen 35° F and 15° F.

Unfortunately, thermometer reading does not allow one to say that 100°F is five times warmer than 20°F. In the same way, the researcher cannot conclude that a respondent who awards a rating of 6 is three times more favourable towards the product under study than another respondent who awards it a rating of 2. This deficiency of interval numbers occurs because such numbers are built on an arbitrary (not absolute!) zero point, which means that the applicability of multiplication and division operations is prohibited. In the Fahrenheit reading, for example, 0°F and is merely an arbitrary zero point and does not mean no heat at all.

Ratio numbers

Ratio numbers differ from interval numbers in one major aspect: ratio numbers are built on a fixed origin or non-arbitrary zero point – one for which there is universal agreement as to its position. It is permissible to carry out multiplication and division on ratio numbers, which are regarded as the most superior and versatile among all numbers. Weight, height, currency, speed and time are all measured with ratio numbers. A 150 lb person can be conclusively said to be twice as heavy as another person who weighs 75 lb.

Ratio numbers can be converted to interval numbers and to ordinal numbers, but the reverse is not true. Equivalently a higher-level number can be down-graded into a lower-level number, but a lower-level number cannot be upgraded. To illustrate this point, we consider the possible answers to question: 'How much do you personally earn per month?' as follows:

Ordinal numbers	Interval numbers	Ratio numbers
Very high . 1	Less than $500 1	$2,122
High 2	$500–$999 2	
Average . . 3	$1,000–$1,999 . . . 3	
Low 4	$2,000–$2,999 . . . 4	
Very low . . 5	$3,000 and above . . 5	

The value expressed in ratio number (that is, $2,122) can be downgraded into an interval or ordinal number if so desired, but it is quite impossible to do so in the reversed direction.

Whenever possible, it is desirable to secure marketing research data in the highest possible level to allow a wider scope of data analysis.

Type	Example	Permissible Operations	Test of Significance
Nominal	Bank account number Sex	■ Number of elements in each category ■ Mode	■ Chi–square test
Ordinal	Ranking of products	■ Mode ■ Median ■ Percentile ■ Rank–order correlation	■ Non–parametric statistical test ■ Sign test
Interval	Thermometer Calendar	■ Mode ■ Median ■ Arithmetic mean ■ Variance ■ Standard deviation	■ t–test ■ F–test ■ Other parametric statistical tests
Ratio	Weight Height Age Currency	■ Mode ■ Median ■ Arithmetic mean ■ Geometric mean ■ Harmonic mean ■ Coefficient of variation	■ All of the above

Figure 8.1 *Comparison of various types of numbers*

A brief comparison of the four types of numbers discussed above is given in Figure 8.1.

Rating scales

Various research techniques are available for measuring consumer behaviour. Disguised methods involving the use of projective techniques have been discussed in Chapter 5. Alternatively, researchers use rating scales for attitude measurement. In essence, a rating scale refers to a measurement situation which employs ordinal, interval or ratio numbers. The respondent places a mark at a specific point along a numerically valued continuum, or ticks off the response(s) from among the numerically ordered series of categories provided, to express his or her attitude towards, the object (or an attribute of the object) under investigation.

The types of rating scales employed in marketing research are:
- graphic rating scale
- pictorial rating scale
- itemized (or verbal) rating scale
- paired-comparison scale
- rank-order rating scale
- constant sum scale
- semantic differential scale
- Stapel scale
- Likert summated scale
- Thurstone scale.

Graphic rating scale

In graphic rating scale, the respondent places a mark at the appropriate point along a continuum that runs from one extreme end of the attitude in question to the other extreme end. Many variations of graphic rating scales

Rating Scale

- Graphic Rating Scale
- Pictorial Rating Scale
- Itemized Rating Scale
- Paired–Comparison Scale
- Rank Order Rating Scale
- Constant Sum Scale
- Semantic-Differential Scale
- Staple Scale
- Likert Summated Scale
- Thurstone Scale

do exist. The continuum line may be presented horizontally or vertically; and it can be supplemented by hatch marks, with or without scale points provided. Verbal descriptions can be used either along the continuum line or at the end points only.

Illustrative example 4

Now that you've used this hair conditioner in the past two weeks, can you please rate its performance in terms of making your hair soft and manageable?

Version A: No scale points provided

Least reliable |———x————————————| Most reliable

Version B: Scale points provided

Least reliable |—|—|—|—|—|—|—|x—|—| Most reliable
                1 2 3 4 5 6 7 8 9 10

In constructing a graphic rating scale, extreme descriptions such as 'never' and 'the worst possible' should be avoided lest it forces the respondent into the centre of the scale.

The graphic rating scale is easy to set up and analyse. If numeric intervals are not indicated, one needs to measure the length of interval from the left end-point to the mark inserted by the respondent and assign a number of score that reflects that length.

Pictorial rating scale

This scaling method displays a sequence of facial expressions or word descriptions symbolizing the varying extent of like/dislike, agreement/disagreement and so on. The respondent chooses the one option that best describes his feeling or reaction towards the object of study:

Of the piece of cake which you've just tasted, can you please indicate which of the following facial expressions best describes your reaction to its level of sweetness?

Another way is to present a set of word descriptions in varying print sizes for the respondent to express the intensity of his attitude or feeling:

In your opinion, do you think that abortion should be legally allowed?

☐ ☐ ☐ ☐ ☐ ☐

YES YES YES NO **NO** **NO**

Pictorial rating scale is most appropriate when the study involves kids, the inarticulate respondents or persons who speak languages different from those of the interviewer.

Itemized (or verbal) rating scale

Itemized rating scale (or verbal rating scale as is sometimes known) is one where the respondent is presented with a set of response categories, ordered by the scale positions so as to reflect the degree of attitude held. Itemized rating scale is most commonly used in marketing research.

Illustrative example 5

How likely would you buy this product if it is available in the market at $4.95 per bottle?

I definitely would buy 1
I probably would buy 2
I might or might not buy 3
I probably would not buy 4
I definitely would not buy 5

When constructing an itemized rating scale, the following major issues will need to be considered:

- number of categories
- odd or even number of categories
- balanced or unbalanced scales
- forced or unforced scales
- comparative or non-comparative scales.

Number of categories

There is no fixed rule governing the exact number of response categories required. The researcher can create as many response categories as he deems appropriate, ranging from the simple dichotomous (e.g. Yes-No answer) to as many as 100 in number. A longer list of response categories provides a better precision of the scale. Researchers typically prefer between four and seven categories with five categories being the norm. As a general rule, the more homogeneous the universe under study, the larger the number of response categories is needed; and vice versa.

Most attitudinal questions are asked on a five-point or seven-point scale. The Top Box score for a particular question indicates the percent of all respondents that answer the question by checking/circling the most favourable scale point for that question. The Top 2 Box score refers to the percentage of respondents that check/circle the most favourable and the next most favourable scale points.

There may be reasons for using the Top Box score rather than the Top 2 Box score as a measure for assessing performance in the future. First, recent research evidence suggests that customers who are 'Very Satisfied' (Top Box) are much more loyal than those who are 'Satisfied' or 'Very Satisfied' (Top 2 Box). People who are merely 'Satisfied' are much more likely to defect to a competitor when the right opportunity arises. Second, the Top 2 Box score is an 'easy' score to achieve which may overstate the percent of customers who are truly satisfied. In the

example below, for instance, while the Top 2 Box score of 80 per cent is commendable, the Top Box score of 5 per cent leaves much room for improvement. But a manager looking only at Top 2 Box score may never have realized that.

Illustrative example 6

'Overall, how satisfied are you with CentreBank?'

	percentage of responses
Very satisfied	5
Satisfied	80
Somewhat satisfied	10
Neither satisfied nor dissatisfied	2
Somewhat dissatisfied	1
Dissatisfied	1
Very dissatisfied	1

Odd or even number of categories

The next consideration concerns even or odd number of response categories. An even number of response categories refers when half of the response categories are positive (favourable) statements while the remaining half are negative (or unfavourable) statements. An odd number of categories, on the other hand, includes an additional category which is usually identified as the neutral position.

Illustrative example 7

Even number of categories	Odd number of categories
Strongly agree 1	Strongly agree 1
Somewhat agree 2	Somewhat agree .. 2
Somewhat disagree .. 3	Neither agree nor disagree 3
Strongly disagree ... 4	Somewhat disagree 4
	Strongly disagree .. 5

The inclusion of a neutral category is often debated. Some researchers argue that it would lure the respondent to remain non-committal. Others maintain that neutral feeling or reaction towards an attribute does exist, and if a neutral category is not provided, the respondent would be forced into given an untrue answer. Yet others are indifferent and claim that the two methods do not produce appreciably different results.

Balanced or unbalanced scale

In a balanced scale, the number of favourable response categories equals to that of unfavourable response categories. Otherwise, we have an unbalanced scale. Generally speaking, when prior knowledge through exploratory research suggests a high likelihood of favourable (or unfavourable) responses to the attitude under study, it will be appropriate to adopt an unbalanced scale.

In some cases, scales may be unbalanced in that they may have a greater number of favourable scale points than unfavourable scale points (or vice versa), so that the central point may not be neutral. For example, an unbalanced scale of the type shown below may be used if we know a priori that more respondents will have favourable than unfavourable responses. In this case providing three favourable scale points helps in obtaining a more precise measurement on the 'extent' of respondents' favourable attributes and feelings than would be possible if there were only two favourable scale points. This is also useful in conservative markets where respondents are more guarded in offering praise. Moreover, this scale helps increase the 'spread' or variance of responses which, in turn, provides stronger measures of association.

Forced or unforced scales

The provision, or the lack of it, of 'don't know' or 'no opinion' category provides the distinction between a forced scale and an unforced scale. If such a category is not provided, thus forcing the respondent to take one side or the other, we have a forced scale. Otherwise, we have an unforced scale. A 'don't know' answer should not be looked upon as a neutral response, since a

---

Unbalanced Scale

An example
When prior knowledge (or exploratory research) suggests a high likelihood of favourable responses.

Unbalanced Scale	
Good 75%	Excellent. 1
Neither 20%	Very Good 2
Bad. 5%	Good 3
	Neither 4
	Bad. 5

An example
When prior knowledge (or exploratory research) suggests a high likelihood of unfavourable responses.

Unbalanced Scale	
Good 5%	Good 1
Neither 20%	Neither 2
Bad. 75%	Bad. 3
	Very bad 4
	Extremely bad 5

respondent who is willing to express his feeling towards the research question may fail to do so due to a genuine lack of knowledge about the attribute under study.

Comparative or non-comparative scale

Hitherto, all the rating scales discussed require the respondent to rate an object independently without any reference to or comparison with a specified standard. These non-comparative scales, as they are commonly called, allow the respondent to arbitrarily apply different standards or reference points to evaluate the object under study. In a way, they present ambiguities and uncertainties in the computation and interpretation of the scores given.

To overcome this, researchers sometimes apply a standard or reference point to facilitate comparison, so as to yield more meaning of the scale values. A comparable scale is thus resulted.

Illustrative example 8

Comparative scale

'How would you describe the chocolate flavour of this drink, compared with the other brand of drink that you have tried?'

Non-comparative scale

'How would you describe the chocolate flavour of this drink?'

Paired-comparison scale

Paired-comparison scale is a special kind of comparative scale where the respondent is presented with one pair of objects at a time. This means that if the study involves N objects, each respondent is required to undertake $k = (1/2) N (N-1)$ paired comparisons. Note that when N increases, k increases even more rapidly.

Number of objects (N)	Number of paired-comparisons (k)
5	10
10	45
15	105
20	190

But once N gets large beyond a certain point, the number of paired comparisons becomes too large for the respondent to manage. In this case, each respondent will be asked to deal with a subset of these paired-comparisons, and each paired-comparison will involve an equal number of respondents.

Paired-comparison scale offers the following advantages:

- As it pairs off two objects at a time for direct comparison, such approach usually yields more reliable results than when a large number of objects are evaluated simultaneously.
- When the number of objects is large, it avoids respondent fatigue.
- It requires overt choice and places the compared experience as close together in time as possible.

On the other hand, paired-comparison scale suffers from the following disadvantages:

- As the number of objects increases, the number of paired comparisons required becomes too large to be manageable.
- The test situation lacks reality, for there normally exists more than two objects for comparison in the marketplace.
- While one object is preferred over the other, one cannot assert that either one is *liked* in the absolute sense, for it could be just that the other one was less disliked.

Rank-order rating scale _____

This technique requires the respondent to rank more than two objects (or alternatives) based on some criterion – e.g. good taste, ease of application, attractiveness etc. It is a simpler scale than the paired-comparison scale as its procedure can easily be understood by the respondent.

Rank-order rating scale offers the following advantages:

- Its concept is simple, thus it can be suitably used for self-administered questionnaire.
- Compared to paired-comparison method, it demands less time from the respondent.
- It provides a more realistic market situation.

On the other hand, the key disadvantage of the rank-order rating scale is that it involves ordinal numbers and so is less amendable to mathematical and statistical manipulations.

Constant sum scale

With this technique, the respondent is asked to allocate a fixed number of points – typically 10 to 100 points – to a set of alternatives or objects based upon some predetermined criterion. The points awarded represent the ranks assigned to these alternatives or objects, and also the quality of differences which the respondent places on them. This technique is popular in marketing research for its simplicity and ease of application.

Semantic differential scale

As the term suggests, this scaling technique *measures* the difference between words. Developed by Osgoods and his colleagues (1957), it combines the verbal and diagrammatic techniques using a seven-point, neutral-centred and bi-polar scale. It was primarily used to measure the connotative meaning of concepts. The respondent places a cross 'X' in the position which indicates his or her thinking about a product or service in terms of the 'construct' or 'dimension' along a bi-polar adjective. Osgoods developed twenty bi-polar adjectives which have wide applications:

- active/passive
- cruel/kind
- curved/straight
- masculine/feminine
- untimely/timely
- unsuccessful/successful
- important/unimportant
- angular/rounded
- calm/excitable
- false/true

Constant Sum Scale

An example:

Please allocate 100 points among the product features listed below to reflect how important each product feature is to you in buying a new automobile.

Economy	21
Style	10
Comfort	15
Safety	32
Social Status	4
Price	18
Total	**100**

- The points allocated show rank order
- Total points allocated must add up to exactly 100

- savoury/tasteless
- hard/soft

- new/old
- good/bad
- weak/strong

- usual/unusual
- colourless/colourful
- slow/fast
- beautiful/ugly
- wise/foolish

The mechanics of operating semantic differential scales are relatively simple. In a survey for evaluating the image of a bank, for example, the bi-polar adjectives shown at the foot of the page can be used.

The two end positions indicate *extremely*, the next inner pairs indicate *very*, the middle pairs indicate *somewhat* while the unique middle position indicates *neither nor*. Referring to the illustration below, the bank under study is perceived to be *extremely* secure; *very* conservative; *somewhat* friendly; and *neither large nor small*. The seven positions hold score values from 1 to 7, with larger values assigned to responses nearer the favourable adjectives. The position (that is, left or right-hand side) of the positive adjective of the bi-polar scale should be randomized in order to minimize biased response arising from a fixed positioning.

The semantic differential scales have been used with great success in marketing research studies concerning product image, brand image, advertising image, corporate image, etc. Respondents very often find these areas of studies difficult to articulate their feelings, and semantic differential scale is just the right method for use.

Two general approaches are adopted for the analysis of semantic differential data, namely: aggregate analysis and profile analysis. In aggregate analysis, the scores across all adjective pairs are added up for each respondent to arrive at a summated score. On the basis of total scores calculated, the individual or group of individuals can then be compared to another individual or group of individuals. Two or more objects (e.g. products, brands, stores, etc.) can also be compared for a same group of individuals. Aggregated analysis is most useful for predicting preference or brand share.

In profile or disaggregate analysis, the average scores pertaining to the various groups of individuals are calculated for each pair of polar adjectives and plotted on a master graph known at a 'snake' diagram (see Figure 8.2). Profile analysis is widely

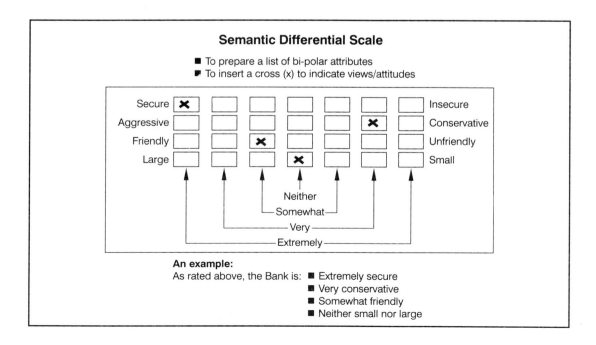

used in applied studies to isolate strong and weak attitudes towards products, brands and the like. Marketing strategies could then be devised to offset the weak attributes on the one hand, and to capitalize on the strong attributes on the other.

Illustrative example 9

Two groups – housewives and businessmen – of 100 respondents each were interviewed to offer their ratings on BIKO Company in terms of four pairs of bi-polar adjectives: powerful-weak, old fashioned-modern, reliable-unreliable and rude-polite.

The rating given by the housewives (denoted by HW) and by the businessmen (denoted by BM) on each pair of bi-polar adjectives are tabulated in terms of their frequencies as follows:

POWERFUL	_ : _ : _ : _ : _ : _ : _	WEAK
HW	20 42 10 5 4 12 7	(Av = 5.05)
BM	40 30 15 5 5 5 0	(Av = 5.80)

OLD-FASHIONED	_ : _ : _ : _ : _ : _ : _	MODERN
HW	5 10 20 25 21 14 5	(Av = 4.09)
BM	8 9 12 20 25 20 6	(Av = 4.29)

RELIABLE	_ : _ : _ : _ : _ : _ : _	UNRELIABLE
HW	52 12 8 10 8 5 5	(Av = 5.55)
BM	10 15 12 22 35 6 0	(Av = 4.25)

RUDE	_ : _ : _ : _ : _ : _ : _	POLITE
HW	15 15 25 20 10 10 5	(Av = 3.45)
BM	5 5 15 20 15 20 20	(Av = 4.75)

The above average scores were calculated by summing up the weighted scores and then dividing it by the number of respondents. For example, the average score offered on powerful-weak attribute is :

Housewive group:

$(20 \times 7) + (42 \times 6) + (10 \times 5) + (5 \times 4) + (4 \times 3)$
$+ (12 \times 2) + (7 \times 1)/100 = 5.05$

Businessman group:

$(40 \times 7) + (30 \times 6) + (15 \times 5) + (5 \times 4) + (5 \times 3)$
$+ (5 \times 2) + (0 \times 1)/100 = 5.80$

These results are plotted on the snake diagram as shown in Figure 8.2.

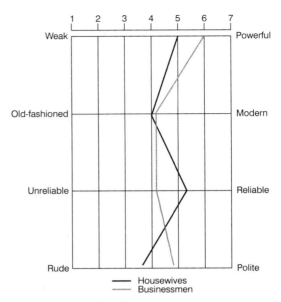

Figure 8.2 *Snake diagram*

Semantic differential scales have the advantages of simplicity and versatility. A controversy which long exists is whether semantic differential scale is ordinal or interval. An increasing number of researchers today accept it as interval data. Such acceptance permits the mean values to be calculated, and in turn broadens the scope of data analysis.

Stapel scale

This is a modified version of a semantic differential scale, using a ten-point scale ranging from –5 to +5 to measure direction and intensity of attitude simultaneously. It uses a single word adjective instead of the polar pair of adjectives or descriptive phrases. Each point on a Stapel scale is assigned a number

Illustrative example 10

Q. Based on the associates you had with research companies in Singapore, how would you rate Pulse Research (Pte) Ltd in terms of . . .

a reliability of data?
b quality of staff?
c reasonable prices?

Circle the number +5 if you think the company can provide very reliable data, and circle the number −5 if you think it would provide very unreliable data, and so on.

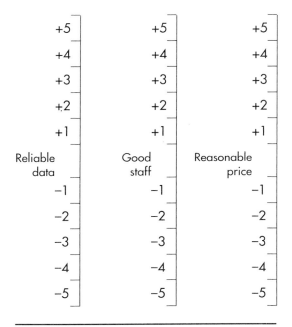

An obvious advantage of the Stapel scale is that there is no need to worry about phrase bi-polarity – a +5 score is truly opposite to a −5 score and so on. The Stapel scale also shows strong promise for measuring beliefs over the telephone, a communication model which is less workable with semantic differential scales.

The Stapel scale is used to develop profile analysis in the same fashion as the semantic differential scale. It is simple to construct and avoid the need to develop bi-polar adjectives for the many items. Despite this, Stapel scale is used less frequently than the semantic differential scale in marketing research, though both produce quite similar results, as methodological research studies have indicated.

Likert summated scale

In both semantic differential and Stapel scales, the respondent evaluates an object in terms of specific adjectives or phases. In practice, however, the respondent may be reluctant or unable to indicate his attitudes in this straightforward manner. Less direct attitude scales are sometimes used.

One such scale developed by Likert is based on summated ratings. A list (or series) of attitude statements about the object under study is compiled and the respondent indicates his or her degree of agreement or disagreement with each of these statements that are related to the object in question on a five-point scale:

- strongly agree
- somewhat agree
- neither agree nor disagree;
- somewhat disagree
- strongly disagree.

It is important to note that the numeric values (or codes) associated with each response category have opposite signs for favourable and unfavourable statements. For a favourable statement, the numeric values are in descending order; while for an unfavourable statement, they are presented in ascending order. The response categories of a Likert scale are simple and straightforward phrasal representations, a reason why the Likert scale is suitable for all methods of data collection. In the Likert scale, favourable statements and unfavourable statements are interspersed in an irregular order for two reasons: first to balance the loading of the statements so as to give respondents the feeling of impartiality, and secondly to induce them to read the statements more carefully before giving a response.

A step-by-step description of how the list of statements in a Likert Scale is developed is given below:

1 A large collection of statements – usually numbering 50 to 100 – relevant to the attitude in question are compiled from depth interviews or exploratory research.

Illustrative example 11

Q. There is a list of statements about National Service. As I read out each statement, can you please tell me whether you agree or disagree with it? (PROBE: Strongly or Somewhat?)

	Agree strongly	Agree somewhat	Neither agree nor disagree	Disagree somewhat	Disagree strongly
National Service inculcates a sense of national loyalty	+2	+1	0	−1	−2
It is a waste of time to do National Service	−2	−1	0	+1	+2

These statements are phrased in a clearly favourable or unfavourable format.

2 This list of statements is then tested on a sample of, say 50 to 100 respondents, who are required to indicate whether they agree (strongly or somewhat) or disagree (strongly or somewhat) to each statement. The sample must exhibit a fair representation of the population under study.

3 The five response categories are assigned with score values (e.g. +2, + 1, 0, −1, −2) in descending order for favourable statements, and in ascending order for unfavourable statements.

4 Each respondent's score is then calculated by adding up the item scores given by him or her to all statements.

5 The final step involves item analysis to decide on statements that discriminate most between the high scorers and the low scorers. For each statement, the top 25 per cent of respondents giving the highest total scores and the last 25 per cent giving the lowest total scores are identified. The mean numerical value is then computed for these top scorers as well as for these bottom scorers. The difference between these two values, called the absolute difference, is used to determine whether or not the statement should be included in the Likert scale. Statements which yield high absolute differences are considered to be discriminating statements and hence should be included. On the contrary, statements which yield low absolute differences are discarded from the final list. An example of the calculated absolute difference for a particular statement is given in Table 8.1.

Table 8.1

	Scale value (x)	Top no.	Scorers' score	Bottom no.	Scorers' score
Strongly agree	+2	10	20	2	4
Somewhat agree	+1	5	5	4	4
Neither agree nor disagree	0	4	0	5	0
Somewhat disagree	−1	3	−3	6	−6
Strongly disagree	−2	3	−6	8	−16
Total		25	16	25	−14
Mean			+0.64		−0.56

Absolute difference (+0.64) − (−0.56) = 1.20

Table 8.2

Statements	Respondent A		Respondent B		Respondent C	
#1	Disagree somewhat	(−1)	Disagree somewhat	(−1)	Neither	(0)
#2	Neither	(0)	Disagree strongly	(−2)	Agree somewhat	(+1)
#3	Agree strongly	(+2)	Neither	(0)	Disagree somewhat	(−1)
#4	Neither	(0)	Agree somewhat	(+1)	Neither	(0)
#5	Disagree strongly	(−2)	Agree somewhat	(+1)	Disagree somewhat	(−1)
Total score		−1		−1		−1

An obvious shortcoming of the Likert scale is that the aggregated total score for respondents may be identical, but their patterns of responses are mostly different. (See Table 8.2.)

In the hypothetical example above, the total scores given by the three respondents A, B and C are the same, but nevertheless, the patterns of their scores offered to the statements are markedly different.

Fortunately, this shortcoming does not pose a severe problem in application because the major interest of the researcher lies in the responses to each statement rather than to a combined set of statements. Perhaps a common argument against using the Likert scale is that it produces ordinal data only. But many researchers today assert that the Likert scale closely resembles an interval scale and regard it so for data analysis. To summarize, researchers find the advantages of the Likert scale outweigh the disadvantages of other indirect scaling techniques.

Thurstone scale

The Thurstone scale was developed by L. L. Thurstone as an acceptable approximation of an interval scale. Like the Likert scale, the Thurstone scale is not universal, which means that a new list of statements needs to be constructed each time with a change of topic under study. A step-by-step construction of the Thurstone scale is described below:

1 The researcher develops and/or assembles an aggregate of statements – as many as 100 to 200 statements – relevant to the subject under study, after consultation with a group of knowledgeable people, or conduct of a literature search, or a combination of both.
2 A panel of between fifteen and twenty judges is invited to sort out the statements into an odd number of piles – usually eleven piles – from *most favourable* to *least favourable* about the subject, with the middle pile representing the *neutral* position. Only the end piles and the middle position pile are anchored with word description:

Most favourable   Neutral   Least favourable

It is presumed that the judges will perceive the eleven piles as representing equal distance apart, with respect to the degree of favourability or disfavourability. For this reason, the Thurstone scale is also known as the 'Method of equal-appearing interval'.
3 Scale values 1, 2, 3, . . ., 11 are assigned from the least favourable pile to the most favourable pile in that order. Note that these values are interval numbers.
4 The pattern of ratings offered to each statement by the judges is examined. A statement showing wide variation of ratings reflects substantial disagreement among the judges and is thus discarded. In

the example shown in Table 8.3, statement S_1 is discarded while statement S_2 is retained.

5 The next step is to determine, for each selected statement, the pile that it should belong to. This pile should be the one where the median rating is located. In the above example, the median rating for S_2 falls in the fifth pile and hence S_2 is allocated to this pile.

6 Sometimes, it may so happen that two or more statements are allocated to the same pile. This is not permissible in the Thurstone scale. When this happens, we retain the statement with the narrowest dispersion of rating in the pile as it reflects the highest level of agreement among the judges.

7 The final step is to assign a numerical value to each statement. A common practice is to adopt the median rating. In this example, the value (or median) for the fifth pile is 5.6.

In applying the Thurstone scaling method, the statements are presented in random order to the respondent who is required to indicate which ones he or she agrees or disagrees with. If the respondent agrees with four statements whose corresponding numerical values are 2.8, 3.3, 1.2 and 1.5 respectively, the rating offered by this particular respondent is calculated as 1/4 (2.8 + 3.3 + 1.2 + 1.5), or 2.2.

The Thurstone scale is generally administered by personal interviews. When first developed by Thurstone, the scale had eleven positions and this is still the most common practice, though any number of positions is also used. A key point to note is that an odd number of positions is preferred to provide a central, neutral situation.

The Thurstone scale has a host of limitations:

1 It is time-consuming to prepare a long list of statements.
2 The panel of judges should be carefully selected to truly represent the target population.
3 The judges themselves may be influenced by their own attitudes.
4 The Thurstone scale fails to indicate the degree of intensity of agreement or disagreement with the various statements.
5 Different groups of respondents can produce the same overall score, even though they may differ in judgement towards individual statements.

Employee attitude survey

Successful service and customer-driven organizations nowadays pay as much attention to their employees as they do their customers. The reason is obvious. It is very easy for dissatisfied employees to channel down their dissatisfaction to customers, either intentionally or unintentionally. When the internal health of an organization is excellent, employees are focused on meeting the internal and external customer needs. On the contrary, when the internal health of an organization is failing, employees are focused on their problems and frustrations, and not on customers.

Table 8.3

Statement	Pile no.											Total
	1	2	3	4	5	6	7	8	9	10	11	
S_1	2	3	3	2	2	3	2	2	2	1	3	25
S_2	1	1	1	6	6	5	4	0	0	1	0	25

This signifies the importance and pressing needs of employee attitude survey to measure employees' attitudes and productivity, without which it would be almost impossible for the top management of an organization to create and sustain a positive, productive workplace. The Gallup Organization helps organizations to undertake employee attitude and productivity measurement with the widely known Gallup Workplace Audit (GWA). Briefly, a GWA is designed to measure the internal health of an organization utilizing a process which provides managers the information to create a more productive, mission-driven, customer-oriented environment, thus resulting in a sustainable external environment. While nearly every GWA is unique in itself, Gallup has identified a group of core questions (see below) which consistently identifies high levels of influence on employee satisfaction, loyalty and workplace productivity.

GALLUP WORKPLACE AUDIT (GWA)

CORE QUESTIONS

(To be included in surveys)

Overall Satisfiction Question

Overall, on a one-to-five scale, how satisfied are you with Gallup as a place to work? (Circle one)

Extremely Dissatisfied 1

Dissatisfied 2

Neither Satisfied nor Dissatisfied 3

Satisfied 4

Extremely Satisfied 5

Strongly Agree = 1
Agree = 2
Neither Agree Nor Disagree = 3
Disagree = 4
Strongly Disagree = 5

1 At work, I have the opportunity to do what I do best every day 1 2 3 4 5

2 My supervisor or someone at work seems to care about me as a person . 1 2 3 4 5

3 I know what is expected of me at work 1 2 3 4 5

4 In the last seven days, I have received recognition or praise for good work 1 2 3 4 5

5 At Gallup, my opinions seem to count 1 2 3 4 5

6 There is someone at work who encourages my development 1 2 3 4 5

7 In the last six months, someone at work has talked to me about my
progress 1 2 3 4 5

8 This last year, I have had opportunities at work to learn and grow 1 2 3 4 5

9 My associates (fellow employees) are committed to doing quality work . . . 1 2 3 4 5

10 The mission of Gallup makes me feel my job is important 1 2 3 4 5

11 I have the materials and equipment I need to do my work right 1 2 3 4 5

12 I have a best friend at work 1 2 3 4 5

End-of-chapter revision

Review questions

8.1 What is meant by measurement and why is it important to marketing research?

8.2 What types of data are of most interest to marketing research? How are they distinguished?

8.3 Distinguish among the four scales of measurement. Give examples of the types of marketing phenomena which each scale might be used to measure.

8.4 What is a nominal scale? What statistics can be used with a nominal scale?

8.5 What is an ordinal scale? What statistics can be used with an ordinal scale?

8.6 What is an interval scale? What statistics can be used with an interval scale?

8.7 Explain what a ratio scale is. What are its advantages over other scales of measurement?

8.8 Develop four different scales for measuring customer preferences for a set of competing brands: one nominal, one ordinal, one interval and one ratio.

8.9 Develop four different scales for measuring customer satisfaction: one nominal, one ordinal, one interval and one ratio.

8.10 Define and describe the following:
a graphic rating scale
b non-comparative rating scale
c itemized rating scale
d pictorial rating scale.

8.11 What are the major issues/decisions to be made in constructing an itemized rating scale?

8.12 Discuss some of the issues involved in the construction of an itemized rating scale.

8.13 Distinguish between balanced and unbalanced scales.

8.14 When should an odd or even number of response categories be used? Explain.

8.15 When should forced or unforced scales be used? Why?

8.16 What advantages and limitations exist for rank-order scales?

8.17 What is a paired comparison? What are its advantages and disadvantages?

8.18 Compare the merits and demerits of rating scales against those for ranking scales. Which one provides more information?

8.19 Describe the semantic differential scale.

8.20 What does the semantic differential scale tell about a person's attitude?

8.21 Develop a set of items (adjectives, phrases and the like) for use in a semantic differential scale to study the attitudes of university students towards:
a nearby canteens
b smokers
c their own university
d automobiles.

8.22 What is profile analysis? Explain the profile analysis method of evaluating data from semantic differential scale.

8.23 How does the Stapel scale differ from the semantic differential scale?

8.24 Describe the Likert scale. What are its advantages?

8.25 What are the steps involved in constructing a Likert scale?

8.26 How does one construct a Thurstone equal-appearing interval scale?

8.27 Indicate the type of scale that would be employed for each of the following characteristics. Present a precise question and the planned data processing associated with each characteristic. Clearly indicate why this results in the scale type stated.
a Colour of a refrigerator.
b Age of a drill press.
c Occupation.
d Advertising budget of a firm.
e Readership of a magazine.
f Brand loyalty.

8.28 Assume that two groups – a group of housewives (HW) and a group of businessmen (BM) – are asked to rate the Mighty Electric Company on the basis of the bi-polar adjective pairs:
a Powerful – Weak
b Reliable – Unreliable
c Modern – Old fashioned.
The frequencies of each group of 100 respondents are shown below:

Powerful	_ : _ : _ : _ : _ : _ : _							Weak
HW	20	42	10	5	4	12	7	
BM	40	30	15	5	5	5	0	

Reliable	_ : _ : _ : _ : _ : _ : _							Unreliable
HW	52	12	8	10	8	5	5	
BM	10	15	12	22	35	6	0	

Modern	_ : _ : _ : _ : _ : _ : _							Old-fashioned
HW	5	14	21	25	20	10	5	
BM	5	20	25	20	12	10	8	

a Using a seven-point scale (where, for example, 7 = extremely powerful and 1 = extremely weak), find a summary rating index for each group of raters for each set of adjective pairs.
b What assumptions are made by using the integers 7, 6, . . . 2, 1 in the scale?

c In which adjective pairs are the rating indices between the groups most similar; most dissimilar?
d What would your answer to (a) be if the weights +3, +2, +1, 0, -1, –2 and –3 were used instead of the weights 7, 6, . . . 1? Would rank order between pairs of summary indices (for each adjective pair) be affected and, if so, how?

8.29 A random sample survey covering 400 respondents was conducted for an evaluation study on two local supermarket chains A and B, in terms of some predetermined attributes, based on a seven-point semantic differential scale. The number of respondents who offered their scores for the respective attributes are given below:

Clean	_ : _ : _ : _ : _ : _ : _							Dirty
Chain A:	82	89	62	61	54	30	22	
Chain B:	51	67	99	77	45	43	18	

Old-fashioned	_ : _ : _ : _ : _ : _ : _							Modern
Chain A:	31	77	87	85	55	47	18	
Chain B:	25	62	83	83	60	57	30	

Inconvenient location	_ : _ : _ : _ : _ : _ : _							Convenient location
Chain A:	30	42	63	69	75	71	50	
Chain B:	21	24	60	77	79	72	67	

Courteous staff	_ : _ : _ : _ : _ : _ : _							Rude staff
Chain A:	32	70	82	66	55	61	34	
Chain B:	36	42	57	67	87	69	42	

Analyse the above data (give calculations up to two decimal places) with an appropriate chart.

8.30 Name the type of number (nominal, ordingal, interval, or ratio) being used in the following questions, and explain your answers.
a Which of the five major TV channels do you watch most frequently?

_____	TV 8
_____	TV5
_____	TV 3
_____	Premier 12
_____	Prime 12

b The temperature tomorrow will reach a high of ?

_____	0°F–20°F
_____	21°F–40°F
_____	41°F–60°F
_____	61°F–80°F
_____	81°F–100°F

c How many potted plants are there in your household?

d How much taller are you now than last year? _____ inches

e How would you rank the following fast food chains, where 1 is the most preferred and 5 is the least preferred?

_____	McDonald's
_____	KFC
_____	Pizza Hut
_____	Long John Silvers

8.31 Assume that a watch manufacturer wishes to know the criteria adopted by the customers in selecting a watch. Construct a semantic differential scale to establish the importance of the various attributes and how a particular brand of watch is provided on those attributes.

True-false questions

Write True (T) or False (F) for the following:

8.32 An ordinal scale has no unit of measurement.

8.33 Ratio scale values possess all the properties of arithmetic operations.

8.34 Only qualitative classification can be achieved on the ordinal scale.

8.35 Measurement of attitudes is always done on a ratio scale.

8.36 A respondent has indicated that his income is $45,000 per year. This information is expressed in the ratio scale of measurement.

8.37 Data from lower scales of measurement allow the use of more powerful methods of statistical analysis.

8.38 Word association test results are generally analysed by determining the frequency with which various responses or response types are given.

8.39 In the cartoon test, respondents are asked to sketch pictures that are relevant to the subject of interest.

8.40 In a balanced scale, the number of favourable categories is equal to the number of unfavourable categories.

8.41 The 'score points' in a basketball game is measured on an interval scale.

8.42 The Thurstone scale is an acceptable approximation of an interval scale.

8.43 The snake diagram is often used to display the findings of a rank-order rating scale.

8.44 Nominal numbers are categorical data which have no numerical value.

8.45 Ordinal numbers are the most primitive and least sophisticated among all types of number.

8.46 The primary functions of nominal numbers are identification and classification of objects/events.

8.47 Statistical measures (e.g. standard deviation, correlation coefficient) are performable with interval numbers.

8.48 Interval numbers are built on a fixed origin or non-arbitrary zero point.

Multiple-choice questions

8.49 Differences in kind rather than degree are measured on the:
a nominal scale
b ordinal scale
c interval scale
d ratio scale.

8.50 The direction but not the amount of difference can be measured on the:
a nominal scale
b ordinal scale
c interval scale
d ratio scale.

8.51 An arbitrary origin and unit of measurement are characteristics of the:
a nominal scale
b ordinal scale
c interval scale
d ratio scale.

8.52 Widely used statistical techniques require measurements at a level not lower than the:
a nominal scale
b ordinal scale
c interval scale
d ratio scale.

8.53 The absolute origin is a characteristic of the:
a nominal scale
b ordinal scale
c interval scale
d ratio scale.

8.54 Adjectives opposite in meaning and separated by a seven-point scale are characteristics of the:
a semantic differential scale
b Thurstone scale
c Likert scale
d Stapel scale.

8.55 In which communication medium would word association not be appropriate?
a Postal questionnaire
b Personal interview
c Depth interview
d Telephone interview.

8.56 'Compared to Diet Coke, how would you rate the taste of Diet Pepsi?' This statement would be appropriate for a rating scale of the:
a semantic differential type
b non-comparative type
c comparative type
d semi-comparative type.

8.57 In a pair-comparison rating scale, there are six objects to be compared. How many comparisons will be necessary?
a 24
b 15
c 12
d 20.

8.58 What scale of measurement do practitioners typically assume for Likert scale results?
a nominal
b ordinal
c interval
d ratio.

8.59 'Our brand currently ranks third in terms of consumer preference.' This implies:
a a ratio scale
b an interval scale
c an ordinal scale
d a nominal scale.

8.60 'Our brand has the unit sales which is twice that of its nearest competitor.' This implies:
a a ratio scale
b an interval scale
c an ordinal scale
d a nominal scale.

8.61 'Darlie is the most refreshing toothpaste.'
Strongly agree 5
Agree 4
Neither agree nor disagree . . . 3
Disagree. 2
Strongly disagree 1
is an example of a:
a graphic rating scale
b semantic differential scale
c Stapel scale
d Likert scale.

8.62 When seeking an appropriate average for nominal data, which would be the statistical measure appropriate to the level of measurement scale:
a median
b arithmetic mean
c mode
d percentile.

8.63 Pictoral rating scale is most appropriate when the respondents are:
a kids
b inarticulate persons
c persons who speak languages different from the interviewer
d all of the above

8.64 Semantic Differential method is of a
a seven-point scale
b five-point scale
c three-point scale
d none of the above

8.65 Likert Scale used in attitude measurement is
a seven-point scale
b five-point scale
c three-point scale
d none of the above

9

Product research and test marketing ___

One of the major application areas of marketing research is in product research. Consumers are being bombarded with new brand-name choices as a record number of new products hit store space. Almost daily, new products make entries into the marketplace while old products exit from it. To keep abreast of this development, marketers are required to constantly evaluate the performances of existing products as well as assess the potentials of new ones.

Product research is the application of market research techniques to business problems in developing new products and modifying existing ones to satisfy consumers' needs and to make profits. It encompasses all forms of marketing research activities which are relevant in supporting the product under study, from inception as product ideas to withdrawal from the product mix. This chapter is primarily concerned with research on new products and their evaluation in a prelaunch situation. However, most of what will be covered is also relevant to existing products, where modifications are being applied. This is particularly pertinent to Singapore, a market for which relatively few products are locally developed and an abundant number of mature products are introduced from overseas.

Basically, product research is necessitated by economically-related factors, including product life cycle, rising cost of new product development and high rate of new product failure. First, all products pass through the

various stages of product life cycle: introduction, growth, maturation, decline and possibly, disappearance. Today's popular products will become obsolete with the passage of time and eventually will be abandoned. To remain competitive and successful, a company requires up-to-date information on the ever-changing needs of consumers – their habits, behaviour, lifestyles and so on. From this viewpoint, marketing research holds the key to the success or failure of a new product. Secondly, the cost of new product development is escalating at such a rapid rate that today it constitutes a major expenditure item of a company. Finally, the failure rate of new products remains high. Of the thousands of new products introduced every year, most fail and are withdrawn. An estimate has put the new product failure rate at between 50 per cent and 90 per cent, depending on which stage of the product life cycle is being considered. Inadequate market analysis, largely due to the deficiency of marketing research data, was identified in a study to be the most significant single factor that contributes to new product failure (see Figure 9.1).

New product development process

Figure 9.2 depicts a schematic diagram of new product development process.

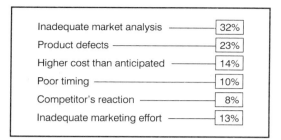

Figure 9.1 *Main reasons for new product failures.* Source: *B. Cochram and G. Thomson (1964) Why New Products Fail. The Conference Board Record, October, pp. 11–18.*

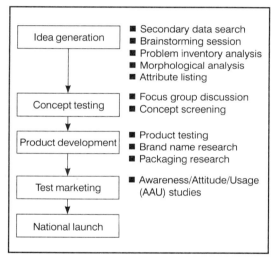

Figure 9.2 *New product development process*

Common research methods accompanying each stage of the process are also indicated.

Idea generation

The product development process begins with idea generation. The objective here is to explore ideas for new products, or in the case of existing products, to identify product improvement, cost reduction, formula change, product repositioning, new attributes and usage patterns. A variety of research procedures can be useful: second-ary data search, brainstorming session, problem inventory analysis, morphological analysis and attribute listing. Each is briefly described below.

Secondary data search

A comprehensive search from secondary data sources can help identify the unfilled need that may exist in the marketplace, and lead to explore new business opportunities that prevail. The search for new product ideas may be stretched across oceans and borders. By copying an idea that has worked well elsewhere, companies can spare themselves months of research time and perhaps millions of dollars. Also, it is a wise step to hedge against the high risk of new product failure. In a survey of senior marketing executives at a new products conference held in Canada not long ago, 86 per cent said they deemed foreign products as a valuable source of ideas.

Brainstorming session

Originated by Alex F. Osborn through his best-seller *Applied Imagination* (1952), this technique quickly gained international prominence. In essence, a brainstorming session serves to reap as many ideas as possible, some perhaps are combinations or variations of ideas gathered from the earlier part of the brainstorming session. Participants are urged that the greater number of ideas generated during the session, the more successful it would be. They are also reques-ted to refrain from criticizing any sugges-tions put forward by the participants, lest it would cause fear of provoking negative reactions amongst the participants.

Problem inventory analysis

Using focus group discussion as its tool, this procedure involves thorough examination of every aspect of consumerism – customers' wants, needs, problems, complaints, wishes, etc. – to explore the underlying causes of discontent.

Morphological analysis

This approach involves two sequential steps. The first step is to identify the relevant dimensions of the product under study. The second step is to enumerate relevant variables with each dimension earlier identified. For a household cleaning product, a total of six dimensions may be identified, together with some of their respective variables are listed below:

Dimensions	Relevant variables (some examples)
1 Type of cleaning instrument	Broom; mop; sponge; vacuum cleaner
2 Product ingredients	Alcohol; disinfectant; pine oil
3 Objects to be cleaned	Brushes; carpet; fences; stoves; windows
4 Packaging design	Bag; bottle; tube; unbreakable
5 Substances to be removed	Dust; germs; mud; rust
6 Texture of the product	Cream; crystals; powder; wax

Finally, new product ideas are generated by taking a combination of variables, one each from the six dimensions.

Attribute listing

Here, all attributes of an existing product are examined with the intention of introducing possible modifications or alterations to generate new product ideas. The options are:

- *Modification.* Should the shape, colour, odour or sound be changed?
- *Size variation.* Should the product be made smaller, bigger, lower, shorter or more condensed?
- *Substitution.* Should any part(s) of the product be replaced by other materials or processes?
- *Rearrangement.* Should the components, sequences or patterns of the product be interchanged?

New product ideas thus generated are further screened and eliminated to a manageable number for subsequent research.

Concept testing

A concept test involves the evaluation of consumer responses towards a product idea or concept before the product is physically developed. At this stage of new product development, the product concept has been generated, but it is short of a tangible (or usable) product. The product concept may simply be a written description outlining how to apply/use the product, the proposed price, and the benefits which the product will yield. At best, pictures of drawings are used to help visualize the written description. Potential consumers are asked to indicate whether or not the product concept has been fully understood and at the same time, to evaluate the product's attributes. In sum, a concept test is designed with the following objectives in mind:

1 To determine customers' understanding of, and attitudes towards the product concept or idea.
2 To measure customers' reactions towards the product's attributes (e.g. packaging, colour, size, etc.).
3 To predict the trial rate of the intended product.
4 To determine whether the product concept warrants further development.
5 To provide guidance on how the product concept might be improved or redefined.

The types of questions asked in a concept test can be of almost infinite variety (see Figure 9.3.)

The buying-intent question is perhaps the most critical of all questions presented in a concept test. It provides a measurement of interest, and is generally accepted as a valid indicator of consumer response to the new

Question items	Typical questions
Buying-intent	'If this product were available at a local store, how likely are you to buy it?'
Frequency of purchase	'How often would you buy the product?'
Place of purchase	'Where would you shop for the product?'
Uniqueness of the concept	'Comparing with other existing products, how different do you think the product is from them?'
Overall impression	'From what you have read about this product, which word or phrase best describes your reaction towards it?'
Price/value reaction	'Which of the statements shown in this card best describes how you feel about the product?'
Product replacement	'Do you feel that the product might partly or totally replace a product that you are using now?' If YES 'What product would it be?'
Product gap	'Do you feel that this product might solve a problem or need which you now have and isn't being satisfied by the existing products?' If YES 'What problem or need?'
Product attribute	'What do you particularly like about the chocolate content of the product?'
Concept comprehension	'Was there anything in the description of this product that was confusing or difficult for you to understand?' If YES 'What was confusing or difficult to understand?'
User	'Do you think that you would be more likely to buy this product for yourself, or as a gift for someone else, or both?'
Like/dislike	'What, if anything, do you think you might like about this product?' 'What, if anything, do you think you might not like about this product?'

Figure 9.3 *Typical questions in concept testing*

product and a predictive value on product sales.

The following table presents the hypothetical results of the buying-intent question in a concept test:

Buying intent	%
I definitely would buy	20
I probably would buy	30
I might or might not buy	24
I probably would not buy	21
I definitely would not buy	5
	100

Most marketers undertake analysis of the buying-intent responses by looking at the 'top box' (*definitely buy*) score or the 'top two boxes' (*definitely buy* and *probably buy*) score. Empirical studies, however, have revealed that non-discriminating respondents tended to mark the top-box(es) for product concept presented to them. They marked *definitely/probably buy* even though they did not buy when the product was actually introduced. On the contrary, some respondents who marked *definitely/probably would not buy* eventually turned out to be buyers. In view of this, some marketers moved from the top boxes system to a procedure which assigns appropriate weights to the *discriminator* response. The example below assumed that among respondents who say they *would definitely buy* the product, about three-quarters of them will actually buy, while 2 per cent of those who say they *definitely would not buy* the product will actually buy and so on. In this manner, the purchase level is estimated at 21.43 per cent.

	Test responses	Weights assigned	Revised scores
	(a)	(b)	(a) × (b)
I definitely would buy	20%	0.75	15.00%
I probably would buy	30%	0.15	4.50%
I might or might not buy	24%	0.05	1.20%
I probably would not buy	21%	0.03	0.63%
I definitely would not buy	5%	0.02	0.10%
Total			21.43%

Concept testing presents a number of problems. First and foremost, there is difficulty in describing the product concept adequately in a short written statement. Realism in the testing situation is lacking. Both sampling and non-sampling errors may give rise to problems related to reliability and validity. Finally, a subsequent change of consumer preferences and competitive offerings can affect the degree of predictive validity.

Product development

Once a concept test suggests strong and favourable conditions for the proposed product, marketers hasten to product development research which encompasses product testing, brand name research and packaging research.

Product testing

Product testing shares many things in common (e.g. objectives, techniques, types of questions asked) with concept testing. Much of what had been described earlier of concept testing applies to product testing as well. Product testing is designed to examine how users perceive a product's value, attributes and benefits, and in what ways these perceived values and attributes relate to actual need and demand. The basic features which differentiate between product testing and concept testing are summarized below:

1 Concept testing typically deals with verbalized or pictorial material only; whereas product testing deals with physical objects that can be tried out and, if necessary, compared to existing products.
2 The *stimuli* used in concept testing is imaginary or intangible, whereas in product testing it is more realistic. This explains the higher research cost for product testing.
3 The role of product testing is primarily to provide answers to such questions as:
   - Which product is better?
   - To what extent is it better – just a little or a lot?
   - Why is one product better than the others?
   - What are the particular likes/dislikes about the product?

Product testing can be carried out under one of the two environments, namely: central location and in-home placement. In the former, product tests take place in a controlled setting (e.g. a shopping mall, a supermarket or market) where *passers-by* are recruited to try the test product. Such studies offer a low-cost alternative, but lack the realism in life since the test products are prepared by trained kitchen personnel (in the case of edible products) instead of by the consumers themselves. A sample copy of the questionnaire used for central location studies is provided in Appendix A at the end of this chapter.

In-home placement test, on the other hand, requires that the test products be placed at the respondent's home for use over a specified period of time. Test products are usually presented *blind*, that is, all the identifying labels or marks are removed. In-home placement tests provide more realism than central location studies, but are more costly (See Appendix B at the end of this chapter for a typical questionnaire used for in-home placement test.)

Three distinct approaches may be adopted to measure the performance of the test product:

1 *Testing against a standard product.* In this case, a standard product is used besides the test product. It may be a competitive product, or the brand leader in the marketplace. The test product usually is an improved product or a product being developed for introduction into the marketplace.
2 *Horse-racing alternatives.* Several products developed by a company are tested against one another to determine which one attains the highest level of consumer acceptance.
3 *Testing against a historical standard.* The test is executed against the performance of a successful product on the market, but which may not be directly involved in the test. However, this method is seldom used due to its limited practical use.

The common types of product test are:

- monadic test
- paired comparison test
- preference and discrimination tests.

1 *Monadic test.* In a monadic test, the respondent evaluates one test product only with no reference whatsoever to other products. The respondent is required to recall a similar product that he or she uses most often when evaluating the test product. Monadic tests can also be operated on a number of test products. In this case, monadic tests are performed on several groups of respondents, with each group involved in one test product only. Care should be taken that these groups of respondents matched each other and are of considerably large size. The monadic test is a realistic kind of product test since in real life, consumers usually try new products one at a time and evaluate them against the products they frequently use when making purchase decisions.

As the respondent needs to test only one product, monadic testing may be very costly due to the high interviewing costs in recruiting respondents.

2 *Paired comparison test.* Paired comparison test obtained its name from the way the product test is performed. A pair of products are presented *blind* to the respondents at the same time. Such tests are commonly used by manufacturers who wish to evaluate a new product against either their own existing product or a competitor's product. A paired comparison test sharpens consumers' perception of the test product and establishes clear preferences of consumers. Unfortunately, the procedure used is somewhat distant from real life than that used in a monadic test, because products are usually judged based on current (or recent) experiences of a similar product. Care must also be exercised to ensure that the trial order of the two products is rotated.

There are three major types of paired comparison tests: Side-by-side, staggered and non-directive.

- Under a *side-by-side* paired comparison test design, the respondents are given two products (usually masked) for use one at a time and are then asked to choose the one that is preferred. The time gap between using the two test products should be short to avoid the possible occurrence of history effect. This design, however, lacks realism as consumers rarely use products side-by-side and hence is not widely used.
- A *staggered* (or *sequential*) paired comparison test involves conducting a monadic test for each of the two products. After each monadic test, respondents forward their reactions and opinions towards the product used. When both the monadic tests end, the respondents are further requested to indicate which one of the two products they prefer, and reason(s) for their preference. Economy is achieved here since this test design yields both

single-product evaluation and double-product comparison. Moreover, the problem of sample differences does not occur as only one group of respondents is involved throughout. A staggered pair comparison test has its drawbacks too. In a test situation, the products may be used in more rapid succession than in normal circumstances. Also, the element of order effect may constitute another weakness, as empirical results have shown that preference is biased in favour of the product tried first. A possible way to tackle this problem is to adopt the *split-ballot* technique, when one product is tried first by one-half of the respondents, and the other product is tried next by the remaining half of the respondents.

- A *non-directive* paired comparison test is a special kind of paired comparison test. Its distinct feature is that when the test products are placed for use, respondents are unaware of the fact that follow-up interviews will be conducted of them at a later date. The respondents would probably deem the placed products as free samples and have no reasons to think that they are in fact participating in any kind of marketing research study. Some time after the product placement, usually two weeks, the respondents are revisited to offer their experiences associated with the products used. This approach is designed to detect whether the respondents observe any differences between the test products and, if so, what differences were observed.

Paired comparison tests claim the following benefits over monadic tests:

- Since direct comparison can sharpen product perception, paired comparison techniques are more sensitive.
- Paired comparison tests are less costly as they involve one sample of respondents only, and are more accurate as they exercise good control over differences among respondents.

- Paired comparison tests improve diagnostic information on the test products.
- Paired comparison tests are closer to the way a product is actually chosen.

3 *Preference and discrimination tests.* Preference and discrimination tests are designed to gauge consumers' capability in differentiating between products. Here, the consumers indicate a definite preference for the test products, or mention a significant difference between the new product A and the old product B. The two main types of product discrimination tests are: triangular (triadic) and double-pair test. In a triangular discrimination test, three products – two are in fact identical (labelled A) and the other is different (labelled B) – are presented *blind* to the respondents. The split ballot technique is employed – one group of respondents gets triad A-A-B and the other group gets triad A-B-B. The respondent is informed that two of the three products presented are identical and the other one is different, and he is required to indicate which one it is. (*Note*: The probability of selecting the correct one through pure guess is one-third, or $p_0 = 0.33$.)

Illustrative example 1:

A sample of 200 consumers are interviewed in a triangular discrimination test involving two products A and B. The results of the test are tabulated below:

	Triad A-A-B	Triad A-B-B
Mention A is different	60	44
Mention B is different	40	56
Sample size (n)	100	100

Eighty-four (or 42 per cent) of the respondents give correct answers and are deemed to be able to discriminate the products. To test statistically the significance of the observed discrimination, we proceed as follows:

$H_0:p = p_0 (= 0.33)$, i.e. there is no clear discrimination

$H_1:p \neq p_0 (= 0.33)$

The test statistic, t, is calculated as follows:

$$t = \frac{p - p_0}{\sqrt{\dfrac{p_0 (1 - p_0)}{n}}} = \frac{0.42 - 0.33}{\sqrt{\dfrac{0.33 (1 - 0.33)}{200}}}$$

$$= 2.707$$

This is a two-sided test. Since 2.707 > 1.96 (at 95 per cent confidence level), the null hypothesis $H_0:p = 0.33$ is rejected. We conclude that there is a clear discrimination of the products by the respondents.

A repeated paired discrimination test, as its name implies, involves a repeat of an identical side-by-side paired comparison test on the same respondent. The pair of products used in the first and second tests are the same, but the respondents are not informed of this. The respondent is asked to indicate which product he or she prefers at each test.

On the basis of random choice, one would expect a quarter ($p_0 = 0.25$) of the respondents to pick one preferred product, say A, twice in a row by chance. The overall *true preference* is then measured by the extent to which the proportion of respondents making clear preferences exceeds 25 per cent.

Illustrative example 2:

A manufacturer of chocolate bars has formulated an *improved* version, labelled A. He wishes to determine whether this improved version is preferred to the existing version B.

A repeated paired discrimination test conducted on 300 customers provided the following final results:

Product preferred in first test	Product preferred in second test	No. of respondents
A $\longleftrightarrow$ A		96
A	B	80
B	A	59
B	B	65
		300

Thus 96 (or 32 per cent) of respondents consistently preferred version A in both tests. To test whether there is a clear preference for version A, we proceed as follows:

$H_0:p = p_0 (= 0.25)$, i.e. there is no clear preference for A

$H_1:p < p_0 (= 0.25)$

we have

$$t = \frac{p - p_0}{\sqrt{\dfrac{p_0 (1 - p_0)}{n}}} = \frac{0.32 - 0.25}{\sqrt{\dfrac{0.25 (1 - 0.25)}{300}}}$$

$$= 2.8$$

This is a one sided test. Since 2.8 > 1.64 (at 95 per cent confidence level), the null hypothesis $H_0:p = 0.25$ is rejected and we conclude that there is a clear preference for the modified version A by the respondents.

Brand name research

Some companies adopt a standard brand name for all their products (e.g. Heinz) while others (e.g. Beecham, Unilever) give each branded line a distinctive name. Whichever the approach it may be, a brand name is intended to convey or support the product concept, as well as emphasize the *unique* selling proposition of the product. A brand name should accomplish the following objectives well:

- Provide connotations of the *uniqueness*, *distinctiveness* and *benefits* of the product.
- Be *catchy*.
- Be *easy to remember*.
- Create *a favourable impression*.

Association test, pronunciation test, memory test, communication power test and preference test are some approaches adopted to evaluate brand names.

Association test uses research techniques such as word matching, free association, sentence completion, story completion, etc. The pronunciation test requires the respondents to read out a list of brand names (including those brand names under consideration), and in the process any hesitation, wrong pronunciation and any variation in emphasis are noted. Often, a tape-recorder is used for playback purposes. The memory test is intended to assess how well a brand name is recalled or remembered from a list of names read. (*Note*: The order in which the specific names are recalled is vital and should be recorded.) The communication power test requires that the respondents associate the product category with the brand names read; and/or associate the brand names with some product attribute statements. The preference test technique is best illustrated by the following example.

Illustrative example 3:

Preference test

A bank commissioned a research organization to conduct a brand name preference test on ten brand names denoted by BN_1, BN_2, ..., BN_{10}. It specifies that the name selected should be the most appropriate one in terms of *being connotative of security, being modern, being easy to pronounce* and *easy to remember*. The relative weights given to these four elements are shown below.

	Weights assigned
Connotative of security	0.45
Connotative of being modern	0.30
Easy to pronounce	0.15
Easy to remember	0.10
Total	1.00

Ten cards each representing a suggested name were prepared. A sample of 200 bank account holders participated in the test.

For each criterion above, the respondents were asked to place each card into one of nine piles with scale points 1, 2, ..., 9 where 1 indicates the least favourable and 9 the most favourable in terms of the criterion being evaluated.

A set of hypothetical ratings given to BN_1 are tabulated as follows:

BN_1 – Scores offered by 200 respondents

Criteria considered	No. of respondents offering scores as indicated									
	1	2	3	4	5	6	7	8	9	Total
Connotative of security	10	16	27	38	34	25	26	12	12	200
Connotative of being modern	39	31	30	29	28	17	16	5	5	200
Being easy to pronounce	8	16	10	20	20	25	26	35	40	200
Being easy to remember	12	18	27	30	42	25	21	13	12	200

The average score for BN_1 in respect of each criterion is shown below:

	Average score
Connotative of security	4.91
Connotative of being modern	3.73
Easy to pronounce	6.11
Easy to remember	4.84

For example, the average score for BN_1 in respect of *connotative of security* is calculated as follows:

$$(1/200) \times [(1 \times 10) + (2 \times 16)$$
$$+ (3 \times 27) + (4 \times 38) + (5 \times 34)$$
$$+ (6 \times 25) + (7 \times 26) + (8 \times 12)$$
$$+ (9 \times 12)] = 4.91$$

Multiplying the average score by its corresponding weight and summing them up, we obtain the weighted score for BN_1:

$$(4.91 \times 0.45)$$
$$+ (3.73 \times 0.30)$$
$$+ (6.11 \times 0.15)$$
$$+ (4.84 \times 0.10) = 4.729$$

Similar calculations are carried out for the other brand names. Finally, the brand name that secures the highest weighted score will be selected.

Packaging research

In ancient times, the role of packaging was product protection and economy, but in modern marketing, such role has expanded manifoldly. Product package has emerged as an important promotional tool to attract purchase, stimulate repurchase, and facilitate storage, transportation and distribution. All these functions call for creative consideration of package design, so much so that marketing research studies are extensively undertaken to determine whether a particular package design meets marketing, economic and environmental needs.

Two types of packaging tests are identified – consumer test and dealer test. In a consumer test, the areas of study would include:

- Testing of advertising copy on the package.
- Association tests for symbols, colours, etc.

- Home usage test (e.g. size, shape, ease of handling, etc.).

Dealer tests, on the other hand, are designed to gather dealers' reactions and opinions on:

- Packaging attraction power.
- Ease of handling, stacking, marking or displaying.
- Incentives to promote sales.

Brand equity research ▬▬▬

The measurement and management of 'brand equity' have become increasingly important issues to a wide range of manufacturers and service providers over the past few years. Companies that market consumer products particularly fast-moving consumer goods (FMCG), have historically concentrated on building sustainable brands. Increasingly, however, companies in many industries are viewing the products and services they sell – and themselves – as 'brands'. The challenge that companies face is how to define and how to measure brand equity.

The Gallup Organization has been conducting brand measurement and brand equity research since the 1930s, whilst *brand equity* has became a widely used term with a multiple of definitions. The Gallup Organization reckons that the most useful definition of 'brand equity' would appear to be: brand equity is the added value which a brand endows a product of service.

Apparently, the benefits of brand equity encompass the following:

1 Brand equity enhances customer loyalty. Brands with high equity are preferred, sought out, and more regularly purchased.
2 Brand equity provides marketers and retailers with the opportunity to obtain high margins, since consumers will pay more, work harder, an/or travel further for high equity brands.

3 Brand equity provides a platform for growth via brand extension and expansion of the brand's franchise.
4 Brand equity provides marketers with valuable leverage throughout their distribution channels. Brands with high equity have an advantage in gaining distributor attention, co-operation, and shelf display space for implementing and extending a company's marketing programmes.
5 Brand equity offers a distinct competitive advantage in that it functions as a barrier to entry into a product category by competing brands.

The Gallup Organization approaches brand equity, and hence its measurement, as the integration of several interrelated key brand characteristics. These characteristics are illustrated in the diagram of the Gallup Brand Equity Measurement Model below.

Gallup's Brand Equity Measurement (BEM) Model involves the assessment and analysis of a range of component measures described below:

● *Brand loyalty: purchase behaviour, purchase intent, preference, willingness to switch advocacy.* Brand loyalty is the degree to which the brand is preferred and selected over its competitors. It is both the primary objective and the major benefit of brand equity, and is situated at the centre of the Gallup BEM Model. Research questions include: measurement of past purchase behaviour/intent to purchase the brand and its competitors; measurement of brand preference and strength of loyalty for the brand and competitor's brands; and measurement of stated and/or demonstrated willingness to switch to a different brand.

● *Brand presence: awareness, familiarity.* Brand presence is the degree to which the brand 'stands out' from its competition. Research questions include: measurement of the first brand (top-of-mind brand) which is mentioned in a given category; measurement of all brands metioned on an unaided basis (unaided awareness)/or an aided basis (aided awareness); measurement of brand marketing communications (including brand advertising) awareness on an unaided and aided basis; and measurement of claimed/reported familiarity with various brands in a given category.

● *Brand position: association, differentiation, image.* Brand position is the degree to which the brand is uniquely positioned and perceptually differentiated from its competitors. Research questions include: measurement of the extent of association between the brand and its competitors on key product/service attributes, claims, and benefits; measurement of the extent of perceived differention between the brand and its competitors; and measurement of the extent of association between the brand and its competitors on key emotional, image, personality and trust/esteem characteristics.

● *Brand experience: satisfaction.* Brand experience is the degree to which customers have had positive or negative experiences with brand purchase and use. Research questions include measurement of brand purchase and usage satisfaction, including both product and service elements.

● *Brand value: perceived price, perceived value, price elasticity, extendibility, willingness to 'work' for.* Brand value is the

**The Gallup Brand Equity Measurement Model
The components of Brand Equity**

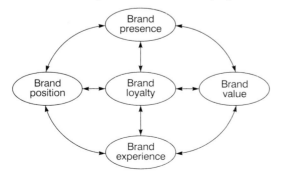

degree to which the brand adds perceived value to a product or service, and/or to a range of proposed product offerings. Research topics include: measurement of the perceived purchase price and the perceived comparative price for competing brands; measurement of the perceived value (price relative to benefits received) for the brand and its competitors; measurement of the elasticity of demand in response to price alternatives for the brand and its key competitors; measurement of the potential for a brand to be extended to other products within an existing category, or into new categories; and measurement of willingness to go out of one's way to obtain, use or purchase the brand.

Test marketing

Before a new product is introduced nation-wide, it is customary to test, on a small portion of the market, its acceptance level as well as the commercial viability of the marketing plan. This procedure, known as test marketing, provides an opportunity to test a new product or a marketing plan under realistic market conditions. Test marketing serves the management with three major functions:

1 To measure sales and profit, and in such a way as to obtain a reasonable prediction for performance at a higher level, be it regional, national, or multi-national.
2 To understand the contributing factors underlying a particular performance, diagnosing those in order to optimize success at a higher geographical level.
3 To provide management with the opportunity to pretest alternative marketing strategies. This involves using different media and promotional mixes in various test markets.

It must be emphasized that, in view of the usually high cost of a market test, only products which have shown a good chance

of being successful in the earlier test (i.e. concept test, product development test) can proceed to this stage. With test marketing, business firms can minimize losses, though not necessarily maximize profits. It also allows the firm a final chance to test its new product, pricing and distribution plans before national introduction. Typical information gathered in test marketing includes:

- Awareness level.
- Purchase and repurchase rate.
- Users' experience with the product.
- Users' perception of the product.
- Market share.
- Users' profile and lifestyles.
- Product usage pattern.
- Reasons for not using product.

Basically in a market test, one is looking for measures of long-term rather than short-term performance; and constant rather than variable factors. The constant (and thus controllable) factors are the product, its price and packaging, advertising and promotion, whereas the variable factors are related to the reactions of retailers and of competitors. In most cases, long term viability of a product depends on repeat purchase, so it is important to isolate this element from initial penetration and trial levels.

The design for test marketing should consider three fundamental issues:

1 The number of test markets to be chosen.
2 The criteria used for selecting test markets.
3 The time duration of the test.

Generally, at least three test markets should be chosen. The more test markets chosen, the more reliable would be the test results; but this will be accompanied by increased costs. Intention to include more test markets should be weighed against the increased benefits that can be expected. As a general rule, when substantial regional differences are observed in relation to the product, a larger number of test markets should be selected.

No single test market or a small group of test markets can truly represent the total intended market for the product. Finding test markets that are demographically representative of national (or regional) markets can be extremely difficult, since no one city or state entirely represents the whole nation. Given the small number involved, the test markets must be selected to best meet the test needs. At the outset, the test market should not be overtested and should be *normal* in that it is not being dominated by any single industry or institution. Next, a test market should be self-contained in terms of media; not only that it should have as little media spillover into neighbouring areas as possible, but also it should receive minimum media impact from outside. Another point is that the test market should be similar in most aspects to the ultimate market it intends to reach.

There is no fixed rule as to how long a market test should last. A typical market test would run from six to twelve months, or for a duration long enough to observe repurchase behaviour. In other words, the shorter the repurchase period of the product, the shorter the test marketing period should be. Soft drinks, biscuits, cigarettes and perishable food experience short repurchase intervals, while toothpaste, hair cream, etc., are usually purchased at relatively long intervals. The latter category of products would require a longer market test. Also, the speed at which competitors react can influence the time duration of the market test. Competitors who come to learn of the market test may beat the firm to the market with a similar product. The Campbell Soup Co. spent eighteen months developing a blended fruit juice called Juiceworks. By the time the product reached the market, three competing brands were already on store shelves. Campbell dropped its product. Also, competitors can deliberately create confusion to test market results by staging unusual promotional activities, implementing new price strategies, or buying all (or a huge amount) of the test product in order to obscure realistic sales figures. Apart from secrecy

consideration, cost is yet another factor that favours a shorter test period. Being an expensive undertaking, a market test should only be considered if the value of research information exceeds the cost it would incur. As a matter of fact, not all new products are test marketed. Highly expensive items (e.g. microwave ovens, cranes, automobiles) are rarely test marketed because the cost would be too prohibitive. Other considerations, including the seasonality of the product, distribution strength or experience with the product category, may also influence the decision on test marketing.

The discussion below compares the approaches used in test marketing and their strengths and weaknesses with reference to the issue described earlier. These approaches are all in common use in the USA, much of Western Europe and Australia. These approaches are:

- town tests
- area tests
- mini tests
- mix tests
- simulated test markets.

They differ considerably in complexity, depth and breadth of measurement, and in cost. One key principle of all these methods is that they measure a *Buying response* rather than an *Intention to buy*. The more sophisticated methods will also attempt to isolate the characteristics of buyers' behaviour which aid more accurate extrapolations.

1 *Town tests.* The town test involves selling-in a new product to as many retailers in one town as possible. Advertising exposure can be achieved by in-store promotions, coupons, local radio, poster and press advertising. Success of the new product in terms of penetration and repeat purchase is gauged by interviewing respondents in the target group, or by using a form of panel and additionally by conducting audits of shop sales.

   Clearly, this form of test depends heavily for its validity on the degree to which the area can be *closed off*, such that interviewers do most of their shopping at retailers who have stocked the new product. Given the closed system, the town test has the attraction of being similar to real selling thus likely to give valid results.

This approach is appropriate to products which are stocked in a range of outlets and whose performance will be affected by the method of display. Furthermore, an assessment of how prepared retailers are to take on the new product is also obtained. Its disadvantages include relatively high cost (in distribution), slowness of getting results, lack of confidentiality, problems of using a *typical* town and the lack of ability to include television advertising.

2 *Area tests*. In many countries (not Singapore), television advertising can be bought on a regional basis. This being the case, it is possible to sell-in a new product to the trade in one television area and then test the new product with the benefit of television advertising, thus providing, in most cases a more realistic situation.

Clearly, these tests can save the vast waste of resources required to go national at once, backed up with an expensive television campaign. However, they are costly and will likely run for between two and six months, and may share the disadvantages found in town tests.

3 *Mini tests*. These can either involve normal retailers or special mobile vans. In the former system, a panel of people who do their shopping at a particular set of selected retailers is recruited and their subsequent purchase behaviour in those shops are recorded.

While the principle of both approaches is the same, the van method offers more confidentiality. In this latter system, a van calls at a panel of households on a regular basis. The advantage of these systems is that prelaunch buying behaviour can be compared to post-launch behaviour. Estimates of trial repeat purchase and cannibalization can thus be obtained.

Generally speaking, mini tests are most appropriate where the products in question tend to be generally stocked in supermarkets and where the target market shops, in the main, in this type of store. It is not normally possible to use television backup.

4 *Mix tests*. In these tests, the basic procedure is to first display the product and/or advertising concept to a large group of target respondents in a central location. Those people who react favourably to the product are given it to use at home. Later a recall is made on those respondents in order to obtain estimates of likely repurchase levels. The test will cover areas such as intention to purchase, product evaluation, perceived value for money, and substitute/competitive usage.

One of the key elements in interpreting the test results in terms of sales estimation is establishing back data for similar products in similar markets where the tests have been carried out. Responses to scales, such an *intention to purchase*, will vary by product field and by country so the interpretation must take this into account.

As well as obtaining consumer behaviour estimates on trial, repeat purchase and purchase frequency, these tests can also incorporate likely shop distribution levels into their calculation for sales estimates.

5 *Simulated test markets*. To a certain extent simulated test markets have a degree of similarity with mini tests. The difference is really in the data analysis rather than the nature of interviewing. In a mini test, the settled level of purchase after a number of visits is used as the estimate.

Simulated test markets use a mathematical model for repeat purchase estimates from the first few purchase occasions. Thus, it is often a much shorter test sometimes involving only a couple of contacts with respondents. Examples of such procedures are Sensor and Assessor, the background and approach of which are described below. No attempt is made to compare the virtues of each method as these are relatively specialized models and must be judged on their own merits with respect to individual research problems and marketing circumstances.

- *Sensor*: Here respondents are recruited at central locations, exposed to advertising and then taken to a simulated shop display with the test brand and its competitor's. They are given coupons worth a certain sum of money to spend on the products on display.

  It has been claimed that the percentage buying in this forced penetration has been found empirically to estimate trial in the marketplace around a year after launch under conditions of 100 per cent awareness and distribution. Trialists try the product in homes and are later recalled on. An additional number of non-trialists are also placed with the product to simulate a sampling exercise.

  On recall, preference questions are covered, an opportunity to buy the test product with the respondent's own money is given and a brand price trade off (to look at price sensitivity) is included. Diagnostic questioning is also included. Long-term repeat purchase is obtained by three kinds of model; from the preference questions, from a Markov model applied to repeat buyers and the trade-off model. The Parfitt-Collins equations are used to obtain a market share estimate. If deemed necessary due to additional product placements, more than one recontact can be made.

- *Assessor*: like sensor, assessor involves a *laboratory* phase then call-back after placement. It attempts to measure all elements of the marketing mix i.e. product, positioning, advertising, pricing, packaging, brand name, etc.

  First, a set of perceptual, behavioural and motivational data is obtained from a *laboratory* test which covers screening, advertising viewing and a simulated shop purchase situation. The screening stage questionnaire covers product usage, habits, last brand purchased and demographics. The next phase in the laboratory test covers (i) perceptions of brands on a list of attributes related to perception and preference, (ii) comparison of test and evoked brands on preference strength (chip game) and other specific open-ended responses.

Respondents who buy the test brand in the test take it home for usage. Non-buyers are also sampled. The respondents are later reinterviewed at home. This interview covers usage reverification, rating of test product on product attributes, comparison of test and evoked brands, opportunity to repurchase, future purchase intention, details of test product usage patterns and intention towards future repurchase. The advantages of simulated test market design are that they need shorter time than area or shop tests to complete. Also they are logistically less troublesome for the manufacturer as they do not have to get the test brand into distribution with promotional support and so on. They afford a greater degree of confidentiality as well. However, their relevance will depend on how the market or a new product about to enter is defined.

It is evident that all the approaches described above have their strengths and weaknesses in terms of methodology, realism, confidentiality and cost. There is no way in which any can be selected as *the best* approach. Each will perform differently depending on which market conditions prevail. Also, overall research objectives with respect to the elements of marketing mix under test will determine which approach is applied. There is, in addition, of course the cost of the exercise. Test market costs are not proportional to the market size but tend to be proportional to risks in general. Thus, one must clearly trade off the cost and risk before determining first whether to test market and then how to test market.

National launch

As mentioned previously, a new product is usually displayed in some test markets that demographically represents the entire national market. Test marketing, therefore, is a cautious and usually prudent step, and it assumes that results gathered from the test markets can be projected nationwide. Upon successful completion of test marketing, the full-scale nationwide launch of the new product will then follow.

Classification of new products by market

When conducting either a *real life* market test or a simulated market test, it is vital to clearly define the market within which the product is competing. This is necessary so as to know which other products should be monitored and, where relevant, what type of stores to use.

Often the views of manufacturers, the retailers and the consumers of a new product are different. For example, the retailers' view will strongly influence where he or she positions the product in the store. For instance, margarine as a product category competes with butter and also oils and fats. Margarine brands clearly compete with one another but will also depend on their formulation with one or other of these additional products. Thus, the competitive context for a new brand of margarine will depend on its proposed advertising platform and end use. Therefore, different margarines will require different competitive products to be monitored during the test.

The evolutionary nature of the market must also be taken into consideration. A new brand of specially produced crisp bread would compete with all crisp breads (at least). Let us assume that two or three imitators come along and create a new submarket. If a new brand were then proposed, this new submarket may well become the likely competitive context.

Thus, it is critical that the correct scenario be defined before a market test is designed. The following outlines the most common market types in which a new product or brand can find itself being positioned:

- *Tightly defined markets.* This is likely to be a market which is similarly defined by manufacturer, retailer and consumer. In other words, a group of brands fulfilling a similar purpose which compete for purchases are found in the same location in-store. These would include washing powder, dog food, take-home ice-cream and mouthwash. However, there is a definite distinction between those markets where purchases are made at fixed and more regular intervals (e.g. dog food, washing powder) and those markets where purchases are made less regularly. In the latter case, there is scope for increasing the market size or increasing purchase frequency.
- *Loosely defined markets.* An example here would be household cleaners. This market has a lot of specialized products, such as window, floor and toilet cleaners, but also a great many general purpose cleaners. Consumers often have a repertoire of products that they use for these tasks. Frequency of purchase is often low and replacement is not automatic when the pack is used up. A similar lack of definition can be found in many food products. Competitors for a new product may come in different packs and preparations e.g. chilled, frozen and tinned, and thus be found in different parts of the store. In these instances it is almost impossible to obtain share estimates (even if these were meaningful) because total market volumes are difficult to estimate. One can only really hope for a fix on volumes.
- *Products which cover different markets.* Examples of these would be perfumed deodorants, which would ostensibly be used as a deodorant but might also be used as a perfume substitute. Also, breakfast cereals which are eaten as a

snack food as well as at breakfast time would qualify as this type of product. If new products are tested in only one of these market scenarios, it is likely the potential market volume will be underestimated. In this case, the manufacturer should be aware of the situation, particularly when the test estimates fall just short of his or her break-even volume.

● *Unique new products.* These are in most markets relatively rare. They do not compete with any other brand. The launch of the first fabric conditioner in any country would be an example.

The role of test market projects in Singapore

When contemplating a test market exercise in Singapore, the marketer has to consider the type of market his or her product is about to enter and the range of research methods available against the background of Singapore's own characteristics. This will assist in determining whether a prelaunch test is necessary and appropriate and if so, which method(s) should be employed.

Singapore differs from the vast majority of countries where products are test marketed in terms of its scale. It is small in terms of population and market size, but so are New Zealand and Ireland where this research is not frequently conducted. However, it is also very compact geographically. It is this latter factor more than any other which makes some of the test market approaches difficult to implement. Yet, at the same time, it is potentially beneficial to other approaches.

The Singapore population is a heterogeneous one. However, it is well distributed across the island in that there are very few areas where certain sectors of the population (e.g. high income groups, ethnic groups, age groups, etc.) tend to concentrate. Thus, there would be little problem in finding test areas with population/consumer profiles to match the total population. This is a problem in the UK, for example, where many ideally positioned test towns possess idiosyncratic profiles, thus making them risky for test operations.

Another factor that needs to be taken into account in Singapore the range and repertoire of outlets used by the consumer. Generally, a lower proportion of purchases are made in supermarkets compared to other countries where many of these test operations are used. This has ramifications on the realism of certain types of test.

A key area of test marketing which cannot be controlled on a restricted area basis is television advertising, a key component in the overall mix. This may be possible in years to come, should cable television become widely available. However, in the meantime, it puts some of the test market methods at a disadvantage.

Appendix A: Central location studies (beverage taste test questionnaire)

INTRODUCTION: Good morning/afternoon/evening. My name is ... and I work as an interviewer for Consumer Research Ltd, which is a private independent marketing research company undertaking surveys on various topics. We are currently doing a beverage taste test and would be grateful for your co-operation.

A well-established manufacturer of beverages is interested in obtaining the opinions of consumers about these two products, labelled here M6 and L5. You have been selected for the survey and we would like to invite you to try these two products and give us your opinions of them.

FOR OFFICE USE: QUOTA REQUIREMENTS

Test No.	Order of Trial	No. of Respondents
A	Try M6 first Try L5 second	100
B	Try L5 first Try M6 second	100

- ALLOW RESPONDENT SUFFICIENT TIME TO THOROUGHLY TASTE FIRST PRODUCT.
- ALWAYS PLACE FIRST PRODUCT TESTED TO RESPONDENT'S LEFT AS HE OR SHE SEES IT.
- ALWAYS RETURN FIRST PRODUCT TESTED TO THAT POSITION.

Q1.	SHOWCARD A Thinking of the product you've just tried, can you tell me which one of the statements in this card best describes your interest in buying it if it is available in the market?	Definitely would buy. . . . Probably would buy . . . . Might or might not buy . . Probably would not buy . Definitely would not buy .	1 2 3 4 5
Q2.	SHOWCARD B Can you show me on this card, how you would say you like this product, in general?	Do not like it at all . . . . . Like it a little . . . . Like it. . . . . Like it very much . . . . . . There is nothing better . . Don't know	1 2 3 4 5 6
Q3.	What do you particularly like about the products? (PROBE: Anything else?)		
Q4.	What do you particularly dislike about the product? (PROBE: Anything else?)		

Q5.	SHOWCARD C Which phrase from this card best describes how you feel about the sweetness of this product?	Much too sweet . . . . Somewhat too sweet. . . . About right amount of sweetness . . . . Not quite sweet enough . Not at all sweet . . . . Don't know	1 2 3 4 5 6
Q6	SHOWCARD D Which phrase from this card best describes how you feel about the strength of flavour of this product?	Much too strong . . . . . . Somewhat too strong . . . About right . . . . Somewhat too weak. . . . Much too weak . . . . Don't know	1 2 3 4 5 6
Q7– Q12	● REQUEST RESPONDENT TO TAKE A DRINK OF PLAIN WATER BEFORE CONTINUING WITH THE SECOND TEST PRODUCT. ● ALLOW RESPONDENT SUFFICIENT TIME TO THOROUGHLY TASTE THE SECOND PRODUCT. ● ALWAYS PLACE SECOND PRODUCT TESTED TO RESPONDENT'S RIGHT AS HE OR SHE SEES IT. ● ALWAYS RETURN SECOND PRODUCT TESTED TO THAT POSITION. (REPEAT Q1–Q6 FOR SECOND PRODUCT TESTED)		

Q13	Now, you have tried both products here. Taking everything into consideration, which product would you say you preferred more in general – the first you tested or the second? (PROBE: Would you say that you preferred it a lot more than the other one you tested or only a little more?)	Prefer 1st product tested:
		  a lot more . . . .
		  only a little more . . . .
		Prefer 2nd product tested:
		  a lot more . . . .
		  only a little more . . . .
		Prefer both equally. . . . .
		Neither preferred. . . . . .
		Don't know . . . .
			
			1
			2
			
			3
			4
			5
			6
			7

Q14	Thinking of the level of sweetness, which one would you say you preferred more, the first product you tested or the second?	First product tested. . . . . Second product tested . . Prefer both equally. . . . . Neither preferred. . . . . . Don't know	1 2 3 4 5

Q15	Which has the more appealing colour, the first product you tested or the second?	First product tested . . . . . Second product tested . . Don't know	1 2 3
Q16	Which has the better flavour, the first product you tested or the second?	First product tested . . . . . Second product tested . . Don't know	1 2 3
Q17	Which is more like a natural orange juice, the first product you tested or the second?	First product tested Second product tested Don't know	1 2 3

Appendix B In-home placement test (shampoo product questionnaire)

FIRST VISIT TO HOUSEHOLD

Introduction: Good morning/afternoon/evening. My name is ... and I work as an interviewer for Consumer Research Ltd, which is a private independent marketing research company undertaking surveys on various topics. We are currently doing a shampoo product survey and would be grateful for your co-operation.

I have here a bottle of shampoo (LABELLED LR) which I would like you to try for the next two weeks. Please use this shampoo as you would normally use your regular brand and keep the bottle for me when I come back in two weeks' time.

HAND OVER FIRST TEST PRODUCT (LR) TO HOUSEHOLD FOR USE

SECOND VISIT TO HOUSEHOLD

Q1	May I have the bottle of shampoo I gave you to try?		
Q2	How many times have you used this shampoo? IF SHAMPOO NOT USED, TERMINATE INTERVIEW OR ARRANGE FOR REVISIT.		
Q3	What, if any, do you particularly like about this shampoo? (PROBE: Anything else?)		
Q4	What, if any, do you particularly dislike about this shampoo? (PROBE: Anything else?)		
Q5	Would you say that this shampoo . . . . . . (READ OUT)? (PROBE: Very/Somewhat)	Cleans hair well Very . . . . Somewhat . . . . Does not clean hair well Very . . . . Somewhat	1 2 3 4
Q6	Would you say the lather of this shampoo is . . . . . . (READ OUT)?	Too much . . . . Just right. . . . . Too little . . . . No opinion	1 2 3 4
Q7	Would you say this shampoo is . . . . . . (READ OUT)?	Easy to rinse off Very . . . . Somewhat . . . . Not easy to rinse off Somewhat . . . . Very . . . . No opinion	1 2 3 4 5

Q8	Does this shampoo leave your hair . . . . . . (READ OUT)? (PROBE: Very/Somewhat)	Feeling soft
		    Very . . . .
		    Somewhat . . . .
		Not feeling soft
		    Somewhat . . . .
		    Very . . . .
		No opinion . . . .
			1
			2
			
			3
			4
			5

Q9	Does this shampoo leave your hair . . . . . . (READ OUT)? (PROBE: Very/Somewhat)	Shiny
		    Very . . . .
		    Somewhat . . . .
		Dull
		    Somewhat . . . .
		    Very . . . .
		No opinion . . . .
			1
			2
			
			3
			4
			5

Q10	Would you say this shampoo . . . . . . (READ OUT)? (PROBE: Very/Somewhat)	Prevents dandruff
		    Very . . . .
		    Somewhat . . . .
		Does not prevent dandruff
		    Somewhat . . . .
		    Very . . . .
		No opinion . . . .
			1
			2
			
			3
			4
			5

Q11	Would you say this shampoo causes your scalp . . . . . . (READ OUT)?	To itch . . . . Not to itch. . . . . No opinion	1 2 3
Q12	Would you say this shampoo leaves your hair . . . . . . (READ OUT)?	Easy to manage. . . . . . . Not easy to manage. . . . No opinion	1 2 3
Q13	Does this shampoo . . . . . . (READ OUT)?	Have a pleasant fragrance Not have a pleasant fragrance . . . . No opinion	1 2 3

Q14	Is the fragrance of this shampoo . . . . . . (READ OUT)? (PROBE: Very/Somewhat)	Strong
		    Very . . . .
		    Somewhat . . . .
		Not strong
		    Somewhat . . . .
		    Very . . . .
		No opinion . . . .
			1
			2
			
			3
			4
			5

Q15	Is this shampoo of . . . . . .
	(READ OUT)? (PROBE: Very/Somewhat)
		Good quality
		   Very . . . .
		   Somewhat . . . .
		Not good quality
		   Somewhat . . . .
		   Very . . . .
		   No opinion . . . .
			1
			 2
			
			 3
			 4
			 5

Q16	How interested would you be to buy this shampoo for regular use?
	(PROBE: Very/Somewhat)
		Interested
		   Very . . . .
		   Somewhat . . . .
		Not interested
		   Somewhat . . . .
		   Very . . . .
		   No opinion . . . .
			1
			 2
			
			 3
			 4
			 5

	• IMMEDIATELY AFTER THE INTERVIEW, HAND OVER SECOND PRODUCT TO HOUSEHOLD FOR USE. • INTRODUCTION: I have here a bottle of another shampoo (LABELLED SP) which I would like you to try over the next two weeks. Again, please use it as you would normally use your regular shampoo and keep this bottle for me until I come back in two weeks' time.		
	• THIRD VISIT TO HOUSEHOLD REPEAT Q1–16 ON SECOND PRODUCT PLACED. • IN ADDITION, PROCEED TO ASK THE FOLLOWING QUESTIONS.		
Q17	Taking everything into consideration, which one of the two shampoos do you prefer, the first or the second that you tried?	Prefer 1st shampoo. . . . . Prefer 2nd shampoo	1 2
Q18	Why do you say so? _____ _____ _____ _____ _____ _____		

End-of-chapter revision

Review questions

9.1 What are the steps in new product development in which marketing research typically plays an active role?

9.2 What are the major sources of new product ideas?

9.3 Describe the essential characteristics of each of the following methods of generating new product ideas:
  a Attribute listing.
  b Morphological analysis.
  c Brainstorming session.
  d Focus group discussion.

9.4 What is meant by concept testing? How is it useful to marketing researchers?

9.5 What research techniques are used in concept testing?

9.6 What is a 'top-box' score? Why may top-box score be poor predictor or trial rate?

9.7 What steps might a research analyst take to improve the predictive validity of top-box scores as indicators of probable trial rate? Explain with a real or hypothetical example.

9.8 What would you say are the major problems involved in concept testing?

9.9 What is a product concept?

9.10 How do monadic, comparative, sequential monadic tests differ?

9.11 What are the reasons for preferring comparative to monadic tests (in general)?

9.12 What is meant by position bias in a product comparison test? Give a real or hypothetical example to illustrate how an unethical marketing researcher might take advantage of this phenomenon.

9.13 What is test marketing? What are the main purposes of test marketing?

9.14 For what kinds of investigation can test markets be used?

9.15 What potential problems may be encountered in a test marketing effort?

9.16 What information can test marketing provide?

9.17 How long should a test market run?

9.18 Name the factors which may affect the choice of a test market.

9.19 In product testing, there are a number of ways in which tests may be conducted. Discuss the following issues:
  a Central location test vs In-home placement test.
  b Monadic test vs Comparative test.

9.20 Your company intends to introduce a new brand of rice cooker. Describe how you would go about conducting product research studies to obtain marketing information needed to support/implement the intention.

9.21 Your company has developed a new shampoo. You are required to conduct a survey to determine the potential market of this new product. Describe briefly the type(s) of research you would conduct.

9.22 Your company has developed three new cake mixes of different tastes. Research is required to determine which is most preferred by consumers. Describe in some details the research you would conduct.

True-false questions

Write True (T) or False (F) for the following:

9.23 In product comparison tests, position bias is least likely to occur when the products are very similar.

9.24 Problem inventory analysis is a method used for concept testing.

9.25 The stimuli used in concept testing is imaginary or intangible.

9.26 Morphological analysis involves an examination of all the attributes of an existing product with a view to introduce possible modifications or alterations.

9.27 The 'Top two boxes' score refers to the sum of 'definitely buy' score and 'probably buy' score.

9.28 Product testing deals with verbalized or pictorial description of the new product.

9.29 In a non-directive paired comparison test, the respondents are informed of follow-up interviews at the time when the test product is placed for their use.

9.30 Test marketing is undertaken after the new product is introduced nationwide.

9.31 The question on buying-intent is generally the most crucial question presented in product concept testing.

9.32 In a central location test, the test products are placed at the respondent's home for use over a specified period of time.

9.33 In a preference/discrimination test, the respondent evaluates one test product only without reference whatsoever to any other products.

9.34 The shorter the repurchase period of the product, the shorter the test marketing period should be.

Multiple-Choice Questions

9.35 _____ is used in idea generation.
   a Secondary data search.
   b Brainstorming session.
   c Morphological analysis.
   d All of the above.

9.36 Which of the following is not part of the product development process?
   a Idea generation.
   b Concept testing.
   c Test marketing.
   d Questionnaire pretest.

9.37 The disadvantages of concept testing include:
   a difficulty in providing a brief description of the product concept
   b lack of realism in the testing situation
   c a change of consumer preference and competitive offerings
   d all of the above.

9.38 _____ may be used in product testing.
   a Monadic test.
   b Paired-comparison test.
   c Preference and discrimination tests.
   d All of the above.

9.39 A concept test is designed with the following objectives in mind.
   a To determine customers' understanding of the product concept or idea.
   b To measure customers' reactions toward the product concept or idea.
   c To predict the trial rate of the intended product.
   d All of the above.

9.40 Monadic test can take the following forms:
   a side-by-side comparison
   b staggered comparison
   c non-directive comparison
   d none of the above.

10

Advertising research

Advertising is a paid form of communications. It has become an important part of modern economic life. Ogilvy Mather maintained that advertising constitutes an integral component of a product, and is to be regarded as production cost rather than as selling cost (Ogilvy Mather [1984] Ogilvy on Advertising. *World Executive's Digest*, February, p. 122.)

The benefits of advertising are manifold:

- It helps the consumer to be a productive shopper by providing information up front.
- It adds value to a brand.
- It creates higher interest and trial rate of the product advertised.
- It stimulates demand, thus helping to reduce the product's unit cost.
- It helps change consumer's perception and attitudes.
- It helps to close the sale faster.
- It helps media owners improve their services through advertising revenues.

Indeed each year, huge outlays are being channelled into advertising with an attempt to persuade people to buy goods and services. In 1997, an estimated S$1,275.2 million were spent in Singapore on advertising equivalent to a per capita expenditure of S$425 (US$300).

Scope of advertising research

With advertising playing a vital role in marketing, the importance of advertising research cannot be overstated. As a matter of fact, one of the major application areas of marketing research is in the field of advertising. John Wanamaker, a prominent retailer, once said: 'I know half the dollars I spend on advertising is wasted – I just don't know which half.' Advertising research is therefore needed to obtain an objective evaluation of advertising as a method of communication and persuasion, and its ingredients

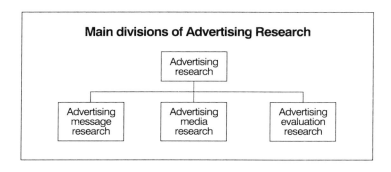

lie in measuring the comprehension of advertisement messages, the impact of the advertisement (e.g. sales volumes) and the preference for the advertising media used. Advertising research can be broadly classified into three main divisions (see previous page).

Advertising message research

Advertising message research focuses on how the advertisement can project the desired message. More specifically, it explores how well the advertisement messages are understood and believed; how much interest and impact have been created and the like. Such facts will be established in advertising message research to guide designers in producing effective advertisements.

Essentially, advertising message research necessitates the conduct of tests to be run either on the entire advertisement or on some specific parts of an advertisement. The most widely used is *copy test*. (*Note*: The term *copy* is used in this context to cover all aspects of the test advertisement, including advertising messages, graphics, pictures, scenes, colour, action, dramatization and so on.) The advertisement involved in a copy test can be a mere written concept, a set of storyboards, drawings, sketches, a rough animated version, or a finished advertisement. A copy test can be one of the following two types:

1. Pretest – when the test is conducted *before* media dollars have been spent on releasing the advertisement.
2. Post-test – when the test is conducted *after* media dollars have been spent on releasing the advertisement.

Advertisement pretesting

Advertising pretesting focuses on developing ideas and methods of presentation. It helps the advertiser to decide whether improvements to the advertisement (e.g. copy, illustration, headline, etc.) are needed. It involves copy testing which not only allows for an evaluation of consumer response to the advertising copy being investigated, but also gauges the extent to which the intended message is being communicated. It is used most effectively at the conceptual stage of copy development to allow for consumer feedback on concepts portrayed by preliminary advertisement copy. In this respect, advertising pretest is extremely useful in avoiding cost wastage on ineffective advertisements.

Research techniques that are commonly used in advertising pretesting are listed in Figure 10.1

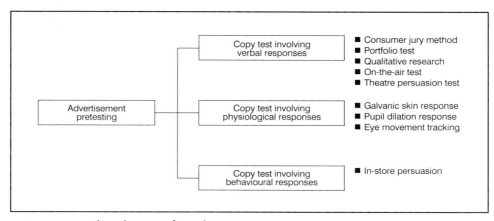

Figure 10.1 *Research techniques for advertisement pretesting*

Consumer jury method.

A panel comprising fifty to a hundred target customers views the test advertisements and ranks them in order of preference, interest or the influence to buy the product. A typical portion of the questionnaire used in the consumer jury test appears below:

What do you think are the intended messages of the advertisement?
How well would you say the advertisement illustrates its messages?
What do you like most about the advertisement?
Which one of these advertisements would you like to read most? Version A . . . . 1 Version B . . . . 2 Version C . . . . 3 Version D 4
Which advertisement interests you most in buying the product? Version A . . . . 1 Version B . . . . 2 Version C . . . . 3 Version D 4

The jurors rank the advertisements in the order of the above dimensions. They may view advertisements individually or collectively; and the evaluation process may take place at home or under controlled conditions.

There are some limitations in the consumer jury method. Among them are:

a Difficulty in selecting a panel of jury members who would be truly representative of the target population.
b Intergroup influence can bias results.
c In the event that the number of advertisements to be tested is considerably large, the jurors will have difficulty in ranking the advertisements on the identified dimensions accurately.

Portfolio test.

This requires a sample of consumers to look through a package usually consisting of six to eight print advertisements, called a portfolio. Respondents are allowed sufficient time to read these advertisements. The portfolio is then taken away and the respondents are asked to recall the specifics about the advertisements including what products and brands they remember seeing. Recall measures are generally unaided. In the case of recall failure, the portfolio is again presented to the respondents. The effectiveness of the test advertisement is measured by such attributes as: claim of credibility in the advertisement, ability to recall the advertisement and the details, general reaction to the advertisement as well as intention to use the advertised product.

Despite its wide application, the portfolio test has its problems. Researchers are particularly concerned that the level of advertisement recall may be much influenced by consumers' interest in the products appearing in the test advertisements.

Qualitative research.

Focus group discussions and depth interviews are the main tools used in qualitative research for obtaining consumers' spontaneous feedback of an advertisement at the development stage. In particular, anything about the advertisement which the consumers consider vague or confusing will be explored; and any unfavourable selling point which the consumers *take away* from the test advertisement can be revealed. Major drawbacks inherent in the test advertisement can be detected early for rectification. Additionally, these tools are used to test against advertising strategies.

On-the-air test.

Besides qualitative research, small-scale quantitative research techniques are employed to gather *early feedback* regarding test advertisements. The better known technique is the on-the-air test, or the day-after recall method. The procedure of the on-the-air test is: first, the test advertisement is broadcast in three or four test markets (e.g. cities, towns, etc.); and secondly, selected respondents are interviewed on the following day over the phone to ascertain:

a Whether they watched the particular programme in which the test advertisement was telecast; if so, whether they could recall seeing the test advertisement.
b What they recalled about the test advertisement, and what the test advertisement had said.
c How they rated the test advertisement in terms of being informative, believable, understandable, humorous, etc.

The interview usually begins by adopting an unaided approach, followed by aided prompts whenever necessary.

Theatre persuasion test.
In the theatre persuasion test, a group of target consumers is invited to a theatrette. Earlier, they had been told that they will be shown pilot episodes of new television programmes with the intention to disguise the survey purpose. Before the show begins, the audience is presented with a list of product brands (including the brand shown in the test advertisement) and asked to indicate their preferred brand. It is announced that a lucky draw will be held, and the winners will each receive one free unit of their preferred brand of product. The lucky draw is then held and subsequently the winners are announced and awarded their prizes. After this, the television programmes are shown, with several advertisements, (including the test advertisement) inserted in between. At the end of the show, the audience is once again asked to indicate their preferred brand, followed by a similar lucky draw and prizes. Brand preferences both *before* and *after* the show are calculated and compared.

Galvanic skin response.
This method is used to record the perspiration rate of the subjects to reflect their emotional

reactions towards the test advertisement. The instrument employed is the psychogalvanometer. The recordings are performed mechanically to permit the subjects little or no chance to consciously distort their responses. However, the use of this method is not widespread.

Pupil dilation response.
The pupilometer is used in laboratory setting to measure the movement of the eye pupil of the subject. The premise of this method is that the faster the subject's pupil dilates, the greater is his interest in the stimulus (e.g. a test advertisement), where brightness and distance of the test environment remain unchanged. This method is not popularly used.

Eye movement tracking.
The eye camera was first developed in 1800 to track eye movements in relation to the parts of the test advertisement watched. The recorded path of eye movements is super-imposed onto the test advertisement so as to yield the following observations:

a Which specific parts of the test advertisement have been seen.
b In what sequence is the test advertisement seen (i.e. where it starts and ends).
c For how long each part of the test advertisement is watched.

In-store persuasion.
The procedural steps of in-store persuasion technique are described below:

a Intercept a quota sample of shoppers (called Sample A) as they enter a retail store.
b Show these shoppers a stack of print advertisements – including the test advertisement – and allow them as much time as required to look through the advertisements.
c Give each shopper a coupon booklet with discounts off several products, inclusive of the product carried in the test advertisement.

d Intercept Sample A of shoppers again as they leave the retail store, and note down whether they have purchased the product carried in the test advertisement. The purchase incidence is thus calculated.

e Repeat the same treatment to another quota sample of shoppers (called Sample B), who are not shown the stack of print advertisements. Likewise, the purchase incidence is calculated.

f Compare the purchase incidences between Sample A and Sample B and apply the appropriate test to determine if the observed difference is statistically significant.

Advertisement post-testing

As opposed to advertisement pretesting, advertisement post-testing takes place after the advertisement has commercially been run. Advertisement post-testing is primarily designed to determine unaided and aided awareness levels of the test advertisement among target consumers. Most of the research techniques for advertisement pre-testing are applicable to post-testing as well. In addition, advertisement post-testing employs one or more of the following methods:

● recognition test.
● recall test.
● triple association test.

Recognition test.
This is used to determine the incidence and the intensity of reading an advertisement which is inserted in the recent issue of a magazine (or periodical). In the case of a weekly or fortnightly magazine, the test commences three to six days after the magazine has been placed on sale and usually lasts for one to two weeks. For a monthly magazine, the test usually begins two weeks after on-sale date and stretches for about three weeks. A recognition test normally involves personal interviews with 100 to 150 *qualified* readers of a given issue

of the magazine. During the interview, the following typical questions will be asked:

Have you read this issue of . . . (READ OUT NAME OF MAGAZINE)?	
Yes	1
No	2
IF YES	
Can you tell me whether you remember having previously seen this advertisement (POINT OUT ADVERTISEMENT UNDER STUDY TO THE RESPONDENT)?	
Yes	1
No	2
How much of this advertisement did you read or see?	
Non-reader. . . .	1
Noted	2
Associated	3
Read most	4

The last question is most crucial, the responses to which are classified into four different levels of reading intensity:

1 Non-readers – refers to those who did not remember having previously seen the advertisement.

2 Noted – refers to those who remembered they had previously seen the advertisement.

3 Associated – refers to those who remembered they had seen the advertisement and could associate it with the advertised product or the advertiser.

4 Read most – refers to those who read half or more of the written material in the advertisement.

Recognition tests have the advantage of simplicity and claim valid measurement of readers' interest and awareness of advertisements. They are subject to some limitations. First, the respondent may confuse the specific advertisement with other similar or identical advertisements seen elsewhere, or make false claims about seeing the advertisement. Secondly, how much the respondent is interested in the advertised product can influence memory recall of the test advertisement. Finally, there is no proof to exhibit a direct positive relationship between recognition of the test advertisement and sales of the product advertised.

Recall test.
Like recognition tests, recall tests measure the penetration level of advertisements. In a recall test, the respondent who is not shown the entire advertisement in advance is asked what he can recall or remember about an advertisement.

The procedure of an advertisement recall survey comprises the following steps:

- Conduct the survey after the advertisement has been commercially run recently.
- Show the advertisement to the respondent (probably covering advertiser's name).
- Determine awareness level.
- Ask respondent what he or she remembers about the advertisement.
- Ask respondent about questions on the intended messages of the advertisement (eg. understandability; believability, interest and impact).

Triple association test.
This test aims to assess respondents' abilities to associate the triplets – product category,

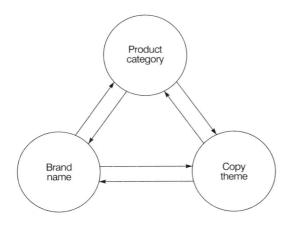

brand (or advertiser) and copy theme – in any order. Two of the triplets are read or shown to the respondent, who is required to give the remaining part of the triplets.

Consider the following example:

> Which airline can you name that says 'It's a great way to fly' in its advertisement?

The two triplets in the above question are:

- Product category – in this case, airline industry; and
- Copy theme – in this case the slogan: 'It's a great way to fly'

The missing triplet is the brand or the advertiser. The response 'Singapore Airlines' (SIA) would yield the correct association.

Advertising media research

The primary goal of advertising media research is to help formulate a sound advertising plan to promote products and services. More specifically, advertising media research is designed to prevent unnecessary wastage in advertising and to compare advertising media (e.g. television, radio, newspapers, etc.) for optimum allocation of the advertising expenditure.

Basic information sought in advertising media research includes:

1 *Media distribution.*
This refers to the circulation of a newspaper/magazine, or the number of television/radio sets owned in homes.

2 *Media audience.*
This refers to the number of people exposed to the advertising medium.

3 *Advertising exposure.*
This refers to the number of people who noted the advertising units. Note that the size of advertising exposure is typically lower than media audience, since people who are exposed to an advertising medium may not notice a specific advertisement carried in it.

4 *Advertising perception.*
This refers to the number of people who have conscious awareness and perception of the advertisement in question. In print advertising, perception is affected by the size, colour and position of the advertisement. Note that advertising perception is typically less than advertising exposure.

5 *Advertising communication.*
This refers to the number of people who comprehend specific things about the advertisement. Again, note that advertising communication is typically less than advertising perception.

6 *Advertising purchase.*
This refers to the number of people who make purchases of the product resulting from seeing the specific advertisement.

The selection of advertising media involves three basic considerations:

● Which general category or categories of media should be used? Should it be television, newspaper, magazine, radio, poster or a combination?
● Which media class within a particular medium type would be most appropriate? For example, if the firm opts for television advertising, would network or spot programmes be better?
● Which particular medium should be selected? In the case of daily newspapers, would the best be *The Straits Times*, *Business Times* or another newspaper?

Newspaper as an advertising medium

Two major types of information are essential in newspaper advertising: circulation and readership. They are not always directly associated: an increase/decrease in circulation does not necessarily mean a corresponding increase/decrease in readership of the same newspaper, and vice versa. Sometimes a copy of the newspaper may be read by one person or it may be shared by a group of readers. This explains why circula-

tion data fails to provide a good estimation of readership, or reflect the extent of advertisement exposure. Between circulation data and readership data, the latter is a more important indicator used in advertising media research.

Circulation data is preferred because it is usually readily available. In Singapore, the Media Circulation Services (S) Pte Ltd publishes twice yearly (January and June) audited circulated figures of print media publications. On the contrary, readership data is usually unknown and will have to be gathered from sample surveys. A fundamental problem in readership measurement is the basic question of who constitutes a newspaper reader. A common practice is to define a reader as one who claims to have read, in full or in part, the specified newspaper during a reference period. Conventionally, the accepted reference period is yesterday (i.e. the day before the interview) in the case of daily newspapers. A respondent is a *reader of a daily newspaper* if he reads that newspaper on the day prior to the date of interview; and is a *reader of a weekly newspaper* if he reads it in the past seven days, not counting the day of the interview.

For the purpose of data collection, mastheads of the newspapers under study are presented in a portfolio for identification purposes. The interviewer flips through the mastheads and the respondent indicates whether or not he or she has seen/read the respective newspapers during the specified reference period.

Television as an advertising medium

Data on television audience is sought for two fundamental purposes: to fix advertisement charges and to list out the popular programmes. In Singapore, a television viewer is defined as one who watched any television programme shown *yesterday*, that is, the day prior to the date of interview.

Programme rating is established via a more detailed form of data input. In one case the respondent is provided with a roster of television programmes shown in the past three days and is asked to answer a series of questions as shown below:

- Here is a list of television programmes shown for the past three days. Please look through these programmes and tell me which ones you have actually watched.
- Thinking back to yesterday, which of these programmes did you watch?
- Thinking back to the day before yesterday, which of these programmes did you watch?
- Thinking back to three days ago, which of these programmes did you watch?

Apart from the above method, other methods used for compiling television audience data are: coincidental telephone interviewing, the audimeter device, the people meter and the diary method.

1 *Coincidental telephone interviewing.*
A sample of respondents is contacted by telephone during broadcasting hour. The typical questions asked include the following:

Can you please tell me whether or not you are watching television now?

               Yes 1
               No 2

IF YES

Which channel/programme are you watching now? _____

ENTER CHANNEL NO: _____

Can you tell me who the sponsor of this programme is? _____

OR

Can you tell me what products are being advertised in this programme?

Coincidental telephone interviewing frees the respondent from the need to recall past events or behaviour, and generally yields more accurate results. Speed and cost economy are other advantages. Coincidental telephone interviewing, however, suffers from some weaknesses:

- Persons living in non-telephone homes are not included.
- Programmes shown at very early/late hours are inappropriate for inclusion in the survey, lest the respondents will be unduly disturbed.
- Brief or short programmes are hard to monitor as only a small number of interviews could be achieved within that time span.

2 *Audimeter device.*
Perhaps the most technical and sophisticated method of television audience measurement is the audimeter device. Invented by A. C. Nielson Company – the world's largest research firm – the audimeters are attached to the television sets of panel households. The audimeters automatically record the time when the television set is turned on, the channel watched and for how long. Such information is instantly transmitted via telephone to the central computer for data analysis. Unfortunately, the audimeter does not indicate who in the household (in fact, there may be none!) are watching. Descriptive analysis of television audience in terms of their basic characteristics (e.g. age, sex, occupation, martial status, income, etc.) is therefore not possible.

3 *People meter.*
The deficiency of audience information in the audimeter device mentioned above is solved by the people meter which records not only the basic information obtainable from the audimeter, but also data on individual viewers. The people meter is activated by each household member pressing a button when he/she watches television, and pressing it again when he or she ceases to watch it.

4 *Diary method.*
Each panel household is given a specially designed diary so that its members will each

record his television viewing behaviour. In addition to providing information on the size and profiles of viewers, the diary method is less expensive. A further feature of the diary information is that it is susceptible to reach/frequency analysis. The panel method permits an examination of how the audience of different programmes builds up and thereby indicates ways and means to efficiently increase the coverage of television schedules. The main disadvantage of the diary method is that panels may forget to record the programmes watched.

Radio/Rediffusion as advertising medium

A radio/Rediffusion listener is defined in almost the same way as a television viewer, that is, one who listened to the radio/Rediffusion broadcast *yesterday* – the day preceding the date of interview.

Cinema as an advertising medium

The reference period used for defining a cinema audience differs slightly from that used in the media earlier discussed. In Singapore, the *past seven days* notion is adopted; hence a cinema audience is one who has visited a cinema in the past seven days, not counting the date of interview.

Media planning

Media planning involves the selection of the appropriate advertising medium space and time in the light of achieving advertising objectives. The basic issues addressed in media planning include:

1 What are the media types and vehicles to be selected?
2 How much media space and time should be bought?
3 What amount of expenditure should be spent?
4 Who constitute the media audiences?
5 What is the audience size?

In addition, consideration is duly given to relative impact, reach and audience duplication, all within the context of the budget for the period. A media planner needs to know the advertiser's strategy for his product or service, the advertiser's objectives in advertising, and the competitive environment that prevails. All such information, together with details of the advertising budget allocated and the time-table, are usually provided by the advertiser in an advertising brief.

We shall now introduce two indices which are frequently used to compare the cost effectiveness of media advertising. They are:

- Cost-per-thousand circulation index.
- Cost-per-thousand reader index.

Cost-per-thousand circulation index

The calculation of cost-per-thousand circulation is given by the formula below:

$$\text{Cost per '000 Circulation} = \frac{\text{Advertisement Cost}}{\text{Circulation}} \times 1,000$$

The resulting figure represents the average advertising cost that the advertiser has to bear for placing the advertisement in every 1,000 circulated copies of the publication. As a general rule, the publication which offers the lowest cost-per-thousand circulation is chosen as the advertising vehicle by advertisers.

Illustrative example 1

The advertising rates for a full-page coloured advertisement in the three magazines A, B and C as well as their circulation figures are given below:

	Advertisement rate	Circulation
Magazine A	$3,000	150,000
Magazine B	$1,800	72,000
Magazine C	$1,500	62,500

Their respective costs-per-thousand circulation indices are:

Magazine A:
$$(\$3,000/150,000) \times 1,000 = \$20$$

Magazine B:
$$(\$1,800/72,000) \times 1,000 = \$25$$

Magazine C:
$$(\$1,500/62,500) \times 1,000 = \$24$$

On the basis of cost-per-thousand circulation index, Magazine A emerged the best buy.

Cost-per-thousand reader index

More often than not, a copy of the publication is passed on by its primary reader to many other readers. Since advertising is targeted at potential customers, obviously readership data is more important than circulation data to the advertiser. For this reason, the cost-per-thousand reader index is more commonly used.

Cost per '000 readers

$$= \frac{\text{Advertisement Rate}}{\text{Readership}} \times 1,000$$

The figure represents the average amount of money which the advertiser needs to spend on the advertisement in reaching 1,000 readers. Obviously, the medium which exhibits the lowest cost-per-thousand readers will emerge the best buy, all other factors being equal.

Illustrative example 2

The table below indicates the readership of three daily newspapers P, Q and R together with the advertisement rates charged by them for a one-quarter page black-and-white advertisement.

	Advertisement rate	Readership
Newspaper P	$3,000	720,000
Newspaper Q	$1,000	210,000
Newspaper R	$1,700	380,000

The respective cost-per-thousand reader indices are:

Newspaper P:
$$(\$3,000/720,000) \times 1,000 = \$4.17$$

Newspaper Q:
$$(\$1,000/210,000) \times 1,000 = \$4.75$$

Newspaper R:
$$(\$1,700/380,000) \times 1,000 = \$4.47$$

Thus Newspaper P, despite its highest advertisement rate, presents the best media buy in terms of cost-per-thousand readers.

The cost-per-thousand index only provides a crude measurement of the exposure value of media vehicles. Other factors are also important consideration, such as the characteristics and lifestyles of media audience. An elite magazine would certainly possess a higher exposure value for an expensive car advertisement than another magazine which is targeted at the lower income group. The exposure value of a medium (e.g. a magazine) would thus need to be revised by its editorial value-prestige, fashion, etc. – over other factors. By and large, television and radio are most effective in reaching teenagers; colour magazines work best for illustrations of fashions and dresses; while newspapers and radio are useful for *sales* announcements.

A comparative study of the strengths and weaknesses of each media type is presented in Figure 10.2 and Appendix A.

Media mix

Media planning becomes even more complex when advertisers consider using multiple media simultaneously in their

Medium	Strengths	Weaknesses
Newspaper	■ Flexibility (size, colour) ■ Timeliness ■ Lower production cost ■ Informative, long copy advertisement	■ Short life span ■ Poor reproduction quality ■ Small 'pass–along' audience
Television	■ Combines sight, sound and motion ■ Appealing to the senses ■ High attention ■ High reach	■ High production cost ■ Venue restriction ■ Fleeting exposure
Radio	■ Mass use ■ Low cost	■ Audio presentation only ■ Swift message ■ Lower attention than television
Magazine	■ High quality ■ Long life span ■ Good 'pass–along' audience	■ Long purchase lead time ■ Some waste in circulation

Figure 10.2 *Strengths and weaknesses of media types*

advertising plan. Media mix refers to the combination of media types used by the advertiser and serves the following purposes:

1 To reach audience unreached by the first medium.
2 To provide repeat exposure in a less expensive, secondary medium after optimum reach is fulfilled in the first medium.
3 To utilize some of the intrinsic values of a medium to extend the creative effectiveness of the advertising campaign (e.g. music on radio, long copy in print media).

Microscheduling

It is the interest of marketers to schedule their advertisements at the most propitious selling times. This involves the art of micro-scheduling, the primary objective of which is to allocate the purchased advertising over a span of time in a manner which will produce maximum impact. Take for example, an advertiser who wishes to schedule thirty television spots within a month. He or she now has three options:

1 To concentrate all spots over a fraction of the month

2 To continuously space the spots throughout the entire month.
3 To intermittently space the spots throughout the entire month.

For each option, the frequency of showing the spots may take either one of the following four forms:

● a level frequency
● a rising frequency
● a falling frequency
● an alternating frequency.

These yield a combination of twelve different patterns of microscheduling as shown in Figure 10.3.

Advertising evaluation research

This area of advertising research addresses two principal questions:

1 Were the advertisements seen?
2 If so, has the advertisement worked?

Typical questions which are asked in advertising evaluation research include:

● Did the chosen media reach the target audience?

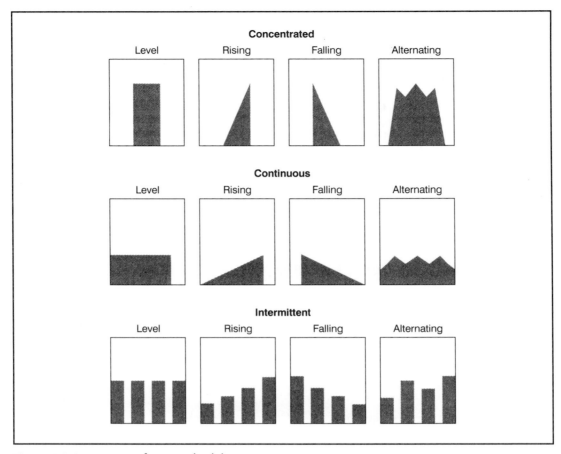

Figure 10.3 *Patterns of microscheduling*

- Is the target audience aware of the brand?
- Can the target audience remember the brand?
- Does the target audience have favourable attitudes towards the brand?
- Has the target audience bought/used the product?

An advertisement is considered successful if it has contributed to sales growth, increase in market share or a rise in the level of product awareness.

Bearing in mind that the primary objective of advertising is to generate higher sales, one may wonder why the evaluation of advertisements should not just be confined to measuring the sales effect brought about by advertising. There exist some prohibiting reasons. Advertising is but one of the many elements in the marketing mix, and as such, it cannot possibly claim the entire credit for any increased sales of a product. Other important factors contributing to increased sales include distribution, in-store promotions, shelf position and retailers' co-operation. It is therefore almost impossible to isolate advertising from other marketing variables in terms of sales output. Secondly, how competitors react towards the advertisement can cause confusion in the measurement of sales. A competitor may choose to increase, decrease or completely stop its advertising, while another competitor may decide to introduce a new product or launch a sales discount on their existing products. All these moves by the

competitors can distort the sales performance considerably to obscure the evaluation
of the advertisement. Finally, even if the
advertisement has its sole effect on sales
output, the impact of the advertisement
cannot be reflected instantly. Advertising
has a known cumulative effect. The impact
of a single advertisement on sales performance is based, at least in part, on all the
advertising efforts for the product made in
the past. It is hard, if not impossible, to
isolate the sales effect of a single advertisement, especially for a well-established
brand.

Appendix A: Advantages and disadvantages of main media

Newspaper

Advantages

1 A newspaper has a physical form. It can be held in hand, cut out, and referred to again by the prospect.
2 Relatively low cost per thousand.
3 Reach all demographic groups as they are usually a mass medium.
4 Booking and copy deadlines relatively short.
5 There is size flexibility. Advertisements of various sizes are acceptable.
6 Long copy is possible.
7 Repetition is possible and this is necessary for creating awareness.
8 Newspapers can assist in selling a product by specifying the places of purchase or by giving instructions on the use of the product.
9 Copy can be amended at short notice.
10 Readers are subject to an atmosphere of urgency which enhances the credibility of ads. Credibility of ads is further enhanced by the authoritative and informative nature of newspapers.
11 Prominence is attainable through specific positions, size, colour, shape, scented ink, fluorescent ink and iron-on ink.
12 Comparatively lower production cost than television or cinema. Amendments can be done cheaply.
13 Provide the immediacy that is necessary for day-to-day merchandise promotions.
14 Enable retailers to display to consumers the wide variety of merchandise they have to offer, providing the necessary information to stimulate action.

Disadvantages

1 Short lifespan
2 Static and hence difficult for products that require demonstration.

Television

Advantages

1 Audio-visual. Especially good for products that require demonstration.
2 Mass medium.
3 The combination of sight, sound, motion and colour can be impactful. The emotional appeal element is present.
4 Facilititates repetition, which is essential because a television spot is a fleeting thing and can create an impression only by repetition.
5 Audience is usually at leisure in the comfort of the home.

Disadvantages

1 Television commercials lack permanence. Advertisers must limit their messages to simple, easy to follow stories – single points delivered quickly. If the product to be sold is an involved one, the short life of the commercial seriously restricts the selling story.
2 Television commercials lack physical form. There is nothing left after the recital. Nothing remains in hand to remind, to inform, and to answer the buyer's questions.
3 The size and makeup of the viewing audiences vary greatly depending upon the scheduling and programme time. By buying into other than prime time, the advertiser cuts down on the audience and loses much coverage. On the other hand, prime time commercial breaks result in commercial clutter.
4 Audience fragmentation due to availability of different channels.
5 Surveys show that 'heavy' television viewers tend to belong to lower economic and educational brackets than newspaper readers.
6 Misidentification is one of television's major problems compounded by clutter. Surveys show that a significant number of viewers either cannot identify the sponsor of a given commercial, or they misidentify

the sponsor as one of that advertiser's competitors.

7 People do not approach the television medium in a specific frame of mind 'to stop' television advertising. But they do shop when they read the supermarket advertisements in a newspaper before food buying, or when they check the car advertisements in classified when they want a car, or the property advertisements when they need a house.

8 Remote control facility allows for 'zapping' during commercial breaks.

9 Studies show that when the commercials come on, there is an exodus from the television room – no doubt due to commercial clutter.

10 High production and airtime costs are difficult for the small budget advertiser.

Radio

Advantages

1 Audibility – while a disadvantage for an advertiser with an involved selling message, can be an advantage for the mass product, the simple sales story. No great personal effort, other than listening, is required.

2 Radio has timeliness. It can deliver the message now.

3 Each demographic segment of the listening public can find programmes to suit its interest. Thus, advertisers can buy airtime selectively.

4 To some extent, radio can reach commuters during 'drive time' between work and home.

5 Fast, low-cost commercial production.

Disadvantages

1 Audience fragmentation due to availability of stations.

2 Radio lacks permanence. A commercial, once delivered is gone forever. If you are not listening at the right time, you never hear it, and the advertiser does not benefit.

3 Radio lacks physical form.

4 Radio is audible. No personal effort is needed to get the message. Indeed, many people have the radio playing for background and may not really be listening.

5 In-car listening has many distractions imposed by the need to concentrate on driving, changing scenery, etc.

6 No visual message.

7 Needs quiet surroundings.

8 Message is limited by short segments.

Magazine

Advantages

1 Selective audience.

2 Magazines generally have a long lifespan.

3 A good visual medium, magazines reproduce advertisements in brilliant accurate full colour.

4 Magazines reach many of the same people issue after issue. There is an excellent reader loyalty factor. Since advertising fundamentally operates on the principle of presenting the same selling story to the same people as often as necessary to produce the sale, magazines allows the advertiser a continuity of exposure to its readers.

5 There is pass-along readership which increases the audience size and the opportunity for advertisement exposure.

6 Long copy is possible.

Disadvantages

1 Limited coverage.

2 Long deadlines.

3 High duplication with newspapers.

4 Magazines are read where buying impulses cannot be acted upon.

Outdoor

Advantages

1 This medium is suitable for rapidly building name awareness.

2 Allows an advertiser to maintain market presence.
3 The outdoor medium does have specific concentration areas, due to placement of its poster panels in high traffic locations.
4 Point of sale applications is one of the most effective ways to use outdoor, e.g. food posters near supermarkets.
5 Outdoor provides all-day, everyday continuity.
6 Dramatic, colour impact.

Disadvantages

1 Car, bus or train, moving at normal speed gives commuters little more than a few seconds to get the message.
2 Viewing conditions severely limit the visual treatment and the copy options outdoor advertisers can use. The message has to be extremely short.
3 Such variables as the visual approach to the billboard, speed of traffic, distance from the viewer, angle and elevation of the board, clutter characteristics of the area where the board is located, weather conditions, darkness all affect the results that may be attainable from outdoor advertising.
4 Outdoor advertising has to compete with many distractions – traffic and directional signs on the road, conversation and the radio, the scenery itself.
5 Low selectivity of contacts.
6 Long lead time.

Yellow Pages

Advantages

1 The directory reaches every home and place of business where there is a telephone as well as public telephone locations.
2 The classification of businesses makes it possible for a business to be found quickly and easily.

3 The directory is usually at hand. People do not normally throw it away.
4 The directory is used when buyers are ready to buy or when they need a service.
5 It is used across all demographic groups.

Disadvantages

1 No copy changes are possible. Once the telephone directory is printed and distributed, that is it for another year.
2 The Yellow Pages are a purely directional medium, best used for emergencies – when the water pipe breaks, the car will not start, etc. Advertisements in the phone directory do not create business the way sales advertisements in newspapers do, i.e. they do not create desire.
3 All competitors displayed together.
4 Long lead time for production.

Direct mail

Advantages

1 Low cost per thousand for shared mail advertisers. This system can provide saturation coverage of a targeted area.
2 Can provide selective audiences, with predetermined interests.
3 Provides massive coverage of an entire market, or whatever smaller segment that may be desired.
4 It allows advertisers to achieve cost-effectiveness with their advertising, not just on mail rates (bulk rates), but also in production.
5 Direct mail circulars provide traceable instant result.
6 Easy to provide means for reader action – return envelopes, etc.

Disadvantages

1 Postage costs can be quite high if the advertiser cannot tie in with a shared mail promotion and has to mail solo.

2 Consumer acceptance can be a problem as a large proportion of people think of direct mail as just junk to throw out.
3 Difficulty in maintaining good mailing lists.
4 Inflexible day of delivery.
5 Distribution to apartments is not to doorstep but in the mail boxes – may be thrown away even before reaching the home.
6 Some may end up in vacant households.

Cinema

Advantages

1 Audio-visual
2 Captive audience.
3 Suitable for reminder advertising.

Disadvantages

1 Audience tends to be young. Hence, comprehensive coverage is limited.
2 Small coverage at a particular time.

End-of-chapter revision

Review questions

10.1 What is advertising research? Why is it used so much in business?

10.2 What are the main divisions of advertising research?

10.3 How might the results of advertising campaigns be measured?

10.4 What is meant by advertisement pretesting?

10.5 Name and evaluate the methods used in advertisement pretesting.

10.6 What are the advantages and disadvantages of unaided recall?

10.7 What are the advantages and disadvantages of aided recall?

10.8 Recognition and recall are two different measures used in post-testing. Give an example of each and evaluate the two measures.

10.9 What are the characteristics of research designs used to provide information on:
a local television viewing?
b local radio audience?
c newspaper readership?
d cinema viewers?

10.10 What methods may be used to measure the size of television audiences? Briefly explain each method.

10.11 What are the advantages of using audimeters over roster-recall method to measure television audiences? What are the disadvantages?

10.12 Select an advertisement from a recent magazine.
a State what you believe to be the main objective of the advertisement.
b Prepare a series of questions for the target audience that will best reveal whether the objective was realized.
c State the relative merits of structured-disguised, structured-undisguised, unstructured-disguised, unstructured-undisguised questions for this question.

10.13 What is the purpose of advertising media research?

10.14 What is a media mix?

True-false questions

Write True (T) or False (F) for the following:

10.15 Advertising pretesting is designed to determine the levels of unaided and aided recalls of the advertisement shown.

10.16 The goal of advertising media research is to help formulate a sound advertising plan to promote products and services.

10.17 An increase in newspaper circulation always means a corresponding increase in newspaper readership, and vice versa.

10.18 Readership data is a more important indicator than circulation data in advertising media research.

10.19 Advertising post-testing focuses on developing ideas and methods of presenting advertisements.

10.20 The level of advertising recall is very much influenced by consumers' interest in the advertised product.

10.21 Media planning involves the selection of the appropriate advertising medium, space and time to achieve the intended advertising objectives.

10.22 To compute the cost-per-thousand circulation index, two types of information are necessary: circulation figure and advertising rate (or cost).

10.23 The people meter records not only the information obtainable by the audimeter, but also data on the viewers.

10.24 An advertising media which offers a higher cost-per-thousand reader index will be more cost efficient.

10.25 Media mix deals with the allocation of the purchased advertising over a span of time with a view of producing maximum impact.

10.26 Advertising media research aims to help formulate a sound advertising plan to promote products and services.

Multiple-choice questions

10.27 Which of the following is used in advertisement post-testing?
a Recognition test.
b Recall test.
c Triple association test.
d All of the above.

10.28 The formula for cost-per-thousand reader index takes into account:
a the characteristics of readers
b the lifestyles of readers
c the editorial content
d none of the above.

10.29 The limitation of magazine as an advertising medium is:
a short life span
b poor reproduction quality
c small pass-along readership
d none of the above.

10.30 Which one of the following methods is not used in advertising research?
a Consumer jury method.
b Portfolio test.
c On-the-air test.
d Product concept test.

10.31 Advertising media research seeks to gather information on:
a media distribution
b advertising exposure
c advertising communication
d all of the above.

10.32 The limitations of television as an advertising medium include:
a high production cost
b fleeting exposure
c venue selection
d all of the above.

10.33 The advantages of newspaper as an advertising medium are:
a flexibility in size and colour
b timeliness
c low production cost
d all of the above

11

Data processing and presentation

Data gathered in the field is *raw*. Like raw material which requires to undergo some production process, raw data needs to be converted into a form suitable for analysis and interpretation. Data processing is, therefore, the link between data collection and data analysis. This can be achieved through a series of logical steps exhibited in Figure 11.1.

Editing

The initial step in data processing is to edit raw data in the completed questionnaires. In essence, data editing is performed to pre-pare the data for coding and transfer to storage. This step requires a thorough examination of raw data for completeness, consistency, accuracy, respondent eligibility and so on.

1 *Check for completeness.* This is to ensure that, first, no sections or pages of the questionnaire are missing and, secondly, that no answer to any question item is inadvertently omitted, either in whole or in part. A blank question will always be taken to mean that the interviewer has forgotten to ask the question. When the missing data is obvious from the answers given to other related question items, the editor can insert the missing data without further inquiry. If the missing data is not obvious, the editor may resort to one of the following measures to treat missing data:
   - Obtain the missing data from interviewer while the interview is fresh in his or her mind

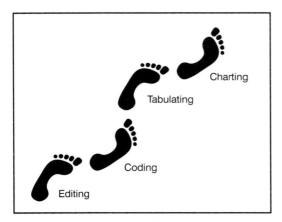

Figure 11.1 *Steps in data processing and presentation*

Editing

- Questionnaire complete?
- Data consistent?
- Data accurate?
- Respondent eligibility?
- Standard measurement unit?

- Ring up the respondent provided that the telephone number is recorded in the questionnaire.
- Send a mail requesting the respondent to supply the missing information.
- Ask interviewer to make a revisit.

2 *Check for data consistencies.* This serves to uncover inconsistent or contradictory answers, and to rectify errors thereof. A respondent who indicated that he has never attended school on one part of the questionnaire but later reported his occupation as medical doctor would constitute an obvious case of data

inconsistency, and would indeed put the analyst in a dilemma situation.

3 *Check for accuracy.* The editor carefully screens through the data to search for inaccuracy, if any. An important area here it to spot possible interview bias in data entry, for example, when a fixed pattern of responses consistently appear in the questionnaires.

4 *Check for respondent eligibility.* The editor checks for qualified respondent as defined for the sample. Sometimes a secretary may complete a mail questionnaire intended for the company's chief executive.

Background data

Record sex
Male . . . 1
Female . . . 2
Record race
Chinese . . . (1)
Malay . . . 2
Indian . . . 3
Others . . . 4
Record age
12 – 14 years . . . 1
15 – 19 years . . . 2
20 – 24 years . . . 3
25 – 29 years . . . 4
30 – 34 years . . . (5)
35 – 39 years . . . 6
40 – 44 years . . . 7
45 – 49 years . . . 8
50 – 54 years . . . 9
55 – 59 years . . . A
60 years and above . . . B
Record house type
Public flat (1–3 rooms) . . . 1
Public flat (4–5 rooms) . . . (2)
Pte housing estate/flat . . . 3
Attrap/zinc-roofed house . . . 4
Shophouse . . . 5
Others . . . 6
Day of interview: 23/3/94 (Wed)
A. What is your language stream?
No formal schooling . . . 1
English . . . (2)
Chinese . . . 3
Malay . . . 4
Tamil . . . 5
Others (Specify: _____) 6

B. What is your marital status?
Single . . . 1
Married . . . 2
Divorced/Separated/Widowed . . . 3
C. What is the highest educational qualification you attained?
None . . . 1
PSLE . . . 2
GCE 'O' level . . . 3
GCE 'A' level/Poly Diploma . . . (4)
Degree . . . 5
D. What is your occupation?
Sr. Accountant
SHOWCARD
E. (a)
Please would you show me on this card the total income earned per month by all the people in your household?
E. (b) If working
Please would you show me on this card how much you *yourself* earned per month?

	Household Income	Personal Income
$ 300 & below	1	1
$ 301 – $ 500	2	2
$ 501 – $ 750	(3)	3
$ 751 – $1,000	4	(4)
$1,001 – $1,500	5	5
$1,501 – $2,000	6	6
$2,001 – $3,000	7	7
$3,001 – $4,000	8	8
$4,001 & above	9	9

F. What is your home/office telephone number?
1234567

Questionnaires completed by ineligible persons are to be discarded.

5 *Standardize measurements.* It is utterly important that the responses be recorded in uniform units of measurement. For example, the responses offered on income may be given as daily wage, weekly income, fortnightly income or monthly income. It is important to convert all related numbers to a common base.

A hypothetically completed questionnaire for data editing is shown on the previous page. Attempt to edit it as a practice.

There are two kinds of editing, namely, *field editing* and *central editing*. The former is intended to uncover errors in recording responses during the data collection stage. Note that field editing does not apply to postal surveys. Central editing is executed at a later stage when the completed questionnaires are returned to the office. Central editing is usually performed more comprehensively than field editing because longer time is permissible. We shall next describe the three modes of editing – manual, mechanical and computer editing.

Manual editing

This is performed by a group of editors, usually the field supervisors. At the outset, these editors are given a set of editing instructions specifying in detail the rules and guidelines to be followed in editing. For research studies of a relatively small size, it is common to employ one editor to maintain consistency. When two or more editors are involved, it will be advisable to assign each editor a subset of question items in the questionnaires to maintain consistency throughout the editing process. When an error is detected, the editor inserts the correction alongside the original entry which should never be erased. This allows the editor's work to be checked in turn when needed.

Manual editing poses a number of limitations. First, it is a time-consuming and costly exercise. Secondly, professional editors would find it a very tedious operation, while the inexperienced ones dread it and consider the job to be extremely demanding. Finally, the editors are also liable to make mistakes and there is no guarantee that all erroneous responses will be detected.

Mechanical editing

In mechanical editing, information contained in the questionnaires is transferred onto punched cards. These cards are then sorted (usually by a counter sorter) into different piles so that those which do not comply with the editing instructions will fall into the *error* pile. These cards are then traced to their original questionnaires for further examination. With the development of modern technology (e.g. the computer), mechanical editing has become almost obsolete.

Computer editing

Computer editing, as its name suggests, involves the use of computer facilities to detect inconsistencies in the questionnaires. Being the most sophisticated and efficient means of editing, it allows a large number of editing instructions to be executed simultaneously. Speed and accuracy are achieved. It is common nowadays to introduce computer editing at data input stage, to readily inform the researcher of any inconsistent data that may occur.

Coding

Coding is the process of identifying and assigning a numeric or character symbol to previously edited data. For a highly structured questionnaire, these codes or numbers have already been indicated by the interviewers either by encircling or ticking off the appropriate codes or boxes. This happens in the case of precoding. With an unstructured questionnaire, the survey responses will need to be classified before coding begins. We call it post-coding, or simply, coding.

Post-coding is a delicate operation which requires experienced research staff and which calls for considerable attention. It requires first the establishment of a coding frame for each question item and secondly the assignment of numbers or codes to the various categories listed in the coding frame. The researcher carefully studies the responses given and thereafter groups them into homogeneous categories. After each category is assigned a code number, the coding frame is formed. For practical reasons, the coding frame is usually constructed based on 10 per cent of the questionnaires.

A coding frame should observe the following rules:

1 All responses of a similar nature should come under the same category or class.
2 All categories combined, they must be universally exhaustive, that is, any response should be classifiable under at least one category.
3 In the case of a single-choiced question, all categories must be mutually exclusive, that is, if a response is classified under a certain category, it will not be classifiable under any other categories.

Question number	Column position	Description/Meaning of codes	
–	1-3	*Job number*	098
#1	4	*House type*	
		HDB flat (1-3 rm)	1
		HDB (4 and 5 rm)	2
		Private apartment/house	3
#2	5	*Ethnic group*	
		Chinese	1
		Malay	2
		Indian	3
		Others	4
#3	6	*The Straits Times readership*	
		Reader	1
		Non-reader	2
#4	7	*Lianhe Zaobao readership*	
		Reader	1
		Non-reader	2
#5	8	*Total time spent in reading newspaper(s)*	
		10 mins or less	1
		Over 10 mins to 20 mins	2
		Over 20 mins to 30 mins	3
		Over 30 mins to 1 hour	4
		Over 1 hour	5
#6	9	*No. of automobiles owned*	
		None	1
		One	2
		Two	3
		Three or more	4

Figure 11.2 *A code book*

For data analysis purposes, the number of categories in a coding frame may be reduced by combining some of the categories. The reverse, however, is not possible. A logical thing to do, therefore, is to create a large number of categories wherever possible. (See example below).

Illustrative example 1:

Monthly household expenditure on public utilities

Larger number of categories		Smaller number of categories
$25 or below 1	}	
$26–$75 2		$75 and below. . . . 1
$76–$125 3	}	
$126–$175 4		$76–$175 2
$176–$225 5	}	
Above $225 6		Above $175 3

Code book

A code book documents, in code form, all the needed information about the variables in the data set. Specifically, it identifies the variables, their location as appeared in the data collection form and in the computer. Specimen of a partial code book is shown in Figure 11.2.

Tabulating

Tabulating refers to simply counting the number of elements/cases that fall into each coded category. Its primary objective is to organize data by groups so as to present information in a quantifiable and readily understandable format. Whether tabulation should be carried out manually or mechanically will largely depend on the amount of data involved, as well as the availability of suitable computer programmes.

Forms of tabulation

Data tabulation may take the form of a simple tabulation or a cross-tabulation. Each of these is described below.

Simple tabulation

Also known as marginal tabulation, simple tabulation involves counting single variable, and presents an empirical distribution of the number of observations (or elements) that fall into each category of response. It is sometimes called a frequency distribution. Assume that in a survey on smokers, the following items of data were included in the questionnaire – sex, age and a classification of heavy/light/non-smoker. Corresponding to these items, three simple tabulations are produced as shown in the hypothetical example below.

Illustrative example 2:

Simple tabulation by sex

Class	Frequency
Male.	500
Female	450
Total	950

Illustrative example 3:

Simple tabulation by age

Class	Frequency
12–29 years	447
30+ years	503
Total	950

Simple tabulation provides much of the needed information, many research studies, however, go beyond it for more detailed data analysis.

Cross-tabulation

Simple tabulation, as earlier mentioned, displays research findings in terms of one variable item at a time. When there is a need to establish the relationship between two or more variables, cross-tabulation is called for. Simply put, cross-tabulation is a technique organizing data by specific groups, categories or classes to facilitate comparison. In cross-tabulation, two or more of the variables are treated simultaneously; the number of cases that have the joint characteristic are counted. An example of a two-way cross-tabulation (i.e. two variables are involved) is presented in Table 11.1.

The most common form of cross-tabulation is the two-way variety, but whenever necessary, more than two variables may be presented in a cross-tabulation for measurement. One such example is the three-way cross-tabulation given in Table 11.2. It is obvious that a three-way cross-tabulation

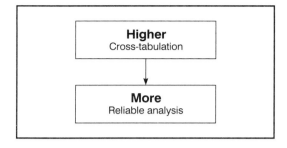

provides much more detailed information than a two-way cross-tabulation and a simple tabulation; but it should also be borne in mind that the more complex the cross-tabulation is, the more difficult, if not confusing, it would be in interpreting the data.

Charting

Tabulation is followed by charting, and together they are commonly called data presentation. A chart offers a graphical and visual picture of tabulated data to help put across important points to data users. We shall now describe the most widely used type of charts:

1 Line graph.
2 Bar chart.
3 Pie chart.
4 Pictogram.
5 Map or cartogram.

Table 11.1 *Number of smokers by sex*

Smoking	Total	Male	Female
		Sex	
Total	950	500	450
Heavy smokers	167	161	6
Light smokers	42	29	13
Non-smokers	741	310	431

Table 11.2 *Number of smokers by sex and age*

Smoking	Total	Male Total	Male 12–29	Male 30+	Female Total	Female 12–29	Female 30+
Total	950	500	235	265	450	212	238
Heavy smokers	167	161	81	80	6	1	5
Light smokers	42	29	17	12	13	8	5
Non-smokers	741	310	137	173	431	203	228

Line graph

Line graph is most useful for describing one or more variables over a period of time, and for exhibiting relationships between variables. In a line graph, the relationship between two variables (one along the horizontal axis and the other along the vertical axis) is displayed by a series of connected lines (see Figure 11.3).

Bar chart

This is one of the most popular graphical presentations. Vertical or horizontal bars are used to represent frequencies and percentage numbers. Unless otherwise indicated, the length of each bar is proportional to the magnitude of the value it represents. Bar charts can be easily constructed and readily interpreted. When the bars are presented horizontally or vertically, we call it a horizontal bar chart (Figure 11.4) or a vertical bar chart (Figure 11.5) respectively. The choice of a horizontal or vertical bar chart is optional. When the bars are further subdivided into components, we then have a component bar chart (Figure 11.6). When two or more sets of bar charts are integrated into a single chart, we call it a multiple or composite bar chart (Figure 11.7), which is especially useful in highlighting changes of variables occurring over time.

Pie chart

Like component bar charts, pie charts are used primarily to exhibit the relationship of each individual component in relation to the whole. While the former use length to facilitate comparison, pie charts involve area (Figure 11.8). A pie chart is most appropriate for demonstrating market shares. Visual comparison of areas, however, presents some difficulties and this explains why pie charts are not considered as a superior form of graphical presentation.

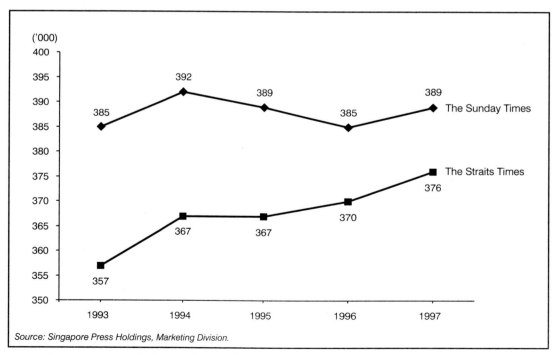

Source: Singapore Press Holdings, Marketing Division.

Figure 11.3 *Average daily circulation of the Straits Times/Sunday Times, 1993–7*

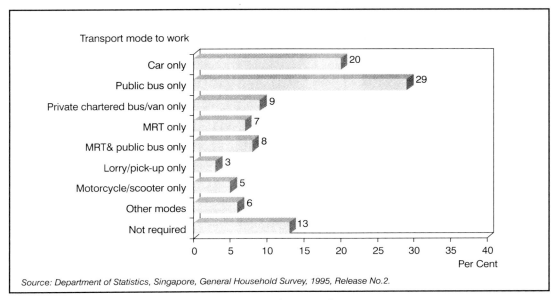

Figure 11.4 *Working persons by transport mode to work*

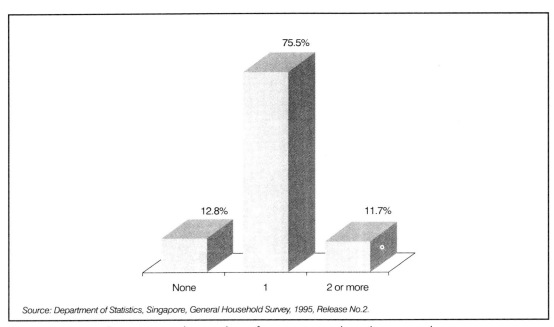

Figure 11.5 *Working persons by number of transport modes taken to work*

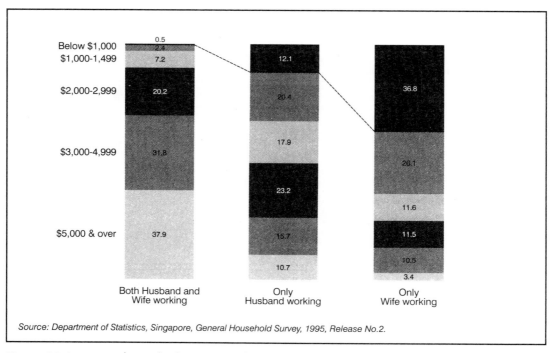

Figure 11.6 *Married couples by incomes from work*

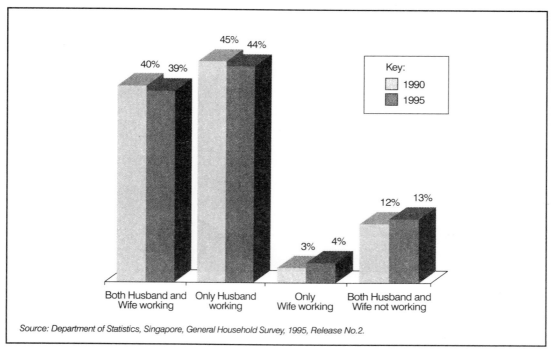

Figure 11.7 *Married couples by working status*

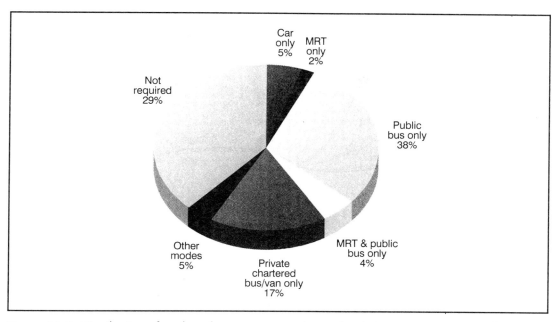

Figure 11.8 *Distribution of students by transport mode to school. Source: Department of Statistics, Singapore*

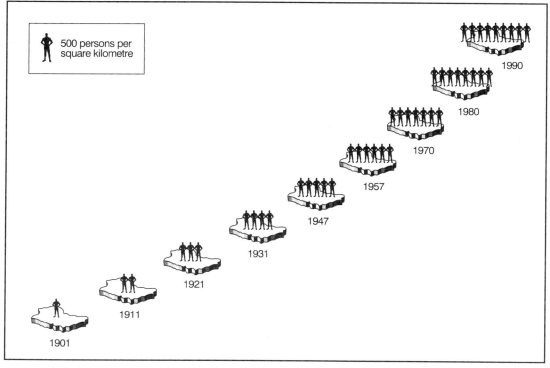

Figure 11.9 *Population density of Singapore. Source: Department of Statistics, Singapore*

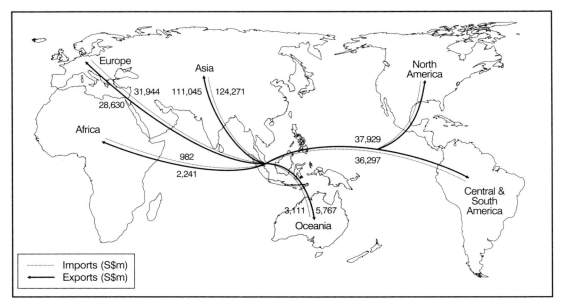

Figure 11.10 *Singapore trade with major regions, 1997.* Source: *Yearbook of Statistics Singapore, 1996*

Pictograms

In pictograms, simple and clear symbols are used to facilitate a vivid impression of the data displayed (see Figure 11.9). The quantity which each symbol represents should be specified. Larger quantities are reflected by a large number of symbols, rather than larger-sized symbols. It is permissible to display a partial symbol when the quantity involved is smaller than the value represented by a whole symbol.

End-of-chapter revision

Review questions

11.1 Name and discuss the steps involved in data processing. Demonstrate the importance of each step.

11.2 Define the term *editing* with respect to marketing research data collected. Explain the main purpose behind editing.

11.3 What are the differences in emphasis between a field editing and a central editing?

11.4 Why is it important that central editing be carried out, if possible, by just one person?

11.5 Discuss the different methods for handling missing data.

11.6 What is computer editing?

11.7 What is meant by coding? Why should responses be coded?

11.8 Differentiate between precoding and post-coding of questionnaire-collected data. Under what situations would each be most appropriate?

11.9 What are the basic rules that should be observed in the establishment of categories in coding?

11.10 What is a frequency distribution?

11.11 What is a cross-tabulation table? What is the objective of cross-classification analysis?

11.12 What is the role of graphic presentation in a research report?

11.13 What is a line chart? For what kinds of information is it generally employed?

11.14 What is a horizontal bar chart? For what kinds of information is it effective?

11.15 What is a vertical bar chart? When is it particularly used?

11.16 What is a pie chart? For what kinds of information is it particularly effective?

True-false questions

Write True (T) or False (F) for the following:

11.17 Editing is a classification system for open-ended questions.

11.18 Coding is the process of identifying and assigning a numeric or character symbol to the edited data.

11.19 Classifications of data are established during the coding operation.

11.20 Editing is carried out to ensure that information gathered is accurate, complete and usable.

11.21 Field editing should be performed as soon as possible after central editing.

11.22 Post-coding is usually carried out for multiple-choice type of questions.

11.23 When several coders are employed, it is best to split the work so that each coder is responsible for the set of questions within a particular portion of the questionnaire.

11.24 Editing involves the assignment of a numeral or alphabet to each response category.

11.25 Data consistency is a concern at the coding stage.

11.26 A simple tabulation is also known as a frequency distribution.

Multiple-choice questions

11.27 Data must be examined to ensure that the information collected is accurate, complete and usable. This is known as:
a checking
b coding

c editing

d tabulation.

11.28 Editing involves checking the raw data for:

a completeness

b consistency

c accuracy

d all of the above.

11.29 Field editing should be carried out:

a during the interview

b as soon as possible after the interview has taken place

c before making initial contact with the respondent

d none of the above.

11.30 If possible, when carrying out central editing, it is best to have:

a just one editor

b at lease four or five editors

c some actual respondents present in order to help explain confusing answers

d none of the above.

11.31 The process of assigning responses to appropriate categories is known as:

a coding

b tabulation

c editing

d statistical summarization.

11.32 Which of these questions are least likely to be precoded?

a Dichotomous.

b Undisguised.

c Open-ended.

d Multiple-choice.

11.33 In order to represent relationship between variables, it may be desirable to carry out:

a one-way tabulation

b two-way tabulation

c one-way coding

d two-way editing.

11.34 Questions that are least likely to be precoded are:

a multiple-choice questions

b open-ended questions

c dichotomous questions

d closed-ended questions.

11.35 The fundamental rule for establishing a coding scheme is that the categories must be:

a exhaustive and compatible

b exhaustive and mutually exclusive

c independent and mutually exclusive

d compatible and typical.

12

Data analysis and interpretation: describing data

Most research studies do not end at data processing and tabulation. The need to transform research data into statistical language often arises, especially so when data is obtained from a sample. With sample data, many questions are left unanswered. For example, when the results showed that 25 per cent of sample households owned motor vehicles, how confident can we be then to say that the incidence of car ownership in all households is not below 20 per cent or above 30 per cent, or some other distant value? Still, if the readership of a daily newspaper were 45 per cent and 48 per cent, as derived from

two random sample surveys conducted independently at different points of time, to what extent are we assured that the observed difference of 3 per cent in readership is truly statistically significant, and not merely due to chance variation between the two selected samples?

Treatment of the above questions leads to data analysis and data interpretation, at the heart of which lies the statistical methods and applications. Briefly put, data analysis is concerned with categorizing, ordering and summarizing data while data interpretation is essentially a follow-up which first involves

Data
Analysis & Interpretation

RAW DATA

WELCOME TO ANALYSIS & INTERPRETATION

Editing

Coding

Tabulation

Summary

Raw data from a study is of little use until it's converted into a form suitable for analysis and interpretation.

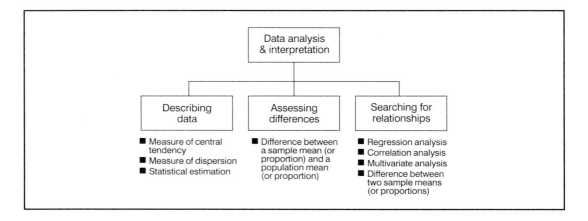

Figure 12.1 *Main divisions of data analysis and interpretation*

the search for the meaning and applications of the research results, and secondly makes references relative to the problem being studied, and ultimately draws conclusions about these relationships.

The main divisions of data analysis and interpretation, together with the respective statistical tools and techniques adopted, are listed in Figure 12.1.

We shall discuss data description in this chapter.

Measure of central location ▰▰

This is the basic device used in describing data. A measure of central location (commonly called the average or mean) is the value or item which describes or represents the distribution of the given set of data. Statistical analysis of data normally begins by computing the measures of central location.

Generally speaking, the measure of central location possesses the following features:

- It is intended to be representative of the whole set of data.
- Different data sets can each be represented by a common denominator (in this case, the mean or average) to facilitate comparison.
- It is used as the basis for further analysis about the given data set.
- It is a measure of central tendency.

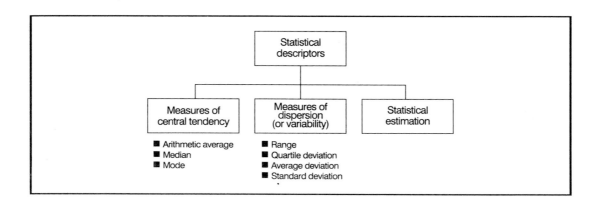

These inherent features explain why averages play an important role in marketing research studies. The three types of averages commonly in use are:

1 The arithmetic mean.
2 The median.
3 The mode.

Arithmetic mean

The arithmetic mean is the best known and most widely used among all types of averages. It is calculated by summing up the values of all the items in the given data set and after which dividing the result by the number of items. By convention, we use the letter X_i to stand for an individual score; the capital Greek letter Σ (*sigma*) for the summation process and the letter N for the number of items. The formula for the arithmetic mean is:

$$\overline{X} = \Sigma X_i/N$$

where $\overline{X}$ = the arithmetic mean
N   = the number of items
X_i = the individual scores
       (or values).

For grouped data, the formula for the arithmetic mean is given by:

$$\overline{X} = \Sigma f_i m_i/N$$

where $\overline{X}$ = the arithmetic mean
N = the number of items
m_i = the mid-point of the *i*th class
f_i = the number of items in the *i*th class.

Illustrative example 1:

mid-semester test results

The mid-semester test results of an MBA class of twenty students are appended below. (*Note*: Listed in the order of their registration numbers).

7.0	7.0	8.5	6.0
6.5	8.0	5.5	6.5
7.5	6.5	6.5	6.5
9.0	8.5	7.0	6.0
5.5	1.0	7.5	8.5

The arithmetic mean $(\overline{X})$ of the mid-semester test results is therefore 6.6 (see below)

$$\overline{X} = 132.0/20 = 6.6$$

The advantages of the arithmetic mean are:

1 It is easy to understand.
2 It is simple to calculate.
3 It deals with all the data in the set, and can be determined with mathematical exactness.
4 It is commonly used as the basis for further analysis about the given data set (i.e. it possesses certain useful mathematical properties).

Its disadvantages are:

1 It may not be truly representative of the data set in that it may not correspond with any particular item.
2 It may give undue weight to, and be unduly influenced by, items with extremely high or low values.

Median

The median is the value of the middle item in an ordered data set. To locate the median, it is first necessary to arrange all the items in the data set in order of size or values. The median is then the middle observation. Thus there will be an equal number of items above as well as below the median. If the data set has even number of items, two items will appear in middle position of the data set, and the median may in this case be taken as the average of these two items.

The median is not as sensitive as the arithmetic mean to extreme values in the data set. Thus, if there exist a few 'outliers' in the data set, the use of median would be more preferred.

Illustrative example 2:

mid-semester test results

Referring to the previous example, arrange the test scores in descending order (option A) or ascending order (Option B).

	Option A	Option B
1st position	9.0	1.0
2nd position	8.5	5.5
3rd position	8.5	5.5
4th position	8.5	6.0
5th position	8.0	6.0
6th position	7.5	6.5
7th position	7.5	6.5
8th position	7.0	6.5
9th position	7.0	5.5
10th position	7.0	6.5
11th position	6.5	7.0
12th position	6.5	7.0
13th position	6.5	7.0
14th position	6.5	7.5
15th position	6.5	7.5
16th position	6.0	8.0
17th position	6.0	8.5
18th position	5.5	8.5
19th position	5.5	8.5
20th position	1.0	9.0

(Median line between 10th and 11th positions)

There are two middle positions, that is, the 10th position (with a test score of 7.0) and the 11th position (with a test score of 6.5).

The median (Me) of the mid-semester test results is therefore 6.75

$$Me = (7.0 + 6.5)/2 = 6.75$$

For grouped data, the median is expressed by:

$$M_e = L_e + [(N/2 - \Sigma f_i)/f_e] \times C$$

where
M_e = the median
L_e = the lower limit of the median class*
N = the total number of items
Σf_i = the total number of items less than the lower limit of the median class

f_e = the number of items in the median class
C = the interval of the median class.

The median class refers to the interval class which the median falls into.

The advantages of the median are:

1 It is simple to understand.
2 It is easily calculated. In many cases it may be observed instantly.
3 It is not affected by extreme items.
4 It can be obtained even when the values of some items are not known.

The disadvantages of the median are:

1 The data must be arrayed in order of size. This may present some administrative difficulty especially when the data set is voluminous.
2 If the number of items is few, it is not likely to be representative of the data set.
3 It is not suitable for arithmetical calculation, and has limited use in practical work.

Mode

The mode (or norm) is that value of the item which occurs most often in the data set. It represents the position of greatest numerical density, or the most predominant value.

For grouped data, the formula for computing the mode is given by:

$$M_0 = L_0 + \{(f_0 - f_1)/[(f_0 - f_1) + (f_0 - f_2)]\} \times C$$

Where
M_0 = the mode
L_0 = the lower limit of the modal class*
f_0 = the number of items in the modal class
f_1 = the number of items in the pre-modal class
f_2 = the number of items in the post-modal class
C = the interval of the modal class.

The modal class refers to the interval class which the mode falls into.

The advantages of the mode are:

1 It is easy to understand.
2 It is not affected by extreme values.
3 Often, it can be instantly identified from the data set.
4 Since it is the value which has occurred with the highest frequency, it is the most descriptive average.

Despite these advantages, the mode is less often used than the arithmetic mean and the median for the following reasons:

1 It may not be representative if there are only a few items.
2 It may be difficult to determine for large class intervals.
3 Like the median, it cannot be used for arithmetic manipulation.
4 Like the median, it is a position average; so it is essential to arrange the data in the form of a frequency distribution (or array).
5 Sometimes a data set contains two, three or many modes possibly due to the inclusion of different subgroups of the population (e.g. young vs old persons) in the sample. Interpretation of data would then require further in-depth analysis.

Illustrative example 3:

mid-semester test results

Referring to the previous example, group the test scores as follows:

Test score	No. of students
9.0	1
8.5	3
8.0	1
7.5	2
7.0	3
6.5	5
6.0	2
5.5	2
1.0	1

Since the test score of 6.5 appears the highest number of times, the mode (M_0) of the mid-semester test score is therefore 6.5:

$$M_0 = 6.5$$

See Figure 12.2 for the main features of mean, median and mode.

	Mean	Median	Mode
1	Defined as the arithmetic average — 'centre of gravity'.	Defined as the value of the middle point of a given array.	Defined as the most frequent value in the point of greatest density.
2	Required metric data.	Requires at least ordinal data.	Can be computed for all types of data.
3	Requires measurement on all units.	Does not require measurement on all units.	Does not require measurement on all units.
4	Uniquely defined.	Indeterminate under certain conditions.	Not unique for multi-modal distributions. Also, there is no mode in the rectangular distribution.
5	Affected by few extreme values and blunders.	Not affected by few extreme values and blunders.	Not affected by few extreme values and blunders.
6	Generally most stable under sampling fluctuations.	Less stable under sampling fluctuations.	Less stable under sampling fluctuations.
7	Can be manipulated algebraically: Means of sub-groups can be properly weighted.	Cannot be manipulated algebraically: Medians of sub-groups cannot be weighted and combined.	Cannot be manipulated algebraically: Modes of sub-groups cannot be weighted and combined.

Figure 12.2 *Features of mean, median and mode*

Measure of dispersion (or variability) ▅▅▅▅

While measures of central tendency locate the *centre* of a data set, measures of dispersion gauge the *spread* of it. Two data sets can have the same measure of central location and yet are vastly different in terms of their *spreads*. In the example below, the central values (e.g. mean, mode, and median) of all three frequency distributions are the same, but Team A obviously has less spread (or variability) than Team B which in turn, has less spread than Team C. If we only consider the mean of these three frequency distributions in data analysis, we will miss an important aspect.

Illustrative example 4:

team performance and dispersion

A class of thirty students are divided into three teams, each with ten students. In a recent examination, the performance scores of the students in these three teams are listed below.

Team A	Team B	Team C
5.2	4.1	1.5
5.4	4.7	4.4
5.5	4.9	4.7
5.8	5.5	5.6
5.8	5.8	5.8
6.0	6.0	6.0
6.0	6.0	6.0
6.0	6.0	6.0
6.1	7.1	8.6
6.2	7.9	9.4

The central values of Teams A, B and C are identical as shown below.

	Team A	Team B	Team C
Arithmatic mean	5.8	5.8	5.8
Median	5.9	5.9	5.9
Mode	6.0	6.0	6.0

However, if the performance scores of the students are plotted by individual teams along the X-axis, we discover that Team A students are more uniform in their performance (as their scores cluster more closely together) than Team B students, which in turn are more uniform in their performance than Team C students.

To amplify what is known of a distribution, it therefore becomes necessary to examine the dispersion of the data set; and ascertain whether its items are clustered closely about the average or are scattered in distance from it. If the items are highly clustered, the average can be regarded as a fairly good representation of the items in the data set, otherwise the average, as a central measure of the data set, will bear little significance. In sum, the uses of a dispersion measure are:

1 It gives additional information to judge the representation and reliability of the measure of central tendency.
2 Because a set of widely dispersed data is often subject to some peculiar problems of its own, it is important to recognize this phenomenon before we can effectively tackle these problems.
3 It enables us to compare dispersions of various samples.

Measures of dispersion commonly used in marketing research studies are:

1 The range.
2 The quartile deviation.
3 The average deviation.
4 The standard deviation.

Range

The range is simply the numerical difference between the largest value and the smallest value in the data set. It represents the maximum breadth of a data set, and ignores all other values in the data set. The range is the crudest measure of dispersion, and is of

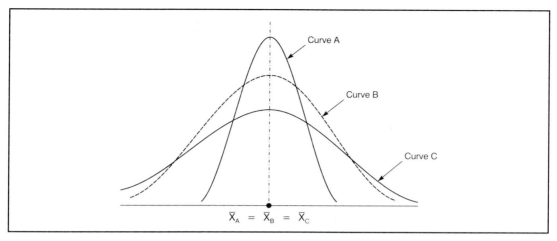

Figure 12.3 *Frequency distributions with same mean but different dispersions*

limited use particularly when some exceptionally low and/or exceptionally high values are present in the data set.

___

Illustrative example 5:

team performance and dispersion

Referring to the previous example, the range of performance scores of each of the three teams of students is calculated below.

Range (Team A) = 6.2 − 5.2 = 1.0
Range (Team B) = 7.9 − 4.1 = 3.8
Range (Team C) = 9.4 − 1.5 = 7.9

The range of Team A is smaller than Team B, which in turn is smaller than Team C. Thus, it can generally be said (apart from extreme case) Team A students are less dispersed in performance scores than Team B and Team C students.

___

Quartile deviation ___

As has been just mentioned, the range can be unduly distorted by the mere presence of an unusually large or small end value. To overcome this, the quartile deviation is sometimes used.

If we denote:

Q_1 = the value which is one-quarter of the way up of an ordered data set
Q_3 = the value which is three-quarter of the way up of this data set

then the quartile deviation is given by the following formula:

$$Q.D. = (Q_3 − Q_1)/2$$

Note that the quartile deviation takes no account of extreme values.

___

Illustrative example 6:

team performance and dispersion

Referring to the previous example:

Team A	Team B	Team C	
5.2	4.1	1.5	
5.4	4.7	4.4	
5.5	4.9	4.7	1st Quartile
5.8	5.5	5.6	
5.8	5.8	5.8	Median

6.0	6.0	6.0
6.0	6.0	6.0
6.0	6.0	6.0 ← 3rd Quartile
6.1	7.1	8.6
6.2	7.9	9.4

The quartile deviation (Q.D.) of the performance scores of the three teams are:

Q.D. (Team A) = (6.0 − 5.5)/2 = 0.25
Q.D. (Team B) = (6.0 − 4.9)/2 ≐ 0.55
Q.D. (Team C) = (6.0 − 4.7)/2 = 0.65

Average deviation

The average deviation is the arithmetic mean (or average) of the total deviations of each of the item value in the data set from the mean. The following procedure is carried out to calculate the average deviation:

1 Compute the arithmetic mean ($\bar{X}$) of the data set.
2 Compute the deviation of each item value from this mean.
3 Sum up these deviations (ignoring the algebraic signs).
4 Divide this sum by the number of items in the data set.
The formula for average deviation is symbolized by:

$$\text{A.D.} = \frac{\Sigma \,|X_i - \bar{X}|}{N}$$

where $X_i - X$ is taken to be the absolute (i.e. positive) difference between X_1 and X.

The average deviation is an absolute measure and as such, is not always suitable for comparing two distinct data sets. Thus, we need to convert the average deviation to the form of a coefficient, called the coefficient of average deviation, which is now a relative measure and is expressed by the formula:

$$\text{Coef. of A.D.} = \frac{\text{Average Deviation}}{\text{Arithmetic Mean}}$$
$$= \text{A.D.}/\bar{X}$$

The coefficient of average deviation is appropriate in comparing the extent of dispersion between various data sets. Generally, the larger the coefficient of average deviation, the greater is the dispersion of one data set over the other.

Illustrative example 7:

Team performance and dispersion

Performance score			Deviation from mean (positive number)		
Team A	Team B	Team C	Team A	Team B	Team C
5.2	4.1	1.5	0.8	1.9	4.5
5.4	4.7	4.4	0.6	1.3	1.6
5.5	4.9	4.7	0.5	1.1	1.3
5.8	5.5	5.6	0.2	0.5	0.4
5.8	5.8	5.8	0.2	0.2	0.2
6.0	6.0	6.0	0.0	0.0	0.0
6.0	6.0	6.0	0.0	0.0	0.0
6.0	6.0	6.0	0.0	0.0	0.0
6.1	7.1	8.6	0.1	1.1	2.6
6.2	7.9	9.4	0.2	1.9	3.4
		Total	2.6	8.0	14.0

The average deviation (A.D.) of the performance scores of the three teams are:

A.D. (Team A) = 2.6/10 = 0.26
A.D. (Team B) = 8.0/10 = 0.80
A.D. (Team C) = 14.0/10 = 1.40

Coef. of A.D. (Team A) = A.D./$\bar{X}$
= 0.26/5.8
= 0.045

Coef. of A.D. (Team B) = A.D./$\bar{X}$
= 0.80/5.8
= 0.138

Coef. of A.D. (Team C) = A.D./$\bar{X}$
= 1.40/5.8
= 0.241

Standard deviation

The standard deviation is a measure of the spread of data about the arithmetic mean and is the most preferred measure of dispersion. To calculate the standard deviation, the difference of each item from the arithmetic mean is squared. These squared differences are added together; the result of which is then divided by the number of items. In this way, we have just computed the variance of the data set as expressed below:

$$\text{Variance } S^2 = \frac{\Sigma (X_i - \bar{X})^2}{N}$$

The standard deviation, σ, is equal to the square root of the variance, that is,

$$\sigma = \sqrt{\frac{\Sigma (X_i - \bar{X})^2}{N}}$$

$$= \sqrt{\frac{\Sigma X_i^2}{N} - \left(\frac{\Sigma X_i}{N}\right)^2}$$

Performance score			Square of deviation from mean		
Team A	Team B	Team C	Team A	Team B	Team C
5.2	4.1	1.5	0.64	3.61	20.25
5.4	4.7	4.4	0.36	1.69	2.56
5.5	4.9	4.7	0.25	1.21	1.69
5.8	5.5	5.6	0.04	0.25	0.16
5.8	5.8	5.8	0.04	0.04	0.04
6.0	6.0	6.0	0.00	0.00	0.00
6.0	6.0	6.0	0.00	0.00	0.00
6.0	6.0	6.0	0.00	0.00	0.00
6.1	7.1	8.6	0.01	1.21	6.76
6.2	7.9	9.4	0.04	3.61	11.56
	Total		1.38	11.62	43.02

The standard deviation, σ, of the performance scores of the three teams are:

$$\sigma \text{ (Team A)} = \sqrt{1.38/10} = 0.37$$

$$\sigma \text{ (Team B)} = \sqrt{11.62/10} = 1.08$$

$$\sigma \text{ (Team C)} = \sqrt{43.02/10} = 2.07$$

The standard deviation constitutes an important measure of dispersion because it is a key parameter of the normal curve. In normally distributed population, once its standard deviation is known, we are able to determine what percentage of the population falls within any specified interval measured in terms of standard deviation.

It is possible to compare the dispersions of two or more data sets by virtue of the coefficient of standard deviation as expressed symbolically in the following:

$$\text{Coefficient of standard deviation} = \sigma/\bar{X}$$

Here again, the larger the coefficient, the wider is the dispersion of a data set than that of the other data set.

Statistical estimation

We begin this section by making certain definitional distinctions related to samples and populations. By convention, sample measures are termed *statistics*, while comparable measure pertaining to the population are called *parameters*.

Statisticians use Greek or capital letters as symbols for parameters, and Roman or lower case letters as symbols for statistics. Figure 12.4 lists these symbols and summarizes the definitions we have studied so far.

Population parameters are usually unknown, and have to be estimated from

Population	Sample
N : Population Size	n : Sample size
μ : Population mean	X̄ : Sample mean
σ : Population standard deviation	s : Sample standard deviation

Figure 12.4 *Symbols used in statistical estimation*

their respective statistics. Statistical estimation of a parameter may take two forms:

1 Point estimation: where a single sample value is obtained to provide an estimation of an unknown parameter.
2 Interval estimation: where an interval is determined to gauge the range of an unknown parameter, with a specified level of confidence.

The sample mean, sample standard deviation, and other values derived from the set of sample data, are typical examples of point estimations for the corresponding parameters. Unfortunately, a point estimate is often insufficient because nothing is said about how reliable it is for a parameter. Its value will be much enhanced if there exists an additional measure to illustrate how close the point estimate is likely to be the true value of the parameter.

Interval estimation will service such need. An interval estimate indicates the error (or accuracy) in two ways: the extent of its range of values, and the probability of the true population parameter lying within that range. This can be done by using the characteristics of the sampling distribution of the statistic. As such, it will be appropriate here to digress somewhat and review some of the notions encountered in sampling distribution.

Normal distribution

A very important continuous probability distribution in statistics is the normal distribution (see Figure 12.5). The key features of a normal distribution include:

● It is symmetrical and bell-shaped.
● Its curve has a single peak; hence unimodal.
● Its mean lies at the centre of the curve.
● Its mean, the median and the mode are of the same value.
● The two tails of the distribution extend definitely and nearly touch the horizontal axis.

Regardless of the values of μ and σ, the total area under the normal curve is always equal to unity, and hence we may think of areas under the curve as probabilities. Mathematically, it is true that:

1 Approximately 68 per cent of the values in a normally distributed population lie within one standard deviation (plus and minus) from the mean.

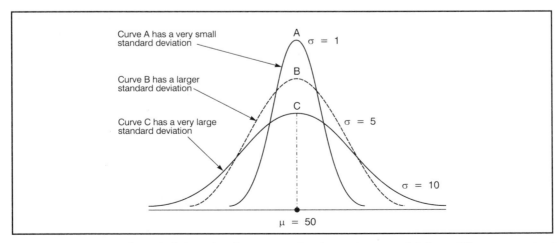

Figure 12.5 *Normal probability distributions with identical mean (μ) but different standard deviations (σ)*

2 Approximately 95.5 per cent of the values in a normally distributed population lie within two standard deviations (plus and minus) from the mean.

3 Approximately 99.7 per cent of the values in a normally distributed population lie within three standard deviations (plus and minus) from the mean.

These three mathematical statements are represented graphically below.

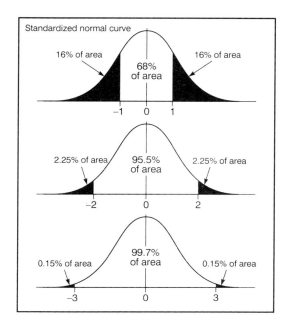

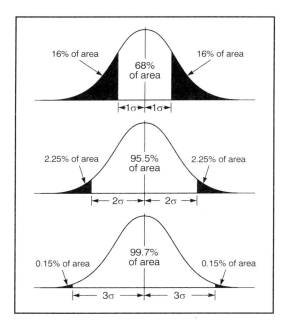

Standardized normal curve

This is a special form of the normal curve. The standardized normal curve has a mean of zero and a standard deviation of one. It is a purely theoretical distribution but nevertheless is the most useful distribution in inferential statistics. The data from an observed normal distribution can be converted to the standardized normal curve by using the following formula:

$$Z_i = (X_i - \mu)/\sigma$$

Sampling distribution of means

The sampling distribution of a sample statistic is the relative frequency distribution of the values of the statistics generated by taking repeated random samples of the same size, and computing the value of the statistic for each sample. In particular, if the sample statistic under study is the mean, we have the so-called sampling distribution of the mean ($\bar{X}$).

We have earlier mentioned that the sample mean $\bar{X}$ is often used as a tool for making an inference about the corresponding population parameter μ. The following theorum, commonly known as the Central Limit Theorum, provides information about the actual sampling distribution of $\bar{X}$:

If the sample size is sufficiently large, then the mean $\bar{X}$ of a random sample from a population will have a sampling distribution which is approximately normal, regardless of the shape of the relative frequency distribution of the original population. As the sample size increases, the better will be the normal approximation to the sampling distribution.

Some other known characteristics of the sampling distribution of $\bar{X}$ are listed below:

1 The sampling distribution of $\bar{X}$ has a mean which is equal to the mean of the population from which the sample was selected. That is, if we denote $\mu_{\bar{x}}$ as the mean of the sampling distribution of $\bar{X}$, then

$$\mu_{\bar{x}} = \mu$$

2 The sampling distribution of $\bar{X}$ has a standard deviation which is equal to the standard deviation of the population from which the sample was selected, divided by the square root of the sample size. That is, if we let $\sigma_{\bar{x}}$ denote the standard deviation of the sampling distribution of $\bar{X}$, then

$$\sigma_{\bar{x}} = \sigma / n$$

With the foregoing review, we now continue with the discussion on interval estimation. In statistics, the probability that we associate with an interval estimate is called the confidence level. This probability indicates how confident we are that the interval estimate will include the population parameter. In statistical estimation, the most commonly used confidence levels are 90 per cent, 95 per cent and 99 per cent.

Interval estimation of a population mean: large sample case

If $\bar{X}$ denotes the sample mean derived from a relatively large sample, the interval estimation of the population mean μ is represented by the following inequalities:

$$\bar{X} - Z \cdot \frac{\sigma}{\sqrt{n}} < \mu < \bar{X} + Z \cdot \frac{\sigma}{\sqrt{n}}$$

when the sample size n > 30.

The corresponding values of Z associated with the different confidence levels are:

Confidence level (%)	Z values
90	1.64
95	1.96
99	2.58

The value $\bar{X} - Z \cdot \sigma / n$ and $\bar{X} + Z \cdot \sigma / n$ are called lower confidence limit and upper confidence limit respectively; while the interval bounded by them is called the confidence interval.

In most practical applications, the value of the population standard deviation σ will be unknown. For larger sample (i.e. n > 30), however, the sample standard deviation S provides a good approximation to σ and may be used in the above formula. Thus, the confidence interval of μ becomes:

$$\bar{X} - Z \cdot \frac{S}{\sqrt{n}} < \mu < \bar{X} + Z \cdot \frac{S}{\sqrt{n}}$$

Illustrative example 8

A sample survey was conducted to establish the amount of travelling time spent by university students between home and the campus. Of the 100 university students interviewed, the mean and the standard deviation of the reported travelling times were $\bar{X} = 22.16$ minutes and $S = 4.8$ minutes respectively. What can be said of the average travelling time per student in the university?

Using the above formula, the interval estimation of the average travelling time per student, denoted by μ, is:

$$\bar{X} - Z \cdot \frac{S}{\sqrt{n}} < \mu < \bar{X} + Z \cdot \frac{S}{\sqrt{n}}$$

$$22.16 - Z \cdot \frac{4.8}{\sqrt{100}} < \mu < 22.16 + Z \cdot \frac{4.8}{\sqrt{100}}$$

$$22.16 - Z \cdot (0.48) < \mu < 22.16 + Z \cdot (0.48)$$

At 90 per cent confidence level, Z = 1.64. Hence

$22.16 - 1.64 \, (0.48) < \mu < 22.16 + 1.64 \, (0.48)$

$21.37 < \mu < 22.95$

At 95 per cent confidence level, $Z = 1.96$. Hence

$22.16 - 1.96 \, (0.48) < \mu < 22.16 + 1.96 \, (0.48)$

$21.22 < \mu < 23.10$

At 99 per cent confidence level, $Z = 2.58$. Hence

$22.16 - 2.58 \, (0.48) < \mu < 22.16 + 2.58 \, (0.48)$

$20.92 < \mu < 23.40$

The respective confidence intervals are illustrated schematically below:

90% confidence:

21.37   22.16   22.95

95% confidence:

21.22   22.16   23.10

99% confidence:

20.92   22.16   23.40

It is readily noted that, the higher the confidence level, the wider the confidence interval becomes.

Interval estimation of a population mean: small sample case

When the sample size is small (n 30), the estimation procedures adopted in the previous section would not be applicable for two reasons:

1 The Central Limit Theorum applies only to large samples, hence we can no longer assume that the sampling distribution of mean ($\bar{X}$) is approximately normal. For small samples, the sampling distribution of mean ($\bar{X}$) will depend on the particular form of the relative frequency distribution of the population.
2 The sample standard deviation (S) is no longer a close approximation of the population deviation σ for small sample size.

Fortunately, another distribution exists which is appropriate for use of small samples. It is called the t-distribution. It is, however, misleading to associate the t-distribution with small sample statistics, as sample size is just one of the two conditions that lead to the use of the t-distribution. Another condition is that the population standard deviation must be unknown. In using the t-distribution, we assume that the population is normal or approximately normal.

Like standard normal distribution, the t-distribution is symmetrical, mould-shaped and have a mean of zero. In general, the

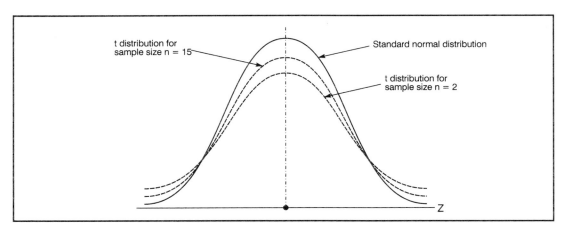

Figure 12.6 *Standard normal distribution and t-distributions for n = 15, n = 2*

t-distribution is flatter than the normal distribution, and there is a different t-distribution associated with every possible sample size. The distribution of t depends on a quantity called the degree of freedom (d.f.) which is equal to n – 1, where n represents the sample size. As the sample size gets larger, the t-distribution loses its flatness and becomes approximately equal to the normal distribution. For sample size n > 30, the t-distribution is so close to the normal distribution that we will use the latter to approximate it (see Figure 12.6).

The confidence interval of a population mean in small sample cases is given by the inequalities:

$$\bar{X} - t_{a/2} . S/\sqrt{n} < \mu < \bar{X} + t_{a/2} . S/n$$

with (n – 1) degrees of freedom.

Illustrative example 9

A random sample of twenty-five households in Felix Town yielded a mean household income of $1,240 per month, and a sample standard deviation of $95. What is the mean income of all households in Felix Town?

This problem requires the use of a t-distribution because the sample size is less than thirty and the population standard deviation is unknown. The sample data given is summarized as follows:

$$n = 25$$
$$\text{d.f.} = 24$$
$$\bar{X} = \$1,240$$
$$S = \$95$$

The estimated standard error of the mean of the population is:

$$\hat{\sigma}_x = \hat{\sigma}/n = S/n$$
$$= \$95/25$$
$$= \$19$$

At 95 per cent confidence level and 24 degrees of freedom, the value of t is 2.064 (see Appendix: Table II).

The confidence interval of the population mean is:

$$\$1,240 - 2.064 . \hat{\sigma}_{\bar{x}} < \mu < \$1,240 + 2.064 . \hat{\sigma}_{\bar{x}}$$
$$\$1,240 - 2.064(\$19) < \mu < \$1,240 + 2.064(\$19)$$
$$\$1,200.78 < \mu < \$1,279.22$$

Interval estimation of a population proportion: large sample case

Researchers often need to estimate the proportion of elements in a population which possess a certain characteristic. Examples are: the proportion of smokers, the proportion of households owning video cassette recorder, the proportion of readers of a newspaper or magazine, and so on. We will now consider the method of estimating the population proportion based on information obtained from a sample.

Let $\hat{p}$ denote the sample proportion. For sufficiently large samples, the sampling distribution of $\hat{p}$ is approximately normal, with

mean

$$\mu_{\hat{p}} = p$$

standard deviation

$$\sigma_p = \sqrt{p(1-p)/n} \quad \sqrt{\hat{p}(1-\hat{p})/n}$$
$$= \sigma_{\hat{p}}$$

The confidence interval for p in a large sample case may be constructed by adopting a procedure which is analogous to that used for estimating a population mean. The interval estimation for p is:

$$\hat{p} - Z_{a/2} . \sigma_{\hat{p}} < p < \hat{p} + Z_{a/2} . \sigma_{\hat{p}}$$

or

$$\hat{p} - Z_{\alpha/s} . \sqrt{\hat{p}(1-\hat{p})/n} < p < \hat{p}$$
$$+ Z_{a/2} . \sqrt{\hat{p}(1-\hat{p})/n}$$

For a 95 per cent confidence interval for p, we have $\alpha = 0.05$ or $\alpha/2 = 0.025$, and Z = 1.96

Illustrative example 10

A sample survey on 1,000 workers was conducted to determine the incidence of public bus usage. The sample data indicated that $\hat{p}$ = 15.5 per cent of workers were bus commuters.

Since σ_p is unknown, its approximation to $\sigma_{\hat{p}}$ is used.

$$\sigma_p = \sigma_{\hat{p}} = \sqrt{\hat{p}(1 - \hat{p})/n}$$

$$= \sqrt{0.155(1 - 0.155)/1.000}$$

$$= 0.0114$$

AT 95 per cent confidence level, Z = 1.96. Hence the interval estimation of p is given by:

$$\hat{p} - Z_{a/2} \cdot \sigma_{\hat{p}} < p < \hat{p} + Z_{a/2} \cdot \sigma_{\hat{p}}$$

$$0.155 - 196(0.0114) < p < 0.155$$

$$+ 1.96(0.0114)$$

$$0.1326 < p < 0.1774$$

$$13.26\% < p < 17.74\%$$

Thus, we can say with 95 per cent level of confidence that the incidence of workers who use public buses lies between 13.26 per cent and 17.74 per cent.

Interval estimation of the difference between two population means: large sample case

The technique used here is a simple extension of that used for large sample estimation of a population mean. This arises when, for example, we wish to compare the rentals of residential units in two districts, A and B, or the mean sales produced by sales staff at a publishing company.

Let us denote:

μ_1 = mean of Population A

μ_2 = mean of Population B

$\bar{X}_1$ and $\bar{X}_2$ the respective sample means
S_1 and S_2 the respective sample standard deviations
n_1 and n_2 the respective sample sizes. (See below.)

	Population A	Population B
Sample size	n_1	n_2
Sample mean	$\bar{X}_1$	$\bar{X}_2$
Sample standard deviation	S_1	S_2

Our problem here is to estimate $(\mu_1 - \mu_2)$ based on the observed difference between the sample means $(\bar{X}_1 - \bar{X}_2)$.

We recall from statistical theory that for sufficiently large sample sizes (i.e. $n_1, n_2 > 30$), the sampling distribution of $(\bar{X}_1 - \bar{X}_2)$ is approximately normal, with

mean

$$\mu_{\bar{x}_1 - \bar{x}_2} - \mu_1 - \mu_2$$

standard deviation

$$\sigma_{\bar{x}_1 - \bar{x}_2} = \sqrt{\frac{\sigma_1^2}{n_1} + \frac{\sigma_2^2}{n_2}}$$

where σ_1^2 and σ_2^2 are the variances of the two populations from which the samples were selected.

For large samples estimation of $(\mu_1 - \mu_2)$, we make the following two assumptions:

1 The two random samples are independently selected from the target populations. By this, we mean that the choice of elements in one sample does not affect, and is not affected by, the choice of elements in the other sample.
2 The sample sizes n_1 and n_2 are sufficiently large ($n_1, n_2 > 30$).

Under the foregoing assumptions, the confidence interval for $(\mu_1 - \mu_2)$ is given by:

$$(\bar{X}_1 - \bar{X}_2) - Z_{\alpha/s}\,\sigma_{(\bar{X}_1 - \bar{X}_2)} < (\mu_1 - \mu_2) < (\bar{X}_1 - \bar{X}_2)$$
$$+ Z_{\alpha/2}\sigma_{(\bar{X}_1 - \bar{X}_2)}$$

or

$$(\bar{X}_1 - \bar{X}_2) - Z_{\alpha/2}\sqrt{\frac{\sigma_1^2}{n_1} + \frac{\sigma_2^2}{n_2}}$$
$$< (\mu_1 - \mu_2) < (\bar{X}_1 - \bar{X}_2)$$
$$+ Z_{\alpha/2}\sqrt{\frac{\sigma_1^2}{n_1} + \frac{\sigma_2^2}{n_2}}$$

When σ_1^2 and σ_2^2 are unknown, we use the sample variance S_1 and S_2 to approximate, and the confidence interval for $(\mu_1 - \mu_2)$ may now be expressed as:

$$(\bar{X}_1 - \bar{X}_2) - Z_{\alpha/s}\sqrt{\frac{S_1^2}{n_1} + \frac{S_2^2}{n_2}}$$
$$< (\mu_1 - \mu_2) < (\bar{X}_1 - \bar{X}_2)$$
$$+ Z_{\alpha/s}\sqrt{\frac{S_1^2}{n_1} + \frac{S_2^2}{n_2}}$$

Illustrative example 11

A research company is asked to estimate the difference of hourly wages of production workers in Town A and Town B. Simple random samples of hourly wages in both towns are chosen. The results of this survey are:

	Town A	Town B
Sample size	$n_1 = 250$	$n_2 = 225$
Sample mean wages	$\bar{X}_1 = \$6.20$	$\bar{X}_2 = \$6.00$
Sample standard deviation	$S_1 = \$0.30$	$S_2 = \$0.40$

The standard deviations of both populations are not known. Therefore, we use S_1 and S_2 as their approximations.

$$\sigma_1 = S_1 = \$0.30$$
$$\sigma_2 = S_2 = \$0.40$$

The standard error of the difference between two means can be estimated as follows:

$$\sigma_{\bar{X}_1 - \bar{X}_2} = \sqrt{\frac{\sigma_1^2}{n_1} + \frac{\sigma_2^2}{n_2}}$$
$$= \sqrt{\frac{(0.3)^2}{250} + \frac{(0.4)^2}{225}}$$
$$= \sqrt{0.00107}$$
$$= 0.0327$$

At 95 per cent confidence level, $Z_{\alpha/2} = 1.96$. The confidence interval of the difference between population means, denoted by $\mu_1 - \mu_2$, is thus given by:

$$(\bar{X}_1 - \bar{X}_2) - 1.96\,\sigma_{\bar{X}_1 - \bar{X}_2} < \mu_1 - \mu_2$$
$$< (\bar{X}_1 - \bar{X}_2) + 1.96\,\sigma_{\bar{X}_1 - \bar{X}_2}$$

$$\$0.20 - 1.96\,(\$0.0327) < \mu_1 - \mu_2$$
$$< \$0.20 + 1.96\,(\$0.0327)$$

$$\$0.136 < \mu_1 - \mu_2 < \$0.264$$

Interval estimation of the difference between two population means: small sample case

This section presents a method for estimating the difference between two population means from small samples. The following specific assumptions about the relative frequency distribution of the two populations from which the samples are drawn must be made:

- Both populations have relative frequency distributions which are approximately normal.
- The variances σ_1^2 and σ_2^2 of the two populations are equal.
- The two random samples are independently selected.

When the above assumptions are satisfied, we may construct the confidence interval for

$(\mu_1 - \mu_2)$ based on small samples (say $n_1 < 30$ and $n_2 < 30$) as follows:

$$(\bar{X}_1 - \bar{X}_2) - t_{(1-\alpha/2)} \sqrt{S_p^2(1/n_1 + 1/n_2)} < \mu_1 - \mu_2$$

$$< (\bar{X}_1 - \bar{X}_2) + t_{(1-\alpha/2)} \sqrt{S_p^2(1/n_1 + 1/n_2)}$$

where $S_p^2 = [(n_1 - 1)S_1^2 + (n_2 - 1)S_2^2]/(n_1 + n_2 - 2)$ is called the pooled variance.

Illustrative example 12

	Population A	Population B
Sample size	$n_1 = 10$	$n_2 = 14$
Sample mean	$\bar{X}_1 = \$500$	$\bar{X}_2 = \$450$
Sample standard deviation	$S_1 = \$42$	$S_2 = \$36$

Note that we have made the following assumptions:

1 Population A has a relative frequency distribution which is normal with mean μ_1 and variance σ^2.
2 Population B has a relative frequency distribution which is normal with mean μ_2 and variance σ^2.

In order to estimate the variance, σ^2, common to both populations A and B, we pool the information available from both samples and compute. The pooled variance is:

$$S_p^2 = [(n_1 - 1)S_1^2 + (n_2 - 1)S_2^2]/n_1 + n_2 - 2$$

$$= [(10-1)(42)^2 + (14-1)(36)^2]/(10 + 14 + 2)$$

$$= [15{,}876 + 16{,}848]/22$$

$$= 1{,}487.45$$

Hence we have:

$$\sqrt{S_p^2(1/n_1 + 1/n_2)} = \sqrt{1{,}487.45(1/10 + 1/14)}$$

$$= \sqrt{1{,}487.45 \, (0.188)}$$

$$= \sqrt{279.64}$$

$$= 16.72$$

At 95 per cent confidence level and degree of freedom df $= n_1 + n_2) - 2 = 22$, the corresponding t value is 2.074. Therefore, the confidence interval for $(\mu_1 - \mu_2)$ is:

$$(\bar{X}_1 - \bar{X}_2) - 2.074 \, (16.72) < \mu_1 - \mu_2$$

$$< (\bar{X}_1 - \bar{X}_2) + 2.074 \, (16.72)$$

$$50 - 34.68 < \mu_1 - \mu_2 < 50 + 34.68$$

$$15.32 < \mu_1 - \mu_2 < 84.68$$

Interval estimation of the difference between two population proportions: large sample case

This section presents the method used to estimate the difference between two population proportions, P_1 and P_2. If we denote the sample proportions as $\hat{P}_1$ and $\hat{P}_2$, then for sufficiently large sample sizes n_1 and n_2 (say $n_1, n_2 > 30$), the sampling distribution of $(\hat{P}_1 - \hat{P}_2)$ is approximately normal with:

mean

$$\mu_{\hat{P}_1 - \hat{P}_2} = (P_1 - P_2)$$

standard deviation

$$\sigma_{\hat{P}_1 - \hat{P}_2} = \sqrt{\frac{P_1(1 - P_1)}{n_1} + \frac{P_2(1 - P_2)}{n_2}}$$

$$= \sqrt{\frac{\hat{P}_1(1 - \hat{P}_1)}{n_1} + \frac{\hat{P}_2(1 - \hat{P}_2)}{n_2}}$$

It follows that a large sample confidence interval for $(P_1 - P_2)$ may be obtained as:

$$(\hat{P}_1 - \hat{P}_2) - Z_{(1-\alpha/2)} \, \sigma_{\hat{P}_1 - \hat{P}_2} < (P_1 - P_2) < (\hat{P}_1 - \hat{P}_2)$$

$$+ Z_{(1-\alpha/2)} \, \sigma_{\hat{P}_1 - \hat{P}_2}$$

or

$$(\hat{P}_1 - \hat{P}_2) - Z_{(1-\alpha/2)} \sqrt{\frac{\hat{P}_1(1 - \hat{P}_1)}{n_1} + \frac{\hat{P}_2(1 - \hat{P}_2)}{n_2}}$$

$$< (P_1 - P_2) < (\hat{P}_1 - \hat{P}_2) + Z_{(1-\alpha/2)}$$

$$\sqrt{\frac{\hat{P}_1(1 - \hat{P}_1)}{n_1} + \frac{\hat{P}_2(1 - \hat{P}_2)}{n_2}}$$

Illustrative example 13

The performances of two trimming machines A and B were monitored during a specific period. Machine A turned out 30 defective items in a lot of 500, while Machine B turned out 18 defective items in a lot of 720. Construct a 90 per cent confidence interval for the difference between the proportions of defective items which were turned out by Machines A and B.

	Machine A	Machine B
Number of items sampled	500	720
Number of defective items	30	18

The sample proportion of defective items which are turned out by Machine A is:

$$\hat{P}_1 = 30/500 = 0.06$$

Likewise, the sample proportion of defective items which are turned out by Machine B is:

$$\hat{P}_2 = 18/720 = 0.025$$

We can now compute

$$\sqrt{\hat{P}_1(1-\hat{P}_1)/n_1 + \hat{P}_2(1-\hat{P}_2)/n_2}$$

$$= \sqrt{(0.06)(0.94)/500 + (0.025)(0.975)/720}$$

$$= \sqrt{0.0001467}$$

$$= 0.0121$$

The 90 per cent confidence interval is then:

$$(\hat{P}_1 - \hat{P}_2) - 1.64(0.0121) < P_1 - P_2 < (\hat{P}_1 - \hat{P}_2) + 1.64(0.0121)$$

$$0.035 - 0.020 < P_1 - P_2 < 0.035 + 0.020$$

$$0.015 < P_1 - P_2 < 0.055$$

We are 90 per cent confident that the interval between 1.5 per cent and 5.5 per cent covers the true difference of the proportions of defective items turned out by the two machines.

Common errors in data analysis and interpretation

Errors in the analysis and interpretation of data often arise due to a number of reasons, for example, the misunderstanding of the function of graphs, diagrams, charts; the misconception about the number system and so on.

Some of the common errors in data analysis and interpretation are listed below:

- graphical illusion
- mix-up in row and column percentages
- insufficiency of cross-tabulations
- fallacy of open-ended responses
- misuse of arithmetic operations.

The following diagrams are examples of graphical illusion.

The conclusions in the following three graphs are obviously contradictory, though all were derived from the same set of data. Why is this so? The answer lies in the understanding of the function of a graph. In essence, a graph provides information on two or more objects, say A and B, such as 'A has more than B', or 'A has same as B' or 'A has less than B'. It, however, does not provide information on the difference between two or more objects, such as 'A has a lot more than B'.

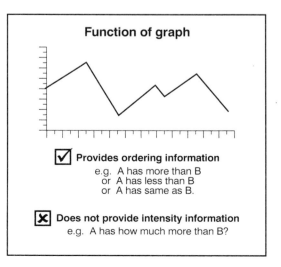

Function of graph

☑ **Provides ordering information**
  e.g. A has more than B
  or A has less than B
  or A has same as B.

☒ **Does not provide intensity information**
  e.g. A has how much more than B?

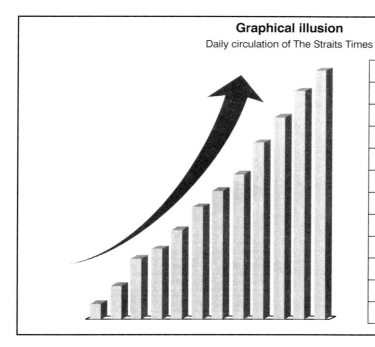

1983	238,797
1984	248,800
1985	263,828
1986	269,412
1987	279,919
1988	292,555
1989	301,581
1990	310,495
1991	328,012
1992	342,050
1993	356,573
1994	367,821

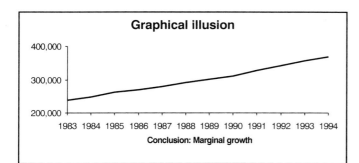

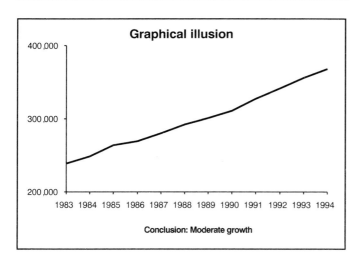

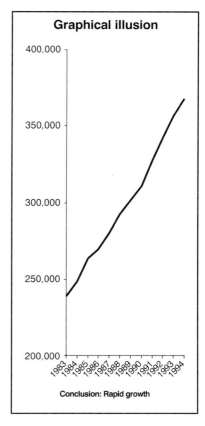

Illustrative example 14:
graphical illusion

The average temperatures in Singapore during the day and during the night are tabulated below:

Day temperature 24Č
Night temperature 30Č

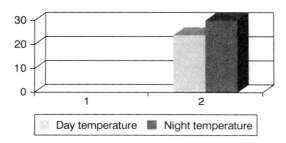

Conclusion I: The day temperature and the night temperature in Singapore are MARGINALLY different.

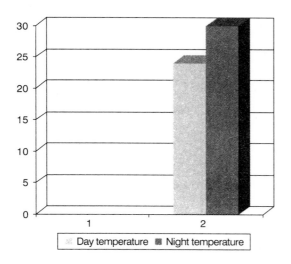

Conclusion II: The day temperature and the night temperature in Singapore are MARKEDLY different.

Illustrative example 15:
mix-up in row and column percentages

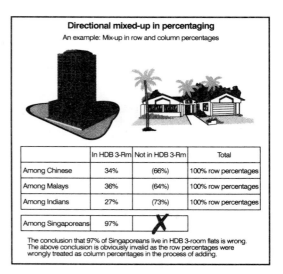

	In HDB 3-Rm	Not in HDB 3-Rm	Total
Among Chinese	34%	(66%)	100% row percentages
Among Malays	36%	(64%)	100% row percentages
Among Indians	27%	(73%)	100% row percentages
Among Singaporeans	97%	X	

The conclusion that 97% of Singaporeans live in HDB 3-room flats is wrong. The above conclusion is obviously invalid as the row percentages were wrongly treated as column percentages in the process of adding.

The above conclusion is obviously invalid as the row percentages were wrongly treated as column percentages in the processing of adding.

Illustrative example 16:
mix-up in row and column percentages

The incidence of readers and non-readers of a magazine among the single (unmarried) persons, the married persons and the divorced/separated persons in a town are tabulated below.

	Among Single	Among Married	Among Divorced/ Separated	TOTAL	
Readers	30%	45%	85%	160%	X
Non-Readers	70%	55%	15%	140%	X

Conclusion: Among all persons, 160 per cent are readers and 140 per cent are non-readers.

The above conclusion is invalid as the column percentages were wrongly treated as row percentages in the process of adding.

Illustrative example 17:

mix-up in row and column percentages

Illustrative example 18:

insuffiency of cross-tabulation

A study was conducted to evaluate the awareness level of a certain Family Planning Compaign. The study results were presented as a two-way tabulation by sex of respondents:

	Male 182 (100%)	Female 178 (100%)
Aware	86 (47%)	62 (35%)
Not aware	96 (53%)	116 (36%)

Conclusion I: Males were more likely to be aware of the campaign than females (47 per cent vs 35 per cent respectively.)

The results were also presented as a two-way tabulation by education of respondents:

	Educated 207 (100%)	Non-educated 153 (100%)
Aware	124 (60%)	24 (16%)
Not aware	83 (40%)	129 (84%)

Conclusion II The educated respondents were more likely to be aware of the campaign than the non-educated respondent (60 per cent vs 16 per cent respectively.)

The results were presented as a three-way tabulation by sex and education of respondents:

	Educated		Non-educated	
	Male 127 (100%)	Female 80 (100%)	Male 55 (100%)	Female 98 (100%)
Aware	124 (60%)	48 (60%)	10 (18%)	14 (14%)
Not aware	83 (40%)	32 (40%)	45 (82%)	84 (84%)

Conclusion III: As indicated in Conclusion II, the educated respondents were more likely to be aware of the campaign than the non-educated respondents.

Conclusion IV: Contrary to Conclusion I, males were about as likely to be aware of the campaign as females. Conclusion I is invalid as it was derived by sex of the respondents only, without additional cross-tabulation by education of the respondents. In this case, it happened that most of the male respondents in the survey were educated, hence the invalidity of Conclusion I.

Illustrative example 19:

fallacy of open-ended questions

Consider the following survey question:

'What are the things you dislike about the biscuits you've just tried?'

The two sets of responses tabulated from (I) an open-ended question format; and (II) a closed-ended question format are tabulated below.

	(I) Open- ended question	(II) Closed- ended question
The chocolate melts easily	15.0%	33.8%
The sweet sickly taste	6.6%	44.6%
The biscuits are too soft	6.2%	51.4%
The biscuits are too hard	4.8%	31.1%
The biscuits are too dry	2.6%	39.2%
The biscuits get crushed in the packet	1.8%	54.1%
The packets don't keep the biscuits fresh	1.8%	54.1%
The chocolates tend to stick together	0.4%	46.8%

Note that the percentage figures tabulated from the open-ended question format are drastically lower than the corresponding percentage figures tabulated from the closed-ended question format. This will almost always be the case as, in an open-ended question format, the respondent will give only a limited number of responses (in this case the things he or she dislikes about), and so will be less conprehensive and accurate. As a matter of fact, open-ended questionnaire format belongs to qualitative approach and the set of responses obtained is not appropriate for making quantitative measurements.

In the above example, the manufacturer of the biscuits under study would not be unduly concerned about the complaint that 'the biscuits get crushed in the packet' from the responses to the open-ended question (only 1.8 per cent mentioned it). However, this would be a mistake as it turned out to be the most frequently mentioned dislike about the biscuits among the respondents, as is vividly reflected in responses to the closed-end question (54.1 per cent mentioned it).

Illustrative example 20:
misuse of arithmetic operations

Ten housewives with hair dandruff were asked to use two brands of shampoo, P and Q, for two specified periods separately. After each specified period, they were asked to evaluate the effectiveness of the shampoo based on the following question:

'How effective would you say the shampoo you've just used to get rid of your dandruff is. Would you say that it is . . . (READ OUT)?'

Very effective (VE) 1
Somewhat effective (SE) 2
Neither effective nor ineffective (N) . . 3
Somewhat ineffective (SI) 4
Very ineffective (VI) 5

The set of responses offered by the ten respondents is tabulated below:

Respondent	Responses for P	Responses for Q
1	VE	VE
2	SE	VE
3	SE	SE
4	SE	VE
5	SE	SI
6	SE	VE
7	N	SI
8	N	VE
9	N	SE
10	N	VE

Case I: Using the numerical scales shown below, the bigger the number, the more effective is the shampoo being evaluated.

VE	SE	N	SI	VI
5	4	3	2	1

Respondent	Points awarded P	Q
1	5	5
2	4	5
3	4	4
4	4	5
5	4	2
6	4	5
7	3	2
8	4	5
9	3	4
10	3	5
Total	38	42

Conclusion: Since Q was given a higher point than P, so Q is more effective than P. Also, since $(42 - 38)/38 = 11$ per cent, Q is 11 per cent more effective than P.

Case II: Using the numerical scales shown below, the smaller the number, the more effective is the shampoo being evaluated.

VE	SE	N	SI	VI
1	2	3	4	5

Respondent	Points awarded P	Q
1	1	1
2	2	1
3	2	2
4	2	1
5	2	4
6	2	1
7	3	4
8	2	1
9	3	2
10	3	1
Total	22	18

Conclusion: Q is more effective than P, as Q is awarded a smaller number than P. Also, since $(22 - 18)/18 = 22$ per cent, Q is 22 per cent more effective than P.

Case III: Using the numerical scales shown below, the bigger the number, the more effective is the shampoo being evaluated.

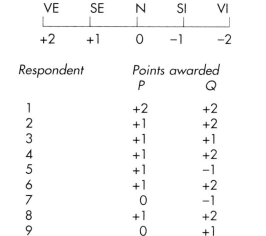

VE	SE	N	SI	VI
+2	+1	0	−1	−2

Respondent	Points awarded P	Q
1	+2	+2
2	+1	+2
3	+1	+1
4	+1	+2
5	+1	−1
6	+1	+2
7	0	−1
8	+1	+2
9	0	+1
10	0	+2
Total	+8	+12

Conclusion: Q is more effective than P, as Q is awarded a higher point than P. Also, since $(12 - 8)/8 = 50$ per cent, Q is 50 per cent more effective than P.

Case IV: Using the numerical scales shown below, the bigger the number, the more effective is the shampoo being evaluated.

VE	SE	N	SI	VI
+1	+1	0	−1	−1

Respondent	Points awarded P	Q
1	+1	+1
2	+1	+1
3	+1	+1
4	+1	+1
5	+1	−1
6	+1	+1
7	0	−1
8	+1	+1
9	0	+1
10	0	+1
Total	+7	+6

Conclusion: P is more effective than Q, as P is awarded a higher point than Q. Also, since $(7 - 6)/6 = 17$ per cent, P is 17 per cent more effective than Q.

The above four conclusions are not consistent, and are even contradictory. The reason is because the numbers used in the numerical scales are ordinal numbers, and as such, they are not permitted to apply the arithmetic operations (i.e. addition, subtraction, multiplication and division) on them.

End-of-chapter revision

Review questions

12.1 What is meant by central tendency of data?

12.2 Define the following terms for a set of data and provide the formula for each.
   a Arithmetic mean.
   b Median.
   c Mode.

12.3 How do extreme values influence the mean, median and mode?

12.4 Why is it necessary to measure dispersion? What are the measures commonly used?

12.5 Describe and provide the formula for each of the following:
   a standard deviation
   b variance
   c range.

12.6 What is the difference (if any) between a parameter and a statistic?

12.7 How would you calculate a point estimate for a population mean from a simple random sample? A population proportion?

12.8 What is an interval estimate?

12.9 What is a confidence interval? What affects the size of a confidence interval?

12.10 In a probability sample of 1,500 consumers, 35 per cent claim to have tried a well-known aspirin. At the 95 per cent confidence level, what is the confidence interval for the proportion of population who have tried the product?

12.11 A probability sample of 200 consumers reveals that 42 per cent prefer a generic product over a nationally-known counterpart. What is the 99 per cent confidence interval for the proportion of the population who favour the generic product? How would the confidence interval change if the sample size were doubled? tripled?

12.12 The proprietor of Bee Tin Restaurant has just tested two new mango puddings. Of 100 customers who tried version A, 70 per cent said it was 'delicious'. Of 100 customers who tried version B, 52 per cent said it was 'delicious'. At the 0.05 significance level, is there a difference between the results?

True-false questions
Write True (T) or False (F) for the following:

12.13 For a set of data, the median is the value that occurs most frequently.

12.14 To calculate the arithmetic mean, data must be in either the interval or ratio scale of measurement.

12.15 The confidence interval is just a statistical way of expressing how to estimate.

12.16 Measures of central tendency provide indication on the spread of a data set.

12.17 The mode is not affected by extreme values in the data set.

12.18 To calculate the arithmetic mean, the data must be arrayed in order of size.

12.19 The first step in significance testing is to formulate the null hypothesis H_o.

12.20 The significance level of a statistical test is the probability of rejecting a null hypothesis that is false.

12.21 If two sample means are significantly different at the 0.05 level of significance, they will be significantly different at the 0.10 level as well.

12.22 When comparing two sample proportions, any difference that is found to be significant in a two-tail test would be significant at one-half that level in a one-tail test.

12.23 The Chi-square technique can be used to compare two or more sample proportions.

12.24 Both the expected and observed frequencies in a Chi-square goodness-of-fit test must sum up to the total number of cases.

12.25 In testing a directional null hypothesis, the hypothesis could not be rejected if extreme sample results are obtained in either direction.

12.26 There is a different t-distribution for each possible sample size.

12.27 With increasing sample size, the t-distribution tends to become flatter in shape.

12.28 The standard deviation is the numerical difference between the largest value and the smallest value in the data set.

12.29 Approximately 68 per cent of the values in a normally distributed population lie within two standard deviations on each side of the mean.

12.30 The Central Limit Theorum applies to small samples only.

Multiple-choice questions

12.31 The measure of central tendency that describes the value observed most often is known as the:
a median

b mean
c mode
d range.

12.32 To calculate the median, data must be at least of the:
a interval scale
b ordinal scale
c nominal scale
d ratio scale.

12.33 The difference between the two extreme values in a set of data is known as the:
a mode
b variance
c median
d range.

12.34 For a given level of confidence, using a larger sample size will:
a decrease the width of the confidence interval
b increase the width of the confidence interval
c have no effect on the width of the confidence interval
d none of the above.

12.35 Which of the following is a necessary condition for using a t-distribution table?
a n is small
b s is known but σ is unknown
c The population is infinite.
d All of the above.

12.36 Which one of the following is not a correct description of the normal distribution?
a It is symmetrical and bell-shaped.
b It has only one peak.
c Its mean is located at the centre.
d Its mean, mode and median are not identical.

13

Data analysis and interpretation: testing hypotheses

The development of mean, median or mode and the estimation of population parameters as discussed in Chapter 12 constitute the elementary level of data analysis. Advanced levels of data analysis are required to ascertain differences and establish associations between population groups, and involve the application of more sophisticated statistical techniques. In this chapter, we shall discuss tests of significance – the statistical technique employed for ascertaining differences between two population groups.

Any sample statistic is subject to random error. It, therefore, becomes necessary to examine whether an observed difference between two population groups is due to some established facts, or mere occurrences of sample variation. Conventionally, we say that if the observed difference is such that it can occur by mere chance fewer than five out of 100 times, it is considered as real (or statistically significant). On the contrary, if the difference can occur more than five out of 100 times, it is attributed to sampling error (or not statistically significant). This constitutes the basic concept on which the significance testing technique is founded. In significance testing, we are interested in making a decision about a parameter value, rather than in obtaining an estimate of its value.

Steps in significance testing ▬

In significance testing, we begin with an assumption (called a hypothesis) that we make about a population parameter. We next proceed to collect sample data, compute the relevant sample statistics and finally use it to judge how likely it is that our hypothesized (population) parameter is correct. In the process, the observed difference between the hypothesized value and the sample value is noted. As a general rule, the smaller the difference, the greater the likelihood that our hypothesized value for the population parameter is correct; and conversely, the larger the difference, the smaller this likelihood. The steps involved in the test of significance technique are summarized below:

1 Formulate the null and the alternative hypotheses.
2 Specify the desired level of significance.
3 Select the appropriate statistical test.
4 Determine the critical value (the decision rule).
5 Calculate the observed value of the test statistic.
6 Accept or reject the null hypothesis.

A flow diagram of significance testing procedure is depicted in Figure 13.1.

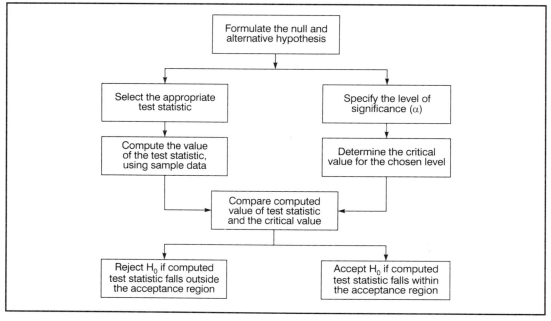

Figure 13.1 *Flow diagram for significance testing*

1 *Formulate the null and the alternative hypotheses.* In statistical terms, a hypothesis is a statement, or assumption about the parameter value of a population. The hypothesis to be tested is called the null hypothesis, symbolized by H_0. The null hypothesis generally takes the form of no change from the past; no difference between a parameter and a constant number; or no difference between two parameters. The philosophy of significance testing maintains that the researcher first formulates the null hypothesis, which he or she believes to be true and is ready to accept it until evidence to the contrary becomes statistically overwhelming. Some examples below will help illustrate the kinds of null hypothesis that can be formulated:

a We wish to establish and compare the proportions of public transport commuters among the HDB flat dwellers (p_1) and non-HDB flat dwellers (p_2). A null hypothesis could be written as: 'There is no difference between the proportion of HDB dwellers who use public transport and that of non-HDB flat dwellers who do so.' The null hypothesis would be written as $H_0: p_1 = p_2$.

b We want to investigate the examination results between students in express classes ($\bar{X}_1$) and those in normal classes ($\bar{X}_2$). The null hypothesis might be written as 'Express class students and normal class students score about the same examination result'. Thus $H_0: \bar{X}_1 = \bar{X}_2$.

c The proportion of households owning a microwave oven (p) is equal to, or less than 15 per cent. The null hypothesis would then be written as $H_0: p \leqslant 15\%$.

If the sample results do not support the null hypothesis, we then turn to something else – the alternative hypothesis, symbolized as H_1. Thus the null hypothesis and the alternative hypothesis should be formulated in the manner that the rejection of the null hypothesis H_0 will automatically lead to the acceptance of the alternative hypothesis H_1, and vice versa. The alternative hypothesis that corresponds to the null hypothesis in the foregoing examples would be:

a The public transport usage rate among HDB flat dwellers is significantly different from that among non-HDB flat dwellers; i.e. $H_1:p_1 \quad p_2$.

b The examination results scored by the express class students and the normal class students are significantly different; i.e. $H_1:\bar{X}_1 \quad \bar{X}_2$.

c More than 15 per cent of households own microwave ovens; i.e. $H_1:p > 15\%$.

Null hypothesis may be directional or non-directional. A directional hypothesis specifies that one quantity is greater or less than another. In item (c) above, the hypothesis is directional. A directional hypothesis can be rejected by the results in just one direction, that is, by a much higher than 15 per cent of sample households owning a microwave oven as in the case of item (c). This is also known as a one-tailed test.

A non-directional hypothesis, on the other hand, is a statement that one quantity is equal to another, such as item (a) above. It can be rejected by a result in either one of two directions: When the public transport usage rate among HDB flat dwellers is much higher than that among non-HDB flat dwellers; or when the public transport usage rate among HDB flat dwellers is much lower than that among non-HDB flat dwellers. This is also known as a two-tailed test. The choice of a directional or non-directional test will depend on the purpose for which the statistical test is being done.

2 *Specify the desired level of significance.* Having formulated the null and the alternative hypothesis, the next step is to decide on the level of risk we are willing to tolerate. Two kinds of errors can occur in hypothesis testing: one arises from the decision to reject a null hypothesis which in fact is true (referred to as a *Type I* error) and the other arises from the decision to accept a null hypothesis which in fact is false (referred to as a *Type II* error).

	H_0 is True	H_0 is False
Reject H_0	Type I error	Correct
Accept H_0	Correct	Type II error

Figure 13.2 *Types of error in significance testing*

The probability of committing a Type I error is called the level of significance of the test, and is designated by the Greek letter *alpha* α. That means if we set $\alpha = 0.05$ and reject the null hypothesis at this level, there is a 5 per cent chance that our conclusion would be a mistake. A small α-value means a higher level of confidence in the test will be secured. Significance level to be set will depend on how much risk one wants to take in rejecting null hypothesis when it is true.

The probability of committing a Type II error is designated by the Greek letter *beta* β. Obviously it is desirable to keep both α and β the smallest possible, but for a sample of a given size, a decrease in α will result in an increase in β, and conversely, an increase in α will result in a decrease in β. The conventional practice is to fix α, and let β vary. The various levels of significance most commonly used in hypothesis testing are $\alpha = 0.10$, 0.05 and 0.01, which correspond to the confidence levels of 90 per cent, 95 per cent and 99 per cent respectively.

In a standard normal distribution, the values of Z for 0.05 and 0.01 levels of significance are shown on p. 288.

3 *Select the appropriate statistical test.* Once the level of significance has been decided upon, next in hypothesis testing is to determine the appropriate test statistic, or its probability distribution. We have a choice between normal distribution and the t-distribution and the rules governing such choice follow the same as discussed in the previous chapter on statistical estimation.

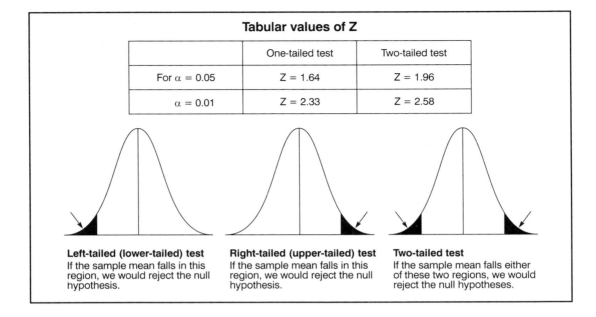

Tabular values of Z

	One-tailed test	Two-tailed test
For $\alpha = 0.05$	Z = 1.64	Z = 1.96
$\alpha = 0.01$	Z = 2.33	Z = 2.58

Left-tailed (lower-tailed) test
If the sample mean falls in this region, we would reject the null hypothesis.

Right-tailed (upper-tailed) test
If the sample mean falls in this region, we would reject the null hypothesis.

Two-tailed test
If the sample mean falls either of these two regions, we would reject the null hypotheses.

4 *Determine the critical value.* The critical value is the value which the test statistic would have to exceed for the null hypothesis to be rejected. This is a statement of the conditions under which the null hypothesis will either be accepted or rejected. The critical value can be found in the appropriate statistical table: cumulative normal distribution, t-distribution, chi-square distribution or F-distribution. In the case of non-directional hypothesis, there will be two critical values at opposing directions.

5 *Calculate the observed value of the test statistic.* Given the appropriate statistical test, a test statistic will be calculated to test the null hypothesis. The test statistic is a value computed from the sample and upon which the decision concerning the null and the alternative hypotheses is based. Depending on the purpose of the test, the test statistic could be any one of the following: a Z-statistic, a t-statistic, a chi-square statistic or an F-ratio, to mention just a few.

6 *Accept or reject the null hypothesis.* The critical value is used to define the regions of acceptance and rejection of the null

hypothesis. When the observed sample value falls within the rejection region, the null hypothesis is rejected; otherwise, the null hypothesis is accepted. It follows that the higher the desired level of significance, the less likely would be the observed value of a test statistic to fall within the rejection region. For example, at $\alpha = 0.05$ (95 per cent confidence level) the critical value will be larger than that at $\alpha = 0.10$ (90 per cent confidence level). Thus, if the evidence observed from the sample enables us to reject a null hypothesis at a given level, we will be able to reject it at other lower levels.

7 *Choice of appropriate technique.* In significance testing, the large number of statistical techniques available has further complicated the task of selecting the most appropriate one for use in a particular situation. Below are five key questions that will aid in making the choice:
  1 What does the test intend to show: group differences or association between variables?
  2 What scale of measurement is involved: nominal, ordinal, interval or ratio?

3 How many samples are involved? Alternatively, does the difference being observed concern a sample value and a population value, or two or more sample values?
4 Where it concerns two or more samples, are these samples related or independent?
5 How many samples are being studied?

Statistical tests for nominal data

As mentioned earlier, the appropriate test will vary according to the scale level of the data. We shall now begin the discussion with the weakest scale of measurement, i.e. the nominal data. A flow diagram for choosing the appropriate test for nominal data is shown in Figure 13.3.

Chi-square analysis

Chi-square analysis is most commonly used in marketing research for handling

hypothesis testing involving nominal data. The symbol χ^2 is used to designate chi-square, the distribution of which has values which depends on the number of degrees of freedom (d.f.). As seen in Figure 13.4, a chi-square distribution is very skewed when it involves a smaller d.f. As d.f. increases, the distribution becomes more symmetrical.

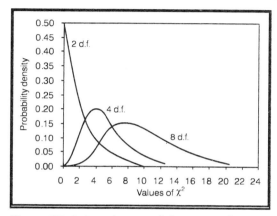

Figure 13.4 *Distribution of chi-square for various degrees of freedom*

The test statistic used in chi-square analysis takes the following form:

$$\chi^2 = \sum_1^n (O_i - E^i)^2/E_i$$

where χ^2 = the chi-square value
O_i = the observed frequency in the *i*-th category
E_i = the expected frequency in the *i*-th category
n = the number of categories

Chi-square goodness-of-fit test

This is often used to test whether a sample comes from a universe which has a given distribution (e.g. normal distribution). A beverage manufacturer may wish to explore whether the sales of soft drinks vary significantly when a switch is made from the old to the new package design. He or she calculates the difference, if any, between the

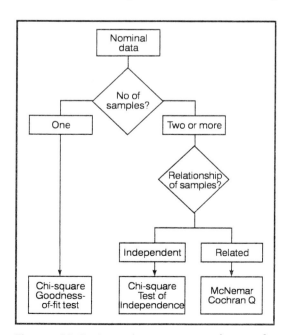

Figure 13.3 *Appropriate statistical tests for nominal data*

expected patterns of sales, and judges whether the observed difference between the two patterns can arise by chance alone, or is due to sampling variation.

Illustrative example 1

A beverage bottler has developed a new drink and considers bottling it in three different package sizes: 5, 10 and 20-ounce. Records of past sales indicated the purchase patterns to be as follows:

Package sizes	Percentage of sales
5-ounce	40
10-ounce	25
20-ounce	35
Total	100

Step 1: the null hypothesis. The null hypothesis H_0 states that there is no difference in the sale patterns between old packaging and new packaging. The alternative hypothesis H_1 states that there is a difference.

Step 2: the level of significance. It was decided to set it at $\alpha = 0.05$. This is a two-tailed test (non-directional).

Step 3: the statistical test. The appropriate test is the chi-square goodness-of-fit test because the data is nominally-scaled, and they are from a single sample. The number of degrees of freedom (d.f.) is $n - 1 = 2$, where n denotes the number of categories.

Step 4: the decision rule. For degree of freedom d.f. $= 2$ and at $\alpha = 0.05$ level of significance, the critical value read from the critical value table is 5.99. The null hypothesis H_0 will be accepted if the computed test statistic of χ^2 is less than 5.99; otherwise H_0 will be rejected and the alternative hypothesis H_1 will be accepted.

Step 5: calculate the test statistic. Before we calculate the test statistic of χ^2, we present the *expected* and the *deserved* frequencies of past sales as follows:

Package sizes	Expected frequencies (E_i)	Observed frequencies (O_i)
5-ounce	$8532 \times 40\% = 3413$	3157
10-ounce	$8532 \times 25\% = 2133$	2560
20-ounce	$8532 \times 35\% = 2986$	2815
Total	8532	8532

$$\chi^2 = \sum (O_i - E_i)^2/E_i$$
$$= (3157 - 3413)^2/3413$$
$$+ (2560 - 2133)^2/2133$$
$$+ (2815 - 2986)^2/2986$$
$$= 114.47$$

Step 6: draw a statistical conclusion. Since the computed χ^2 value (114.47) is much larger than the critical value (5.99), we reject the null hypothesis H_0 and conclude that the sales patterns between the old bottling and the new bottling are statistically different.

Chi-square tests of independence

The goodness-of-fit test described above is applicable for situations where only one variable (e.g. package size) is tested. With two variables, the test of independence is used instead. This test is most appropriate for analysing cross-tabulations, or for establishing whether two variables are independent. Two variables are said to be independent when no relationship exists between them; that is, the distribution of one variable cannot in any way affect the distribution of the other variable. Note, however, that this test does not measure the extent of dependence (if it so exists) between the two variables.

Illustrative example 2

In a study to determine whether workers' contribution to a charity fund is related to their respective occupations, a quota sample of 320 workers – consisting of 120 production workers, 140 clerical and sales workers and 60 managerial staff – was surveyed. The amount of contributions offered by them is shown in Table 13.1.

Step 1: the null hypothesis. The null hypothesis H_0 states that there is no direct relationship between the amount of contribution and the occupation. The alternative hypothesis H_1 states that there will be a relationship between these two variables.

Step 2: the level of significance. Suppose that a significance level of $\alpha = 0.05$ was chosen for the test. This is the same as stating that the probability of a Type I error is 0.05.

Step 3: the statistical test. The chi-square test of independence is appropriate as the data is nominally-scaled, and the two variables are independent. This is a two-tailed test (non-directional). The number of degrees of freedom is:

$$d.f. = (n - 1) \times (m - 1)$$
$$= (4 - 1) \times (3 - 1)$$
$$= 6$$

where   n represents the number of rows
m represents the number of columns.

Step 4: the decision rule. For degree of freedom d.f. = 6 at the 0.05 level of significance, the critical value read is 12.59. Thus the null hypothesis H_0 will be accepted if the computed test statistic of χ^2 is less than 12.59; otherwise, H_0 will be rejected and the alternative hypothesis H_1 will be accepted.

Step 5: calculate the test statistic. In order to compute the test statistic χ^2, we derive the expected frequencies as shown in Table 13.2.

Table 13.1

Amount of contribution	Observed frequencies (O_i)			
	Production workers	Clerical/sales workers	Managerial staff	All workers
Less than $10	66	69	25	160 (50%)
$10–$15	31	35	14	80 (25%)
$16–$20	15	20	13	48 (15%)
Above $20	8	16	8	32 (10%)
Total	120	140	60	320 (100%)

Table 13.2

Amount of contribution	Expected frequencies (E_i)			
	Production workers	Clerical/sales workers	Managerial staff	All workers
Less than $10	60	70	30	160
$10–$15	30	35	15	80
$16–$20	18	21	9	48
Above $20	12	14	6	32
Total	120	140	60	320

For example, the value in the first column and first row of the table is obtained as follows:

$$120 \times 50\% = 60$$

The observed value of the statistic may now be computed:

$$
\begin{aligned}
\chi^2 &= \sum (O_i - E_i)^2 / E_i \\
&= (66 - 60)^2 / 60 + (69 - 70)^2 / 70 + \ldots \\
&\quad + (16 - 14)^2 / 14 + (8 - 6)^2 / 6 \\
&= 6.29
\end{aligned}
$$

Step 6: draw a statistical conclusion. Since the computed χ^2 value (6.29) is smaller than the critical value (12.59), the null hypothesis H_0 is accepted, and we can conclude that the amount of contribution and the occupation type are not related.

McNemar test

A modification of the chi-square test, this test is employed when the samples are not independent. The McNemar test is appropriate for analysing before-and-after research design situations. A typical example would be to test the effectiveness of a particular treatment (e.g. a discount coupon offer) on purchase rate.

In the McNemar test, the null hypothesis H_0 takes the form that among customers who change their purchase rates, the probability that a customer will change from low to high purchase rate is the same as the probability that a customer will change from high to low purchase rate, which is 0.5.

The test statistic used in McNemar test takes the form:

$$X_2 = \frac{(|B + C| - 1)^2}{B + C}$$

where χ^2 = the observed chi-square value
  B = the number of customers who changed from behaviour P (e.g. low purchase rate) to behaviour Q (e.g. high purchase rate)

C = the number of customers who changed from behaviour Q (e.g. high purchase rate) to behaviour P (e.g. low purchase rate)

Illustrative example 3

A marketing research study was undertaken to evaluate the effectiveness of a recent television advertisement. A sample of 400 respondents was interviewed to indicate their purchase behaviour of the product advertised, both before and after the advertisement. The following table shows the results obtained:

Before advertisement	After advertisement Low purchase rate	High purchase rate	Total
Low purchase rate	190 (A)	80 (B)	270
High purchase rate	40 (C)	90 (D)	130
	230	170	400

Step 1: the null hypothesis. The null hypothesis H_0:$P(B) = P(C)$, i.e. the advertisement did not cause a change in the purchase rate.

Step 2: the level of significance. Suppose that a significance level of $\alpha = 0.05$ was chosen for the test. This is a two-tailed test (nondirectional). The number of degrees of freedom is:

$$
\begin{aligned}
\text{d.f.} &= (n - 1) \times (m - 1) \\
&= (2 - 1) \times (2 - 1) \\
&= 1
\end{aligned}
$$

Step 3: the statistical test. The McNemar test is appropriate because the data is nominally-scaled, and the study involves a before-and-after measurement of two related variables.

Step 4: the decision rule. At $\alpha = 0.05$ level of significance, the critical value of χ^2 is 3.84 for d.f. = 1. Therefore, we will reject the null hypothesis H_0 if the calculated χ^2 is greater than 3.84 and will accept it if otherwise.

Step 5: calculate the test statistic. To calculate χ^2 from the sample date, we have:

$$B = 80$$
$$C = 40$$

Hence

$$\chi^2 = \frac{(|B - C| - 1)^2}{B + C}$$

$$= 12.68$$

Step 6: draw a statistical conclusion. Since the computed χ^2 value (12.68) exceeds the critical value of χ^2 (3.84), the null hypothesis H_0 is rejected. We conclude that the advertisement was successful in increasing the purchase rate of the product under study.

When more than two related samples are involved in the analysis, the McNemar test can no longer be used. In these situations, the Cochran Q test is adopted, the discussion of which is, however, beyond the scope of this book.

Statistical tests for ordinal data

This section deals with statistical tests specifically designed for ordinal data analysis. The choice of an appropriate statistical test for ordinal data is suggested by the flow diagram in Figure 13.5.

Kolmogorov-Smirnov test

Like the chi-square goodness-of-fit test, the Kolmogorov-Smirnov test is used to investigate the degree of agreement between the *observed* distribution and some specified *theoretical* distribution. But unlike the

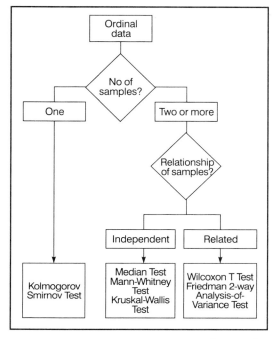

Figure 13.5 *Appropriate statistical tests for ordinal data*

goodness-of-fit test, it takes advantage of the ordinal nature of the available data and is concerned with:

- specifying the cumulative percentage distribution that would occur under the null hypothesis
- comparing this cumulative percentage distribution with the observed cumulative percentage distribution.

Note that the ordinal aspect of the two derived cumulative percentage distributions is preserved. The test statistic used in a Kolmogorov-Smirnov test is:

$$D = \max |F_0(X) - S_n(X)|$$

where D = the test statistic
$F_0(X)$ = the specified cumulative percentage distribution under null hypothesis H_0 for any value X, and is the proportion of cases expected to have scores equal to, or less than X

$S_n(X)$ = the observed cumulative percentage distribution of a random sample of n observations, where X is a possible score.

Note, therefore, that D represents the maximum difference (ignore sign) between the two corresponding values $F_0(X)$ and $S_n(X)$ for any value X.

Illustrative example 4

A manufacturer of domestic paints is considering developing a new colour paint in four different shades – very light, light, medium and dark. A sample of 240 paint users was shown the photographs of each shade and asked to indicate their preferences. The results are tabulated below:

Shade	No. of respondents
Very light	90
Light	70
Medium	50
Dark	30
Total	240

Is there evidence to suggest any particular preference for shades among the respondents?

Step 1: the null hypothesis. The null hypothesis H_0 is that there is no preference for the various shades. The alternative hypothesis H_1 would indicate that there is a preference for the various shades.

Step 2: the level of significance. It was decided to set the level of significance at $\alpha = 0.05$. This is a two-tailed test (non-directional).

Step 3: the statistical test. The Kolmogorov-Smirnov test is used because the data are ordinally-scaled, and we are interested in comparing an observed frequency distribution with a theoretical frequency distribution.

Step 4: the decision rule. At $\alpha = 0.05$, the critical value of D for large samples (say over 35) is given by the formula $1.36/\sqrt{n}$, where n is the sample size. In our example, the critical value is $1.36/\sqrt{240} = 0.088$. Therefore, the null hypothesis H_0 will be rejected if the computed value of D exceeds 0.088; otherwise, the null hypothesis H_0 will be accepted. Incidentally, the following formula can be used to calculate the appropriate critical value of D for large samples at other levels of significance:

α-level	Formula for D
0.20	$1.07/\sqrt{n}$
0.15	$1.14/\sqrt{n}$
0.10	$1.22/\sqrt{n}$
0.05	$1.36/\sqrt{n}$
0.01	$1.63/\sqrt{n}$

Step 5: calculate the test statistic. We proceed as follows:

	Observed frequency	Expected frequency	Observed percentage	Expected percentage
Very light	90	60	0.38	0.25
Light	70	60	0.29	0.25
Medium	50	60	0.21	0.25
Dark	30	60	0.12	0.25
Total	240	240	1.00	1.00

Their cumulative percentages are calculated as follows:

	Observed cumulative percentage $S_n(X)$	Expected cumulative percentage $F_n(X)$	Difference $F_n(X) - S_n(X)$
Very light	0.38	0.25	−0.13
Light	0.67	0.50	−0.17
Medium	0.88	0.75	−0.13
Dark	1.00	1.00	0

The value of the test statistic is therefore:

$$D = -0.17$$
$$= 0.17$$

Step 6: draw a statistical conclusion. Since the calculated D value (0.17) exceeds the critical value (0.088), the null hypothesis H_0 is rejected. We conclude that there is a significant preference for the various shades.

Median test

The median test is appropriate for determining whether two random samples were drawn from the same population, or from two different populations with the same median value. The procedure of the median test is as follows:

1 Combine the two sample groups into one single distribution.
2 Calculate the Grand Median (G.M.) of the combined distribution.
3 Compare this Grand Median with each value in the two samples, and establish the following contingency table:

	Sample I	Sample II	
No. of values above the Grand Median	a	b	a + b
No. of values below the Grand Median	c	d	c + d
	a + c	b + d	

The test statistic to be used in the median test is given by:

$$\chi^2 = \frac{n(|ad - bc| - \frac{n}{2})^2}{(a + b)(c + d)(a + c)(b + d)}$$

where n = the combined sample size
a, b, c and d represent the values shown in the contingency table above.

The null hypothesis H_0 takes the following form: The probability that observations will be above the Grand Median and the observations will be below the Grand Median should be the same for the two populations.

Illustrative example 5

A country club wishes to determine if there is a real difference in the satisfaction level of its offered services between the golf members and the social (non-golf) members. A random sample consisting of twenty respondents from each membership type was interviewed to respond to a questionnaire on the club's services using Likert-type (i.e. ordinally scaled) statements. A score of 1 is assigned to a *very bad* response and a score of 5 for a *very good* response. The ultimate scores offered by the respondents in each group were recorded as follows:

Golf members:		Social members:	
Respondent number	*Aggregated score*	*Respondent number*	*Aggregated score*
1	27	1	69
2	88	2	24
3	51	3	54
4	52	4	75
5	70	5	82
6	66	6	71
7	33	7	65
8	34	8	53
9	36	9	30
10	93	10	26
11	81	11	77
12	50	12	65
13	60	13	46
14	21	14	45
15	72	15	50
16	58	16	83
17	22	17	56
18	59	18	35
19	20	19	74
20	48	20	68

To begin with, combine the forty scores and rank them from the highest to the lowest as follows:

Rank position	Combined score
1	93
2	88
3	83
4	82
5	81
6	77
7	75
8	74
9	72
10	71
11	70
12	69
13	68
14	66
15.5*	65
15.5*	65
17	60
18	59
19	58
20	56
21	54
22	53
23	52
24	51
25.5*	50
25.5*	50
27	48
28	46
29	45
30	36
31	35
32	34
33	33
34	30
35	27
36	26
37	24
38	22
39	21
40	20

At rank 20–21:

⟵ Grand Median
$= \frac{1}{2}(56 + 54)$
$= 55$

*In case of tie scores, the ties are treated by giving each the average rank for the tie score.

We now establish the 2×2 contingency table as follows:

	Golf members	Social members	
No. of values above the Grand Median	9	12	21
No. of values below the Grand Median	11	8	19
	20	20	

We are now set to perform the test of significance.

Step 1: the null hypothesis. The null hypothesis H_0 states that there is no real difference between golf members and social members in the satisfaction level of the club's services. The alternative hypothesis H_1 states that there is a difference.

Step 2: the level of significance. Set the level of significance at $\alpha = 0.05$. This is a two-tailed test. The number of degrees of freedom d.f. is:

$$\text{d.f.} = (n - 1) \times (m - 1)$$
$$= (2 - 1) \times (2 - 1)$$
$$= 1$$

Step 3: the statistical test. Here the median test is used because the data measured is ordinal, and we want to determine whether or not the two independent samples were drawn from the same population with the same median.

Step 4: the decision rule. The critical value for degree of freedom d.f. = 1 and the specified level of significance $\alpha = 0.05$ is 3.84. Therefore the null hypothesis H_0 will be rejected if the calculated χ^2 is larger than 3.84.

Step 5: calculate the test statistic. From the data given above, we have:

$$\chi^2 = \frac{n \left(|ad - bc| - \frac{n}{2} \right)^2}{(a + b)(c + d)(a + c)(b + d)}$$

$$= \frac{40 \left(|9 \times 8 - 12 \times 11| - 20 \right)^2}{21 \times 19 \times 20 \times 20}$$

$$= 0.40$$

Step 6: draw a statistical conclusion. Since the calculated χ^2 (0.40) is smaller than the critical value of χ^2 (3.84), the null hypothesis H_0 is accepted and we can conclude that there is no significant difference in the satisfaction levels between golf members and social members.

Mann-Whitney U test

For truly ordinal data (Likert-scale data is only *theoretically* ordinal data), the Mann-Whitney U test is a more powerful test than the median test. It is an alternative to the t-test when the assumptions underlying the parameter t cannot be fully met, or when measurement is at best ordinal. The test statistic to be used in Mann-Whitney U test is given by:

$$U = \text{Min} (U_1, U_2)$$

where
$$U_1 = n_1 n_2 + [n_1(n_1 + 1)/2] - R_1$$
$$U_2 = n_1 n_2 + [n_2(n_2 + 1)/2] - R_2$$
n_1 = the sample size of the first sample
n_2 = the sample size of the second sample
R_1 = sum of the ranks of first sample
R_2 = sum of the ranks of second sample.

A close examination of the above formulae reveals that the more similar the evaluations given by the two samples, the smaller will be the R-values, and the larger will be the U-values. It therefore follows that, in Mann-Whitney U test, we are in fact testing the probability of obtaining a value which is the smaller of the two U-values, if the two samples are indeed similar in their evaluations.

Illustrative example 6

Referring to the same example above, we have:

n_1 = the number of golf members sampled
   = 20

n_2 = the number of social members sampled
   = 20

R_1 = the sum of the ranks of golf members sampled
   = 442.5

R_2 = the sum of the ranks of social members sampled
   = 377.5

The procedure of the test is set out below:

Step 1: the null hypothesis. The null hypothesis H_0 is that there is no real difference in the evaluation of the club's services as expressed by the golf members and the social members.

Step 2: the level of significance. It was decided to set the level of significance at $\alpha = 0.05$. This is two-tailed test (non-directional).

Step 3: the statistical test. The Mann-Whitney test is appropriate as the measurement level is at least ordinal and converted into ranks. Also, the samples are independent.

Step 4: the decision rule. At $\alpha = 0.05$, $n_1 \doteq 20$ and $n_2 = 20$, the critical value for the Mann-Whitney statistic is $U_c = 127$ for a two-tailed test. The null hypothesis H_0 will be rejected if the computed U-value is 127 or less; otherwise it will be accepted. Note that this decision rule is just the reverse of the decision-making procedure that is followed for most of the other tests of significance.

Step 5: calculate the test statistic. We carry out the following computations:

$$U_1 = n_1 n_2 + [n_1(n_1 + 1)/2] - R_1$$
$$= 20 \times 20 + [20(20 + 1)/2] - 442.5$$
$$= 167.5$$

$$U_2 = n_1 n_2 + [n_2(n_2 + 1)/2] - R_2$$
$$= 20 \times 20 + [20(20 + 1)/2] - 377.5$$
$$= 232.5$$

Hence

$$U = \text{Min}(U_1, U_2)$$

$$U = \text{Min}(167.5, 232.5)$$
$$= 167.5$$

Step 6: draw a statistical conclusion. Since the computed U (167.5) exceeds the critical U_c (127), it falls outside of the critical region and the null hypothesis H_0 is accepted. We therefore conclude, as in Illustrative example 5, that the evidence does not support a significant difference in the evaluation of the club's services as expressed by the golf members and the social members.

Kruskal-Wallis test

An extension of the Mann-Whitney U test, Kruskal-Wallis test is used when more than two independent samples are involved. In the country club example, the Kruskal-Wallis test will be applicable if, instead of subdividing the members into two groups based on membership types (golf versus social members), the subdivisions of club members are formed according to more than two age groups.

Wilcoxon T test

Also called the signed rank test, it is used in situations which involve ordinal data on two dependent samples. The test is suitable for pretest and post-test research designs. Furthermore, it can be used for metric data (ie interval or ratio data) when the assumption underlying the parametric t or z test cannot be met.

Illustrative example 7

Suppose that the country club in the previous example wished to evaluate whether its advertisement campaign has helped increase the awareness level of its services. A sample of ten members were interviewed to provide scores on a number of questions, both before and after the advertisement campaign. The combined scores for each respondent are computed and provided below:

Member's serial number	Combined scores	
	Before advertisement	After advertisement
1	77	82
2	76	79
3	84	79
4	69	71
5	63	73
6	75	76
7	72	74
8	61	76
9	72	76
10	71	78

Step 1: the null hypothesis. The null hypothesis H_0 states that the advertisement campaign has not helped increase the awareness level of the club's services, as there is no significance difference in the awareness of club's services before and after the advertisement campaign. The alternative hypothesis H_1 states that there was an improvement in the awareness level of the club's services after the advertisement campaign.

Step 2: the level of significance. Set the level of significance at $\alpha = 0.025$. This is a one-tailed test, since the direction of the difference is predicted.

Step 3: the statistical test. The Wilcoxon T test is appropriate because the study involves related samples in which the data are ordinally-scaled and the difference can be ranked in magnitude. The test statistic calculated is the T value.

Step 4: the decision rule. At level of significance $\alpha = 0.025$ the critical value of the Wilcoxon T for $n = 10$ is found to be 8 in a one-tailed test. Thus the null hypothesis H_0 will be rejected when the calculated T value is less than 8. This argument is similar to that of the Mann-Whitney U statistic described in the previous section.

Step 5: calculate the test statistic. Before we proceed to compute the T value based on the sample data, we calculate the signed difference between each pair of observations. Then those differences are rank-ordered with regard to their algebraic signs. Finally, the sign of the difference is attached to the rank for the difference (see below).

Respondent number	Score difference	Rank order of score differences
1	5	6.5*
2	3	4
3	−5	6.5*
4	2	2.5*
5	10	9
6	1	1
7	2	2.5*
8	15	10
9	4	5
10	7	8

* In case of tie scores, each is given the average rank for that set.

The test statistic to be used in Wilcoxon T Test is:

$$T = \text{Min}\ (T_1, T_2)$$

where

T_1 = the sum of all ranking orders in respect of positive score differences

$\quad = 6.5 + 4 + 2.5 + 9 + 2.5 + 10 + 5 + 8$

$\quad = 47.5$

T_2 = the sum of all ranking orders in respect of negative score differences

$\quad = 6.5$

Thus

$T = \text{Min}\ (47.5, 6.5)$

$\quad = 6.5$

Note that the larger the difference between the samples, the smaller would be the value of T, since it is defined as the smaller of the rank values.

Step 6: draw a statistical conclusion. Since the computed T (6.5) is smaller than the critical value (8), the null hypothesis H_0 is not accepted. (*Note*: This rejection argument is similar to that of Mann-Whitney U test.) We can therefore conclude that there is no evidence to support the claim that the advertisement campaign has increased members' awareness of the services offered by the club.

Friedman two-way analysis-of-variance test

This test is an extension of the Wilcoxon T test involving more than two dependent samples. The procedure and the formula used for this test can be found in an appropriate statistics text.

Statistical tests for interval and ratio data

The kinds of significance tests discussed so far are concerned with nominal and ordinal data. To end this chapter, we turn to significance tests when interval or ratio data are involved. We noted earlier that interval and ratio data can be downgraded to nominal or ordinal data, so all significance tests which are applicable to nominal or ordinal data are valid for interval or ratio data as well. By downgrading the data, however, much of the valuable information would be lost. Researchers have therefore further developed more powerful statistic tests which are designed specifically for interval and ratio data.

A flow diagram of significance tests for interval and ratio data is presented in Figure 13.6.

Choice between Z test and t test _____

Both the Z-test and the t-test are used for interval or ratio data. Figure 13.7 summarizes when to use the Z distribution and t distribution in making tests of means (or averages). Later in this chapter, we shall examine the appropriate probability distributions for making tests about proportions.

Remember one more rule when using the t test for two population means. We need to further assume that the unknown population variances are equal. If we cannot assume that they are equal, that is σ_1^2 σ_2^2, then the problem is beyond the scope of this book.

Significance test of difference between a population mean and a sample mean

We wish to test the hypothesis that the mean or the hypothetical mean (μ) of a certain population equals some specified value μ_0.

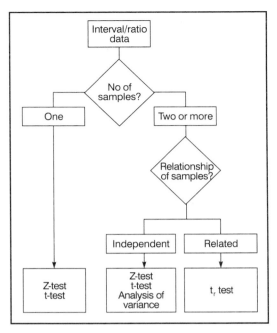

Figure 13.6 *Appropriate statistical tests for interval/ratio data*

The procedure of making the test is illustrated by the example below.

Illustrative example 8

A lamp manufacturer claims that the average life of each lamp is more than 950 hours. A sample of 200 lamps was selected at random and the average length of life was found to be 1,000 hours, with a standard deviation of 60 hours. Is the manufacturer's claim valid?

Step 1: the null hypothesis. The null hypothesis H_0 states that the average life of a lamp is μ = 950 hours or more. The alternative hypothesis H_1 states that the average life of a lamp is less than 950 hours.

Step 2: the level of significance. Set the level of significance at α = 0.10. This is a one-tailed test (directional).

	Population standard deviation is known	Population standard deviation is NOT known
Sample size n@30	Normal distribution Z-table	Normal distribution Z-table
Sample size n<30 and the population is assumed normal or approximately normal	Normal distribution Z-table	t-distribution t-table

Figure 13.7 *Conditions for using probability distributions in testing hypothesis about means*

Step 3: the statistic test. Here the Z test is used because the sample size is larger than thirty.

Step 4: the decision rule. The critical value is Z = 1.96 for a one-tailed test at α = 0.10. the null hypothesis H_0 will be accepted if the calculated Z is less than 1.96. Otherwise the alternative hypothesis H_1 will be accepted.

Step 5: calculate the test statistic. The test statistic Z can be computed by using the formula:

$$Z = \frac{\bar{X} - \mu}{\sigma}$$

where $\bar{X}$ = the sample mean
μ = the hypothesized value of the population mean
σ = the population standard deviation.

As σ is unknown, we use the sample standard deviation instead. Hence:

$$Z = \frac{\bar{X} - \mu}{S/n}$$

$$= \frac{1,000 - 950}{60/200}$$

$$= 11.79$$

Step 6: draw a statistical conclusion. Since the computed Z value (11.79) is larger than the

critical value (1.96), the null hypothesis H_0 is rejected, and we conclude that the average life of a lamp is not likely to be more than 950 hours.

Significance test of difference between two means: large sample

A second type of test concerns testing of differences between two means. In many decision-making situations, we need to determine whether the means of two populations are alike or different. The production manager, for example, may want to test whether female workers yield lower outputs than male workers within the same production department. A human resource director may be interested to determine whether the hourly charges by private tutors are the same in two town centres.

The standard deviations of the two populations are generally not known. Our first step is to estimate them using the standard deviations of the two corresponding samples as follows:

$\hat{\sigma}_1 = S_1$ = standard deviation of one sample

$\hat{\sigma}_2 = S_2$ = standard deviation of the other sample

The estimated standard error of the difference between two means, $\bar{X}_1$ and $\bar{X}_2$ can now be determined:

$$\hat{\sigma}_{\bar{X}_1 - \bar{X}_2} = \sqrt{\frac{\hat{\sigma}_1^2}{n_1} + \frac{\hat{\sigma}_2^2}{n_2}}$$

where n_1 and n_2 are the sizes of the two samples respectively.

The test statistic to be used in making the test is:

$$Z = \frac{\bar{X}_1 - \bar{X}_2}{\sqrt{\frac{\hat{\sigma}_1^2}{n_1} + \frac{\hat{\sigma}_2^2}{n_2}}}$$

Illustrative example 9

A test in marketing research course was set for a group of students, consisting of seventy-two males and sixty-four females. The marks scored by the students are:

Male students	Female students
$n_1 = 72$	$n_2 = 64$
$\sum X_{1i} = 4{,}356$	$\sum X_{2i} = 3{,}744$
$\sum (X_{1i} - \bar{X}_1)^2 = 7{,}492$	$\sum (X_{2i} - \bar{X}_2)^2 = 7{,}862$

Step 1: the null hypothesis. The null hypothesis H_0 states that the male students and the female students have done equally well in the test. The alternative hypothesis H_1 states that the two groups of students scored differently in the test.

Step 2: level of significance. Set the level of significance at $\alpha = 0.05$. This is a two-tailed test (non-directional)

Step 3: the statistical test. The Z test is appropriate because both the sample sizes are larger than thirty.

Step 4: the decision rule. The critical value is Z = 1.96 for a two-tailed test at $\alpha = 0.05$. The null hypothesis H_0 will be accepted if the calculated Z is less than 1.96. Otherwise, it will be rejected and the alternative hypothesis H_1 will be accepted instead.

Step 5: calculate the test statistic. The test statistic, Z, can be computed using the formula:

$$Z = \frac{\bar{X}_1 - \bar{X}_2}{\sqrt{\frac{\hat{\sigma}_1^2}{n_1} + \frac{\hat{\sigma}_2^2}{n_2}}}$$

where

$$\bar{X}_1 = (1/n_1) \sum X_{1i} = (1/72) \times (4{,}356)$$
$$= 60.5$$

$$\bar{X}_2 = (1/n_2) \sum X_{2i} = (1/64) \times (3{,}744)$$
$$= 58.5$$

$$\hat{\sigma}_1^2 = S_1^2 = \frac{\sum (X_{1i} - \bar{X}_1)^2}{(n_1 - 1)}$$

$$= \frac{7{,}492}{71}$$

$$= 105.52$$

$$\hat{\sigma}_2^2 = S_2^2 = \frac{\sum (X_{2i} - \bar{X}_2)^2}{(n_2 - 1)}$$

$$= \frac{7{,}862}{63}$$

$$= 124.80$$

Hence

$$Z = \frac{(60.5 - 58.5)}{\sqrt{105.52/72 + 124.80/64}}$$

$$= 1.08$$

Step 6: draw a statistical conclusion. Since the computed Z value (1.08) is smaller than the critical value (1.96), the null hypothesis H_0 is accepted, and we conclude that the male students and the female students performed equally well in the test.

Significance test of difference between two means: small sample

In the previous example where the sample sizes were large (n_1, $n_2 \geq 30$), we estimated

$\hat{\sigma}_1^2$ and $\hat{\sigma}_2^2$ by using S_1 and S_2 respectively. With small sample sizes, this practice is no longer appropriate. If we can now assume that the unknown population variances are equal, that is $\sigma_1^2 = \sigma_2^2$, the following modifications may be made to perform a small sample test of a hypothesis about the difference between two population means.

If $\sigma_1^2 = \sigma_2^2$, we can proceed to estimate the common variance σ^2. We do this by using a weighted average of S_1 and S_2, where the weights are the numbers of degrees of freedom in a weighted average. S_p^2 is called a pool estimate of σ^2 and is given by:

$$S_p^2 = \frac{(n_1 - 1)\, S_1^2 + (n_2 - 1)\, S_2^2}{(n_1 + n_2 - 2)}$$

Hence the estimated standard error of the difference between the two means X_1 and X_2, is given by:

$$\sigma_{\bar{X}_1 - \bar{X}_2} = \sqrt{S_p^2 \cdot \left(\frac{1}{n_1} + \frac{1}{n_2} \right)}$$

where n_1 and n_2 are the two sample sizes respectively.

The test statistic to be used in the test is:

$$t = \frac{(\bar{X}_1 - \bar{X}_2)}{\sqrt{S_p^2 \cdot \left(\frac{1}{n_1} + \frac{1}{n_2} \right)}}$$

and the distribution of t is based on $(n_1 + n_2 - 2)$ degrees of freedom.

Illustrative example 10

A survey was conducted to determine whether cigarette consumption of smokers differed in two cities, A and B. A sample of 22 smokers in City A and another sample of twenty smokers in City B were selected and the number of cigarette sticks consumed per day during the survey week by each smoker was recorded. The results are summarized below.

City A	City B
$n_1 = 22$	$n_2 = 20$
$\sum X_{1i} = 462$	$\sum X_{2i} = 390$
$\sum (X_{1i} - \bar{X}_1)^2 = 2{,}010$	$\sum (X_{2i} - \bar{X}_2)^2 = 2{,}136$

Is there evidence (at $\alpha = 0.05$) that the mean number of cigarettes consumed by smokers in City A differs significantly from that in City B?

Since the samples selected for the study are small ($n_1 = 22$, $n_2 = 20$), the following assumptions are made:

1. The population of the number of cigarette sticks consumed by smokers in City A and smokers in City B both have approximately normal distributions.
2. The variances of the populations of the number of cigarette sticks consumed by smokers in the two cities are equal.
3. The samples are independently and randomly selected.

Step 1: the null hypothesis. The null hypothesis H_0 states that there is no difference in the cigarette consumption per smoker between City A and City B. The alternative hypothesis H_1 states that there is a difference in the consumption level.

Step 2: the level of significance. Set the level of significance at $\alpha = 0.05$. This is a two-tailed test.

Step 3: the statistical test. The t test is appropriate because the sample sizes n_1 and n_2 are less than thirty and the population standard deviations, assumed equal, are unknown.

Step 4: the decision rule. The critical value with degree of freedom d.f. = $(22 + 20 - 2) = 40$ and the specified level of significance $\alpha = 0.05$ is t = 2.021. The null hypothesis H_0 will be accepted if the calculated t is less than 2.021; otherwise it will be rejected and the alternative hypothesis H_1 will be accepted instead.

Step 5: calculate the test statistic. The test statistic, t, can be computed from the formula:

$$t = \frac{(\bar{X}_1 - \bar{X}_2)}{\sqrt{S_P^2 \cdot \left(\frac{1}{n_1} + \frac{1}{n_2}\right)}}$$

we have

$$\bar{X}_1 = \left(\frac{1}{n_1}\right) \sum X_{1i} = \left(\frac{1}{22}\right)(462)$$

$$= 21.0$$

$$\bar{X}_2 = \left(\frac{1}{n_2}\right) \sum X_{2i} = \left(\frac{1}{20}\right)(390)$$

$$= 19.5$$

$$S_P^2 = \frac{[(n_1 - 1)S_1^2 + (n_2 - 1)S_2^2]}{(n_1 + n_2 - 2)}$$

$$= \frac{[\sum(X_{1i} - \bar{X}_1)^2 + \sum(X_{2i} - \bar{X}_2)^2]}{(n_1 + n_2 - 2)}$$

$$= \frac{[2,010 + 2,136]}{40}$$

$$= 103.65$$

Hence

$$t = \frac{(21.0 - 19.5)}{\sqrt{103.65 \left(\frac{1}{22} + \frac{1}{20}\right)}}$$

$$= 0.478$$

Step 6: draw a statistical conclusion. Since the computed value of t lies within the acceptance region, we accept H_0 and can conclude that there is no difference in cigarette consumption per worker between City A and City B.

Significance test about a population proportion: large sample

The procedure for testing the differences between proportions is analogous to the test for the differences between means. To test a hypothesis about a population proportion P_0 based on a large sample, the test statistic to be used is given by the formula:

$$Z = (P - P_0)/\sqrt{P_0 Q_0/n}$$

where
P = the sample proportion
P_0 = the hypothesized value of the population proportion
$Q_0 = 1 - P_0$
n = the sample size

Illustrative example 11

A television station claimed that the viewership of a particular television programme was $P_0 = 38.0$ per cent or more. A study was made on 542 respondents and the level of viewership of that television programme was calculated to be $P = 40.2$ per cent. Does this evidence indicate that the true proportion of viewership of the television programme is significantly larger than 38 per cent? Test at significance level $\alpha = 0.05$.

Step 1: the null hypothesis. The null hypothesis H_0 states that the viewership of the particular television programme is 38 per cent or more. The alternative hypothesis H_1 states that the viewership is below 38 per cent.

Step 2: the level of significance. It was decided to set the level of significance at $\alpha = 0.05$. This is a one-tailed test.

Step 3: the statistical test. The Z test is used because the study involved a large sample.

Step 4: the decision rule. At $\alpha = 0.05$, the critical value is $Z_c = 1.64$. Therefore, the null hypothesis H_0 will be rejected if the computed value of Z exceeds 1.64; and if the computed value of Z is smaller than 1.64, H_0 will be accepted.

Step 5: calculate the test statistic. The test statistic is computed below:

$$Z = (P - P_0)/\sqrt{P_0 Q_0/n}$$
$$= (0.402 - 0.380)/\sqrt{0.38 \times 0.62/542}$$
$$= 1,055$$

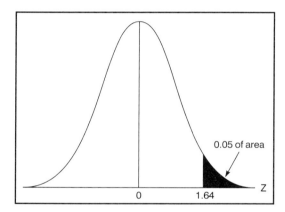

Step 6: draw a statistical conclusion. Since the computed value of Z falls within the acceptance region, we accept H_0 and conclude that the viewership of the television programme was 38 per cent or more.

Significance test for difference between two sample proportions

We will demonstrate, with examples, the following three cases:

- Case 1: Independent proportions.
- Case 2: Correlated but mutually exclusive proportions.
- Case 3: Correlated but overlapping proportions.

Illustrative example 12:
Independent proportions

Two random surveys, conducted three months apart, gathered public opinions on the question: 'If there were a general election tomorrow, would you vote for or against the ruling party?'

The results of the two surveys are provided below:

	1st Survey	2nd Survey
Sample size	1,060	1,020
For ruling party	488 (46%)	408 (40%)
Against ruling party	572	612

Step 1: the null hypothesis. The null hypothesis H_0 states that there is no significant change in the political opinions of the voters.

Step 2: the level of significance. It was decided to set the level of significance at $\alpha = 0.05$. This is a two-tailed test (non-directional).

Step 3: the statistical test. Here the Z-test is used because of the large sample size.

Step 4: the decision rule. The critical value is $Z_c = 1.96$ for a two-tailed test at $\alpha = 0.05$. The null hypothesis H_0 will be accepted if the calculated Z is smaller than 1.96 but greater than –1.96. Otherwise, it will be rejected and the alternative hypothesis H_1 will be accepted.

Step 5: calculate the test statistic. The test statistic to be used is:

$$Z = \frac{P_1 - P_2}{S_{P_1 - P_2}}$$

where $P_1 = \dfrac{488}{1,060} = 0.46$

$P_2 = \dfrac{408}{1,020} = 0.40$

$S_{P_1 - P_2}$ = the standard error of the difference between sample proportions

$$= \sqrt{P(1 - P)\left(\frac{1}{n_1} + \frac{1}{n_2}\right)}$$

But

$$P = \frac{(n_1 P_1 + n_2 P_2)}{(n_1 + n_2)}$$

$$= \frac{1,060 \times 0.46 + 1,020 \times 0.40}{1,060 + 1,020}$$

$$= 0.431$$

Hence

$$S_{P_1 - P_2} = \sqrt{\begin{array}{c}0.431 \times (1 - 0.431) \\ \times \left(\dfrac{1}{1,060} + \dfrac{1}{1,020}\right)\end{array}}$$

$$= 0.0217$$

The value of the test statistic can now be calculated:

$$Z = \frac{P_1 - P_2}{S_{P_1 - P_2}}$$

$$= \frac{(0.46 - 0.40)}{0.0217}$$

$$= 2.76 > 1.96 \ (95 \text{ per cent confidence level})$$

Step 6: draw a statistical conclusion. Since Z > Z_c, the null hypothesis H_0 is rejected, and we conclude that the change in the political opinions between the two surveys is statistically significant.

Illustrative example 13:

Correlated but mutually exclusive proportions

A random sample of 460 shampoo users were interviewed on the question: 'What brand of shampoo do you use most often nowadays?'

The results obtained are tabulated as shown below:

Kao	$P_1 =$	18.8%
Emeron	$P_2 =$	15.1%
Wella	$P_3 =$	12.7%
Vosene	$P_4 =$	7.4%
Colgate	$P_5 =$	5.0%
Countess	$P_6 =$	5.0%
Others	$P_7 =$	36.0%
Total		100.0%

Is the difference of market shares between Kao and Emeron statistically significant?

Note that the respondent was allowed to name one brand only. Thus the above set of percentage values (for market shares are correlated in that a change (increase or decrease) in the value of any percentage value can result in some changes in the values of one or more other percentage values. The sum of these percentage values will always add up to 100 per cent.

Step 1: the null hypothesis. The null hypothesis H_0 states that the difference between the market shares of Kao and Emeron is not statistically significant. The alternative hypothesis H_1 states that there is a significant difference of the market shares between Kao and Emeron.

Step 2: the level of significance. It was decided to set the level of significance at $\alpha = 0.05$. This is a two-tailed test (non-directional).

Step 3: the statistical test. Here the Z test is used because the sample sizes exceed thirty.

Step 4: the decision rule. The critical value is $Z_c = 1.96$ for a two-tailed test at $\alpha = 0.05$. The null hypothesis H_0 will be accepted if the calculated Z is less than 1.96 but more than -1.96. Otherwise, it will be rejected.

Step 5: calculate the test statistic. The test statistic to be used is:

$$Z = \frac{P_1 - P_2}{S_{P_1 - P_2}}$$

where $P_1 = 18.8\%$
$P_2 = 15.1\%$ and

$S_{P_1 - P_2}$ = the standard error of the difference between the two market shares

$$= \sqrt{\frac{[P_1(1 - P_1) + P_2(1 - P_2) + 2P_1P_2]}{n}}$$

$$= 0.027$$

The value of the test statistic can now be calculated:

$$Z = \frac{(18.8\% - 15.1\%)}{0.027}$$

$$= 1.37$$

Step 6: draw a statistical conclusion. Since the computed Z value (1.37) is smaller than the critical value (1.96), we accept the null hypothesis H_0 and conclude that the difference of market shares between Kao and Emeron is not statistically significant.

Illustrative example 14:

Correlated but overlapping proportions

An AAU Dishwashing Liquid random survey was undertaken on 532 housewives who were asked, among other questions, the brand-recall question: 'Would you please name the brands of dishwashing liquid that you can think of?' The following results emerged:

Mama Lemon	$P_1 = 58\%$
Cherina	$P_2 = 37\%$
Sweetheart	$P_3 = 24\%$
Zip	$P_4 = 23\%$
Glo	$P_5 = 17\%$
UIC	$P_6 = 13\%$
Others	$P_7 = 9\%$

Is the difference in the recall levels between Cherina (P_2) and Sweetheart (P_3) statistically significant?

Like the previous example, the above percentages are correlated but the sum of these percentages may exceed 100 per cent because each respondent is allowed to mention more than one brand. In such situation, one additional information is needed from the sample, namely the proportion (denoted by P_{23}) of housewives who could recall both the two brands under study. In this example, we assume $P_{23} = 12.7$ per cent.

Step 1: the null hypothesis. The null hypothesis H_0 is that the observed difference between the recall levels of Cherina and Sweetheart is not statistically significant.

Step 2: the level of significance. It was decided to set the level of significance at $\alpha = 0.05$. This is a two-tailed test (non-directional).

Step 3: the statistical test. Here again the Z test is used because the sample sizes exceed thirty.

Step 4: the decision rule. The critical value is $Z_c = 1.96$ for a two-tailed test at $\alpha = 0.05$. The null hypothesis H_0 will be accepted if the calculated Z is less than 1.96. Otherwise, it will be rejected and the alternative hypothesis H_1 will be accepted.

Step 5: calculate the test statistic. The test statistic to be used is:

$$Z = \frac{P_2 - P_3}{S_{P_2 - P_3}}$$

where $P_2 = 37$ per cent
$P_3 = 24$ per cent

$S_{P_1 - P_2}$ = the standard error of the difference between the two recall levels

$$= \sqrt{\frac{[P_2(1 - P_2) + P_3(1 - P_3) + 2(P_2P_3 - P_{23})]}{n}}$$

$= 0.0252.$

The value of the test statistic can now be calculated:

$$Z = \frac{P_2 - P_3}{S_{P_2 - P_3}}$$

$$= \frac{(37\% - 24\%)}{0.0252}$$

$= 8.33$

Step 6: draw a statistical conclusion. Since the computed Z value (8.33) is larger than the critical value (1.96), the null hypothesis H_0 is rejected and we can conclude that the difference of the recall levels between Cherina and Sweetheart is statistically significant.

End-of-chapter revision

Review questions

13.1 What is the purpose of a hypothesis test of difference between groups?

13.2 What is a null hypothesis? What is an alternative hypothesis?

13.3 Describe the computational steps in the hypothesis-testing procedure?

13.4 What is meant by a Type I error? A Type II error? Why are they important to know?

13.5 What is a one-tailed test? When should it be employed?

13.6 What is a two-tailed test? When should it be preferred?

13.7 Why is the chi-square test called a 'goodness-of-fit' test?

13.8 When is the chi-square goodness-of-fit test applicable? How are the expected frequencies determined? How is the test statistic calculated?

13.9 What conditions would lead to the use of the:
a Kruskal-Wallis test?
b Kolmogorov-Smirnov test?
c Mann-Whitney U test?
d Wilcoxon T test?

13.10 What conditions would lead to the use of:
a χ^2 one-sample test?
b χ^2 two-sample test?
c McNemar test

13.11 A Marketing Manager wishes to determine whether or not strawberry flavour and lemon flavour in a soft drink are equally preferred by consumers. Out of 500 consumers interviewed, 300 expressed preference for strawberry flavour and the remaining 200 indicated preference for lemon flavour. Do these data provide strong evidence that there is a difference in preference between the two flavours?

13.12 A department store ran an alternate promotion offer in a test city for a period of three months. From a random sample of 500 consumers interviewed, the market share was found to increase from 15% to 24%. Is it valid to claim that the alternate promotion offer is more effective than the previous promotion offer?

True-false questions

Write True (T) or False (F) for the following:

13.13 In hypothesis testing, the hypothesis to be tested is called alternative hypothesis.

13.14 A Type II error is made when a true hypothesis is rejected.

13.15 Reducing the probability of making a Type I error also reduces the probability of making a Type II error.

13.16 The null hypothesis is accepted if computed test statistic falls outside of the acceptance region.

13.17 The null hypothesis and the alternative hypothesis should be so formulated that the rejection of the former will automatically lead to the acceptance of the latter.

13.18 A directional hypothesis is also referred to as a one-tailed test.

13.19 Chi-square analysis is most commonly used in hypothesis testing involving interval or ratio data.

Multiple-choice questions

13.20 To the statistician, significance difference means:
   a a real difference
   b a difference due to chance variation
   c an important difference
   d a difference that cannot be avoided.

13.21 The two-tailed test of the difference between means is appropriate to evaluate:
   a the relative difference between two numbers
   b the direction of absolute difference between two numbers
   c the absolute difference between two numbers
   d the direction of relative difference between two numbers.

13.22 The one-tailed test of significance is appropriate to evaluate:
   a the relative difference between two numbers
   b the absolute difference between two numbers
   c the direction of relative difference between two numbers
   d the direction of absolute difference between two numbers.

13.23 The chi-square goodness-of-fit test evaluates the significance of the difference between:
   a two means
   b two percentages
   c more than two means
   d more than two percentages.

13.24 In significance testing, the null hypothesis is a statement that is assumed to be:
   a true regardless of the nature of numerical evidence
   b false regardless of the nature of numerical evidence
   c false unless evidence is overwhelming that it is true
   d true unless evidence is overwhelming that it is false.

13.25 The statement 'H_0:Footballers earn an average of $70,000 per year' implies:
   a a one-tailed test
   b a two-tailed test
   c a three-tailed test
   d none of the above.

13.26 In order to carry out a chi-square analysis of data, it is necessary that the data is in (or converted to) which one of the following scales of measurement?
   a Nominal.
   b Ordinal.
   c Interval.
   d Ratio.

14

Data analysis and interpretation: measuring association _____

Statistical techniques for determining whether an observed difference between variables (or subgroups of population) is statistically significant have earlier been discussed. In this chapter, we shall attempt to measure the intensity of association (if any) between variables. Many statistical techniques are available and the use of the appropriate techniques would depend on:

- the number of variables involved
- the level of measurement
- whether variables are dichotomous or multichotomous.

Figure 14.1 is a flow diagram depicting the most commonly used statistical techniques for measuring the intensity of association between variables.

Indices of association ▇▇▇▇▇▇

The basic tool for measuring the intensity of association between variables is the *index of association*. For an index to be meaningful and measurable, it must have a definite range, with a limiting number each to signify perfect positive association and perfect negative association between variables. The range most commonly used is from −1 to +1. A perfect positive association occurs when the index assumes the maximum

value of +1.0, while a perfect negative association occurs when the index assumes the minimum value of −1.0. The case of no association is represented by the index value of zero. For example, if the association between smoking and liquor consumption registers an index of +0.75 for men and an index of +0.35 for women, we can say that the association between these two variables is higher for men than for women; and that it is positive association for men as well as for women.

As derived from the sample data, the index of association is a statistic, just like the sample mean and the sample proportion. For the study of statistical inference, therefore, we need to perform the appropriate test of significance to determine whether the calculated index differs significantly from the zero value which indicates no association. We shall begin our discussion with the association between two variables, also known as bivariate association.

Indices of association for two dichotomous nominal variables _____

Phi coefficient Φ

When the two variables under study are dichotomous and nominally-scaled, the widely used index of association is the Phi coefficient Φ. Two dichotomous variables, X

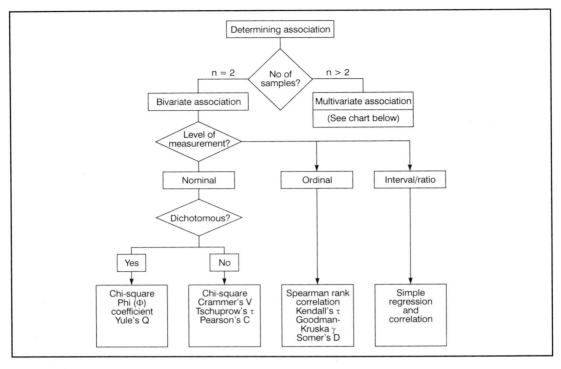

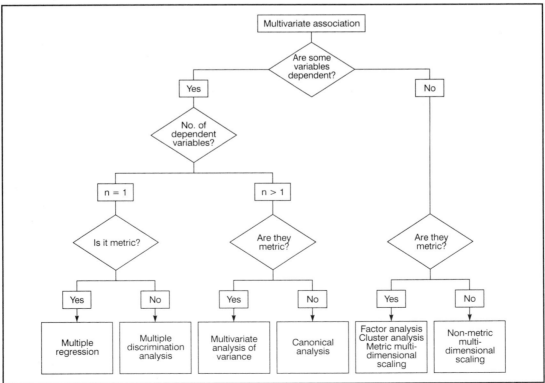

Figure 14.1 *Statistical techniques for determining association*

and Y, can generate a 2 × 2 contingency table (see below) where a, b, c and d represent the number of observations in the four cells:

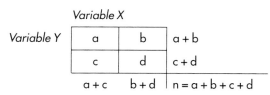

Variable X

Variable Y	a	b	a + b
	c	d	c + d
	a + c	b + d	n = a + b + c + d

The value of Phi coefficient is given by the formula:

$$\Phi = \frac{ad - bc}{\sqrt{(a+b)(c+d)(a+c)(b+d)}}, \; -1 \leqslant \Phi \leqslant 1$$

The absolute value for Φ may also be obtained from the following relationship with chi-square χ^2:

$$\Phi = \sqrt{\frac{\chi^2}{n}} \quad \text{or} \quad \chi^2 = n\Phi^2$$

where n = the sample size and χ^2, as noted earlier, is itself an index of association.

Illustrative example 1

A survey among 300 married couples on the incidence of drinking among husbands and wives produced the following results:

		No. of husbands		
		Drink	Don't drink	
No. of wives	Drink	125	40	165
	Don't drink	60	75	135
		185	115	300

The question posed is: Is there an association between the incidence of drinking between husbands and wives?

$$\Phi = \frac{ad - bc}{\sqrt{(a+b)(c+d)(a+c)(b+d)}}$$

$$= \frac{(125)(75) - (60)(40)}{(125 + 40)(60 + 75)(125 + 60)(40 + 75)}$$

$$= 0.32$$

Step 1: the null hypothesis. $H_0: \Phi = 0$, that is, there is no association on the incidence of drinking between husbands and wives.

Step 2: level of significance. Set the level of significance at $\alpha = 0.05$. This is a two-tailed test. The number of degrees of freedom d.f. $= (2 - 1)(2 - 1) = 1$.

Step 3: the statistical test. The appropriate test is χ^2 since both the variables involved are nominally-scaled and of dichotomous nature.

Step 4: the decision rule. The critical value for d.f. = 1 and at the specified level of significance $\alpha = 0.05$ is $\chi_c^2 = 3.84$. Thus, H_0 will be rejected if the calculated χ^2 is larger than 3.84.

Step 5: calculate the test statistic. From given data, we obtain

$$\chi^2 = n\Phi^2$$
$$= 300 \times 0.1024$$
$$= 30.72$$

Step 6: draw a statistical conclusion. Since $\chi^2 > \chi_c^2$, the null hypothesis H_0 is rejected and we conclude that the association on the incidence of alcoholic drinking between husbands and wives is statistically significant.

Yule's Q

Yule's Q presents a simpler measure of the index of association for two dichotomous, nominally scaled variables. Consider the following 2 × 2 contingency table:

Variable X

Variable Y	a	b	a + b
	c	d	c + d
	a + b	b + d	n = a + b + c + d

The formula used for computing Q is:

$$Q = \frac{ad - bc}{ad + bc}$$

where   Q ranges from −1 (when either a = 0 or d = 0) or +1 (when either b = 0 or c = 0).

Illustrative example 2

Referring to the data given in Illustrative example 1:

No. of husbands

No. of wives		Drink	Don't drink	
	Drink	125	40	165
	Don't drink	60	75	135
		185	115	300

The value of Q is:

$$Q = \frac{(125)(75) - (60)(40)}{(125)(75) + (60)(40)} = 0.592$$

Indices of association for two multichotomous nominal variables

Several measures are available here, most of which are based on the χ^2-statistic. These χ^2-based indices attempt to standardize the χ^2-value and free the index from its dependence on the sample size and/or the number of categories involved in both variables.

Crammer's V

Crammer's V is a good index of association between two multichotomous variables which do not have the same number of categories. The formula for the computation of V is given below:

$$V = \frac{\chi^2}{n.[\min(r - 1), (c - 1)]}; O \leqslant V \leqslant 1$$

where χ^2 = the χ^2-value
n = the sample size
r = the number of rows
c = the number of columns.

Illustrative example 3

A study sponsored by a cosmetics manufacturer yielded the following data on the colour of hair and eyes of the 400 female adults. (*Note*: The expected frequencies corresponding to each cell were computed in the usual manner and are shown in the lower right-hand corner):

Colour of hair

Colour of eyes		Blonde	Brunette	Red	
	Blue	30 _20_	30 _40_	20 _20_	80
	Brown	20 _50_	120 _100_	60 _50_	200
	Other	50 _30_	50 _60_	20 _30_	120
		100	200	100	400

We proceed with the significance testing as follows:

Step 1: the null hypothesis. H_0: The computed value of Crammer's V is not statistically significant. The degree of freedom d.f. = (3 − 1) × (3 − 1) = 4.

Step 2: level of significance. Set the level of significance at $\alpha = 0.05$. This is a two-tailed test (non-directional).

Step 3: the statistical test. Since the two variables are nominally-scaled but not dichotomous, the test statistic to be used is χ^2.

Step 4: the decision rule. From χ^2-tables, the critical value of the test statistic is $\chi^2_c = 9.49$. The null hypothesis H_0 will be rejected if the calculated χ^2 is larger than 9.49.

Step 5: calculate the test statistic.

$$\chi^2 = \Sigma \frac{(O_i - E_i)^2}{E_i}$$

$$= \frac{(30 - 20)^2}{20} + \frac{(20 - 50)^2}{50}$$

$$+ \cdots + \frac{(60 - 50)^2}{50} + \frac{(20 - 30)^2}{30}$$

$$= 49.83$$

Hence:

$$V = \sqrt{\frac{\chi^2}{n \cdot [\min(r - 1, c - 1)]}}$$

$$= \sqrt{\frac{49.83}{400 \times 2}} \quad (r = c = 3)$$

$$= 0.250$$

Step 6: draw a statistical conclusion. Since the calculated χ^2 (49.83) is larger than the critical value (9.49), the null hypothesis H_0 is rejected and we conclude that the computed value of Crammer's V is significant.

Tschuprow's τ

Tschuprow's τ is another chi square-based index of association. It is defined as follows:

$$\tau = \sqrt{\chi^2/n} \sqrt{(r - 1)(c - 1)}; \quad 0 \leqslant \tau \leqslant 1$$

where n = the sample size
        r = the number of rows
        c = the number of columns.

Tschuprow's τ and Crammer's V will always have the same values when r = c.

Pearson's contingency coefficient C

This coefficient is also a chi square-based index of association. Its equation is:

$$C = \sqrt{\frac{\chi^2}{\chi^2 + n}} \quad ; \quad 0 \leqslant C \leqslant 1$$

where n = the sample size.

Indices of association for two ordinal variables

In the case of two ordinally scaled variables, the commonly used indices of association are:

1 Spearman rank correlation coefficient (r_s).
2 Kendall's tau (τ).
3 Goodman-Kruskal gamma (γ).
4 Somer's D.

Spearman rank correlation coefficient

Denoted by r_s, this is the best known index of association between two ordinal variables. The computational procedure for r_s is:

1 Convert the original scores into ranks for each of the two variables beginning with the rank of 1. (*Note:* Tied scores are assigned the average rank corresponding to those scores.)

2 Compute the difference score d_i corresponding to each pair of ranks.

Sample item #	Rank according to variable X	Rank according to variable Y	Rank difference
1	X_1	Y_1	$d_1 = X_1 - Y_1$
2	X_2	Y_2	$d_2 = X_2 - Y_2$
3	X_3	Y_3	$d_3 = X_3 - Y_3$
.	.	.	.
.	.	.	.
n	X_n	Y_n	$d_n = X_n - Y_n$

3 Compute the Spearman rank correlation coefficient r_s as defined by:

$$r_s = 1 - \frac{6 \Sigma d_i^2}{n(n^2 - 1)}$$

where n = the sample size (or number of pairs of responses).

The value of r_s will range from -1 to $+1$.

Illustrative example 4

An insurance company wished to examine the correlation between in-house training and on-the-job performance of its salesmen. A random sample of fourteen salesmen was selected and their rank orders in terms of in-house training and on-the-job performance were tabulated as follows:

Salesman number	In-house training	On-the-job performance	Rank difference (d_i)	d_i^2
1	9	10	−1	1
2	6	4	2	4
3	14	14	0	0
4	1	1	0	0
5	13	12.5	0.5	0.25
6	12	12.5	−0.5	0.25
7	11	7	4	16
8	7.5	6	1.5	2.25
9	5	3	2	4
10	10	8	2	4
11	3	2	1	1
12	2	5	−3	9
13	4	9	−5	25
14	7.5	11	−3.5	12.25
			$\Sigma d_i = 0$	$\Sigma d_i^2 = 79$

Step 1: the null hypothesis. The null hypothesis is $H_0 : r_s = 0$, that is, in-house training and on-the-job performance are not associated.

Step 2: level of significance. Set the level of significance at $\alpha = 0.05$. This is a two-tailed test.

Step 3: the statistical test. Since the two variables involve rank numbers, the Spearman rank correlation method is used.

Step 4: the decision rule. From t-distribution tables, the critical value is $t_c = 2.179$ (d.f. = n − 2 = 12). The null hypothesis H_0 will be rejected if the calculated t value is larger than 2.179

Step 5: calculate the test statistic. We compute r_s as follows:

$$r_s = 1 - \frac{6 \Sigma d_1^2}{n(n^2 - 1)}$$

$$= 1 - \frac{6 \times 79}{14(14^2 - 1)}$$

$$= 0.826$$

We may test the significance of r_s by the use of the following formula:

$$t = \sqrt{\frac{n - 2}{1 - r_s^2}}$$

$$= \sqrt{\frac{14 - 2}{1 - (0.826)^2}}$$

$$= 5.07$$

Step 6: draw a statistical conclusion. Since the calculated t (5.07) is larger than the critical value (2.179), the null hypothesis H_0 is rejected, and we can conclude that the observed correlation between in-house training and on-the-job training is statistically significant.

___

Kendall's tau τ

Kendall's tau τ takes into consideration all possible pairs of respondents, and determine for each pair, whether their relative ordering in one variable is the same as their relative ordering in the other variable. If the relative ordering in both variables are the same, the two respondents in the pair are said to have constituted a *concordant* pair. On the contrary, if their relative orderings are reversed, the two respondents are said to have constituted a *discordant* pair.

For the salesmen data in the previous example , we re-rank the salesmen as shown below.

Salesman no.	Rank on in-house training	Rank on performance
4	1	5
12	2	5
11	3	2
13	4	9
9	5	3
2	6	4
8	7.5	6
14	7.5	11
1	9	10
10	10	8
7	11	7
6	12	12.5
5	13	12.5
3	14	14

Here, Salesman 2 and Salesman 7 constitute a concordant pair since their relative ranking on in-house training moves up from the sixth position to the eleventh position and their relative ranking on performance moves up from the fourth position to the seventh position as well. Salesman 2 and Salesman 12 constitute a

discordant pair, for their relative ranking on in-house training moves down from the sixth position to the second position while that on performance moves up from the fourth position to the fifth position. Note that it is the direction, and not the magnitude of change in relative ranking that is being considered.

Kendall's tau τ is defined as

$$\tau = \left[\frac{4C}{n(n-1)} \right] - 1$$

or

$$\tau = 1 - \left[\frac{4D}{n(n-1)} \right]$$

where
C = the number of concordant pairs
D = the number of discordant pairs
n = the sample size.

___

Illustrative example 5

In a sample of twelve second-year students, the ranks of physics and maths test scores are tabulated below.

Student number	Rank on physics	Rank on maths
1	7	9
2	5	4
3	12	11
4	1	1
5	11	12
6	10	10
7	9	7
8	6	6
9	4	3
10	8	8
11	3	2
12	2	5

The concordant and the discordant pairs of students are identified below:

Student number	Concordant with student number	Discordant with student number
1	2, 3, 4, 5, 6, 8, 9, 11, 12	7, 10
2	1, 3, 4, 5, 6, 7, 8, 9, 10, 11	12
3	1, 2, 4, 6, 7, 8, 9, 10, 11, 12	5
4	1, 2, 3, 5, 6, 7, 8, 9, 10, 11, 12	
5	1, 2, 4, 6, 7, 8, 9, 10, 11, 12	3
6	1, 2, 3, 4, 5, 7, 8, 9, 10, 11, 12	
7	2, 3, 4, 5, 6, 8, 9, 11, 12	1, 10
8	1, 2, 3, 4, 5, 6, 7, 9, 10, 11, 12	
9	1, 2, 3, 4, 5, 6, 7, 8, 10, 11	12
10	2, 3, 4, 5, 6, 8, 9, 11, 12	1, 7
11	1, 2, 3, 4, 5, 6, 7, 8, 9, 10	12
12	1, 3, 4, 5, 6, 7, 8, 10	2, 9, 11

Here C = number of concordant pairs of students

$$= 118/2$$
$$= 59$$

D = number of discordant pairs of students

$$= 14/2$$
$$= 7$$

Step 1: the null hypothesis. The null hypothesis is $H_0 : \tau = 0$, that is, there is no positive association between the physics test score and the maths test score.

Step 2: level of significance. Set the level of significance at $\alpha = 0.05$. This is a two-tailed test.

Step 3: the statistical test. The appropriate statistical test is Z, where

$$Z = \frac{3\tau \sqrt{n(n-)}}{2(2n+5)}$$

Step 4: the decision rule. From the Z-distribution table, the critical value is $Z_c = 1.64$ at $\alpha = 0.05$. Thus H_0 will be rejected if the calculated Z is larger than 1.65.

Step 5: calculate the test statistic. The computed Kendall's tau τ is:

$$\tau = \frac{4C}{n(n-1)} - 1$$
$$= \frac{4 \times 59}{12(12-1)} - 1$$
$$= 0.788$$

Hence we have:

$$Z = \frac{3\tau \sqrt{n(n-1)}}{2(2n+5)}$$
$$= \frac{3 \times 0.788 \sqrt{12(12-1)}}{2(2 \times 12 + 5)}$$
$$= 0.468$$

Step 6: draw a statistical conclusion. Since the observed Z value (0.468) is smaller than the critical value (1.64), we accept null hypothesis H_0, and conclude that the positive association between the physics test scores and the maths test scores is not statistically significant.

Goodman-Kruskal γ

This is another version of the Kendall's tau coefficient, its calculation is best illustrated by an example shown below.

Illustrative example 6

A sample of 100 respondents in a consumer survey was cross-classified according to whether they were heavy, medium or light consumers of coffee and whether they were heavy, medium or light smokers. From the results tabulated below, the researcher would want to establish whether the two issues are related and, if so, to determine the magnitude of association between coffee consumption and cigarette smoking.

Cigarette smoking	Coffee consumption			
	Heavy	Medium	Light	Total
Heavy	20	5	3	28
Medium	15	18	9	42
Light	5	12	13	30
	40	35	25	100

Two respondents are said to constitute a concordant pair if their relative orderings on coffee consumption are the same as their relative orderings on cigarette smoking. For example, P and Q as described below, will constitute a concordant pair:

- P: *medium* coffee consumer and *heavy* cigarette smoker
- Q: *light* coffee consumer and *medium* cigarette smoker.

Conversely, the following two respondents, S and T, will constitute a discordant pair:

- S: *medium* coffee consumer and *heavy* cigarette smoker
- T: *heavy* coffee consumer and *medium* cigarette smoker.

And if the two respondents are tied on any one variable, they neither constitute a concordant nor a discordant pair. This also applies when two individuals are tied on both variables.

The formula for calculating Goodman-Kruskal γ is given by:

$$\gamma = \frac{C - D}{C + D}; -1 \leqslant \gamma \leqslant 1$$

where C = the number of concordant pairs; and
D = the number of discordant pairs.

From our example, the values of C and D are:

$$C = 20(18 + 9 + 12 + 13) + 15(12 + 13)$$
$$+ 5(9 + 13) + 18(13)$$
$$= 1,759$$

$$D = 5(15 + 5) + 18(5) + 3(15 + 18 + 5 + 12)$$
$$+ 9(5 + 12)$$
$$= 493$$

Hence

$$\gamma = \frac{C - D}{C + D}$$

$$= \frac{1,759 - 493}{1,759 + 493}$$

$$= 0.562$$

Somer's D

Unlike Goodman-Kruskal γ, Somer's D explicitly considers ties in the data. The formula for the computation of Somer's D is given by:

$$D = \frac{2(C - D)}{\frac{1}{2}[(n^2 - \Sigma C_i^2) + (n^2 - \Sigma R_i^2)]}$$

where C = the number of concordant pairs
D = the number of discordant pairs
n = the sample size
C_i = the column totals
R_i = the row totals.

Referring to Illustrative example 6, we have:

$$\Sigma C_i^2 = (40)^2 + (35)^2 + (25)^2 = 3,450$$

$$\Sigma R_i^2 = (28)^2 + (42)^2 + (30)^2 = 3,448$$

Hence

$$D = \frac{2(1,759 - 493)}{\frac{1}{2}[(100^2 - 3,450) + (100^2 - 3,448)]}$$

$$= \frac{2,532}{6,551}$$

$$= 0.387$$

Indices of association for two interval/ratio variables

For interval or ratio scaled variables, the most commonly used index of association are regression and correlation. Regression explores the relationship between the variables, whereas correlation measures the association between the variables. Alternatively, regression analysis tells us in what way the variables are related while correlation analysis examines the extent to which these variables are associated. When two variables are involved, we have simple regression analysis and simple correlation analysis respectively.

Simple correlation analysis

When two variables vary in a manner that movements in one variable will cause corresponding movements in the other variable, we say that these two variables are correlated. Many examples of correlation will instantly come to mind. An increase in air temperature will normally be accompanied by an increase in soft drinks sales; while an increase in video-cassette libraries is likely to result in a decrease in cinema attendances. In the first example, the movements in the two variables are in the same direction, that is, an increase (or decrease) in one variable is associated with an increase (or decrease) in the other variable. The two variables are said to be positively correlated. In the second example, the movement of one variable is associated with a movement in the other variable in the reverse direction, and we say that the two variables are negatively correlated.

A useful method of investigating the presence of correlation between two vari-ables is the scatter diagram. A scatter diagram is constructed by plotting the data of a bivariate distribution on a graph with X-value along the horizontal axis against the corresponding Y-values along the vertical axis. The dots in a scatter diagram provide a picture of the two sets of data and help explore the nature of relationship that might exist between the two variables. Some examples of scatter diagrams are shown in Figure 14.2.

Figure 14.2(a) exhibits a distinct tendency for marriage ages of brides and bridegrooms to move in the same direction. Moreover, the dots tended to cluster around a straight line, suggesting a linear positive correlation between the marriage age of bride and that of bridegroom. Figure 14.2(b), on the other hand, displays a linear negative correlation between temperature and the sales volume of beer. An example of non-linear correlation is illustrated in Figure 14.2(c). It presents a scatter diagram where a curve rather than a straight line gives the best indication of the relationship between two variables. This phenomenon is referred to as curvilinear correlation and is outside the scope of this book. Figure 14.2(d) is an example of no apparent correlation between the two variables, where the dots (or points) in the scatter diagram do not appear to move in any obvious direction.

Computation of the correlation coefficient (r)

Assume a sample of n items which has the values in respect of two variables X and Y as follows:

Sample item no.	Variable X	Variable Y
1	X_1	Y_1
2	X_2	Y_2
3	X_3	Y_3
.	.	.
.	.	.
.	.	.
n	X_n	Y_n

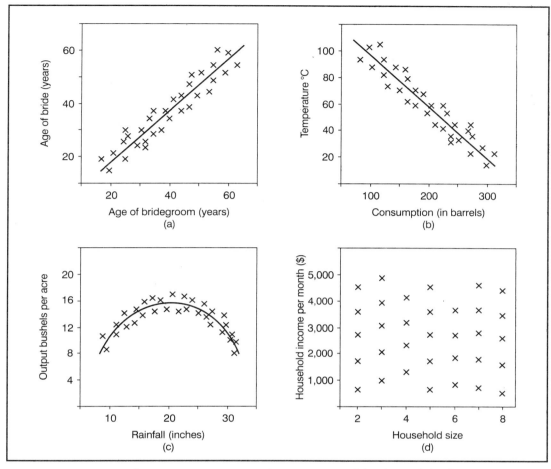

Figure 14.2 *Scatter diagrams: some examples: a. Age of bride and bridegroom; b. Beer consumption and temperature; c. Rainfall and output of wheat; d. Household size and household income*

The formula for the computation of the (linear) correlation coefficient is given by:

$$r = \frac{\sum(X_i - \bar{X})(Y_i - \bar{Y})}{\sqrt{\sum(X_i - \bar{X})^2 - \sum(Y_i - \bar{Y})^2}}$$

where $\bar{X}$ = the arithmetic mean of X_i-values = $(1/n)\sum X_i$

$\bar{Y}$ = the arithmetic mean of Y_i-values = $(1/n)\sum Y_i$

Another version of the formula is:

$$r = \frac{n\sum X_i Y_i - (\sum X_i)(\sum Y_i)}{[n\sum X_i^2 - (\sum X_i)^2].[n\sum Y_i^2 - (\sum Y_i)^2]}$$

The values of r will range from −1 to +1. When r = +1, there is a perfect positive correlation between the two variables. When r = −1, there is a perfect negative correlation between the two variables. When r = 0, there is no relationship between

r-values	Interpretation
0<r<0.30	Whether positive or negative, there is little evidence or correlation, and changes in terms of the first series should not be taken to indicate what changes will result in the second series.
0.30 r<0.50	Whether positive or negative, there is some degree of direct or inverse correlation, and changes in the items of one series not necessarily be taken as a guide to the probable changes in the other.
0.50 r<0.75	Whether positive or negative, there is a dedicated correlation between the two series, and changes in one series may be taken as a rough guide as to probable changes in the other series.
0.75 r<0.90	Whether positive or negative, there is a fairly high degree of direct or inverse correlation between the two series. Estimation of items of one series may be made from known values of the other series with reasonable accuracy.
0.90 r 1.00	Whether positive or negative, there is a considerably high degree of direct or inverse correlation. Estimations of items of one series may be made from known values of the other series with high accuracy particularly where r is greater than 0.95.

Figure 14.3 *Interpretation of r-values*

the two variables. Figure 14.3 provides the interpretative values of r.

Illustrative example 7

A random sample of twelve students whose heights and weights are recorded in the following:

Student number	Height (X_i) (ins)	Weights (Y_i) (lbs)
1	66	142
2	67	139
3	62	105
4	65	122
5	63	112
6	62	110
7	67	145
8	61	98
9	64	116
10	64	120
11	65	128
12	62	103

The scatter diagram plotted is presented below. It allows two types of information. First, we can visually look for patterns that indicate whether the variables are related. Secondly, given that the variables are related, we can see what kind of line or curve describes this relationship.

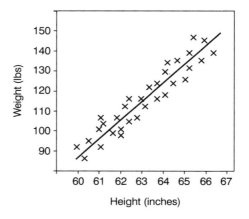

The dots in the above scatter diagram tend to follow a line sloping upwards from left to right. This suggests a high degree of positive correlation between the heights and the weights of students.

To compute the correlation coefficient r, we carry out the following calculations:

$$\bar{X} = \frac{1}{n} \Sigma X_i = 64$$

$$\bar{Y} = \frac{1}{n} \Sigma Y_i = 120$$

Hence

$$r = \frac{\Sigma(X_i - X)(Y_i - Y)}{\sqrt{\Sigma(X_i - X)^2 \cdot \Sigma(Y_i - Y)^2}}$$

$$= \frac{344}{\sqrt{46 \times 2{,}716}}$$

$$= 0.97$$

The square of the r value is also a useful measure in that it signifies the extent of the variance in one variable that is explainable by the other variable. It is called the coefficient of determination whose values vary between 0 to +1.

In the above example, the coefficient of determination is:

$$r^2 = (0.97)^2$$

$$= 0.941 \text{ or } 94.1\%$$

This means either one variable can explain 94.1 per cent of the variation in the other variable.

To test the hypothesis on whether r differs significantly from the zero value, we can use either the F-distribution or the t-distribution test statistics:

$$F = \frac{r^2(n-2)}{1-r^2}$$

with d.f. = 1 and (n − 2) = 10

$$t = \frac{r\sqrt{n-2}}{\sqrt{1-r^2}}$$

with d.f. = n − 2 = 10

Referring to the above example, we have:

$$F = \frac{0.941 \times (12-2)}{1-0.941}$$

$$= 159.49$$

At $\alpha = 0.05$, the critical value of $F_c = 4.96$.

Since F > F_c, the null hypothesis H_0 is rejected and we conclude that there is a significant level of association between the two variables under study.

Simple regression analysis

Apart from ascertaining the direction, as well as the strength of association between two variables, researchers often wish to

Table 14.1

X_i	Y_i	$X_i - X$	$Y_i - Y$	$(X_i - X)(Y_i - Y)$	$(X_i - X)^2$	$(Y_i - Y)^2$
66	142	2	22	44	4	484
67	139	3	19	57	9	361
62	105	-2	-15	30	4	225
65	122	1	2	2	1	4
63	112	-1	-8	8	1	64
62	110	-2	-10	20	4	100
67	145	3	25	75	9	625
61	98	-3	-22	66	9	484
64	116	0	-4	0	0	16
64	120	0	0	0	0	0
65	128	1	8	8	1	64
62	103	-2	-17	34	4	289
			Total:	344	46	2,716

establish the pattern in which an independent variable is related to the dependent variable; and subsequently to predict the scores of the dependent variable, based upon the knowledge of scores of the independent variable. The statistical technique involved is known as simple regression analysis.

In essence, simple regression analysis identifies the relationship between two variables in the form of an equation to predict a dependent variable on the basis of its independent variable. The key task of simple regression analysis lies in establishing the equation between the two variables. Mathematically, we know that when a linear association exists between the two variables X and Y, the equation will be in the form of a straight line $Y = a + bx$, where a and b are constants and:

a = the point where the straight line intercepts the Y-axis

b = the gradient of the straight line.

The computation of the values of a and b are given by the formula:

$$b = \frac{n \Sigma X_i Y_i - (\Sigma X_i)(\Sigma Y_i)}{n \Sigma X_i^2 - (\Sigma X_i)^2}$$

$$a = \frac{\Sigma Y_i - b \Sigma X_i}{n}$$

Illustrative example 8

Referring to the data given in Illustrative example 7, we arrive at the following calculations:

X_i	Y_i	X_i^2	$X_i Y_i$
66	142	4,356	9,372
67	139	4,489	9,313
62	105	3,844	6,510
65	122	4,225	7,930
63	112	3,969	7,056
62	110	3,844	6,820
67	145	4,489	9,715
61	98	3,721	5,978
64	116	4,096	7,424
64	120	4,096	7,680
65	128	4,225	8,320
62	103	3,844	6,386
Total 768	1,440	49,198	92,504

$$b = \frac{n \Sigma X_i Y_i - (\Sigma X_i)(\Sigma Y_i)}{n \Sigma X_i^2 - (\Sigma X_i)^2}$$

$$= \frac{12 \times 92,504 - 768 \times 1,440}{12 \times 49,198 \times (768)^2}$$

$$= 7.48$$

$$a = \frac{\Sigma Y_i - b \Sigma X_i}{n}$$

$$= \frac{1,440 - 7.48 \times 768}{12}$$

$$= -358.72$$

The equation of the regression line is:

$$Y = -358.72 + 7.48X$$

Thus for a student of height $X = 64.5$ ins, his predicted weight will be:

$$Y = -358.72 + 7.48 \times 64.5$$

$$= 123.74 \text{ lbs}$$

Indices of association for mixed scale variables

The indices of association just described relate to two variables of the same level of measurement. We will not elaborate on the indices of association that relate to two variables of different levels of measurements. However, some brief remarks are provided below.

Index of association for nominal-ordinal variables

The appropriate index of association to be used between a nominal variable and an ordinal variable is the Freedman's coefficient of differentiation. Basically, this index demonstrates the extent to which the individuals in each category of a nominal scale tend to consistently rank higher or lower than the individuals in the other categories.

Index of association for nominal-metric variables

The correlation ratio Eta (η) is the only index available for describing the association between a nominal and an interval/ratio variable. It measures the ability to guess a score for individuals in different classes of a nominal scale variable.

Multivariate analysis ▬▬▬

When three or more variables are involved, the study of relationship is collectively called multivariate analysis, which requires a thorough statistical knowledge of the wide range of techniques and their applications. The increased versatility and accessibility of the computer have greatly enhanced an extensive use of these statistical techniques.

Among the pool of statistical techniques available for multivariate analysis, the most commonly used ones are:

1 Multiple regression.
2 Automatic interaction detector.
3 Discriminant analysis.
4 Factor analysis.
5 Cluster analysis.
6 Multidimensional scaling.

Multiple regression ▬▬▬

In simple regression, the prediction of one dependent variable is made based on the variations in one independent variable only, ignoring the potential relationship of all other variables to the dependent variable. The students' weights, in our earlier example, were predicted based upon their respective heights alone. No consideration whatsoever was made on their parents' physical sizes, household conditions (e.g. income), etc. which may also turn out to be relevant factors.

Multiple regression analysis is a statistical tool specially designed to analyse the relationship between a single dependent (criterion) metric variable and several independent (predictor) metric variables. Its function is to help predict, based on the known values of several independent variables, the corresponding value of the single dependent variable under study. The task in multiple regression analysis is to establish a predicting equation which is analogous to the one developed for simple linear regression analysis. Thus:

$$\hat{Y} = a + b_1X_1 + b_2X_2 + \ldots + b_nX_n$$

where $\hat{Y}$ represents the predicted value of the dependent variable, $X_1, X_2, \ldots, X_n$ are the values for the respective independent variables, and a and b_i are constants.

Illustrative example 9

A real estate development corporation wishes to predict the price of homes based on a person's income and age. Data from a random sample of 100 recent homebuyers is shown below:

Respondent no.	Price of home ($'000) (criterion)	Income ($'000) (predictor)	Age (years) (predictor)
1	60	21	40
2	52	18	35
3	96	46	56
.	.	.	.
.	.	.	.
.	.	.	.
100	34	9	28

Source: Burke International Research Corporation (1980) *Marketing Research for Marketing Managers.*

Using a statistical procedure known as least-square analysis, we obtain an equation for the straight line which provides the best fit for the data:

$$\text{Price of home} = 15.2 + 2.01 \text{ (Income)} + 0.49 \text{ (Age)}$$

This equation can be used for forecasting the price of homes likely to be owned by an individual with a certain income and age. Care must be exercised not to use the equation for predicting values not included in the range covered by the original data. The relative importance of the various predictor variables can be assessed by an examination of standardized regression coefficients, which are normally provided in most computer software.

Automatic interaction detector

Automatic interaction detector (AID) is another useful multivariate dependence analysis procedure, which is particularly suitable for exploring complex interactive relationship among a massive set of data. It takes a dependent or criterion (metric) variable and several independent (nominal, categorized) variables or factors, and goes on to show which factors are strongest in explaining the former.

The analysis consists of sequentially generating binary splits for the sample respondents by choosing, at each split, the one factor or independent variable which will be most powerful in terms of explaining

as much variation in the dependent variable as possible. The procedural steps are:

1 Consider each candidate variable, one at a time, and split into all possible dichotomies.
2 For each dichotomy, calculate the between sums of squares (BSS) and select the split that maximizes BSS.
3 The sample respondents are then split into the two groups on the one independent variable which explains the maximum amount of variances.
4 Repeat the above process on each of the two newly formed groups separately.

Illustrative example 10

It is intended to explore the relationship between the likelihood of reading Newspaper ABC and four potential independent (predictor) variables namely: sex, age, household income and occupation of respondents. To simplify data collection, these predictor variables were obtained in the following categories:

Sex	Household Income
Male	Below $1,000
Female	$1,000–$2,000
	$2,001 and over

Age	Occupation
15–25	White collar workers
26–35	Blue collar workers
36–45	Non-working persons
46–55	(e.g. housewives, students, etc.)
over 55	

The criterion variable (in this case, it is the likelihood of reading the Newspaper ABC) was measured in actual percentages. The tree diagram resulting from the AID analysis is shown overleaf.

The diagram shows that likelihood of reading Newspaper ABC is highest (43.6 per cent) among the blue collar workers and non-workers aged between 15 and 35 years, coming from households with income $2,000 and below per month. Altogether they make up 25 per cent (250 from 1,000) of

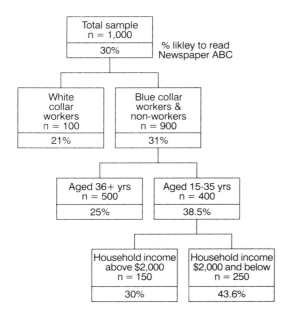

In sum, AID consists of performing sequential one-way analysis of variance on the criterion variable. The algorithm searches through the various categorized predictor variables arriving at that dichotomous split on a single predictor which will account for the largest variation in the criterion variable. It develops sequentially a set of mutually exclusive and exhaustive subgroups of the data, providing the maximum possible improvement in predicting the values of the criterion variable. Quite different from most multivariate approaches, AID takes the form of a hierarchical tree diagram, and is easily comprehended by the non-technician.

Discriminant analysis

Researchers often deal with research studies which address the following questions:

1 What predictor variables, if any, discriminate two groups of persons or users? (e.g. Mercedes Benz owners vs non-Mercedes Benz owners)?
2 Can discriminating variables be selected to predict the likelihood of a person belonging to a certain group of persons or users?
3 Can we estimate the size of different groups of persons or users?

the sample respondents. In other words, if Newspaper ABC is principally targeted at this category of persons, it can expect to gain a trial rate of 10.9 percent (43.6 per cent of 25 per cent) of the total population.

The final segmentation from the tree diagram can be summarized below:

Segment	Segment profile	Size	Likelihood of reading Newspaper ABC (%)
1	White collar workers	100	21
2	Blue collar workers and non-working persons aged 36+ years	500	25
3	Blue collar workers and non-working persons aged 15–35 years living in households earning above $2,000 per month	150	30
4	Blue collar workers and non-working persons aged 15–35 years living in households earning $2,000 and below	250	43.6
		1,000	30

All of these questions can be answered by the use of discriminant analysis. In most cases, the criterion variable will consist of two groups or classifications such as owners versus non-owners, heavy drinkers versus light drinkers. In other instances, more than two groups are involved, such as a three-group classification involving say, heavy, moderate and light beer-drinkers. Discriminant analysis is capable of handling either two groups or multiple (three or more) groups. In the former case, the technique is referred to as two-group discriminant analysis and in the latter case, multiple discriminant analysis (MDA). Discriminant analysis develops a profile of the different group members and uses the profile to predict which subjects are likely to fall into each group. Like regression analysis, it uses data about independent variable(s) to estimate the value of the dependent variable. But unlike regression analysis, the criterion variable is usually non-metric. The independent variables used in discriminant analysis must be metrically scaled.

Discriminant analysis involves deriving the linear combination of the two (or more) independent variables that will discriminate best between the priori defined groups.

$$Z = w_1 X_1 + w_2 X_2 + w_3 X_3 + \ldots + w_n X_n$$

where Z = discriminant score
w_i = discriminant weights
X_i = independent (or explanatory) variables.

The discriminate equation is developed by adopting the statistical decision rule of maximizing the between-group variance relative to the within-group variances. The weights w_i are assigned to the various independent (predictor) variables in such a way that the variance between groups is maximized and the variance within groups is minimized. Essentially, it involves the process of maximizing the value of r where:

$$r = \frac{\text{Variance between groups}}{\text{Variance within groups}}$$

A critical value is determined that separates the groups identified in the dependent variable; and depending on the score derived (from the discriminant equation), each subject is then assigned to one of the categories in the dependent variable: heavy smoker, moderate smoker, and non-smoker.

Illustrative example 11

A research study is intended to discriminate between credit card holders (CC) and non-credit card holders (NCC) based on three predictor variables – number of children

under 12 years, age and household income. A probability sample of 100 NCC and 100 CC respondents was interviewed to obtain data on the three demographic predictor variables as shown below:

Respondent no.	Ownership group	No. of children (X_1)	Age (X_2)	Household income (X_3)
001	NCC	2	38	9.50
002	NCC	4	54	18.65
.	.	.	.	
.	.	.	.	
100	NCC	3	49	31.25
101	CC	0	41	24.20
.	.	.	.	
.	.	.	.	
199	CC	1	26	11.36
200	CC	3	49	31.25

Analysis of the above data using the appropriate computer programme produced the following statistically significant linear combination or discrimination function:

$$Z = 0.42 - 0.18 X_1 + 0.32 X_2 + 0.55 X_3$$

The weights provide an insight into the importance of the three predictor variables in discriminating between owners and non-owners of credit card. To remove the effects of different units of measurement for the three predictor variables, each of the weights above is multiplied by the standard deviation of the corresponding variables. The standardized weights for our example are shown below:

	Weights
No. of children	3.12
Age	4.96
Household income	1.18

Hence age and number of children are relatively more important than household income in determining credit card ownership. Furthermore, age and household income have an influence which is opposite in direction to that of the number of children.

The procedure may be applied to the sample respondents to provide the following *confusion* matrix, where the number of correct classifications is shown in the diagonal line and the number of incorrect ones off the diagonal line. Thus the success of the discriminant equation can be assessed – the percentage of subjects which are properly classified determines the accuracy of the equation.

Actual	Predicted	
	Holders	Non-holders
Holders	85	15
Non-holders	25	75

The above matrix shows that the discriminant equation correctly classified 85 of 100 credit card holders and 75 of 100 non-credit card holders, or an overall accuracy level of 80 per cent.

Factor analysis

Factor analysis is a generic term describing a group of statistical methods whose primary purpose is to condense the data contained in a fairly large number of variables into a smaller set of variables or *factors*. A list of statements which form a broad dimension of attitude may be reduced to a smaller set of new latent variables with a minimum loss of information. Note that a factor is a variable that is not directly observable but instead, needs to be inferred from the input variable.

In generalized term, a factor F_i may be expressed as a linear combination of the n original variables $X_1, X_2, \ldots, X_n$ that measure, or are indicators of, the factor:

$$F_i = a_{i1}X_1 + a_{i2}X_2 + a_{i3}X_3 + \cdots + a_{in}X_n$$

For any variable X_i not relevant to the factor F_i, its respective coefficient $a_{<i1>}$ would either be equal or close to zero. As an example, a set of six original variables X_1, X_2, X_3, X_4, X_5 and X_6 may be reduced to two factors F_1 and F_2 where:

$$F_1 = a_{11}X_1 + a_{12}X_2$$

(Here $a_{13} = a_{14} = a_{15} = a_{16} = 0$)

$$F_2 = a_{23}X_3 + a_{24}X_4 + a_{25}X_5 + a_{25}X_6$$

(Here $a_{21} = a_{22} = 0$)

The two basic reasons for using factor analysis are:

1 To reduce a large number of variables to a more manageable data set, but still retain most of the information found in the original data set.
2 To identity the underlying structure of the data in which a large number of variables may really be measuring a smaller number of basic characteristics of our sample.

Cluster analysis

Cluster analysis consists of a group of techniques whose primary objective is to classify an unorganized set of individual subjects into distinct groups based on some discovered similarities, or common characteristics. These groups are called *clusters* or *target segments* in marketing terminology. The elements within the same cluster are more like each other than those in different clusters. The basis upon which the clusters are formed could involve a wide variety of characteristics ranging from the commonly used socio-economic factors, to the more sophisticated variables such as needs, attitudes and psychological bases. Once meaningful clusters or target segments are found, they can be studied in terms of demographic, socio-economic and psychographic aspects.

When forming the clusters, it is essential to decide on a set of dimensions for the

Cluster No.	City	Cluster No.	City	Cluster No.	City
1	Omaha Oklahoma City Dayton Columbus Fort Worth	7	Sacramento San Benardino San Jose Phoenix Tucson	13	Allentown Providence Jersey City York Louisville
2	Peoria Davenport Binghamton Harrisburg Worcester	8	Gary Nashville Jacksonville San Antonio Knoxville	14	Paterson Milwaukee Cincinnati Miami Seattle
3	Canton Youngstown Toldeo Springfield Albany	9	Indianapolis Kansas City Dallas Atlanta Houston	15	San Diego Tacoma Norfolk Charleston Ft. Lauderdale
4	Bridgeport Rochester Hartford New Haven Syracuse	10	Mobile Shreveport Birmingham Memphis Chattanooga	16	New Orleans Richmond Tampa Lancaster Minneapolis
5	Wilmington Orlando Tulsa Wichita Grand Rapids	11	Newark Cleveland Pittsburgh Buffalo Baltimore	17	San Francisco Detroit Boston Philadelphia
6	Bakersfield Fresno Flint El Paso Beaumont	12	Albuquerque Salt Lake City Denver Charlotte Portland	18	Washington St Louis

Figure 14.4 *Groupings of test market cities using cluster analysis.* Source: *Paul E. Green, Ronald E. Frank and Patrick J. Robinson (1967), Cluster Analysis in Test Market Selection.* Management Science, **13**, April, B393 (Table 2).

subjects or observations to be scored on these dimensions and grouped on the basis of the similarity of their scores. Cluster analysis is ideal for situations where it is desired to segment a market, but a basis for such segmentation does not presently exist. Essentially, this technique attempts to group individuals in a manner such that within-cluster similarities are maximized, while between-cluster similarities are minimized.

Illustrative example 12

Green, Frank and Robinson (1967) used clustering techniques to cluster eighty-eight standard metropolitan areas in the USA for test market purposes. Fourteen separate variables (or characteristics) such as population, retail sales, median age, etc. were considered. Results of their analysis with groupings of comparable cities are shown in Figure 14.4.

Illustrative example 13

A study was undertaken in 1991 to form opinion groups (or clusters) of adult consumers in Singapore, based on their perceptions and attitudes toward advertising. Five opinion groups were identified, namely: (A) the enthusiasts, (B) the followers, (C) the middle-of-the-roaders, (D) the critics and (E) the laggards (see Figure 14.5).

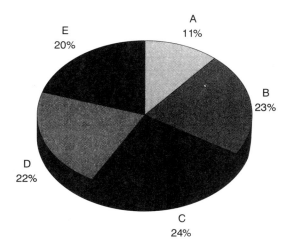

Figure 14.5 *Five opinion groups*
Source: *Wong Toon Quee (1991) The Percep-
tions and Attitudes of Consumers toward
Advertising in Singapore. PhD dissertation.*

A brief description of each opinion group is
given below.

A *The enthusiasts.* They are the most
favourably inclined to advertising among all
opinion groups. Their belief in advertising
are especially strong in the following
aspects: that they have higher trust in
advertised products than in unadvertised
products; that products are as good as they
are advertised to be; that ads do not hide
bad things about the products; and that
advertisements do not lead consumers to
buy things that they may not need. Perhaps
they are the sole believers that heavy
advertising can even help sell poor-quality
products. The enthusiasts represent 11 per
cent of the consumers.

  This opinion group has the largest
percentage of men (59 per cent). It is also
characterized by a high proportion of
married consumers (76 per cent). The
enthusiasts are lower educated than the
other opinion groups. Relatively less
percentage of Chinese was found in this
group (see Figure 14.6).
B *The followers.* This opinion group is slightly
less positive than the enthusiasts about
advertising in general. They are most likely

to dispose with the statement that too much
money is spent on advertising, and the
statement that advertising benefits only the
big companies and not the small ones.
They expressed more trust in advertised
products than unadvertised products.
Twenty-three percent of consumers belong
to this opinion group.

  By and large, they are fairly close to the
typical demography of the overall
consumers, albeit with a slightly higher
presence of the 20 to 29 years old (see
Figure 14.6).
C *The middle-of-the-roaders.* The
middle-of-the-roaders present an almost
consistent picture of neutral responses. A
few exceptions being: they enjoy discount
sales advertisements most among all
opinion groups; they truly believe that
advertisements help them to make the
correct purchases and that advertising
urges manufacturers to improve the quality
of their products. This group comprises 24
per cent of consumers.

  The middle-of-the-roaders has the
largest percentage of women (56 per
cent), and of senior citizens aged 50 years
and over (27 per cent) among all opinion
groups (see Figure 14.6).
D *The critics.* The critics loathe advertisements
that have sex appeal. They are adamant
that too much money is being spent on
advertising, and deny having more
confidence in advertised than in
unadvertised products. They are least
bothered to look at advertisements before
making their shopping trips, and doubtful
of advertising being able to urge the
manufacturers to improve the quality of
their products. Twenty-two per cent of
consumers fall in this group.

  The critics have the highest percentage
of Chinese (86 per cent), and the
unmarrieds. Relatively speaking, there
tended to be a high proportion of better
educated consumers in this group (see
Figure 14.6).
E *The laggards.* The laggards are the least
favourable to advertising among all five
opinion groups. Their ratings were most

	All groups	Opinion group				
		I	II	III	IV	V
No. of respondents	588	63	134	140	133	118
	%	%	%	%	%	%
SEX						
Male	51	59	53	44	57	44
Female	49	41	47	56	43	56
RACE						
Chinese	77	54	81	70	86	82
Malay	15	33	14	16	8	11
Indians/Others	8	13	4	13	6	7
AGE						
15 to 19 years	11	10	9	13	15	8
20 to 29 years	26	19	34	19	23	30
30 to 39 years	25	22	26	26	30	19
40 to 49 years	18	25	13	15	20	22
50 years and above	20	24	8	27	11	21
MARITAL STATUS						
Single	34	21	37	34	40	31
Married	64	76	62	64	59	69
Divorced/Widowed	2	3	1	3	2	1
EDUCATIONAL ATTAINMENT						
None	15	25	15	16	10	16
Primary	25	32	27	29	18	21
Lower Secondary	39	35	36	43	41	36
Upper Secondary	11	2	12	7	13	18
Tertiary/Diploma	10	7	9	5	18	10
HOUSE TYPE						
HDB 1-3 room flat	49	57	54	50	43	45
HDB 4&5 room flat	38	30	35	41	35	43
Private housing	13	13	11	9	23	12

Figure 14.6 *Demographics of opinion groups*

negative in nine of the twenty-four advertising aspects under study, including the following:

- enjoy television advertisements
- right amount of money spent on advertising
- product is priced higher due to advertisements
- advertisements hide bad things about the product.

The laggards represent 20 per cent of consumers. Compared to all other opinion groups, we observed that proportionately more members of this group are females; are residents in government 4–5 room flat; and have upper secondary education (see Figure 14.6).

A number of methods can be used to form clusters. One of the less complicated methods used is known as *hierarchical clustering*. Each respondent is initially assumed to be in a separate cluster (say 200 respondents or clusters). The two respondents who are most alike are combined to form a new composite cluster, resulting in a 199-cluster solution. These 199 clusters are further examined to find the next most alike pair to be combined, to give a 198-cluster solution. This process is repeated until all the original respondents/ clusters have been combined into one. The researcher is then free to choose the level of clustering (between 200 clusters and 1 cluster in this case) that groups the respondents in the way most relevant and practical to the marketing problem.

Multidimensional scaling _____

We have, in Chapter 8, discussed the semantic differential scale, the Likert scale and the Stapel scale which are most widely used to measure attitudes in marketing research. These are regarded unidimensional scales as they measure perceptions or preferences in terms of a single dimension (e.g. high-low quality; modern-old, etc.) at a time. In reality, consumers' perceptions of and preferences for a given product or brand are more often multidimensional than unidimensional. In an automobile study, for example, the vehicle may be perceived along a *durable* dimension, a *luxurious* dimension, a *spacious* dimension, an *economy* dimension, or other dimensions.

The term 'multidimensional scaling' encompasses a family of statistical techniques that enable the researcher to take a series of single dimension relationships and transform them into one multidimensional relationship. It attempts to project consumers' attitudes, perceptions and preferences as points in a geometric space. It maps the alternatives in a multidimensional space in a manner that their relative positions in the space reflect the degree of perceived similarity between alternatives. A major advantage of multidimensional scaling is that it enables relationships to be exhibited pictorially (in space) rather than just numerically. This technique also offers the researchers an insight into the number of salient criteria which underlie a person's judgement. Thus it may be discovered that prestige and comfort are the most salient criteria a person considers when he or she makes a comparison between automobiles and, similarly, mint flavour and price may be the two key criteria underlying his or her judgement about various brands of toothpaste.

The procedure of the multidimensional scaling technique is outlined by Johnson (see R. M. Johnson [1971] Market Segmentation: A Strategic Management Tool. *Journal of Marketing Research*, February, pp. 13–18) as:

1 Obtaining each respondent's opinions of where each product, brand or whatever is being evaluated, stands in the product space.
2 Locating each respondent's ideal point in the product space for such a product.

End-of-chapter revision

Review questions

14.1 What is meant by the nature of association? Briefly describe the objectives in studying association.

14.2 What is understood by the degree of association? How does it differ from causation?

14.3 What are meant by predictor variable and criterion variable?

14.4 What questions must one answer in order to select the appropriate bivariate statistical procedure?

14.5 What is the basic use of a chi-square goodness-of-fit test? How is the value of the test statistic calculated? How are the expected frequencies determined?

14.6 Explain and demonstrate the meaning of correlation coefficient.

14.7 What is meant by the term *dependence* when referring to data analysis?

14.8 What is a scatter diagram? Why is it useful in measuring association?

14.9 What is regression analysis? Linear correlation?

14.10 What is the interpretation of the coefficient of determination?

14.11 A marketing researcher interested in the business publication reading habits of purchasing agents has assembled the following data:

Business publication preferences (first-choice mentions)

Business publication	Frequency of first choice
W	35
X	30
Y	45
Z	55
Total	165

a Test the null hypothesis ($\alpha = 0.05$) that there are no differences among frequencies of choice for publications W, X, Y, and Z.

b Suppose that the researcher had aggregated responses for the publication pairs W-Y and X-Z. Test the null hypothesis ($\alpha = 0.05$) that there are no differences among frequencies of choice for the two publication pairs.

14.12 Assume next that the researcher was able to obtain information regarding whether each purchasing agent held a technical degree or not. The data are as follows:

Business publication	First-choice mentions		Total
	Technical degree	No technical degree	
W	20	15	35
X	15	15	30
Y	25	20	45
Z	30	25	55
Total	90	75	165

a Is there an association between business publication choice and type of college degree ($\alpha = 0.1$)?

b What is the appropriate null hypothesis for this illustration?

14.13 Why is multivariate analysis becoming more often used in marketing research?

14.14 Define the term *discriminant analysis*. Provide a real or hypothetical example in which discriminant analysis might be beneficial in the analysis of marketing research data.

14.15 What kinds of prediction are possible with discriminant analysis?

14.16 What is factor analysis? Why is it useful in the analysis of marketing research data?

14.17 Factor analysis is a data-reducing technique. Explain.

14.18 What is cluster analysis? For what practical marketing applications is it useful?

14.19 What technique is used to measure bivariate association in
a ordinal data?
b interval data?
c nominal data?

True-false questions
Write True (T) or False (F) for the following:

14.20 Discriminant analysis requires ratio scaled data.

14.21 The coefficient of regression can be positive, negative or zero.

14.22 The coefficient of regression is the constant slope of a simple linear regression line.

14.23 In two-group discriminant analysis, the discriminant line is used to predict group membership.

14.24 The index of association is a measure of the intensity of association between variables.

14.25 When an increase in one variable causes a decrease in the other variable, we say that these two variables are positively correlated.

Multiple-choice questions

14.26 In a regression-correlation analysis leading to an equation of the $Y = a + bX$ type, the coefficient of determination (r_2) represents:
a the proportion of the variation in X that is explained by changes in Y
b the proportion of the variation in Y that is explained by changes in X
c the total variation of X and Y
d the proportion of the variation in Y that is explained by the scatter diagram.

14.27 Factor analysis generates a new set of variables or factors, each of which is a _____ of the original variables.
a fraction
b non-linear sum
c linear combination
d derived proportion.

14.28 Which one of the following multivariate techniques facilitates market segmentation by identifying similar individuals?
a Multiple regression analysis.
b Canonical correlation.
c Cluster analysis.
d Conjoint analysis.

14.29 Which one of the following is not a statistical technique of multivariate analysis?
a Factor analysis.
b Multidimensional scaling.
c Scatter diagram.
d Discriminant analysis.

15

The research report

We now come to the final phase of the marketing research process, namely the presentation of survey results in the form of a report. The research report is an extremely important document to serve as the final, formal communication between the researcher and the research client for a particular project. It is the only one step in the entire research process which brings all other steps (e.g. designing questionnaire, gathering data, drawing important conclusions etc.) together and, in fact, documents all of the preceding efforts. Without it, such efforts will have been wasted. Often the research report is the only part of the research study that others will ever see.

The primary purpose of the research report is to communicate the research results, conclusions and recommendations (if required) in a clear and concise manner.

Note that the key word here is communicate and for all intents and purposes the report must be an effective tool of communication to accurately present the findings, conclusions and recommendations, as well as to stimulate the marketers to take some managerial action. To fulfil this function, the researcher's job is to look at the analysis of the information collected and ask the question: 'What does this mean to the management?' Quite apart from being just a communication tool between the research client and the researcher, the research report is also a source document for future reference.

Types of research report

A research report may be technical or popular in orientation, depending on the audience for which it is designed. While both types of report give descriptions on the methodology and findings of a research study, each makes rather different assumptions about the interests and background of the target readers. For this reason, they differ considerably in terms of detail, style of writing, use of technical terms and length.

The technical report

A technical report is generally intended for other researchers or research managers who are interested in the technical details about

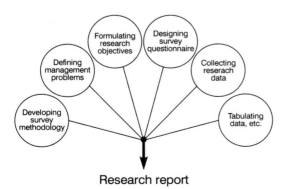

Research report
- It brings all steps together
- It documents all steps
- Difficult task but highly rewarded

1. The instructions from the authority or client may indicate a purely statistical report on the one extreme or a fully-elaborated recommendation of the other.
2. The nature and complexity of the problem will certainly indicate the manner in which the report must be presented.
3. The nature and variety of readers for whom the report is intended will vitally affect its form and content. If a report on the habits of buyers and users of a product it intended for the company's salesmen, it must certainly be less formal and technical, and perhaps briefer and more pictorialised than if solely for use of the sales manager.
4. The size of the report will influence its format, binding and even the nature of the exposition of the findings.
5. The number of copies to be made will determine the method of reporduction and therefore the nature of the illustrative material.
6. The length of the useful life of the report may influence the amount of money and effort to be invested in presentation.

Figure 15.1 *Factors influencing report form. Source: Reprinted from Committee on Reporting of the American Marketing Association (1948) Preparation and Presentation of the Research Report. Journal of Marketing, July, pp. 62–3.*

research design, sampling design, statistical methods, etc., adopted for research study. Such details enable the target readers to evaluate the suitability and accuracy level of the research study on a step-by-step basis.

A technical report should therefore present a detailed account of each step employed in the research project and is free to use technical terms such as standard deviation, analysis of variance, degree of freedom, confidence level and the like. But a brief definition for any technical term with which the reader might not be familiar should be included whenever deemed necessary.

The popular report

A popular report, on the other hand, is intended for a more general audience who is interested in reading the research findings but would not be particularly bothered about the research techniques adopted. A distinct feature of such report is that it makes less use of detailed, complex statistical tables. The writing style of the popular report is designed for rapid reading and easy comprehension of the main findings of the research. With these objectives in mind, the report will normally make more use of flow diagrams, pictures, charts and graphs.

Structure of research report ▬

There is no standard style of format for a research report. The form, length, style and degree of technicality of a research report will depend on the subject, size of the study, type of reader for whom it is intended and, to a lesser extent, the relationship between the research sponsor and the researcher.

The Committee on Report of the American Marketing Association (AMA) has prepared a list of factors which influence the form of the research report (see Figure 15.1).

The major components of an actual report appear below. This is merely a suggested

Research report

Components

☞ Title page
☞ Contents page
☞ Background/Introduction
☞ Survey objectives
☞ Executive summary
☞ Detailed findings
☞ Research methodology
☞ Appendix

format and one may wish to omit or combine some of them as it best suits one's purpose. Each component is now described more fully.

Title page

This is the beginning of the report and serves to inform the reader of the following:

- Title of the survey.
- For whom the research was prepared.
- By whom the report was written.
- The completion date of the report.

Table of contents

The table of contents should list out all the main sections, subsections together with their respective page numbers to allow readers rapid access. Readers who are only interested in specific parts of a lengthy report will use this table to find them. For shorter reports (e.g. six pages), the table of contents may be omitted, so long as distinctive headlines are provided.

Executive summary

The executive summary starts the actual report by presenting a brief abstract of information that is necessary to reach a conclusion. Not all readers have the time to read the report in its entirety. For busy executives, in particular, the executive summary is most essential as it highlights the survey findings in a straightforward and precise manner. It is not uncommon that the executive summary is the only section of the research report read by the busy executives and hence to keep it brief and non-technical would be of utmost necessity. The executive summary would usually consist of an introduction, followed by short statements of research objective, research results and interpretations and recommendations.

Introduction

Sometimes referred to as *background*, this section presents, among other things, the details of the marketing problem as seen by the researcher. The introduction section will usually provide the reader with the following:

- Research purpose.
- Specific research objectives.
- Brief statement on research methodology.
- Survey period, including the size of field staff employed.
- Type and size of respondents interviewed.

Survey findings

This section contains the analysed data of the research study and is the meat of the report covering the original problems, hypotheses and information needs of the research study in considerable detail. The evidence upon which conclusions and recommendations are based is also presented in this section. Being the largest section of a report, it displays a combination of text with relevant charts, tables and diagrams which not only serve as a reference but also a source of support for statements made in the text. There is always a temptation to include every piece of research finding in this section. However, considerable efforts should be made to limit this to the most relevant ones.

Conclusions and recommendations

The researcher's role is not just to present the facts, but also to draw conclusions on the basis of the findings. When the situation warrants it, the researcher is expected to make recommendations on the basis of these conclusions. Understandably, the researcher may lack the broad perspective of the company and cannot be expected to possess full knowledge of all corporate factors involved in a marketing decision. This, however, should not prevent him or her from recommending courses of action that seem appropriate on the basis of the study results. In any case, the manager will still have the final decision on accepting or rejecting the researcher's recommendations. In the event that the research undertook the study in the capacity of a marketing consultant, it is almost certain that the client expects such recommendations as part of the report.

Research report Guidelines
☞ Consider the audience
☞ Be mindful of survey objectives
☞ Be objective
☞ Be selective
☞ Be concise & clear
☞ Avoid technical terms
☞ Use illustrations

Appendix

This section concludes the research report. In a way, the appendix section serves the function of catch-all for the report. It provides the right place for those supportive materials that appear relevant but do not justify space in the main sections of the report. Items such as statistical analysis and calculations, statistical tables, a copy of the questionnaire, storyboards and interviewer instructions are best relegated to this section. The researcher should resist the temptation of putting everything into the appendix section just to make the size of the report appear substantial. The decision-maker does not pay for the research report on the basis of its physical size.

Report writing

Each individual has his or her own writing style and ability. The reports prepared by various researchers will inevitably display differences arising from the varying personalities, imaginations and experiences between them. Notwithstanding what has just been said, it is generally agreed that for effective report writing, a series of guidelines given below should be adhered to.

1 *Consider the audience.* Always bear in mind that the reader, not the writer, dictates the appropriate form of report. The report audience will determine whether a technical report or a popular report, or both, is needed. The management, for example, is less interested in detailed reporting of the research design and methodology and hence a summary of the survey findings would be what is required; this means a popular report.

2 *Be mindful of survey objectives.* A key factor guiding the preparation of the report is the need to present the data collected in a manner that enables the survey objective(s) to be accomplished. If, for example, the survey objective is to provide an evaluation of three potential packaging designs, the ensuing report should provide the information needed to make such an evaluation.

3 *Be objective.* At times, the researcher may discover that the research findings contradict the judgement of his or her research client or unfavourably reflect on the outcome of the latter's promotional effort. While the advertising manager will be delighted to read a report which elaborates favourably on the successful aspects of his or her promotion campaign, he or she would argue or even reject the research report if its findings rated the promotional campaign a failure. In a situation like this, the

researcher's commitment to objective reporting is tested. The professional researcher has the obligation to present the research findings in an objective manner, unprejudiced by the management's belief or expectations.

4 *Be selective*. It is almost impossible (and unwise!) to include in the report every single piece of information gathered from the research study. The danger of an overwritten report is obvious: the more important point will not be given the proper emphasis and they will likely be overshadowed by the details. The researcher must use his or her own judgement in deciding what should and should not be included in the report.

5 *Be concise and clear*. Clarity in writing means efficient communication, a quality which good report writer develop only after considerable experience. A fundamental rule is to keep paragraphs short and concise; each paragraph preferably dealing with only one point. Unnecessarily long sentences should be avoided at all costs, lest ambiguities and confusions occur. Besides, sentences should flow smoothly, linking one point to another in the proper sequence. A wise thing to do is for the researcher to invite a few persons unfamiliar with the study to read through the report and to forward their feedback.

6 *Avoid technical terms*. As earlier mentioned, the research report should consider the experience level of the reader. Technical terms which are unfamiliar to the reader should be avoided, particularly in the case of a popular report. If it is absolutely necessary to introduce these technical terms, some brief descriptions or explanations of such terms should be provided.

7 *Insert visual aids*. To attract and maintain the reader's attention as well as to facilitate easy reading, the report must include visual presentation aids such as graphs, pictures and maps. These visual aids help in the understanding of the research findings and are meant to supplement, rather than to replace written text. Additionally, quotation marks, italics, capitalization, dots, exclamation marks or other symbols may also be appropriately used to indicate emphasis on some key points raised.

Oral presentation

A written report constitutes just one way for the presentation of research findings. The other is oral presentation. While a written report is almost a necessity, an oral presentation is optional, for it is merely used to reinforce what is already in the written report. The setting of an oral presentation can range from a small meeting with top management staff to a more formal presentation comprising a large group of individuals. Generally, oral presentation differs little from the written report insofar as content and form are concerned. Although its primary objective is to support the written report, an oral presentation can achieve a number of things which the written report fails to accomplish. For example, oral presentation allows the reader to ask questions and have points clarified. Also, in the oral presentation, the audience has the opportunity to interact concerning the interpretation of the research findings.

Oral presentation requires the researcher to be a good public speaker, using his or her natural gestures to emphasize important findings, and handing his or her notes and visual aids comfortably. The researcher should constantly establishes eye contact with the audience to gather feedback. A good presenter will always avoid covering everything included in the written report. Too many statistics presented all within a short span of time can be quite complex for the uninitiated and can quickly fade away their interest and attention.

Some tips for a good oral presentation are provided in Figure 15.2.

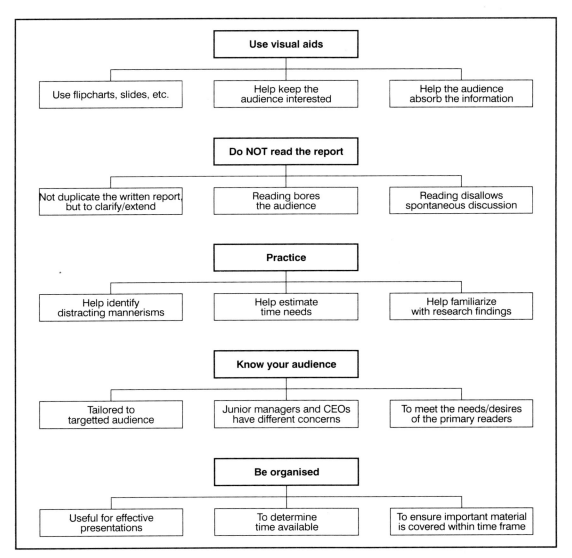

Figure 15.2 *Tips for oral presentation*

Appendix A: The 5Ps of a perfect presentation

1 PREPARATION

Preparation concerns every aspect of getting into a state of readiness for the delivery. In most cases it makes the difference between success and failure or impact and mediocrity. As Winston Churchill said – his best impromptu speeches had been rehearsed many times before the mirror.

2 PURPOSE

Many presenters are too caught up with the contents of their presentation. The purpose is what matters more. Without a clear overall purpose, the delivery will be flat and somewhat pointless. Also within the presentation there may be many different subpurposes, e.g. to get attention, to explain, to reason, to excite, etc. Awareness of such purposes fundamentally influences your presentation and delivers impact.

3 PRESENCE

Effective presenters establish a presence with their mind, an acute awareness of audience existence and they greatly heighten their receptiveness to audience communication. Being present lets you react spontaneously to the situation. And if you have to give the same presentation countless times, there is all the more reason to 'be present'. It forces you to speak as if it was the first time.

4 PASSION

Passion can make your presentation. Absence of passion can break it. Passion in a presenter warms, excites, enthuses, amuses and interests because it reaches beyond the rational self. Cold hard facts and logical analysis without the emotional component seldom move an audience. Passion is closely connected to energy. When you express strong feelings you both use and radiate energy. The audience invariably responds. Good presenters use the right amount of passion to energize themselves and the audience. The result is that their message is heard and people are persuaded, entertained, aroused or amused.

5 PERSONALITY

Your personality is unique and when you exert your personality in a situation you make a difference. Never assume that facts speak for themselves. It is your personality that makes your presentation different and worth hearing. Poor presenters often leave parts of their personalities behind when called upon to present. The result is often a bland information-giver rather than the person who will make the difference. To become a powerful presenter you need to know how you actually come across to others and learn to express your personality in an appropriate way to them.

Source: 6M Management Consultants Pte Ltd.

Appendix B: Advantages and disadvantages of overheads and slides

	Overheads	Slides
Advantages	Can be prepared quickly and economically	Compact: easily carried and stored
	Speaker faces audience, facilitating discussion	Suitable for any size audience
	Easy to carry and store	Projectors are readily available
	Uses ordinary room lighting Can make additions or deletions during the talk	Tend to be considered 'professional'
	Can change the order during the talk	
Disadvantages	Projectors are large and heavy	Relatively expensive
	Projectors may block the listeners' view of the screen	Need extra time for designing
	Can be messy if frequent erasures are made	Need extra time to process
	Mechanics of keeping overheads in focus may distract listeners	Need a really darkened room: inhibits discussion and note-taking
		No changes of any sort possible during the talk

Source: Arleus Frisk SAGE Publications: How to Report on Surveys, p. 31.

End-of-chapter revision

Review questions

15.1 What is the role of the research report?

15.2 What general guidelines exist for the preparation of written research reports?

15.3 Reports are often classified as technical or popular. Comment.

15.4 'In report writing, the researcher's commitment to objective reporting is tested'. Comment.

15.5 Differentiate between the technical report and the non-technical (or popular) report as applied to marketing research.

15.6 What is meant by 'consider the audience' when writing a research report?

15.7 What components are typically included in a research report?

15.8 What should go on the title page?

15.9 What should go in the:
a introduction section?
b methodology section?
c limitation section?
d appendix section?

15.10 What should be included in the body of a report? Explained.

15.11 A management summary is said to be the most important section of the non-technical research report. Discuss.

15.12 A research report should be technically accurate and easily read. Explain the trade-off involved.

15.13 How might an oral presentation supplement a written research report?

15.14 Why are visual aids used in oral presentations?

15.15 The marketing research department of a prominent advertising agency decides to measure the sales response of the magazine advertising Brand S hand soap. The product is to be advertised initially in the 4 July issue of Magazine M, a bi-monthly magazine. The agency selects a simple random sample of 200 subscribing families to Magazine M and interviews each of these sample families on 19 July. The interview is designed to determine:
a whether the family shopper reads the soap advertisement
b whether Brand S soap was purchased within the period 5 July to 18 July.
The results are summarized in Table 15.1.

Table 15.1

	Number purchasing Brand S 5–18 July	Number not purchasing Brand S 5–18 July	Total
Subscribers who read the Brand S advertisement in the 4 July issue of Magazine M.	6	54	60
Subscribers who did not read the Brand S advertisement in the 4 July issue of Magazine M.	11	129	140
Total	17	183	200

a Calculate the percentage difference between those subscribers who read the advertisement and purchased, and those who did not read the advertisement and purchased by each of the following methods:
- absolute difference in percentages
- relative difference in percentages.

b Which method(s) would you recommend the agency to use in preparing a report to the client?

15.16 Is it common for the research report to contain all of the information and data obtained in the study process? Explain.

15.17 'Oral presentation requires the researcher to be a good public speaker.' Explain.

15.18 What can be achieved from an oral presentation of survey findings?

True-false questions

Write True (T) or False (F) for the following:

15.19 A copy of the data collection form is an essential part of a complete research report.

15.20 The higher the executive status of the audience, the shorter a written report will tend to be.

15.21 It is generally not considered appropriate for a research report to include decision; recommendations that are based on the findings.

15.22 Supportive materials that are excessively technical or cumbersome should be placed in the main body of the report.

15.23 When making an oral presentation, one should limit discussion to a few major points.

15.24 The technical report is intended for the general audience who is not particularly concerned with the research techniques adopted.

15.25 The executive summary is the meat of the report and forms the largest section of the entire report.

15.26 The researcher's role is not just to present the survey findings, but also to draw conclusions on the basis of such findings.

15.27 An oral presentation can achieve a number of things which the written report fails to accomplish.

15.28 The researcher is obligated to present the research findings in an objective manner, unprejudiced by the beliefs and/or expectations of the management who commissioned the research.

15.29 A popular report makes less use of detailed, complex statistical tabulations.

Multiple-choice questions

15.30 The reader of a research report can get an idea of the general outline of the report from the:
a introduction
b table of contents
c body
d executive summary.

15.31 The executive summary of a research report will generally:
a be just one or two sentences in length
b range from a few paragraphs to two pages in length
c range from two to five pages in length
d constitute 25 per cent of the report.

15.32 Items like raw data, calculations and statistical analyses should be contained in the:
a methodology section
b introduction
c appendix
d data analysis section.

15.33 Of the following components in a marketing research report, which one would be likely to appear before the others?
a Methodology section.
b Findings.
c Conclusions and recommendations.
d Appendix.

15.34 The title page should include:
  a the title of the survey
  b for whom and by whom the report was written
  c completion date of the survey report
  d all of the above.

15.35 Which of the following is not a part of the appendix?
  a A copy of the questionnaire.
  b Interviewer's instruction manual.
  c Analysis of survey findings.
  d Detailed statistical tables.

Answers to end-of-chapter revision ____

T = True   F = False

1.21	T	2.30	d	3.66	d	4.56	c	5.69	d	7.27	T	8.54	a
1.22	F	2.31	d	3.67	d	4.57	d	5.70	d	7.28	F	8.55	a
1.23	T	2.32	d	3.68	c	4.58	c	5.71	d	7.29	F	8.56	c
1.24	F			3.69	c	4.59	a			7.30	T	8.57	b
1.25	F	3.29	T	3.70	a	4.60	d	6.35	T	7.31	T	8.58	C
1.26	T	3.30	F	3.71	c	4.61	c	6.36	T	7.32	F	8.59	C
1.27	F	3.31	F	3.72	a	4.62	d	6.37	T	7.33	T	8.60	a
1.28	T	3.32	T	3.73	b	4.63	c	6.38	F	7.34	F	8.61	d
1.29	F	3.33	T	3.74	c			6.39	F	7.35	T	8.62	c
1.30	T	3.34	T	3.75	a	5.37	F	6.40	F	7.36	d	8.63	d
1.31	F	3.35	F	3.76	d	5.38	T	6.41	T	7.37	b	8.64	a
1.32	F	3.36	F	3.77	c	5.39	T	6.42	F	7.38	c	8.65	b
1.33	F	3.37	T	3.78	d	5.40	F	6.43	T	7.39	d		
1.34	F	3.38	F	3.79	c	5.41	T	6.44	T	7.40	c		
1.35	T	3.39	T			5.42	T	6.45	F	7.41	c	9.23	F
1.36	a	3.40	T	4.30	T	5.43	T	6.46	F	7.42	d	9.24	F
1.37	d	3.41	F	4.31	T	5.44	F	6.47	T	7.43	d	9.25	T
1.38	c	3.42	F	4.32	T	5.45	T	6.48	T	7.44	d	9.26	F
1.39	a	3.43	T	4.33	T	5.46	F	6.49	F			9.27	T
1.40	d	3.44	T	4.34	T	5.47	T	6.50	T	8.32	T	9.28	F
1.41	d	3.45	F	4.35	F	5.48	F	6.51	F	8.33	T	9.29	F
1.42	c	3.46	F	4.36	F	5.49	T	6.52	T	8.34	F	9.30	F
1.43	b	3.47	F	4.37	T	5.50	F	6.53	T	8.35	F	9.31	T
1.44	b	3.48	F	4.38	F	5.51	F	6.54	F	8.36	T	9.32	F
1.45	d	3.49	T	4.39	F	5.52	T	6.55	T	8.37	F	9.33	F
1.46	d	3.50	F	4.40	T	5.53	T	6.56	c	8.38	T	9.34	T
1.47	d	3.51	T	4.41	F	5.54	T	6.57	c	8.39	F	9.35	d
		3.52	T	4.42	T	5.55	F	6.58	a	8.40	T	9.36	d
2.17	F	3.53	F	4.43	T	5.56	T	6.59	a	8.41	F	9.37	d
2.18	F	3.54	a	4.44	F	5.57	F	6.60	b	8.42	T	9.38	d
2.19	F	3.55	d	4.45	F	5.58	F	6.61	b	8.43	F	9.39	d
2.20	T	3.56	b	4.46	a	5.59	T	6.62	a	8.44	T	9.40	d
2.21	T	3.57	d	4.47	b	5.60	F	6.63	d	8.45	F		
2.22	T	3.58	c	4.48	a	5.61	d	6.64	d	8.46	T	10.15	F
2.23	T	3.59	a	4.49	c	5.62	b	6.65	b	8.47	T	10.16	T
2.24	F	3.60	c	4.50	a	5.63	a	6.66	d	8.48	F	10.17	F
2.25	T	3.61	a	4.51	a	5.64	d			8.49	a	10.18	T
2.26	T	3.62	b	4.52	a	5.65	c	7.23	F	8.50	b	10.19	F
2.27	b	3.63	c	4.53	b	5.66	b	7.24	F	8.51	c	10.20	T
2.28	c	3.64	d	4.54	c	5.67	b	7.25	T	8.52	c	10.21	T
2.29	d	3.65	d	4.55	a	5.68	d	7.26	F	8.53	d	10.22	T
												10.23	T

10.24	F	11.19	T	11.33	c	12.23	T	13.13	F	14.20	F	15.22	F
10.25	F	11.20	T	11.34	b	12.24	T	13.14	F	14.21	T	15.23	T
10.26	T	11.21	F	11.35	b	12.25	F	13.15	F	14.22	T	15.24	F
10.27	d	11.22	F			12.26	T	13.16	F	14.23	T	15.25	F
10.28	d	11.23	T	12.13	F	12.27	F	13.17	T	14.24	T	15.26	T
10.29	d	11.24	F	12.14	T	12.28	F	13.18	T	14.25	F	15.27	T
10.30	d	11.25	F	12.15	T	12.29	F	13.19	F	14.26	b	15.28	T
10.31	d	11.26	T	12.16	F	12.30	F	13.20	a	14.27	c	15.29	T
10.32	d	11.27	c	12.17	T	12.31	c	13.21	c	14.28	c	15.30	b
10.33	d	11.28	d	12.18	F	12.32	b	13.22	d	14.29	c	15.31	b
		11.29	b	12.19	T	12.33	d	13.23	d			15.32	c
		11.30	a	12.20	F	12.34	a	13.24	d	15.19	T	15.33	a
11.17	F	11.31	a	12.21	T	12.35	d	13.25	b	15.20	T	15.34	d
11.18	T	11.32	c	12.22	T	12.36	d	13.26	a	15.21	F	15.35	c

Appendices _____

Table I: *Table of normal distribution (proportion of the area under the normal curve with values as extreme as the observed values of Z)*

Z	0.00	0.01	0.02	0.03	0.04	0.05	0.06	0.07	0.08	0.09
0.0	0.5000	0.4960	0.4920	0.4880	0.4840	0.4801	0.4761	0.4721	0.4681	0.4641
0.1	0.4602	0.4562	0.4522	0.4483	0.4443	0.4404	0.4364	0.4325	0.4286	0.4247
0.2	0.4207	0.4168	0.4129	0.4090	0.4052	0.4013	0.3974	0.3936	0.3897	0.3859
0.3	0.3821	0.3783	0.3745	0.3707	0.3669	0.3632	0.3594	0.3557	0.3520	0.3483
0.4	0.3446	0.3409	0.3372	0.3336	0.3300	0.3264	0.3228	0.3192	0.3156	0.3121
0.5	0.3085	0.3050	0.3015	0.2981	0.2946	0.2912	0.2877	0.2843	0.2810	0.2776
0.6	0.2743	0.2709	0.2676	0.2643	0.2611	0.2578	0.2546	0.2514	0.2483	0.2451
0.7	0.2420	0.2389	0.2358	0.2327	0.2296	0.2266	0.2236	0.2206	0.2177	0.2148
0.8	0.2119	0.2090	0.2061	0.2033	0.2005	0.1977	0.1949	0.1922	0.1894	0.1867
0.9	0.1841	0.1814	0.1788	0.1762	0.1736	0.1711	0.1685	0.1660	0.1635	0.1611
1.0	0.1587	0.1562	0.1539	0.1515	0.1492	0.1469	0.1446	0.1423	0.1401	0.1379
1.1	0.1357	0.1335	0.1314	0.1292	0.1271	0.1251	0.1230	0.1210	0.1190	0.1170
1.2	0.1151	0.1131	0.1112	0.1093	0.1075	0.1056	0.1038	0.1020	0.1003	0.0985
1.3	0.0968	0.0951	0.0934	0.0918	0.0901	0.0885	0.0869	0.0853	0.0838	0.0823
1.4	0.0808	0.0793	0.0778	0.0764	0.0749	0.0735	0.0721	0.0708	0.0694	0.0681
1.5	0.0668	0.0655	0.0643	0.0630	0.0618	0.0606	0.0594	0.0582	0.0571	0.0559
1.6	0.0548	0.0537	0.0526	0.0516	0.0505	0.0495	0.0485	0.0475	0.0465	0.0455
1.7	0.0446	0.0436	0.0427	0.0418	0.0409	0.0401	0.0392	0.0384	0.0375	0.0367
1.8	0.0359	0.0351	0.0344	0.0336	0.0329	0.0322	0.0314	0.0307	0.0301	0.0294
1.9	0.0287	0.0281	0.0274	0.0268	0.0262	0.0256	0.0250	0.0244	0.0239	0.0233
2.0	0.0228	0.0222	0.0217	0.0212	0.0207	0.0202	0.0197	0.0192	0.0188	0.0183
2.1	0.0179	0.0174	0.0170	0.0166	0.0162	0.0158	0.0154	0.0150	0.0146	0.0143
2.2	0.0139	0.0136	0.0132	0.0129	0.0125	0.0122	0.0119	0.0116	0.0113	0.0110
2.3	0.0107	0.0104	0.0102	0.0099	0.0096	0.0094	0.0091	0.0089	0.0087	0.0084
2.4	0.0082	0.0080	0.0078	0.0075	0.0073	0.0071	0.0069	0.0068	0.0066	0.0064
2.5	0.0062	0.0060	0.0059	0.0057	0.0055	0.0054	0.0052	0.0051	0.0049	0.0048
2.6	0.0047	0.0045	0.0044	0.0043	0.0041	0.0040	0.0039	0.0038	0.0037	0.0036
2.7	0.0035	0.0034	0.0033	0.0032	0.0031	0.0030	0.0029	0.0028	0.0027	0.0026
2.8	0.0026	0.0025	0.0024	0.0023	0.0023	0.0022	0.0021	0.0021	0.0020	0.0019
2.9	0.0019	0.0018	0.0018	0.0017	0.0016	0.0016	0.0015	0.0015	0.0014	0.0014
3.0	0.0013	0.0013	0.0013	0.0012	0.0012	0.0011	0.0011	0.0011	0.0010	0.0010

Taken from Fisher and Yates (1974) *Statistical Tables for Biological, Agricultural and Medical Research*. Longman.

Table II: *Table of critical values of t*

Degrees of freedom	Level of significance for one-tailed test					
	0.10	0.05	0.025	0.01	0.005	0.0005
	Level of significance for two-tailed test					
	0.20	0.10	0.05	0.02	0.01	0.001
1	3.078	6.314	12.706	31.821	63.657	636.619
2	1.888	2.920	4.303	6.965	9.925	31.598
3	1.638	2.353	3.182	4.541	5.841	12.941
4	1.533	2.132	2.776	3.747	4.604	8.610
5	1.476	2.015	2.571	3.365	4.032	6.859
6	1.440	1.943	2.447	3.143	3.707	5.959
7	1.415	1.895	2.365	2.998	3.499	5.405
8	1.397	1.860	2.306	2.896	3.355	5.041
9	1.383	1.833	2.262	2.821	3.250	4.781
10	1.372	1.812	2.228	2.764	3.169	4.587
11	1.363	1.796	2.201	2.718	3.106	4.437
12	1.356	1.782	2.179	2.681	3.055	4.318
13	1.350	1.771	2.160	2.650	3.012	4.221
14	1.345	1.761	2.145	2.624	2.977	4.140
15	1.341	1.753	2.131	2.602	2.947	4.073
16	1.337	1.746	2.120	2.583	2.921	4.015
17	1.333	1.740	2.110	2.567	2.898	3.965
18	1.330	1.734	2.101	2.352	2.878	3.922
19	1.328	1.729	2.093	2.539	2.861	3.883
20	1.325	1.725	2.086	2.528	2.845	3.850
21	1.323	1.721	2.080	2.518	2.831	3.819
22	1.321	1.717	2.074	2.508	2.819	3.792
23	1.319	1.714	2.069	2.500	2.807	3.767
24	1.318	1.711	2.064	2.492	2.797	3.745
25	1.316	1.708	2.060	2.485	2.787	3.725
26	1.315	1.706	2.056	2.479	2.779	3.707
27	1.314	1.703	2.052	2.473	2.771	3.690
28	1.313	1.701	2.048	2.467	2.763	3.674
29	1.311	1.699	2.045	2.462	2.756	3.659
30	1.310	1.697	2.042	2.457	2.750	3.646
40	1.303	1.684	2.021	2.423	2.704	3.551
60	1.296	1.671	2.000	2.390	2.660	3.460
120	1.289	1.658	1.980	2.358	2.617	3.373
∞	1.282	1.645	1.960	2.325	2.576	3.291

Taken from Fisher and Yates (1974) *Statistical Tables for Biological, Agricultural and Medical Research.* Longman.

Table III: *Table of critical values of χ^2*

Degrees of freedom	Probability that chi-square value will be exceeded									
	0.995	0.990	0.975	0.950	0.900	0.100	0.050	0.025	0.010	0.005
1	0.0^4393	0.0^3157	0.0^3982	0.0^2393	0.0158	2.71	3.84	5.02	6.63	7.88
2	0.0100	0.0201	0.0506	0.103	0.211	4.61	5.99	7.38	9.21	10.60
3	0.072	0.115	0.216	0.352	0.584	5.25	7.81	9.35	11.34	12.84
4	0.207	0.297	0.484	0.711	1.064	7.78	9.49	11.14	13.28	14.86
5	0.412	0.554	0.831	1.145	1.61	9.24	11.07	12.83	15.09	16.75
6	0.676	0.872	1.24	1.64	2.20	10.64	12.59	14.45	16.81	18.55
7	0.989	1.24	1.69	2.17	2.83	12.02	14.07	16.01	18.48	20.28
8	1.34	1.65	2.18	2.73	3.49	13.36	15.51	17.53	20.09	21.95
9	1.73	2.09	2.70	3.33	4.17	14.68	16.92	19.02	21.67	23.59
10	2.16	2.56	3.25	3.94	4.87	15.99	18.31	20.48	23.21	25.19
11	2.60	3.05	3.82	4.57	5.58	17.28	19.68	21.92	24.72	26.76
12	3.07	3.57	4.40	5.23	6.30	18.55	21.03	23.34	26.22	28.30
13	3.57	4.11	5.01	5.89	7.04	19.81	22.36	24.74	27.69	29.82
14	4.07	4.66	5.63	6.57	7.79	21.06	23.68	26.12	29.14	31.32
15	4.60	5.23	6.26	7.26	8.55	22.31	25.00	27.49	30.58	32.80
16	5.14	5.81	6.91	7.96	9.31	23.54	26.30	28.85	32.00	34.27
17	5.70	6.41	7.56	8.67	10.09	24.77	27.59	30.19	33.41	35.72
18	6.26	7.01	8.23	9.39	10.86	25.99	28.87	31.53	34.81	37.16
19	6.84	7.63	8.91	10.12	11.65	27.20	30.14	32.85	36.19	38.58
20	7.43	8.26	9.59	10.85	12.44	28.41	31.41	34.17	37.57	40.00
21	8.03	8.90	10.28	11.59	13.24	29.62	32.67	35.48	38.93	41.40
22	8.64	9.54	10.98	12.34	14.04	30.81	33.92	36.78	40.29	42.80
23	9.26	10.20	11.69	13.09	14.85	32.01	35.17	38.08	41.64	44.18
24	9.89	10.86	12.40	13.85	15.66	33.20	36.42	39.36	42.98	45.56
25	10.52	11.52	13.12	14.61	16.47	34.38	37.65	40.65	44.31	46.93
26	11.16	12.20	13.84	15.38	17.29	35.56	38.89	41.92	45.64	48.29
27	11.81	12.88	14.57	16.15	18.11	36.74	40.11	43.19	46.96	49.64
28	12.46	13.56	15.31	16.93	18.94	37.92	41.34	44.46	48.28	50.99
29	13.12	14.26	16.05	17.71	19.77	39.09	42.56	45.72	49.59	52.34
30	13.79	14.95	16.79	18.49	20.60	40.26	43.77	46.98	50.89	53.67
40	20.71	22.16	24.43	26.51	29.05	51.80	55.76	59.34	63.69	66.77
50	27.99	29.71	32.36	34.76	37.69	63.17	67.50	71.42	76.15	79.49
60	35.53	37.48	40.48	43.19	46.46	74.40	79.08	83.30	88.38	91.65
70	43.28	45.44	48.76	51.74	55.33	85.53	90.53	95.02	100.40	104.22
80	51.17	53.54	57.15	60.39	64.28	96.58	101.90	106.60	112.30	116.32
90	59.20	61.75	65.65	69.13	73.29	107.60	113.10	118.10	124.10	128.30
100	67.33	70.06	74.22	77.93	82.36	118.50	124.30	129.60	135.80	140.20

Taken from Fisher and Yates (1974) *Statistical Tables for Biological, Agricultural and Medical Research.* Longman.

Index _____